"Yours for Liberty"

# "Yours for Liberty"

*Selections from*

## *Abigail Scott Duniway's*
## *Suffrage Newspaper*

*edited by Jean M. Ward & Elaine A. Maveety*

**Oregon State University Press**
Corvallis

The paper in this book meets the guidelines for permanence and durability of the Committee on Production Guidelines for Book Longevity of the Council on Library Resources and the minimum requirements of the American National Standard for Permanence of Paper for Printed Library Materials Z39.48-1984.

**Library of Congress Cataloging-in-Publication Data**
Duniway, Abigail Scott, 1834-1915.
  "Yours for Liberty" : selections from Abigail Scott Duniway's suffrage newspaper / edited by Jean M. Ward & Elaine A. Maveety.—1st ed.
    p.  cm.
  Includes bibliographical references and index.
  ISBN 0-87071-474-0 (alk. paper)
  1. Women—Suffrage—Oregon—History—Sources. 2. Women—Suffrage—Northwest, Pacific—History—Sources. I. Ward, Jean M. II. Maveety, Elaine A. III. Title.
  JK1911.O7D85 2000
  324.6'23'0979549—dc21

                                                                99-086842

**Oregon State University Press**
101 Waldo Hall
Corvallis OR 97331-6407
541-737-3166 •fax 541-737-3170
http://osu.orst.edu/dept/press

# Table of Contents

## Selections from Duniway's *The New Northwest*

### 1871

### 1872

# 1873

# 1874

## 1877

## 1878

## 1885

## 1886-87

# Introduction

Abigail Jane Scott Duniway (1834-1915), a remarkable woman noted for her long and tireless efforts for woman suffrage and women's rights, was one of relatively few women newspaper editors and publishers of her era. Her weekly paper, *The New Northwest*,[1] was published from 1871 to 1887, at Portland, Oregon, during a time when women constituted only about one percent of all editors in the western states and territories.[2] The newspaper provides a vivid portrait of Duniway and her pioneering work, within a period of exceptional growth and turbulent activity in the Pacific Northwest.

Although securing the ballot for women was her primary goal, Abigail Scott Duniway did not establish *The New Northwest* solely to promote women's rights. The masthead in the first issue, published on May 5, 1871, read:

> *A Journal for the People.*
> *Devoted to the Interests of Humanity.*
> *Independent in Politics and Religion.*
> *Alive to all Live Issues, and Thoroughly*
> *Radical in Opposing and Exposing the Wrongs*
> *of the Masses.*

For this volume, the first published collection of writings from Duniway's paper, the selections are arranged chronologically, and dates of publication are given below the selections in parentheses. Since most of the selections are excerpts from Duniway's editorial columns, travel correspondence and news items, we have provided titles to assist readers with identification of content. With a few exceptions, which are identified, these selections were written by Duniway herself. They bring to life a time when traditional social attitudes and institutions were being challenged, both regionally and nationally.

## Duniway's "Bailiwick": Portland and the Pacific Northwest

The years during which *The New Northwest* was published—1871 to 1887—were years of explosive growth for Portland. Although the city's population in 1870 was only about 8,300, it had been the most important trade, shipping, and financial center in the Pacific Northwest since the 1850s, a status it retained until near the turn of the century. Portland's population doubled in the next ten years and by 1890 was over 46,000.[3]

Portland was a city with deep class and ethnic divisions. The social elite were businessmen and financiers, primarily from the Northeastern United States, native-born, Protestant, and wealthy. They and their wives established their own social clubs, traveled frequently to the East Coast and to Europe, and sent their sons east for schooling. Men such as William Ladd, Henry Corbett, Simeon Reed, John Ainsworth, and Henry Pittock came west in the early 1850s, and their names are permanently recorded in Portland history. Abigail's brother, Harvey W. Scott, who became both wealthy and influential in his role as editor of *The Oregonian*, moved in these circles. These men, and others like them, dominated Portland's civic and cultural organizations, and wielded considerable local, and often national, political influence.[4]

At the other end of the social spectrum, Portland's streets were crowded with saloons and prostitutes. In August of 1871, *The New Northwest* reported that Portland had 149 liquor dealers—roughly one for every sixty persons: men, women, and children—in the city.[5] Prostitution had also reached a serious level; by 1880, Portland was reported to have thirty bordellos.[6]

Abigail Scott Duniway deplored the subjugation of women, which she believed led to prostitution. She was deeply outraged by the prevailing moral code which "stones the woman, lets the man go free" and by the social and economic circumstances that drove these women to desperation and sometimes to acts of violence.

Portland was also a city of immigrants. In 1870, one-half of the city's population was either foreign-born or had at least one foreign-born parent. Foreign immigration was encouraged by businesses seeking cheap labor, and by 1890 the figure peaked at approximately 60 percent of the population.[7] Throughout the 1870s, the largest immigrant group in the city was the Irish, but by 1880, the Chinese, or "Celestials" as they were called in the West, had become the largest immigrant population in Portland.[8]

Racial and ethnic bigotry was part of Oregon's history from the beginning. Exclusionary clauses preventing blacks—whether slave or free—from entering Oregon Territory were passed in the 1840s.[9] When Oregon achieved statehood in 1859, it was "the only free state admitted to the Union with an exclusion clause in its constitution."[10] The exclusion clause was rarely enforced, but it was not repealed until 1926.

In 1870, despite the exclusion laws, Portland had a black population numbering 140 to 150 people.[11] A black church—the "People's Church"—existed in Portland as early as 1862, and the African Methodist Episcopal Zion Church was established in 1869.[12] Portland's small but active black community held events to celebrate emancipation and to mark the Fifteenth Amendment, ratified in 1870. Duniway was among the speakers at these events, which were reported in *The New Northwest.*

By far the most severe racist activities in both Oregon and Washington during the 1870s and 1880s were directed against the Chinese. Beginning in the 1850s, small numbers of Chinese came to the Pacific Northwest and found work as domestics and in agriculture and mining; later they were sought as cheap and reliable labor for railroad-building and in cigar factories, iron and paper mills, and salmon canneries. In 1870, Oregon's Chinese population was 3,330, about 500 of whom lived in Portland.[13] When sections of the railroad in the Willamette Valley were completed, many Chinese migrated to the city seeking new employment.

Even when their numbers were small, the Chinese were subjected to discriminatory taxes and prohibitions on certain types of employment, such as labor on public works projects. Politically motivated ordinances such as Portland Common Council's "cubic air ordinance" of June 1873, which required 550 cubic feet of air space per occupant, were directed at the Chinese, who lived in overcrowded buildings, and allowed the police to arrest and impose expensive fines on the Chinese occupants.[14] On October 28, 1880, *The New Northwest* reported that the Chinese population of Chicago was only 174; but Oregon's Chinese population had by that year increased to over 9,500, about 1,700 of whom were crowded into Portland's waterfront Chinatown. Washington Territory's Chinese population was smaller—only 234 in 1870 and 3,186 in 1880.[15]

As their population grew and the national economy slowed in the early 1880s, hostile feelings and anti-Chinese agitation increased in the Pacific Northwest. Anti-Chinese societies proliferated in Oregon and Washington to demand removal of Chinese from the Northwest. These societies operated outside the law and were actually groups of vigilantes. *The New Northwest* recorded much of this anti-Chinese activity as it simmered during the 1870s and exploded into violence, intimidation, and threats of expulsion in the 1880s.

Duniway and her family employed a Chinese cook and were generally sympathetic to the plight of the "Celestials," believing them to be hard-working people doing necessary labor. *The New Northwest* editorialized against the brutal treatment of Chinese men who were fighting a fire in Portland in December of 1872—a fire which many blamed on Chinese carelessness. In August of 1873, another fire struck Portland. Although it was never proven, this disastrous fire, which destroyed more than twenty blocks of Portland's downtown area, was widely believed to have been set by anti-Chinese vigilantes in an attempt to burn out Chinatown.[16] Abigail Scott Duniway's most complete personal statement on "the Chinese Question," as it came to be known, is recorded in *The New Northwest* of February 11, 1886, in "Letter from the Fireside Number Six," which is reproduced in this volume.

In contrast, Duniway's opinions about Indians varied according to the circumstances and sometimes seemed ambivalent. During the 1870s, when tribes forcibly resisted the breaking of treaties, encroachment on their lands, and removal to reservations, Euro-American settlers in outlying areas of the Pacific Northwest lived with the threat of Indian retaliation. *The New Northwest* carried reports of three major cases of Indian resistance: the Modoc War of 1872, the Nez Percé War of 1877, and the Bannock-Paiute War of 1878. Predictably, in all three conflicts, the paper's sympathies were with the settlers.

Duniway's position on the Indian question evolved over time. "The Indian," she wrote in her November 26, 1875, editorial correspondence for *The New Northwest*, was "better off in his own element, and more prosperous in every way when let alone, than he can ever be among white men." Six years later, further reflection and investigation moved Duniway to endorse the growing public sentiment that "equality of rights" for future generations of Indians might be achieved if they were assimilated into "citizenship and its accompanying responsibilities." Indians should then be granted homesteads "upon the same terms as whites."[17] Her visit to the Indian School at Forest Grove, Oregon, in September of 1880, had convinced her that the "children of the forest" could be assimilated into white civilization if "the tap roots are cut that formerly connected them with the associations of their kind."[18] Away from their families, in this residential setting, the boys were taught farming and trades, and the girls learned housekeeping skills. Duniway praised the efforts of the staff and the behavior of the forty resident children, regretting only that disadvantaged white children were not so well provided for.

When Abigail Scott Duniway reported on the plights of the disadvantaged and the privileges of the elite, she was keeping her pledge to "oppose and expose" the "wrongs of the masses." Even for her own time, Duniway was often "politically incorrect," but she was invigorated by controversy. She formed her own opinions and did not hesitate to take a position on any "live" issue. Social, cultural, and economic challenges in Portland and the greater Pacific Northwest provided an ample source of material to keep her newspaper columns filled for sixteen years.

## Abigail Scott Duniway and *The New Northwest*

With the motto of "Free Speech, Free Press, Free People," Duniway pledged *The New Northwest* to exposing and combating social injustice. The weekly paper, first printed as a four-page and later as an eight-page broadside, included some writings by others,[19] but this volume focuses on pieces written by Duniway herself. As editor, and the primary writer, she contributed reports of local, regional, and national news, advice to correspondents, editorials, short fiction, eighteen serialized novels, and correspondence describing her frequent lecturing trips throughout the Pacific Northwest and her several cross-country journeys to attend and often address national gatherings of the woman suffrage movement. Some of her liveliest writing occurs in her editorial correspondence, detailing her travels.

Contemporary readers may not be aware of Duniway's sense of humor, unless they have read microfilms of *The New Northwest.* Her wit and love of adventure balance and humanize the more usual picture of Duniway as a formidable paragon—the indefatigable champion of women's rights and now the State of Oregon's representative in the National Women's Hall of Fame.

Outspoken and frequently controversial, Duniway certainly had her enemies. Readers learned that she was not above *ad hominem* attack when she felt justified; in fact, she appeared to delight in it. In the beginning, she was relatively inexperienced and somewhat naive but, where a person less dedicated would have failed, Duniway's energy and determination made a success of *The New Northwest.*

For sixteen years, until she sold the newspaper in January of 1887, *The New Northwest* carried Duniway's discussion of questions as varied as the treatment of Chinese, policies related to American Indians, the rights and legal status of women, arguments about Temperance and Prohibition, and the vagaries of religion, including forays into Spiritualism, a popular movement of the period.

Investigation of all these questions was Duniway's declared mission as a journalist, and religion was no exception. She was unconvinced by the "shallow depths" of her childhood lessons in Calvinist salvation and damnation, and dismayed by the practices of many orthodox ministers.[20] When a subscriber to *The New Northwest* asked in 1881 about Duniway's religious views, she answered: "I believe in churches, but not in bigotry; in Christ, but not in creeds;

in religion, but not in self-righteousness; in God, but not in the devil."[21] Membership in a church was unimportant to her and, although she was drawn in later years to the Unitarian Church, and even considered joining, she "couldn't quite get down to it; it seemed so silly."[22]

Duniway's heterodoxy involved exploration of Spiritualism through what she termed first-hand "scientific investigation."[23] She participated in seances, wrote about her investigations, and spoke regularly on woman suffrage at Spiritualist meetings in Oregon. Although she deplored "cheap illiterate" mediums and had doubts about the authenticity of certain physical manifestations, Spiritualism clearly held an appeal for Duniway.[24] Following her daughter Clara's death in 1886, Duniway was convinced that she "heard from her, through private psychic sources."[25]

Duniway prided herself on careful observation and serious investigation, her prerequisites for responsible journalism. For example, to describe technology of the times, she visited hydraulic gold mines in Nevada, went underground in Seattle's coal mines, observed "the slaughtering saw" rip logs into lumber at Knappton, Washington Territory, and made "a close personal inspection" of Astoria's "new electric light plant." To inform her readers of conditions in various institutions, she visited insane asylums, penitentiaries, poor farms, and schools. To report accurately the stories of women charged with crimes, she interviewed them in prison and frequently attended their trials.

Aiming for a primarily female audience, Duniway established a personal relationship with her readers by sharing her own experiences and writing about the things she knew. She identified with farm wives and their common experiences of overwork, loneliness, and too-frequent childbirth. She offered women advice and admonished husbands to get help for their overburdened wives and make sure they had some regular contact with other women. Revealing herself in a way that was unique and interesting for a newspaper editor, Duniway wrote of her recurrent headaches, her weariness and frustrations—and she shared news of her family's celebrations and tragedies.

And the women responded, often writing letters of gratitude which were published in the columns of *The New Northwest*. Mrs. M. A. Canney, writing from Exeter Mills, Maine, told Duniway, "[Y]our little paper comes to me like a bit of delicious cream, and I have such a genuine relish for cream, that I am afraid without it, everything else would look blue."[26] An Oregon woman named "Marie," living in a log cabin on the McKenzie River, was "filled with gratitude" to Duniway for "sending forth a paper devoted to human improvement."[27]

## "I Could Not Choose but Scribble": The Making of a Suffragist Editor

Unlike the vast majority of women reformers of the period, Duniway had her own publication outlets for the advocacy of human rights in general and woman suffrage in particular. *The New Northwest* (1871-87), Oregon's first woman suffrage paper, was followed by *The Coming Century* (1891-92), Duniway's short-lived "Journal of Progress and Reform." From the fall of 1895 until she retired from journalism in early 1897, she was editor of Frances Gotshall's *The Pacific Empire*, a weekly published in Portland which carried the motto, "A Journal of Freedom." In total, about twenty years of Duniway's life were spent as an editor of these human rights publications, and over forty years were devoted to advocacy for woman suffrage.

By conventional standards, Abigail Scott Duniway appears an unlikely candidate for editor of any newspaper, let alone a weekly reform journal. Due to frailty and ill health in childhood, compounded by the strain of hard work on her parents' Illinois farm, her formal education was limited to less than one year of intermittent attendance in rural Illinois schools.[28] She gained her real education through reading books and newspapers, and later by teaching in Oregon schools. Teaching, she said, "left me equipped with a tolerably good English education, and much practical experience, more varied than falls to the lot of almost any other woman I have ever known."[29]

When Duniway began *The New Northwest*, she was, as she conceded later in her autobiography, "wholly ignorant of the publishing business," a predominantly male field into which she was "stumbling blindly."[30] Her financial resources were slim and, at the age of thirty-six, she bore responsibilities as the wife of a semi-invalid husband and the mother of six children, ranging in age from two to seventeen. Moreover, she lived in the Pacific Northwest, far distant from the center of reform movements in the East.

But, for a woman of Duniway's will, these circumstances were challenges to be met, not insurmountable obstacles. She seems never to have lacked confidence in her own abilities, sense of purpose, or vision. She believed that her life experiences as a farmer's wife, milliner, teacher, and novice writer, in combination with "common sense," equipped her to realize her ambition and serve the public "in the capacity of editor and proprietor of a newspaper." Using the "editorial we," a common convention of the time, she told her readers in the first issue of *The New Northwest* that writing "always was our forte."

The virtual absence of a formal education did not mean that Duniway was uninformed or unfamiliar with newspapers and reform activity. During her childhood, a variety of newspapers of the day reached the Scott home in Tazewell County, Illinois, both through subscription and exchange with relatives.[31] In the pages of Horace Greeley's *New York Tribune*, for example, young Abigail Scott read about reform movements, including abolition of slavery and women's rights, and Greeley became a hero in her eyes.

Beyond some early "poesy" published in *The Illinois Journal* when she was a youngster, Abigail Scott's first major writing effort was in 1852, when her parents and their nine surviving children migrated from Illinois to Oregon Territory.[32] Seventeen-year-old Abigail was assigned by her father, John Tucker Scott, to keep a daily journal of the overland trip, a record he hoped to see published as a guide for future immigrants.[33] This assignment proved tedious and sometimes onerous, even heartbreaking when "plains cholera" took the lives of Abigail's mother, Ann Roelofson Scott, and youngest brother, but the journal later served as a resource for several of Duniway's novels.[34]

Abigail's submissions to Oregon Territory newspapers began after she left her first teaching position, at Eola, Polk County, and married Benjamin Charles Duniway, "an attractive young man" who was "considered the best catch around."[35] On August 3, 1853, two months short of her nineteenth birthday, Abigail, or "Jenny" as she was called by her family, married Ben and joined him on his donation claim near Needy, about twelve miles from Oregon City, in Clackamas County. Years later, in a private letter, she described the first four years of marriage on this Clackamas farm, which she named "Hardscrabble," as the hardest years of her life.[36] But, as she noted in one of her published memoirs, "I was not particularly unhappy on the farm. My husband was sober, industrious and kind. My children were a source of abiding joy, and I found enough of mental exercise with them and my crude, untutored pen."[37]

During the years at Hardscrabble, Duniway lived in a log cabin with a lean-to kitchen and bore the first two of her six children, Clara Belle, the Duniways' only daughter, and Willis Scott. During her recovery from Willis's birth, Duniway wrote stories and poems. The Hardscrabble cabin burned to the ground in the summer of 1856, and the next year the Duniways were located at "Sunny Hill Side Farm" in Yamhill County, two miles from Lafayette. At Sunny Hill, Duniway continued to write, and two more sons were added to the family: Hubert Ray and Wilkie Collins, who was named after one of Abigail's favorite authors.

Duniway's early "scribblings," as she referred to them, included pieces for the Oregon City *Argus* and *The Oregon Farmer*, and her first novel, *Captain Gray's Company, or; Crossing the Plains and Living in Oregon*. Her poem, "To a Burning Forest Tree," was credited in the *Argus* to "Jenny Glen."[38] Sent to the editor on a piece of brown wrapping paper, the poem was accompanied by a note from "Jenny": "I have to write with one foot upon the cradle-rocker; I live upon a farm, cook for workmen, make a great deal of butter, and tend two babies." W. L. Adams, editor of the *Argus*, responded that a woman "who can do all this and be sufficiently contented and happy to draw poetry from the surroundings of a home in the timber, must be a wife worth having"; however, Adams later suggested that she try her hand at writing a prose article instead of poetry.[39] Under the signature of "A Farmer's Wife," some of Duniway's prose appeared in *The Oregon Farmer*, and she used her own name—"Abigail J. Duniway"—for her novel.

When *Captain Gray's Company* appeared in April of 1859, Oregon was celebrating its new statehood, and Duniway was only twenty-four. She was not a convert to equal rights and woman suffrage until later in life, and her mission in *Captain Gray's Company* was to protect and strengthen woman's sphere—an approach to gender relations found in most woman's fiction (known as "domestic fiction") of the nineteenth century.

*Captain Gray's Company* drew negative criticism as a foolish and badly written romance. Particularly biting comments came from Asahel Bush,[40] editor of the Salem *Statesman*, and the Reverend Thomas Hall Pearne, editor of *The Pacific Christian Advocate*, who wrote: "We have been sickened with the love stories of the book and generally disgusted with its general lack of good taste and correct grammar."[41] The criticisms of *Captain Gray's Company* left lasting scars; throughout the rest of her life, Duniway apologized for the novel. In 1904, she described the work as a "crude and callow novel" and recalled that she could not bring herself to read a single line when it was serialized in *The New Northwest*.[42]

The year after publication of *Captain Gray's Company*, Duniway again stirred up controversy. In a series of letters to the *Oregon Farmer*, she took farmers to task for not paying attention to the pernicious effects of drudgery and "excessive maternity" on the health of their wives and future generations."[43] The "Farmer's Wife" was "determined to agitate this matter till somebody goes to thinking."

During the 1860 election year campaigns, when Edward Dickinson Baker spoke in Lafayette, only men were expected to participate, but Abigail and six other women, accompanied by their husbands, audaciously attended and were received with "half-audible hisses" from the crowd and a gracious welcome from Baker. This was Duniway's first political meeting, and she was eager to hear the eloquent Baker, a close friend of Abraham Lincoln and the man who had helped the Scott family climb out of financial difficulty in Illinois. During her editorship of *The New Northwest*, Duniway gave lectures on "The Life and Times of Col. E. D. Baker," and she credited him with trying to convince her that woman suffrage was an important issue.

The Civil War years were difficult times for the Duniways, and two events in 1862 shaped their future: the loss of Sunny Hill Side Farm and Ben's serious injury in an accident. Against Abigail's better judgment, Ben had gone security on promissory notes for a friend and, when the friend defaulted, the debt fell to the Duniways. A flood in late 1861 swept away their harvest, and the notes signed by Ben could not be paid. The farm was sold to make payment on their debts, and the Duniways moved to a small house in Lafayette, where Ben worked

as a teamster to earn money for purchase of another farm. But, in the fall of 1862, Ben was thrown to the ground by a runaway team of horses, and a heavy wagon rolled over him. He suffered permanent injury to his back and chest, and could do only light work for the rest of his life.

Abigail became the primary breadwinner for the family. For three years at Lafayette, she took in boarders and taught school in her home, rising at three in the summer and four in the winter to care for the household before the day of teaching began. She sold her Lafayette school in 1865, and the family moved to Albany, where she opened a private school and bore two more children: Clyde Augustus and Ralph Roelofson.

*Duniway as a teacher, 1862-63*

After a year or so of teaching in Albany, Duniway determined to open a millinery shop to improve the family's financial situation. About 1866, the year of her fifth pregnancy, she moved her Albany school to Broad Albin Street, converted it to a shop, and went into partnership with a Mrs. Jackson, whom she later bought out.[44]

In her Broad Albin Street shop, Duniway came to realize how unjustly women were treated as she witnessed, on a daily basis, the humiliation many of her customers suffered because of their "supported and protected" status under the law. She observed and grew to know women from all walks of life

*Duniway with baby Clyde, 1867*

who had no financial independence, were not educated to support themselves and their families, and were subject to the authority—sometimes the abuse—of their husbands. She learned of the tragedies of "grass widows," women who were separated or divorced from their husbands, and she saw "there was no Canada for fugitive wives"—a metaphor that appears frequently in her writings.

As a businesswoman, Duniway was converted to the cause of women's rights and woman suffrage, but this conversion did not come easily. "I was not a willing convert to belief in equal rights for women," she wrote in a reminiscence. "Blessed with a kind father and a sober, upright husband, I grew up from childhood imbued with the teaching that it was a woman's lot to engage in a lifetime of unpaid servitude and personal sacrifice. . . . I schooled myself to imagine that I was filling my Heaven-appointed sphere, for which final recompense awaited me in the land of souls."[45] Abigail credited her "good" and "sensible" husband Ben with finally convincing her that conditions would never improve for women until they had the right to vote.[46] She had come a long way from the "Farmer's Wife" of 1859 who wrote that women should be content "to use *cradles* for ballot-boxes, in which they have a right to plant, not votes, but *voters.*"[47]

By 1870, Duniway's conversion was complete, and she pursued ways to help support her family *and* serve the cause of women's rights. In a meeting with two friends in Albany, she presented her idea of starting an equal rights newspaper in Oregon. They "expressed their doubts as to the financial success of the proposed newspaper enterprise" but agreed to join in organizing "the nucleus of a State Equal Suffrage Association," actually the second such organization formed in Oregon.[48]

When Duniway learned that a woman suffrage convention was to be held in San Francisco in May of 1871, she determined to combine a buying trip for her millinery shop with attendance at the meeting. Business took her to San Francisco earlier than expected during the winter of 1870-71 and, armed with credentials from Oregon, Duniway met in San Francisco with a number of California suffrage leaders over the holidays.[49] This was the first of many journeys she would make for the equal suffrage cause.

In her autobiography, Duniway noted that, on New Year's Eve, 1870, she addressed a San Francisco audience in her first "set speech outside of an Oregon classroom."[50] The speech was well received, and she was invited to remain in California for a time and lecture on a salaried basis. "I wrote," Duniway recalled, "as was a faithful married woman's habit, to my semi-invalid husband, asking permission to accept the position, which would include the salary, much-needed between seasons in the millinery business in Oregon."[51]

While in San Francisco, Duniway pursued her interests in journalism and spent time with Emily Pitts-Stevens, editor of *The Pioneer*, a San Francisco equal-rights weekly. The first issue of *The Pioneer* for 1871 was filled with Duniway: the text of her January 4th address to the San Francisco County Woman Suffrage Association, her column entitled "Oregon Department," one of her poems, and an essay on a day spent with Emily Pitts-Stevens. Most surprising was the announcement that A. J. Duniway would serve as Oregon editor for *The Pioneer*.[52]

In "Our Editorial Bow," Duniway explained to readers of *The Pioneer* that "a bargain was concluded the week before between ourself and Mrs. Emily Pitts Stevens," and said "bargain resulted in the placing of our name, in connection with hers, as Oregon editor of *The Pioneer*—the Human Rights and Universal Suffrage Organ for the Pacific Coast."[53] Duniway continued: "As our many friends in Oregon well know, it has been our aim for the past two years to establish such a newspaper just as soon as necessary arrangements could be completed for that purpose." Here was an opportunity to combine forces in one paper: "In union there is strength; in consolidation, money; in harmony, wisdom; in all, success." In her closing, Duniway promised: "I shall return home—you see I sometimes forget the new distinction of the editorial 'we'—as soon as possible after the meeting of the Human Rights Convention in San Francisco."

But Duniway's stay in California was cut short. In mid-January, a telegram from Ben arrived: "Come home immediately; business requires it." At home, she "found no visible need of anything but the salary I had relinquished in blind obedience to what I considered an unreasonable mandate."[54] One can imagine the words that flew in the Duniway household![55]

On January 25, 1871, the Portland *Oregonian* announced that "Mrs. A. J. Duniway of Albany arrived in this city yesterday morning to ascertain what interests can be raised here in behalf of the removal of *The Pioneer* newspaper from San Francisco to this city."[56] Further, *The Oregonian* added, "In anticipation of success she will move shortly to this city."

*The Pioneer* did not relocate to Portland but, within the short period of three months in early 1871, Abigail Scott Duniway moved her family from Albany to Portland and established *The New Northwest*. Funds from the sale of some Duniway property, coupled with $3,000 borrowed by Abigail, provided financing to purchase a press and type, rent a house, and hire a foreman. The two-story frame house at Third and Washington streets provided space on the first floor for family living and a millinery shop, with room on the second floor for printing the newspaper.

*The New Northwest* was a Duniway family enterprise. Abigail was editor of the paper, and Ben assisted with business matters. All the children, except for the two youngest, helped out and received wages. Willis, age fifteen, who had served as a printer's devil at the Albany *State Rights Democrat*, worked with *The New Northwest* foreman, Isaac Long. Hubert, age twelve, and Wilkie, age ten, were newsboys and learned how to set type. Clara, age seventeen, looked after the millinery shop and assisted her father in the care of Clyde, not yet four, and Ralph, not yet two. Soon, Duniway added a housekeeper and Chinese cook to the household. Family finances improved when Abigail's brother, Harvey W. Scott, collector of customs in Portland and a junior editor for *The Oregonian*, hired Ben Duniway as an "opener and packer" in the customs office "at $1,300 annually," a position he held from about 1873 to 1886.[57]

Abigail Scott Duniway did not seek the advice of her younger brother, Harvey Scott, when she began *The New Northwest*.[58] In the first issue of her paper, she wrote: "If we had been a man, we'd have had an editor's position and a handsome salary at twenty-one." At the age of thirty-six, Duniway was thinking of more advantaged males, such as Harvey, who was then a junior editor and eventually became senior editor and part owner of *The Oregonian*.[59] The next month, for readers who thought her brother or father must be writing the editorials, Duniway explained that she, "as editor and proprietor" of *The New Northwest*, wrote "every line of editorial."[60]

Duniway did, however, obtain the assistance of other family members. Within a few years, she turned to her talented sister, Catherine A. Scott Coburn, a widow with four daughters.[61] Coburn served as associate editor of *The New Northwest* from 1874 to 1879, when two of Duniway's sons—Willis and Hubert—became co-publishers of the paper. A third son, Wilkie, joined the Duniway Publishing Company in 1882. But even with the inclusion of family members, *The New Northwest* was a venture fraught with financial uncertainty.

## On the Road for *The New Northwest*

A major challenge facing Duniway throughout the years that she published *The New Northwest* was finding subscribers and securing renewals. Much of her time was spent on the road, with sample copies of the paper and subscription forms in hand. Readers were encouraged to become "agents" for the paper and earn premiums—from ivory napkin rings to shuttle sewing machines—for subscription sales. And, in efforts to publicize her work, Duniway sent complimentary copies of her paper to influential people throughout the country and exchanged regularly with women's journals and newspapers in the East.

Actual readership of *The New Northwest* included non-subscribers as well as subscribers, but paid subscriptions probably never exceeded about three thousand.[62] In September of 1877, Duniway reported that the paper had grown to be a "permanent institution, popular and respected," and that its indebtedness was $106.[63] For 1880, the Duniway Publishing Company netted $1,600, and profits almost doubled in 1882.[64] Income evidently declined prior to the sale of the paper. For a three-month period in 1886, the year before the paper was sold, *The New Northwest* ledgers showed an average monthly profit of $65.[65]

Early on, Abigail Scott Duniway recognized the necessity of traveling beyond Portland to introduce her paper and carry her message to potential subscribers and supporters. She knew that a reform paper with a woman's rights advocate at the helm held limited appeal for a general readership. Duniway needed to secure a place for *The New Northwest* in the larger landscape of the Pacific Northwest, and she had an opportunity to do so when the paper was but a few months old.

Susan B. Anthony arrived in Portland in the fall of 1871, and Duniway eagerly agreed to serve as business manager for her lecture tour of the Pacific Northwest. Anthony's visit was in response to an invitation extended by Duniway prior to establishing *The New Northwest.* In the summer of 1870, she had written to Laura Curtis Bullard, the new owner and editor of *The Revolution,* founded by Susan B. Anthony and Elizabeth Cady Stanton.[66] She praised the newspaper, introduced herself to its readers, and noted that what Oregon needed was visits from "leaders to put the people to thinking" on the woman question. "How I wish some of our great agitators," Duniway wrote, "such as Mrs. Stanton or Miss Anthony, would come among us for a season to give the cause an impetus."[67]

*Duniway, ca. 1877, reading copy of her **David and Anna Matson** (1876)*

During the months of September, October, and early November of 1871, Duniway frequently traveled with Anthony to reach a variety of audiences in Oregon and Washington Territory, and as far north as Victoria, British Columbia.[68] The women went by stagecoach, steamer, wagon, carriage, horseback, and rail to meet with groups in churches, schoolhouses, hotels, public halls, stores, homes, and even in pool halls and saloons when other doors were closed to them. Ministers who opposed woman suffrage denied them use of churches, and a husband in Port Gamble, Washington Territory, refused them housing because his wife had not asked his permission to have guests. When Anthony spoke to audiences at the Oregon State Fair in October, Abigail and Ben Duniway were present with four of their children, and Anthony spent her only overnight camping experience in a tent with the Duniway family, "packed side by side like herrings."[69] In Salem, Anthony was interviewed by justices of the Oregon Supreme Court; in Olympia, both Anthony and Duniway addressed the Washington Territorial Legislature.

Although travel was difficult, stage roads and frontier hotels primitive, and audiences sometimes unfriendly, Duniway was invigorated by the experience. By the conclusion of the tour, she had made friends and contacts for future suffrage work, signed up many new subscribers for *The New Northwest*, learned about organizing for suffrage, served a successful apprenticeship as a lecturer, and established an association with Anthony that was to last until "Aunt Susan's" death in 1906.[70]

After Anthony's departure, the pace of Duniway's work increased, and she was often on the road herself for *The New Northwest* and woman suffrage. She was the first woman to address the Oregon legislature when she argued for woman suffrage before the House in the fall of 1872.[71] In her autobiography, Duniway described her hectic schedule: "It was no small task to travel, often by night, over the terrible roads of the Pacific Northwest, lecturing three to five evenings every week, writing serial stories for 'The New Northwest,' illustrative, always, of various phases of my theme, and furnishing editorial correspondence often covering a full page of the paper."[72]

Duniway valued labor "above every other accompaniment of physical life." Nor did she spare herself. Although she suffered "periodic attacks of illness," the teachings of her childhood had imbued her with an abiding sense of faithfulness to duty. In 1875, she wrote from Albany, Oregon, to tell readers of *The New Northwest* that she had been sick for the past ten days. But, she went on to report, in that time she had "given four lectures, organized the suffrage society, visited a dozen families, done one day's sewing, written two chapters of the serial story and ever so much other MS, and yet we see no stopping place, although compelled to forego much that our voice and pen are longing to attempt."[73]

Indications that Duniway was growing weary appeared from time to time in *The New Northwest*, and the death of her daughter Clara, in January of 1886, took a heavy toll. On October 7, 1886, a particularly "vigorous growl" from Duniway, then fifty-two, warned readers that if others did not exert themselves to keep the paper afloat with subscriptions, she would sell out and move to Washington Territory, where women already had the vote. Owing to impaired health from "constant office work," Willis and Wilkie Duniway had retired from *The New Northwest* staff in July of that year and moved to Idaho Territory to recuperate, leaving Abigail and her son Hubert to publish the paper. In August, Duniway reported that her husband would also relocate in Idaho, where the Duniways had purchased a 1,280-acre ranch. In her farewell note of January 6,

1887, announcing the sale of the paper, Duniway said that she, too, was headed for Idaho.

Over the next few weeks, Duniway contributed several items to the paper, but *The New Northwest* ended after a brief period under its new owner, Oliver P. Mason, a Portland businessman and close friend of Harvey Scott. Although she spent some time in Idaho Territory, Abigail and eventually Ben left the Idaho ranch and returned to Portland, the center for Duniway's later suffrage efforts.

## Duniway and Two Controversial Movements: Temperance and Woman Suffrage

Duniway gave considerable space in *The New Northwest* to two national movements: Temperance and Woman Suffrage. The Temperance Movement advocated moderation in, or abstinence from, the consumption of intoxicating liquor, thereby protecting women and children from the evils generated by "King Alcohol." The Woman Suffrage Movement sought to place the legally protected power of the ballot in the hands of women. With the ballot, it was believed, women could gain equal education, employment, and property rights. Women's "natural rights" as citizens would be guaranteed, and their votes would improve the human condition.

### Temperance

Despite her philosophical and political differences with the Temperance Movement, especially the prohibitionists, Duniway called herself a "temperance woman" and "looked upon temperance in everything as a question of moral and individual responsibility."[74] Although her position on prohibition evolved over the years, she essentially concluded that prohibition of the sale of alcohol was neither a prevention nor a cure for the disease of alcoholism; the answer was to be found in education and individual responsibility.

Duniway did agree, however, with temperance and prohibitionist arguments that wives were disadvantaged under the law and placed at the mercy of their drinking husbands. A husband and wife were considered "one person in law"; the legal being of the wife was merged in her husband. If the husband became a heavy drinker and no longer provided for his family, the wife had no legal redress, and the family could be ruined. When temperance women asked what could be done to correct these injustices, Duniway's answer was the ballot.[75]

The Temperance Movement with which Duniway was both associated and had her differences was founded early in the nineteenth century by Protestant men concerned about religious and moral issues associated with the increasing consumption of alcohol. Amelia Bloomer, who established *The Lily* as a temperance paper in 1849, later wrote that,

> up to about 1848-49, women had almost no part in all this temperance work. They could attend meetings and listen to the eloquence and arguments of men, and they could pay their money towards the support of temperance lecturers, but such a thing as their having anything to say or do further than this was not thought of.[76]

At the stormy 1853 World Temperance Convention in New York, Susan B. Anthony was denied the right to serve on a committee, and the chair announced that "it was not fit for a woman to be in such places."[77]

Following the Civil War, there was a second great wave of interest in temperance, social purity, and the general suppression of vice, including the sale of alcohol. Women engaged in temperance reform with a new sense of confidence, and a number joined male reformers to rid the nation of "evil drink." Prohibitionists founded the Prohibition Party in 1869 and ran a slate of candidates in the presidential election of 1872, the second year of Duniway's *The New Northwest*. Their platform called for universal suffrage, regulation of business, public education, encouragement of immigration, and constitutional prohibition; however, the party garnered only about five thousand of over six million votes cast in the 1872 election.[78] Duniway, distrustful of the prohibitionists and disenchanted with her old hero, Horace Greeley, who was running as the Democratic candidate, threw her support to Ulysses S. Grant, who was overwhelmingly re-elected.

Although Duniway did not endorse linking woman suffrage with prohibition, she argued for equal rights in temperance meetings. At the meeting of the Oregon State Temperance Alliance in February of 1872, Duniway overcame the "gag law" imposed on women and spoke for equal rights. She presented a resolution that recognized "women as legitimate auxiliaries" in the Temperance Movement and called for "the votes of women upon the subject of Temperance . . . in their various precincts."[79] The resolution passed, 119 to 12, with the clarification from a male delegate that it did "not mean woman suffrage for other than the temperance question."

The next year, following formation of the Oregon State Woman Suffrage Association (OSWSA), conservative members of the Oregon Temperance Alliance tried to block Duniway's participation at their annual meeting. On the grounds that the OSWSA was "a political party," the Committee on Credentials refused to seat her as a delegate. A heated battle ensued, and Duniway was finally admitted. In an unsuccessful attempt to secure endorsement of *The New Northwest* as an official temperance publication, Duniway informed the Temperance Alliance that her newspaper was "in every particular, a strict Temperance sheet. It never had by a single article or even an advertisement, encouraged the sale of intoxicating liquors and she did not intend that it should in the future." In fact, Duniway said, she was willing to see "one of the chief planks in its platform [be] prohibition in the fullest sense of the word."[80] In later years, however, Duniway's public position on prohibition clearly shifted.

Early in her editorship of *The New Northwest*, Duniway was faced with how to interpret the national phenomenon of the Woman's Temperance Crusade and its relationship to the woman suffrage movement. In the winter of 1873-74, women in several small towns of southwestern Ohio and western New York marched against local saloons and other outlets for the sale of alcohol, using prayers, hymns, pledge cards, petitions, pickets, and a nineteenth-century version of the sit-in to purge their towns of demon drink. From its inception in December of 1873, to its conclusion in June of 1874, the Crusade spread to over nine hundred communities in thirty-one states and territories and the District of Columbia.[81]

Despite the power of liquor interests and hostile opposition from immigrant populations in cities such as Chicago, the Crusade did have an impact. Newspaper reports showed 1,260 liquor outlets closed or pledged to stop selling beverage alcohol.[82] In addition, 750 breweries closed, malt liquor production dropped by over 5.5 million gallons, and federal excise tax receipts dropped sharply.[83]

Just before the Crusade reached Portland, Duniway endorsed the effort in her editorial of March 6, 1874, "Praying Down Saloons." Although she was not in Oregon when the Portland Crusaders first took to the streets on March 23rd, *The New Northwest* and *The Oregonian* published regular reports of their activities.[84] Duniway was disappointed that the Crusaders had not opened their eyes "to the *power of the ballot*." In her stinging editorial of July 17, 1874, she argued that the Crusaders had been misled by the clergy: "The first prayer that will be effectually answered will be made with ballots in your hands to keep company with the prayers in your hearts."

On the heels of the Woman's Crusade, the National Woman's Christian Temperance Union (WCTU) was founded in the fall of 1874. Under the leadership of Frances Willard, who served as president from 1879 until her death in 1898, the WCTU grew to be the largest women's organization in the country.[85] Willard's commitment to woman suffrage led her to establish a WCTU Department of Suffrage in 1882 and, through her efforts, the Prohibition Party endorsed woman suffrage the same year.

Frances Willard stopped in Portland during her extensive speaking tour of the western states in 1883. In June, Duniway met Willard at a reception and later, amidst WCTU white ribbons that symbolized purity and banners that called for "Home Protection," she heard Willard address Portland's Woman's Christian Temperance Union Convention and praised her for her eloquence.

In the fall of 1883, following Willard's visit, the women of Washington Territory were granted the ballot. While Duniway rejoiced at the victory, she soon clashed directly with members of the WCTU on the question of "local option," a form of prohibition initiated to give Washington towns the local option to abolish liquor licenses and limit liquor sales to drug stores for "sacramental purposes." Duniway feared retaliation from powerful liquor interests if women in Washington voted for local option: woman suffrage might be repealed. She also believed the prohibition law would prove unenforceable.

In June of 1886, before the vote on local option was taken, Duniway hurried to Washington to warn women not to vote for the proposal.[86] Local option resulted in a mixed vote, with more areas voting against than in favor of the proposed law. The entire issue became moot, however, when the law was declared unconstitutional in September of 1886. The next year, as Duniway feared, Washington women were disenfranchised.

Duniway's refusal to advocate for prohibition and her resistance to combining prohibition with efforts for woman suffrage severed some of her ties with members of the Woman's Christian Temperance Union and displeased national suffrage leaders such as Susan B. Anthony and Anna Howard Shaw.[87] Privately, Duniway wrote to her son Clyde, "People who are drunk on prohibition have no more sense than those who are drunk with whisky."[88]

## Woman Suffrage

In 1886, the year before *The New Northwest* was sold, Lucy Stone, a leader of the American Woman Suffrage Association, lauded Abigail Scott Duniway for going through "more toil and drudgery for the Woman Suffrage cause than any other woman we know" and for being "the pioneer Woman Suffragist of the great Northwest."[89] Historian Eleanor Flexner described Duniway as "the hardiest and most tireless worker the western states produced."[90] Given Duniway's work with *The New Northwest* and other publications, the number of woman suffrage campaigns in which she was involved, and the defeats she experienced, the accolades are richly deserved.

In Oregon, which rejected woman suffrage more times than any other state, Duniway witnessed five failed attempts to give women the ballot—in 1884, 1900, 1906, 1908, and 1910—before final victory in 1912 by a close margin of 4,161 votes. In Washington Territory, she campaigned for woman suffrage and rejoiced in the victory of 1883; however, the territorial supreme court twice voided woman suffrage acts, first in 1887 and again the next year.[91] When Washington became a state, Duniway mourned the defeat of woman suffrage at the polls in 1889 but cheered when Washington gave women the ballot in 1910. She campaigned in the Idaho Territory and celebrated Idaho's victory in 1896.[92]

Oregon's first defeat of woman suffrage in 1884 was Oregon's only campaign during publication of *The New Northwest.* The loss was a heavy blow for Duniway, particularly when she considered the role played by her brother Harvey Scott. From 1877 through 1883, Scott "promoted his sister's lectures, contributed financially to her cause, and gave woman suffrage occasional editorial support" in *The Oregonian.*[93] When Washington Territory granted women the ballot in 1883, Scott agreed with the decision: "[W]oman is capable of exerting an

*Harvey Scott*

influence in public affairs which the state needs, and this influence can be made effective only through suffrage."[94] But Scott's position on woman suffrage shifted in the mid-1880s and, to Duniway's great disappointment, *The Oregonian* did not support woman suffrage in Oregon in 1884. In 1900, when woman suffrage came before Oregon voters for the second time, the increasingly conservative Scott helped defeat the amendment with a major anti-suffrage editorial published the day before the election.[95] Following the defeat, Duniway wrote to Henry Blackwell: "When one's foe is of one's own household, the humiliation is even harder to bear than the onslaught. But one thing is certain, Scott never touched so lively a 'corpse.'"[96] And, she confided to her son Clyde, "Henceforth, until he makes reparation, he is no brother of mine."[97]

In 1902, Scott "called off his dogs" and gave his sister "assurance that the strife has ceased."[98] Harvey Scott kept his promise and remained neutral during Oregon's equal suffrage campaigns of 1906 and 1908, yet the views he expressed in 1900 were well known. Prior to the 1906 election, Scott told his readers: "*The Oregonian* has not changed its mind, but is tired of contention."[99] He did not live to see the defeat in 1910 nor the final victory of 1912—the first year *The Oregonian* actively supported woman suffrage.

Beginning in 1870 and 1871, Abigail Scott Duniway helped establish local and state organizations in an attempt to educate the public and counter the opposition. With friends, she had founded a fledgling equal suffrage association at Albany in 1870. In the fall of 1871, while working alongside Anthony, the great organizer of the woman suffrage movement, Duniway assisted in forming associations such as the Multnomah County Woman Suffrage Association throughout Oregon and Washington Territory. At conventions in Olympia, Seattle, and other locations, Duniway served her organizational apprenticeship under Anthony's guidance, an experience that equipped her for leadership in organizations such as the Oregon State Woman Suffrage Association, officially founded in 1873, at a mass meeting in Portland.[100]

After touring with Anthony in 1871, Duniway also participated in suffrage efforts at the national level. Although she aligned herself closely with the National Woman Suffrage Association (NWSA), headed by Susan B. Anthony and Elizabeth Cady Stanton, Duniway thought highly of Lucy Stone [Blackwell] and Henry Blackwell, leaders in the American Woman Suffrage Association (AWSA). The two organizations were formed in 1869 after a split in the American Equal Suffrage Association caused by opposing positions on the proposed

Fifteenth Amendment and differing strategies for gaining woman suffrage. The NWSA, the more radical of the two, championed all aspects of women's rights and favored a federal amendment for woman suffrage, a goal not achieved until 1920. The AWSA welcomed men to its ranks, endorsed the Fifteenth Amendment, which would extend suffrage to black males, and focused on woman suffrage mainly through state-by-state campaigns. In 1889, Duniway was appointed to the committee that accomplished the 1890 merger of the two organizations as the National American Woman Suffrage Association (NAWSA).

Unlike eastern suffrage leaders, who first emphasized justice (natural rights) arguments and later turned to expediency (benefits to society) arguments for woman suffrage, Duniway used both. Not only should justice be served, she declared, but suffrage was the key to a more independent and equitable future for women, thereby improving society as a whole. At the same time, she was cautious about openly using expediency rhetoric that would fuel the opposition, particularly the liquor interests, who already believed woman suffrage would lead to prohibition.[101]

During the years of *The New Northwest*, Duniway traveled east four times for national woman suffrage conventions held in 1872, 1876, 1884, and 1885. Although she was invited regularly to attend more national meetings, she declined because of expense and family circumstances.[102]

Duniway's introduction to national conventions in 1872 was filled with color and excitement. At the invitation and encouragement of Susan B. Anthony, she attended the NWSA Convention, held in New York City on May 9 and 10. This was a presidential election year, and the NWSA meeting had been called to establish a People's Party of Progression and Human Rights; however, the convention broke apart when Victoria Woodhull established her own People's Party, later named the Equal Rights Party, and departed with her supporters. Following the chaos, Duniway conducted an amusing interview with the incomparable and engaging Victoria Woodhull, who had announced herself as candidate for President of the United States, with Frederick Douglass as her running mate.

Duniway also interviewed her childhood hero, Horace Greeley, another presidential hopeful, but she found "the perturbed old candidate" far from engaging and unwilling to lend his support to woman suffrage. Prior to interviewing Greeley, Duniway had spoken in favor of his candidacy on the floor of the NWSA Convention. After the unsatisfactory interview, she supported the reelection of Ulysses S. Grant, the "Radical Republican" candidate of the Republican Party, over Greeley, the "Liberal Republican" who had been endorsed as the candidate of the Democratic Party.

Duniway then went to Boston for the AWSA Convention, where she met Lucy Stone, Henry Blackwell, William Lloyd Garrison, Mary Livermore, and other reform "luminaries." She reported to readers of *The New Northwest* that her impromptu address to convention participants in Boston's Tremont Temple was "one of the best I ever had the pleasure of making."[103] And, typically, her rhetoric had included "boosterism"—speaking about the advantages of living and working in the Pacific Northwest: "There are many symptoms of rabid Oregon Fever reported among Tremont Temple patients today."

When the November presidential election of 1872 rolled around, Abigail Scott Duniway was at the Morrison Precinct in Portland, ready to cast her ballot for the Republican ticket. Earlier that month, as part of a national suffrage effort, she had urged readers of *The New Northwest* to join her at the polls: "Ladies of Portland, ladies of Oregon, ladies everywhere . . . Go and Vote!"[104] After all, as Susan B. Anthony argued during her 1871 tour of the Pacific Northwest, women were citizens with rights under the Fourteenth and Fifteenth Amendments, and those citizen rights included suffrage.[105] *The Oregonian* reported that four women appeared at the Morrison Precinct: "Mrs. A. J. Duniway, Mrs. M[aria] P. Hendee, Mrs. M. A. Lambert and Mrs. Beatty (colored)."[106] They were accompanied by Mr. Duniway and Mr. Hendee. Although the women's ballots were accepted, they were put *under*, not inside, the ballot box!

In June of 1876, the centennial year, Duniway set out with great enthusiasm for national suffrage meetings in New York City and the Centennial Exposition in Philadelphia. Her goal was to be in the East for Independence Day, but serious flooding in the West delayed her progress. Winding her way across the country, Duniway spent weeks lecturing in the territories of Idaho and Utah, and later in Iowa and Illinois. At last, in October, four months after her departure from Oregon, she arrived on the East Coast.

She participated in the AWSA Convention, attended the Woman's Congress, toured the great Centennial Exposition, visited with national figures in the suffrage movement, and basked in the glow of publishing *David and Anna Matson*, her epic poem based on a prose sketch by Whittier. Readers of *The New Northwest* learned that Duniway had been given a change of name by suffrage friends; however, the change from "A. J. Duniway" to "Abigail Scott Duniway" did not appear in *The New Northwest* until May 1, 1879. In December, Duniway started westward, lecturing along the way, but illness and over-work left her "nearly prostrate" for six weeks in Illinois.

After an absence of ten months, Duniway finally reached Portland in April of 1877, only to discover that her beautiful and talented daughter had been secretly married in the kind of "runaway marriage" that Duniway had warned against in lectures and writings. Clyde Duniway remembered his mother's reaction to the news:

> *Well do I recall the scene in the sitting room when sister Clara and Don H. Stearns confessed that while Mother was absent they had gone to Vancouver, Wash., and had been secretly married. Mother gave way to violent denun-ciations. Clara fainted, and Mother wished that she had died! Then the storm passed and the best was made of the situation.*[107]

Duniway was never again away from home for such a lengthy period.

In March of 1884, the year of Oregon's first vote on woman suffrage, Duniway traveled east again, this time to Washington, D. C., for the NWSA Convention. In her report to the convention, Duniway said she had divided her time about equally between Oregon and Washington, and had spoken in each state about seventy times a year for twelve and one-half years, making, "at a low estimate, 1,750 public speeches, or nearly five years of steady speaking."[108]

At least one convention session was given to the Oregon campaign, and Duniway reported in *The New Northwest*: "Suffice it to say, we are to have help from headquarters, and our visit to Washington will not be in vain."[109] She was elected one of five NWSA vice-presidents at large; with Anthony and other women, she paid a call to the White House, where they met a "badly frightened" President Chester Arthur; and she spoke in support of a Sixteenth Amendment for woman suffrage before the Senate Committee on Woman Suffrage. Following the convention, Duniway visited with Lucy Stone and Henry Blackwell in Boston and lectured on temperance to an audience of 2,500 in Boston's Tremont Temple.

When she arrived back in Oregon at the end of April, Duniway cam-paigned for the June vote on woman suffrage, only to suffer her first Oregon loss. The final vote was 28,176 opposed and 11,223 in favor. "The women of Oregon are beaten at the ballot-box," Duniway told readers of *The New North-west*, "but they are not crushed."[110]

Undaunted, Duniway traveled east again, in December of 1884, to lec-ture in Minneapolis, St. Paul, and Chicago. In October of 1885, she was off again for Minneapolis, this time for the AWSA Convention. She was accompanied by Miss Bessie Isaacs, of Washington Territory, described in Duniway's October 22nd editorial correspondence for *The New Northwest* as "the one genuine, live woman voter of the convention." Washington gave women the vote in 1883, and Duniway expressed pride at being the only delegate at the convention who was able to "introduce a living trophy of work accomplished."

Although she moved within the circles of the national woman suffrage movement, in later years Duniway crossed swords over campaign strategies with some of the eastern women.[111] In particular, she was opposed to what she saw as eastern interference with the campaigns she waged in the Pacific Northwest. "I have found it to be by far the better way to abstain from all sorts of hurrah methods," she wrote, "and let the men feel that we trust them for votes."[112] While Duniway wanted to keep the opposition unaroused and uninformed

*At the home of Mrs. Viola M. Coe (standing left), President of the Oregon State Woman Suffrage Association, Governor Oswald West signs the Oregon Woman Suffrage Proclamation authored by Abigail Scott Duniway, November 1912*

with what she termed her "still hunt" campaigns, eastern leaders called for "hur-rah campaigns" that made frontal attacks on the opposition. A number of suffrage leaders in the Pacific Northwest were loyal supporters of Duniway and agreed with her resistance to eastern interference;[113] some eastern suffrage leaders de-scribed Duniway as irascible and too stubborn to cooperate.[114]

Duniway was seriously ill and could not participate in activities for the Oregon campaign of 1912, but her Clay Street house was draped in yellow banners proclaiming "Votes for Women—Oregon Next" and "Oregon Equal Suffrage Headquarters."[115] For the first time, significant numbers of young col-lege women joined the fold to participate in the rallies, parades, and banquets that marked the campaign. Oregon's hour seemed near; Washington had adopted woman suffrage in 1910, and California had followed in 1911. Before the vote was taken, the "grand old lady," whose illness had been publicized throughout the campaign, was visited by Governor Oswald West, who asked her to write the Woman Suffrage Proclamation for the seventy-five thousand women of Oregon. When the votes were tallied, Oregon had adopted woman suffrage by a margin of 4,161, and Oregon's "Mother of Equal Suffrage" had lived to see the day and sign the proclamation.

When Abigail Scott Duniway was honored in 1913 as the first woman in Oregon to register to vote, she declined to list herself as "retired."[116] Her health improved, and she completed her autobiography, *Path Breaking*. She campaigned vigorously against prohibition, only to see it approved by Oregon in 1914, and served as honorary president for both the State Federation of Women's Clubs and the National Council of Women Voters. In the fall of 1915, Duniway suf-fered from a foot infection that led to blood poisoning and, on October 11th, a few days before her eighty-first birthday, she died in a Portland hospital.

## Reflections

Abigail Scott Duniway was conscious of her place in history and believed she would be remembered by future generations. Portland's Duniway Park and Duniway Middle School are tributes to her legacy and she is, as noted earlier, Oregon's representative in the National Women's Hall of Fame.

It is a surprising revelation, however, to visit Duniway's grave in Portland's Riverview Cemetery, to see the weathered letters on the small stone, nearly flush with the ground, which marks the final resting place of such a larger-than-life figure. How anonymous the little marker seems when contrasted with the towering monument erected to her brother, Harvey Whitefield Scott, who became a wealthy man. His smoothly carved block of gray granite stands high on a sloping hillside, with the matching, full-length, rectangular markers of his family members spread beneath in a semi-circle, while Abigail's grave lies far below in a less prominent area of the cemetery.

In her 1904 essay, "How I Became a Literary Woman," Duniway wrote:

> *The man or woman who expects to make the short life worth the living, must, like Tolstoi, speak the highest truth as he sees it regardless of consequences to self or purse, never losing sight of the fact that the day will come when humanity at large will come up to his ideal.*

*Abigail Scott Duniway, ca. 1905*

Abigail Scott Duniway lived and died a controversial figure, fighting for reform in a flawed society as long as she had strength to fight. Although she did not die in poverty, she was never wealthy. Duniway was a woman who believed in justice and lived by her principles, fully committed to her signature line, "Yours for Liberty." She did her best to leave the world a better place than she had found it.

As we turn to Abigail Scott Duniway's editorial debut in *The New Northwest*, "About Ourself," and register her self-confidence and enthusiasm as she begins her new adventure, we already know the end of the story. It will take more than forty years of struggle before women in all the western states where Duniway campaigned achieve full voting rights. And Oregon, her home state, will be the last in the Far West to approve woman suffrage. Although Duniway is described by historians as "tireless," and "hardy," we know that she got very tired, and she was often not well. But she never gave up; she would not quit. Perhaps, more than her accomplishments, more than her writing, that is what is most memorable, amazing, and inspiring about Abigail Scott Duniway.

# Notes for Introduction

1. The full name of Duniway's newspaper was *The New Northwest*, which is the title we use in our essay. Duniway, however, frequently referred to the paper simply as her *New Northwest* or the *New Northwest*, references we have preserved in selections from the newspaper.

2. Sherilyn Cox Bennion, *Equal to the Occasion: Woman Editors of the Nineteenth-Century West* (Reno: University of Nevada Press, 1990), 2. In her study of eleven western states and territories, Bennion looked at listings of editors in directories for 1870, 1880, 1890, and 1900. She found that, although the directories may not have included all women editors, "the proportion of women remained stable at about 1 percent until the end of the century, when it increased to 2 percent." In total, about three hundred western women edited more than 250 publications between 1854 and 1899. About twelve suffrage papers were published from 1869 to 1914 in the West (2-5).

3. Population figures for Portland are from the Bureau of Municipal Research and Service, Information Bulletin No. 106, *Population of Oregon Cities, Counties and Metropolitan Areas 1850 to 1957* (Eugene: University of Oregon, 1958), 4.

4. For a discussion of these leading citizens of Portland, see Paul G. Merriam, "Urban Elite in the Far West: Portland, Oregon, 1870-1890," *Arizona and the West* 18 (1976): 45-48; E. Kimbark MacColl, with Harry H. Stein, *Merchants, Money, & Power: The Portland Establishment, 1843-1913* (Portland: Georgian Press, 1983); E. Kimbark MacColl, *The Shaping of a City: Business and Politics in Portland, Oregon, 1885 to 1915* (Portland: Georgian Press, 1976).

5. "Temperance and Woman's Rights," *NNW,* 18 Aug. 1871.

6. Charles A. Tracy, III, "Police Function in Portland, 1851-1874, Part III," *Oregon Historical Quarterly* 18 (Fall 1979): 294-295, n. 209.

7. Paul G. Merriam, "The 'Other Portland': A Statistical Note on Foreign-Born, 1860-1901," *Oregon Historical Quarterly 80* (Fall 1979): 261.

8. Merriam, "The 'Other Portland,' " 266, Table 3.

9. For a discussion of Oregon's Exclusion Laws from 1844 to 1857, see Elizabeth McLagan, *A Peculiar Paradise: A History of Blacks in Oregon, 1788-1940* (Portland: Georgian Press, 1980), 23-31.

10. McLagan, 57.

11. Census figures for blacks and mulattos in Portland vary slightly depending on the sources from which they were derived. See McLagan, *A Peculiar Paradise*, 89, n. 18, and K. Keith Richard, "Unwelcome Settlers: Black and Mulatto Oregon Pioneers, Part II," *Oregon Historical Quarterly* 84 (Summer 1983): 177.

    The census figure for Portland's black population in 1880 was 192, and the state of Oregon's total black population was reported as 346 in 1870; 487 in 1880; and 1,186 in 1890. In comparison, Seattle's black population was 19 in 1880, and Washington's total black population was 207 in 1870; 325 in 1880; and 1,602 in 1890. For these population reports, see U. S. Bureau of the Census, *Negro Population in the United States, 1790-1915* (Washington, D. C.: Government Printing Office, 1918), 43-44; 95-105.

12. McLagan, 92.

13. Merriam, "The 'Other Portland,' " 266-267, Tables 3 and 4.

14. For discussion of these discriminatory restrictions and their enforcement, see Hugh Clark, *Portland's Chinese: The Early Years* (Portland: Center for Urban Education, Ethni-City Series, 1975; rev. ed. 1978), 14, and Tracy, "Police Function in Portland, Part III," 305-306.

15. The 1880 Chinese population figures in Oregon and Portland are from Merriam, "The 'Other Portland,' " 266-267, Tables 3 and 4. Chinese population figures for Washington Territory are from Robert Edward Wynne, "Reaction to the Chinese in the Pacific Northwest and British Columbia,

1850 to 1910," Ph.D. diss., University of Washington, 1964: 69. By 1880, Oregon had the second largest Chinese population in the United States (9,515); California, with about 75,000, had the largest number of Chinese (MacColl, *Shaping of a City*, 3).

16. These rumors are noted by both Clark, *Portland's Chinese*, 13, and Tracy, "Police Function in Portland," 307-308.

17. "Reflections on the Indian Question," *NNW*, 9 June 1881.

18. "Editorial Correspondence," *NNW*, 2 Sept. 1880.

19. Duniway opened the pages of *The NNW* to Pacific Northwest women writers such as Frances Fuller Victor, Belle Cooke, Minnie Myrtle Miller (Theresa Dyer), Bethenia Owens-Adair, and Mary P. Sawtelle. For examples of writings by these and other Pacific Northwest women, as well as essays about their lives, see Jean M. Ward and Elaine A. Maveety, eds., *Pacific Northwest Women, 1815-1925: Lives, Memories, and Writings* (Corvallis: Oregon State University Press, 1995).

20. Duniway's maternal grandfather, Lawrence Roelofson, was a founder of the Cumberland Presbytery in Illinois; her uncle, Neill Johnson, was a circuit-riding preacher in Illinois and later one of the founders of the Oregon Cumberland Presbyterian Church; her paternal grandfather, James Scott, gave up his leadership role with the Cumberland Presbyterians to become a deacon in the evangelical Tremont Baptist Church. In both Illinois and the Pacific Northwest, Duniway encountered religious prescriptions for woman's self-sacrifice and self-abnegation. As an advocate of equal suffrage, she was criticized from the pulpit by orthodox ministers; as a suffrage lecturer, doors of churches were often closed to her.

21. "Correspondence," answer to a correspondent from Goldendale, *NNW*, 17 Nov. 1881.

In 1893, Duniway confided to her son Clyde: "I have not been to church since I last wrote. Really, there is nothing in it for one who has sounded all its shallow depths in childhood and found nothing— nothing—a worse than nothing and vanity. And yet there must be something somewhere. Oh that I might find it" (ASD to Clyde Duniway, 31 Jan. 1893, Duniway Papers).

22. ASD to Clyde Duniway, 2 April 1893, Duniway Papers.

Duniway sometimes attended Unitarian services and was impressed by the work of Reverend T. L. (Thomas Lamb) Eliot of the First Unitarian Church in Portland, her friend and a supporter of woman suffrage. She wrote to her son Clyde that Unitarian services "are nearer to my style of thought than others" (20 Nov. 1892, Duniway Papers).

23. Duniway frequently referred to her "scientific investigation" and "serious investigation" of Spiritualism. In a letter to her son Clyde, she mentioned that some of her fellow "interested investigators" in Spiritualism included U. S. Senator John H. Mitchell, Governor William Thayer, and son Ralph Duniway's law partner (4 Oct. 1898, Duniway Papers). She also joined with friends such as William U'Ren for seances at the Portland home of Seth and Sophronia Lewelling. See Thomas C. McClintock, "Seth Lewelling, William S. U'Ren and the Birth of the Oregon Progressive Movement," *Oregon Historical Quarterly* 68 (Sept. 1967): 201.

24. Duniway's disgust with "cheap illiterate" mediums was mentioned in her letter to Clyde Duniway, 27 March 1905, Duniway Papers. To Duniway's regret, her sons did not share their mother's fascination with spiritualism and the occult.

25. ASD, *Path Breaking: An Autobiographical History of the Equal Suffrage Movement in Pacific Coast States* (Portland: James, Kerns and Abbott, 1914), 279.

26. "What Our Friends Say," *NNW*, 5 June 1874.

27. "Letter from the Mountains," *NNW*, 14 July 1871.

28. In an interview in 1913, Duniway said she "had never been to school but 5 months" in her life (Interview by Fred Lockley, *Oregon*

*Journal*, 22 June 1913); however, when a correspondent in 1914 inquired about her education, Duniway replied that she was grounded in the "proverbial 'three R's'" by "much less than a year's tuition—all told" (ASD to Barbara Booth, 11 April 1914, Duniway Papers). She assumed that "our busy mother must have taught us at her knee," and she recalled the "old Webster's Elementary Spelling book," which was "the first book I ever owned." Duniway brought this "blue-backed speller" with her to Oregon and used it when she began teaching in 1853.

29. ASD to Barbara Booth, 11 April, 1914. Duniway wrote Booth that, for her first teaching position in Oregon, she recalled "passing a creditable examination and receiving a first class certificate, though I believe I was not questioned severely, except in the proverbial 'three R's.'"

30. *Path Breaking*, 31.

31. For a substantial list of reform and religious papers read by the Scott family in Illinois, see Ruth B. Moynihan's excellent biography of Duniway, *Rebel for Rights, Abigail Scott Duniway* (New Haven: Yale University Press, 1983), 10-11.

32. The Scott family left Tazewell County, Illinois, on 2 April 1852 and arrived at Oregon City on 30 September 1853, after a difficult journey of about 2,400 miles. For detailed information on the Scott party and their overland trip, see David C. Duniway's introduction to "Journal of a Trip to Oregon," in Kenneth L. Holmes and David C. Duniway, eds., *Covered Wagon Women*, Vol. V (Glendale, CA: Arthur H. Clark Co., 1986), 22-38. Another edition of this volume of *Covered Wagon Women*, with an introduction by Ruth B. Moynihan, was published in 1997 by the University of Nebraska Press.

33. Abigail Jane Scott, "Journal of a Trip to Oregon," MS, Duniway Papers. The journal appears in Holmes and Duniway, eds., *Covered Wagon Women*, Vol. V.

A copy of the manuscript was made during the winter of 1852-53 and sent to Grandfather James Scott in Pleasant Grove,

Illinois, but the potential publisher, a relative of the Scotts, considered it "to [*sic*] much out of date . . . [to] pay expenses" (L. S. Turley to James Scott, 28 Feb. [1856?], Edwin Browne Papers; cited by Moynihan in *Rebel for Rights*, 231, n. 20).

34. The journal was a primary source for *Captain Gray's Company* (1859) and *From the West to the West* (1905), and also provided details of the overland journey for *The Old and the New* (1897), her last serialized novel in *The Pacific Empire*.

35. ASD, interview by Fred Lockley, *Oregon Journal*, 22 June 1913.

36. ASD to Clyde Duniway, 17 Dec. 1894, Duniway Papers.

37. "Narrative by Abigail Jane Scott Duniway," *The Oregonian*, 7 Oct. 1900; rpt. in Harvey Scott, ed., and Leslie M. Scott, comp., *History of the Oregon Country*, Vol. III (Cambridge, MA: Riverside Press, 1924), 248-249.

38. Oregon City *Argus*, 12 Sept. 1857. Duniway considered the writing of this poem to be the "portentous hour that I, as a 'literary woman,' must have been born. I scribbled the ode in question, simply because I could not choose but scribble." See "How I Became a Literary Woman," *The Western Lady* (Portland: n. p., 1904), 3.

39. W. L. Adams, *Argus*, 12 Sept. 1857. William Lysander Adams (1821-1906) was the Whig editor of the Oregon City *Argus*, which became the first distinctively Republican newspaper in Oregon. See *Argus*, 16 Jan. 1858; 3 July 1858.

40. Asahel Bush (1824-1913) was a member of what was called the "Salem clique" of Democrats who were in control of Oregon's government prior to the Civil War. He became associated in 1868 with W. S. Ladd in the Ladd & Bush Bank in Salem. In *History of Oregon Newspapers* (Portland: Binfords & Mort, 1939), George S. Turnbull wrote: "Bush was a hard fighter, sharp of tongue and pen, and his struggles with Editors Dryer of *The Oregonian*, Adams of the *Argus*, and others helped fashion the 'Oregon style' of journalism" (81).

41. Thomas Hall Pearne, *The Pacific Coast Christian Advocate*, 14 May 1859. Pearne (1820-1910) was a Methodist minister, one of the early trustees of Willamette University, and an associate of Asahel Bush. In comparison with criticisms of *Captain Gray's Company* from Bush and Pearne, *The Oregonian*, edited by Thomas Jefferson Dryer, was brief and mild: "[I]n hastily looking over pages after the merits we do not find them" (*The Oregonian*, 30 April 1859).

42. "How I Became a Literary Woman," 3. According to Duniway, her "patient sister," Catherine A. Scott Coburn, associate editor, "supervised" publication of *Captain Gray's Company* as a serial in *The NNW*, 21 May 1875 to 29 Oct. 1875.

43. "Letter from a Farmer's Wife," *Oregon Farmer*, 5 June 1860.

44. The Albany *State Rights Democrat* of 24 Nov. 1886 advertised: "Mrs. Jackson and Mrs. Duniway, 1st and Broad Albin Sts. Fashionable Millinery Goods." In *Path Breaking*, Duniway wrote that she "had bought out a partner and was ready to start up with millinery and notions" before she called on Jacob Mayer in Portland to secure goods for her shop (19).

45. "Personal Reminiscences," 56.

46. Duniway's description of the event has the ring of an epiphany and the overtones of a religious experience: "The light permeated my very bones, filling me with such hope, courage and determination as no obstacle could conquer and nothing but death overcome" (*Path Breaking*, 40).

47. ASD, *Argus*, 22 Jan. 1859.

48. *Path Breaking*, 40. A local woman suffrage society had been organized earlier in 1870, at Salem, by Col. C. A. Reed and Judge G. W. Lawson.

49. ASD in Elizabeth Cady Stanton, Susan B. Anthony, and Matilda Joslyn Gage, eds., *History of Woman Suffrage*, Vol. III (1886; rpt. New York: Arno and *The New York Times*, 1969): 768.

50. *Path Breaking*, 68. This New Year's Eve speech might have been given to the San Francisco County Woman Suffrage Association, the same group Duniway addressed on Wednesday evening, 4 Jan. 1871, at Dashaway Hall in San Francisco (San Francisco *Pioneer*, 5 Jan. 1871).

51. *Path Breaking*, 68.

52. San Francisco *Pioneer*, 5 Jan. 1871. *The Oregonian* of 16 Jan. 1871 carried a similar announcement: "Mrs. A. J. Duniway of Albany has taken the position of Oregon editor upon the *Pioneer*, a paper published in San Francisco and devoted to the promotion of woman's rights."

53. ASD, "Our Editorial Bow," "Oregon Department," San Francisco *Pioneer*, 5 Jan. 1871. Microfilm of *The Pioneer* is at the Bancroft Library at the University of California, Berkeley.

54. *Path Breaking*, 68.

55. Although the word "obey" was not included in their wedding vows, the marriage of Abigail Scott and Ben Duniway was evidently not created in heaven. Abigail did not regret that Ben's injury placed her in the public arena as a businesswoman and later as a newspaper editor; however, her interests were quite different from Ben's. He was a man who loved to talk about ranches and horses, including the matched pairs of pintoes he located for circuses; she was a woman who loved to discuss politics and literature. Although Ben was supportive of equal rights for women, his daily life was significantly different from his wife's, and he is mentioned frequently in Clyde Duniway's unpublished "Memories of Abigail Scott Duniway" (1929; rev. 1932) as the available, caring, parental figure. In his last years, Ben was quite ill, and Abigail cared for him at home. The year after Ben's death, Abigail wrote to Clyde: "I know what the light [of love] *is*, but *alas*, I never, never enjoyed it" (ASD to Clyde Duniway, 17 Nov. 1897, Duniway Papers).

56. *The Oregonian*, 25 Jan. 1871. We have found no evidence that Emily Pitts-Stevens intended to move *The Pioneer* to Portland. Her paper, originally *The Mercury*, began in September of 1869, with Pitts-Stevens as editor. Although targeted as a "free love" advocate by her opponents, she remained

editor until September of 1873, when Mrs. C. C. Calhoun became the publisher. *The Pioneer* survived for only a few months under Calhoun.

57. Lee Nash, "Abigail versus Harvey: Sibling Rivalry in the Oregon Campaign for Woman Suffrage," *Oregon Historical Quarterly* 98 (Summer 1997): 146. Nash found documentation for official approval and endorsement of Ben's position in June and July of 1873 (p. 162, n. 18). However, Ben's obituary in *The Oregonian*, reprinted in *The Pacific Empire* under editor Abigail Duniway, made no mention of his work at the customs house. It spoke of Ben as "an excellent farmer" who, "about ten years ago" had gone "to Eastern Idaho, where, with two or three of his sons, he engaged in stock raising" (*The Oregonian*, 5 Aug. 1896; *PE*, 6 Aug 1896).

58. In *Path Breaking*, Duniway wrote that she did not consult with her brother, but he congratulated her on the first issue of *The NNW*: "'You have made a capital paper,' he said, as he surveyed my little 'plant,' his eyes gleaming with pleasure and surprise" (32).

59. Harvey Whitefield Scott (1838-1910) was a junior editor with *The Oregonian* when Duniway started *The NNW*. He had engaged in classical studies and graduated from Pacific University at Forest Grove, the only member of the first graduating class in 1863. Then, while studying law in the offices of Judge E. D. Shattuck, Harvey served as city librarian for Portland (1864-65). Although he was admitted to the Oregon Bar in September of 1865, journalism was his chosen field. From 1865 to 1872, he held what biographer Lee Nash described as "a sort of editorial apprenticeship" with *The Oregonian* and "adhered faithfully to the radical Republican line on political issues" ("Abigail versus Harvey," 144). As a political appointee, he served as collector of customs in Portland from 1870 to 1876. Scott returned to *The Oregonian* as a part owner and chief editor in 1877, a position from which he wielded considerable power until his death in 1910. Those who knew Harvey Scott were

impressed with his photographic memory, carefully constructed prose, and knowledge of Latin, Greek, history, and literature.

60. "Correspondence," *NNW*, 23 June 1871. Harvey Scott did, however, contribute some pieces to *The NNW* during its early years.

61. Catherine Amanda Scott Coburn (1839-1913) was widowed in 1868 and taught school for several years before joining *The NNW*. She was described by contemporaries as a writer who "observes keenly, thinks carefully, feels truly, judges unharshly, depicts clearly." See Helen F. Spalding, "Mrs. Catherine A. Coburn," in Mary Osborn Douthit, ed., *Souvenir of Western Women* (Portland: Anderson & Duniway, 1905), 173. Turnbull said that Coburn, like Duniway, "was a gifted writer" (*History of Oregon Newspapers*, 179). After five years with *The NNW*, Coburn left in 1879 to serve as editor of the Portland *Daily Bee*. She became editor of the *Evening Telegram* in 1880 and joined the editorial staff of *The Oregonian* in 1888.

62. George P. Rowell, in the *American Newspaper Directory* (NY: Rowell, 1884), reported *The NNW* circulation as 980 in 1873; over 1,000 in 1880; nearly 2,000 in 1882; and over 3,000 in 1884. *The American Newspaper Annual Directory* (Philadephia: Ayer) gave the circulation as 1,750 in 1883 and 3,000 in 1885, 1886, and 1887.

The yearly subscription rate, until 1886, was $3.00. In November of 1885, Duniway announced to readers that subscriptions starting in January of 1886 would be reduced from $3.00 to $2.50, if paid in advance.

63. "End of Volume VI," *NNW*, 7 Sept. 1877.

64. Duniway Publishing Company Papers, Oregon Historical Society.

65. "Cash Book of the New Northwest," April, June, July 1886, Duniway Publishing Company Papers, Oregon Historical Society.

66. *The Revolution*, which opposed the Fourteenth and Fifteenth Amendments because women were not explicitly included, began in January of 1868, with Anthony as publisher and Stanton and Parker Pillsbury

as editors. Within two years, the paper was in serious debt, and Theodore Tilton, first president of the National Woman Suffrage Association, arranged for it to be sold in 1870 for one dollar to Laura Curtis Bullard, a wealthy heiress. Within eighteen months, Bullard abandoned the paper, and *The Revolution* was ended. Anthony, however, had assumed the indebtedness of $10,000, which she managed to repay in 1876, after years of lecturing throughout the country.

67. "From Oregon," *The Revolution*, 6 Oct. 1870. In this letter, dated July 12, 1870, at Albany, Duniway included a description of herself: "I am the mother of six children, own and carry on a millinery establishment of no mean proportions, write sketches and 'squibs' for half a dozen newspapers, talk human rights on appropriate occasions, keep pretty well posted in politics, have a life insurance agency, and still have plenty of time to vote without neglecting the baby."

68. For an excellent work on this 1871 tour and Anthony's other visits to the Pacific Northwest, see G. Thomas Edwards, *Sowing Good Seeds: The Northwest Suffrage Campaigns of Susan B. Anthony* (Portland: Oregon Historical Society Press, 1990).

69. Susan B. Anthony, "1871 Diary," Papers of Susan B. Anthony, Box 2, Library of Congress. Anthony's diary notation was: "Camped with the D's this night.—the first time in my life. Mr. D., the Keltys [Sarah Maria Scott Kelty and James Kelty]—3 boys—Clara, Mrs. D. and self. Packed side by side like herrings—can't say I like it better than nice bedroom and hair matress [*sic*]."

Years later, in a letter to Duniway, Anthony recalled the camping experience: "Your little yellow-covered *Pacific Empire* has just attracted my attention, and, sure enough, it does seem like old times to read your report of the Salem State Fair, and remember the tent or wigwam in which all of your family and I bunked on the ground in 1871; that is my only experience of sleeping out of doors during all these years" ("Letter from Susan B. Anthony," *PE*, 31 Oct. 1895).

70. For discussion of the relationship between Duniway and Anthony, see Jean M. Ward, "The Emergence of a Mentor-Protégé Relationship: The 1871 Pacific Northwest Lecture Tour of Susan B. Anthony and Abigail Scott Duniway," *Proceedings of the 1982 Northwest Women's Heritage Conference Sponsored by the University of Washington and the Ford Foundation* (Seattle: University of Washington, 1984), 120-45.

71. Duniway was speaking in favor of a woman suffrage amendment to a temperance bill, a provision to allow women to vote on temperance issues. The bill failed by a close vote of 22 to 21. See "Legislation," *NNW*, 11 Oct. 1872; "Suffrage in the House, *NNW*, 18 Oct. 1872; "Temperance Suffrage Bill," *NNW*, 25 Oct. 1872; *Path Breaking*, 59-61.

72. *Path Breaking*, 52.

73. "Editorial Correspondence," *NNW*, 12 March 1875.

74. *Path Breaking*, 62.

75. To clarify her position, Duniway argued that the only cure for the injustices caused by intemperance "was not the ballot *per se,* but the independence, liberty, and financial and political standing that the ballot represents, which will eventually enable free women to hold men, though without any arbitrary show or exercise of authority, to as strict a line of moral rectitude as men to-day hold women" ("Editorial Correspondence," *NNW*, 10 June 1886).

76. Amelia Bloomer, *Life and Writings of Amelia Bloomer*, ed. D. C. Bloomer (1895; rpt. NY: Schocken Books, 1975), 39.

77. Mari Jo Buhle and Paul Buhle, eds., *The Concise History of Woman Suffrage: Selections from the Classic Work of Stanton, Anthony, Gage, and Harper* (Urbana: University of Illinois Press, 1978), 143.

78. Andrew Sinclair, *Era of Excess: A Social History of the Prohibition Movement* (NY: Harper and Row, 1964), 84.

79. ASD, "Victory!—We Went, We Fought, We Conquered," *NNW*, 1 March 1872; "*Oregonian* Report," rpt. in *NNW*, 1 March 1872.

80. ASD, "Proceedings," NNW, 28 Feb. 1873.

81. Jack S. Blocker, Jr., *Give to the Wind Thy Fears: The Women's Temperance Crusade, 1873-74* (Westport, CT: Greenwood Press, 1985), 5.

82. Jack S. Blocker, Jr., "Separate Paths: Suffragists and the Women's Temperance Crusade," *SIGNS* 10 (Spring 1985): 462.

83. Ruth Bordin, *Woman and Temperance: The Quest for Power and Liberty, 1873-1900* (Philadelphia: Temple University Press, 1981), 26.

84. Beyond the newspaper reports, for additional information on the Woman's Crusade in Portland, see Frances Fuller Victor, *The Women's War with Whisky; or, Crusading in Portland* (Portland: Geo. H. Himes, 1874). Duniway published her criticism of Victor's work, faulting her friend for giving only one side of the Crusade and failing to mention women's rights and woman suffrage (ASD, "Women's War with Whisky," *NNW*, 11 Sept. 1874).

85. In 1879, when Willard was elected president of the WCTU, membership was at 27,000. It soared to 73,000 within four years and reached about 176,000 by the turn of the century. For a discussion of WCTU membership growth, see Barbara Leslie Epstein, *The Politics of Domesticity: Women, Evangelism, and Temperance In Nineteenth-Century America* (Middleton, CT: Wesleyan University Press, 1981), 115.

86. During the summer of 1886, after Washington's local option campaign, Duniway wrote a series of seven essays on "The Temperance Problem" and explained her position. "We could not join in this movement," she wrote, "because . . . it began at the wrong end of the temperance reform. It pictured the drunkard as a martyr to the man who sold him intoxicating liquors, rather than a victim of his own bestiality and moral and physical disease. It sought to distract women from the basic principle upon which alone they might build a platform of liberty and justice" (The Temperance Problem," *NNW*, 8 July 1886).

87. Even Duniway's Oregon suffrage friends,

Dr. Bethenia Owens-Adair and Dr. Mary Thompson, both of whom were prohibitionists, thought Duniway should step down from leadership of the Oregon suffrage movement in 1886. On the national level, Anthony and Shaw were particularly displeased by Duniway's 1889 speech to the National Woman Suffrage Association, in which she announced: "I declare that as a temperance woman, I am opposed to prohibition on principle" ("Ballots and Bullets," NWSA Convention, Washington, D. C., Feb. 1889; rpt. in *Path Breaking*, 188-200).

88. ASD to Clyde Duniway, 24 Nov. 1893, Duniway Papers.

89. Lucy Stone, "One Faithful Worker," *The Woman's Journal;* rpt. *NNW*, 23 Sept. 1886.

90. Eleanor Flexner, *Century of Struggle: The Woman's Rights Movement in the United States*, rev. ed. (Cambridge: Belknap Press of Harvard University Press, 1975), 162.

91. For a discussion of these two Washington Territory cases in 1887 and 1888, see T. A. Larson, "The Woman Suffrage Movement in Washington," *Pacific Northwest Quarterly* 67 (April 1976): 54-55.

92. When leaders of the National American Woman Suffrage Association attributed the 1896 victory in Idaho to the work of the NAWSA Campaign Committee, Duniway reported that she had given over 140 public lectures in Idaho from 1876 to 1895, and had been "obliged to travel an aggregate of over 12,000 miles by river, rail, stage and buckboard" ("An Open Letter," addressed to "Mrs. M. C. Athey, Cor. Sec. Ida. E. S. A.," 6 Jan. 1897, typescript, ASD Scrapbook #2, Duniway Papers).

93. Nash, "Abigail versus Harvey," 147.

94. Harvey Scott, *The Oregonian*, 30 Nov. 1883.

95. Harvey Scott, *The Oregonian*, 3 June 1900.

96. ASD to Henry Blackwell, 22 June 1900, ASD Scrapbook #1, Duniway Papers.

97. ASD to Clyde Duniway, 4 July 1900, Duniway Papers.

98. ASD to Clyde Duniway, 21 Feb. 1902, Duniway Papers.

99. Harvey Scott, *The Oregonian*, 2 June 1906.

100. "Call for a Woman Suffrage Convention," *NNW*, 31 Jan. 1873. As secretary of the Multnomah County Woman Suffrage Association, Duniway announced "a mass meeting of friends of Woman Suffrage in the State of Oregon and Territory of Washington," to be held in Portland on February 14 and 15, "to organize a permanent State Society, to meet once in each year." Supporters from California were also invited to attend and "to co-operate" in this endeavor.

After the February meeting, Duniway reported that Mrs. H. W. Williams, Vice-President of the Multnomah County Woman Suffrage Association, served as president *pro tem* for the session. Mrs. Abby B. Gibson was elected president of the OSWSA, Catherine Scott Coburn was elected secretary, and vice presidents were elected from each Oregon county. The name of the organization was the Oregon State Woman Suffrage Association, and *The NNW* was to be the "organ of the Association" ("The Convention," *NNW*, 21 Feb. 1873). To Duniway's dismay, however, the OSWSA never provided funding for *The NNW*. In 1877, when Hattie A. Loughary was president, the preamble and constitution of the OSWSA appeared on the front page of *The NNW* (2 Feb. 1877).

101. Lauren Kessler, "A Siege of the Citadels: Search for a Public Forum for the Ideas of Oregon Woman Suffrage," *Oregon Historical Quarterly* 84 (Summer 1983): 131. In her content analysis of all sixteen years of *The NNW*, Kessler identified two hundred editorials that directly argued for woman suffrage and found that the economic inequality argument, used sixty-two times, was Duniway's most frequently used argument. Suffrage as a natural right (the justice argument) was a close second and appeared sixty times. Enfranchised women will benefit society (a clear expediency argument) appeared only seventeen times, and Kessler attributes this to Duniway's concern that use of the expediency argument would draw the attention of the opposition, especially the liquor interests.

102. In 1880, for example, Matilda Joslyn Gage urged Duniway to attend the NWSA Convention in Indianapolis and a mass meeting in Chicago, but she found the cost prohibitive and had neither "the time nor strength to work our way across the continent this year" (Matilda Joslyn Gage and ASD, "Letter and Answer," *NNW*, 6 May 1880).

103. ASD, "Editorial Correspondence," *NNW*, 21 June 1872.

104. ASD, "Important," *NNW*, 1 Nov. 1872.

105. During her second 1871 lecture in Portland, Anthony claimed that "by a fair and liberal interpretation of the Fourteenth and Fifteenth Amendments to the Constitution of the United States, the women of this country have the right to vote, or in other words that women are already voters" ("Women Already Voters," *NNW*, 15 Sept. 1871).

In 1872, Susan B. Anthony and a number of other women, including three of her sisters, went to the polls in Rochester, New York, and succeeded in voting in the presidential election. She was arrested, tried, and found guilty of the crime of illegal voting. Before her trial in 1873, Anthony gave lectures in which she posed the question: "Is it a crime for a U. S. citizen to vote?" Two years later, in *Minor v. Happerstett* (1874), the United States Supreme Court settled the question and ruled that citizenship, as defined in the Fourteenth Amendment, did not grant the franchise to women. For particulars on the trial, see *Account of the Proceedings of the Trial of Susan B. Anthony* (Rochester, NY: Daily Democrat and Chronicle Book Print, 1874).

106. "The Votes of the Ladies," *The Oregonian*, rpt. in *NNW*, 8 Nov. 1872.

107. Clyde Duniway, "My Memories of Abigail Scott Duniway" (1929; rev. 1932), Duniway Papers.

108. ASD, "Address before the National Woman Suffrage Association," Washington,

*Abigail Scott Duniway is the first woman to register as a voter in Oregon,
witnessed at her home by Multnomah County Clerk John B. Coffey, 1913.*

D. C., Feb. 1884, ASD Scrapbook #2,
Duniway Papers.

109. ASD, "From Washington," *NNW*, 20
March 1884.

110. ASD, "To Our Patrons," *NNW*, 12 June
1884.

111. These included Clara Bewick Colby and
Anna Howard Shaw. Colby (1845-1916)
established *The Woman's Tribune* in Nebraska
in 1883, later moved to Washington, D. C.,
and brought the paper to Portland in 1904,
only to see it end in five years. Although
originally an arm of the NWSA, *The
Woman's Tribune* lost subscribers to *The
Woman's Journal*, which became the official
newspaper of the suffrage movement at the
time of the 1890 merger of the NWSA and
AWSA. Duniway's hostility to Colby was
clear: "[B]ecause of your ignorance of our
methods, you are doing the Suffrage
movement infinite harm" (ASD to Clara B.
Colby, 22 March 1905, Duniway Papers).
And Duniway wrote to Alice Blackwell:
"Mrs. Colby, whose presence among us is
the greatest menace to our next campaign, is

doing everything in her power to stir up
strife between myself and the
prohibitionists. . . . Our W.C.T.U. was held
well in hand before she came among us"
(ASD to Alice Stone Blackwell, 28 July
1906, Duniway Papers). The Clara Bewick
Colby Collection is at the Huntington
Library, San Marino, California.

Anna Howard Shaw (1847-1919) was
the major target of Duniway's anger about
eastern methods. After the disastrous
campaign of 1906, Duniway wrote to Shaw:
"One more 'hurrah campaign' in Oregon
and we should be in the same boat with
every state like Massachusetts, New York,
Ohio, Pennsylvania, Nebraska, Iowa and
California. Do you not notice? and can you
not learn from experience that the National
method not only never wins a state election
but can never even get a campaign started?"
(ASD to Anna Howard Shaw, 18 Sept.
1906, Duniway Papers). The Anna Howard
Shaw Papers are at the Schlesinger Library,
Radcliffe College.

112. ASD to Mrs. M. C. Athey, 6 Jan. 1897, Duniway Papers.

113. Among them were Emma Smith Devoe and Viola May Coe. Devoe, who led the successful Washington campaign in 1910, was a close friend of Duniway, agreed with her on campaign strategy, and shared Duniway's dislike of Anna Howard Shaw. Devoe managed to keep the eastern forces out of Washington during the 1910 campaign and was president of the National Council of Women Voters, which she founded at Tacoma. The Emma Smith Devoe Collection is located at Washington State Library.

Viola May Coe, another of Duniway's close friends, served often as president or acting president of the Oregon suffrage association beginning in 1905, and she led the successful campaign in 1912, during Duniway's illness. Both Coe and Dr. Marie Equi, of the College Women's Club, supported Duniway in her conflicts with national leaders. In a lengthy letter in 1912, Equi challenged Anna Howard Shaw: "[H]ave you ever won one state in which you have campaigned? Why haven't you? Why did the women of Washington and California keep you out? . . . [Y]ou are the Boss and dislike Mrs. Duniway" (Marie Equi to Anna Howard Shaw, undated copy of 1912 letter, ASD Scrapbook #2, Duniway Papers).

114. Even Susan B. Anthony found Duniway stubborn. Prior to Oregon's 1900 vote on woman suffrage, Anthony wrote to Clara Bewick Colby, then in Washington, D. C.: "I certainly would *not* go, nor *advise you nor any other one* of our Suffrage speakers to step foot into that State, until after the election, unless duly and formally invited by Mrs. Duniway, and pledged to speak on precisely such lines as she directed. . . . [I]n the nature of things, [she] must lead the affairs there and [her] head is so full of crotchets that it is impossible for her to *co-operate* with anybody; she must simply *control*. . . . If the Amendment fails, I do not want you personally or the National generally to have any hand in causing it, whereas, if it wins, I want Mrs. Duniway to have the entire credit thereof. She is amply sufficient, not only unto herself, but unto the whole State of Oregon as well" (Susan B. Anthony to Clara Bewick Colby, 19 May 1899, Clara Bewick Colby Papers).

115. Portland *Telegram*, 1 Feb. 1912.

116. *The Oregonian*, 15 Feb. 1913.

# 1871

## About Ourself

In coming before the reading public in the capacity of editor and proprietor of a newspaper, and presuming to occupy ground which has heretofore been *monopolized by gentlemen*, we feel the responsibility of our position, and realize the necessity of making our work come up practically to the high standard which alone should satisfy the gleaner after truth. As our work belongs to the public, we feel that the public has a right to know something about us; so we will indulge our readers in the following account of our stewardship:

The first nine years of our married life were spent upon a farm, where, surrounded by a growing family, we unhesitatingly performed prodigies of labor, doing anything and everything that came in our way, until health was destroyed and constitution broken. We are naturally acquisitive, calculating and fond of active business life; and though on the farm we had work enough to do, yet every farmer's wife knows that her work is considered wholly unremunerative so far as herself is concerned. We are not complaining, but simply stating facts.

Before marriage we had learned some of the sweets of pecuniary independence, for we had taught school and followed dress-making and millinery. Desiring to please our good husband, we struggled to be contented and remain upon the farm. To relieve our active brain we began to scribble. It always *was* our forte, and if we had been a man, we'd have had an editor's position and a handsome salary at twenty-one. Sketches for newspapers, with occasional poems and letters, occupied us for a while, but health entirely failing, we were compelled to spend hours of each day in a reclining position, surrounded, in a lonely farm house, with the prattle of happy children, and occupied with our own intense thoughts.

We had reached the advanced age of twenty-two years, the age at which most boys enter college, and there we were, a wife and mother, but a broken-down, yet hopeful, spirited child; nothing more, nothing less. When tired out with household cares and no longer able to sit up, we would recline upon the lounge and scribble.

We wrote a book [*Captain Gray's Company*]. We published. It failed. Any body might have known it would who had one particle of public experience. The thing never had a stronger censor than ourself. It was full of ideal nothings and a good deal of good sense, but it contained many imperfections of our own and the

*The Duniway Family, ca. 1868.*
*Left to right: Hubert, Ben, Willis, Clyde (in his father's arms),*
*Ralph (added later), Clara, Abigail, and Wilkie.*

publisher's, and we both lost money. We deserved to lose it.

Misfortunes following us, we left the farm and engaged in teaching school. Here commenced our real battle with public life. Strong men, who might have been better employed in making rails, opposed our work, but we struggled on and succeeded. We taught school for four years, having had under our care during that time some thirteen hundred children. Health failed again and we tried a millinery and dress-making business. We succeeded again, and active business in a new direction again restored our health.

We have served a regular apprentice-ship at working—washing, scrubbing, patching, darning, ironing, plain sewing, raising babies, milking, churning and poultry raising. We have kept boarders, taught school, taught music, wrote for the newspapers, made speeches and carried on an extensive millinery and dress-making business. We can prove by the public that this work has been *well* done. Now, having reached the age of thirty-six, and having brought up a family of boys to set type and a daughter to run the millinery store, we propose to edit and publish a newspaper, and we intend to establish it as one of the permanent institutions of the country.

We started out in business with strong prejudices against "strong-minded women." Experience and common sense have conquered those prejudices. We see, under the existing customs of society, one half of the women over-taxed and under-paid; hopeless, yet struggling toilers in the world's drudgery; while the other half are frivolous, idle and expensive. Both of these conditions of society are wrong. Both have resulted from woman's lack of political and consequent pecuniary and moral responsibility. To prove this, and to elevate woman, that thereby herself and son and brother man may be benefited and the world made better, purer, and happier, is the aim of this publication. We ask no favors of a "generous public." We shall give value received for every dollar we obtain. Half that we have planned to do we cannot now enumerate; but we shall prove to you if you will sustain our paper that we are not only in earnest, but that we know just what we are about.

*(May 5, 1871)*

## Our First Attendance at a Political Meeting

We were living upon a farm, engaged in the multitudinous duties incumbent upon mistress, dairywoman, nurse, washerwoman and maid of all work—a way in which most farmers' wives are supported(?) by energetic and thrifty husbands, who never dream that women earn a dollar. Our good husband generally took us all to town to church on Sundays; but we had no other opportunities for intellectual improvement except the weekly visits of the *Oregon Farmer*, then published at Portland, the *Oregon Argus*, Wm. L. Adams' paper, published at Oregon City. But we somehow learned that the great orator, Col. E. D. [Edward Dickinson] Baker, was to speak in Lafayette on a certain day.[1] A longing desire to hear him took possession of us and we announced to our honored liege that we should *go*.

He demurred at first, but a few cogent reasons for our desire to go, the principal one being that the illustrious statesman was an acquaintance of our childhood, gained the point, and taking the little ones with us, just as we and every other family did when going to church, we repaired to the village. Stopping at the house of Hon. J. R. McBride, we acquainted Mrs. M. with our intention and the motives which prompted it. The move, indeed, seemed a bold one, as we

*Col. Edward Dickinson Baker*

were told that a certain ex-editor, who was to introduce the speaker, always told dirty anecdotes; that ladies were not expected to be present, and, if they went, they would be insulted.

Mrs. M. and her worthy mother agreed to face the storm with us. So it was arranged that while they were preparing luncheon, we should canvass the town for volunteers. Our numbers were mustered by one o'clock, the hour appointed for the speaking, and seven ladies, accompanied by their husbands, repaired to the hall, which was thronged with men to the number of several hundred. As we entered the crowded room half-audible hisses were heard in several quarters. That was eleven years ago—men have improved much in manners since then—and we began to feel a sensation of trepidation rather poorly according with our previous firmness.

Hon. E. D. Baker, the man of iron heart and eagle eye, rose majestically from his seat on the rostrum, and waving his hand over that dense masculine assembly, welcomed the ladies with cheerful speech and happy utterance, ordering room for them near the speaker, in his own gallant way, and order reigned supreme. Some of the stale jokes of the ex-editor, before alluded to, may have been rendered in a "dryer" manner, owing to the presence of ladies, but no other serious result was manifest. As we sat there for hours, listening to the burning eloquence which no pen can delineate, and thought of the hundreds of women whose husbands were present, harkening to the magic of the great man's voice, while they were compelled to stay at home in utter inanition, our first great lesson on *equality before the law* was learned.

Many women were shocked at the audacity of the few who broke the way, but among all those shocked one could not be found who was willing to stay away from the next political meeting. For years ladies have attended these meetings, and spent more time in so doing than they will occupy in voting during their remaining days upon the earth; yet not one of them has neglected a home duty in consequence or forgotten her innate womanhood upon any public occasion. Wish we could say as much for the men.

*(May 26, 1871)*

## Answer to a Timid Woman

A "timid woman" writes: "Would I not run the risk of ruining my character by trying to engage in business? Men are so apt to talk about independent women."

Tut! Tut! Suppose they do! They "talk about" lazy women, idle women, expensive women, proud women, slatterns, wantons and prudes. They criticize everybody, and to set yourself down in silly inanity for fear they'll "talk about you" won't prevent their talking about you, neither will your "timidity" pay your bills. Command respect and you'll get it. Affect timidity and you'll get no substantial sympathy. The gods help those who help themselves.

*(May 26, 1871)*

## Hardships of Farmers' Wives (Washing)

We hope the well meaning farmers of Oregon will be disposed to deal leniently with us while we talk to them in a spirit of good-will about the hardships that are daily endured by the wives of most of them.

A woman who is engaged in the trying task of bearing and bringing up a family of children, should be allowed at least some of the seasons of rest and relaxation which all men, with common consent, accord to their brood animals, that seem to have a direct money value exceeding that of the mother of their children. . . .

No farmer's wife who is a mother should be allowed to do the washing for the family. Thousands of women have actually been crucified by the wash-tub. We are going to say something here that will startle you more, we fear, than our announcement that we shall vote. Washing is not a woman's work. It is peculiarly trying upon the most important functions of the procreative existence. It is especially weakening and trying upon the back and loins. The hot suds excites perspiration, which leaves the system in a condition to engender diseases peculiar to women. It is labor that requires strength equal to black-smithing or making rails. Yet we have known many a strong man who would grudgingly devote a half-hour to the fretful baby who was crying for its natural nourishment, while the weak mother was struggling for life at the wash-tub, overheating the baby's food, sowing seed for her own and her offspring's premature decay—the man never once imagining that it was his duty to let the wife sit or lie down to rest with the baby while he vigorously applied the "grease of his own elbows" to the ridgy washboard.

*(June 2, 1871)*

## Hardships of Farmers' Wives (Isolation)

The farmer, who is always busy with the routine of his business, who never feels the need of society, because his various occupations bring him in daily contact with other men, is prone to forget that his wife is a social being. He seems to fail to consider that she is not a machine, and therefore stands in need of change and recreation. The rainy season of this country is particularly trying upon the mind and body of a farmer's wife. The farm houses are generally remote from each other, and the winter rains make the traveling disagreeable; therefore the wife for months and months remains at home, not seeing the face of a single lady friend.

We have ourself lived, during four consecutive winters, upon a farm where, for four months of each year, we did not see the face of a woman. Nobody need tell us that such a state of life is natural or right. We know better. Let the farmer regularly, willingly and cheerfully dress himself up, at least as often as once a week, and take his family to church or to see the neighbors. If his wife, from her long recluse habits, appears unwilling to get away from home, let him urge her to accompany him; let him help her to dress the little ones and get the house in order for their departure, and let him see that opportunities are regularly given her for social reunion with her friends of both sexes.

*(June 16, 1871)*

## Answer to a Farmer's Wife

"A farmer's wife" says: "My husband won't let me have the *Northwest* any longer because you say so much about the hardships of farmers' wives. He returned your last paper to you with some insulting words on it. I hope it won't hurt your feelings. I send this letter to apologize. Of course I can't take the paper myself, for he won't bring it from the post-office."

You shall have the paper. Send us the name of your nearest neighbor who takes the paper and we will enclose it to him or her. What would your husband say if you should cut off his supply of tobacco or whisky? Don't raise a "muss" with him. Just *manage* him. These pig-headed men must be persuaded that they are enjoying their "rights." Take philanthropic courage from the fact that there are not many such men in the world, and the few there are must be out-generaled.

*(June 16, 1871)*

## Our Editorials Are Our Own

[To] Mrs. H.: You will see our name as *Editor and Proprietor* at the head of our columns. We supposed the word "proprietor" would tell the whole story, but it didn't. It is amusing to watch the conjectures as to whether or not we edit the paper ourself or get some man to write it up. Our brother [Harvey W. Scott] gets the credit for the financial articles, our father for the practical ones, a certain lawyer for the witty ones, a judge for the deep ones, and ourself for some of the selections that some wiseacre deems objectionable.

*Abigail Scott Duniway, Editor of **The New Northwest**, 1871*

We did not proclaim ourself editor until we sounded public opinion as to whom would be attached the credit, but the credit is being scattered so much that nobody has much glory, and so we hereby announce to our correspondent, and to all others who may have been in doubt, that we write every line of editorial upon any and all subjects. Our father, brother, husband, sons and daughter having other business; lawyer friends and worthy judges also being otherwise employed. Correspondents we have, and poets—but our editorials are our own.

*(June 23, 1871)*

## A Tribute to Horace Greeley

How many and varied are our impressions concerning this remarkable man! We well remember the first time we saw a copy of his New York *Tribune*. We had heard our father denounce it as an "incendiary, abolition affair," and that was enough to make us anxious to investigate the publication. We were but fourteen then, but had developed precocious curiosity, inherited, we suppose, from our unfortunate ancestor, the mother of all men as well as women.

A milk-and-water specimen of humanity [J. R. Lowrance], for whom we never entertained the smallest iota of personal respect, a thin-haired, thin-visaged and flabby-looking clergyman, who made his home at our house, and whom we grumblingly worked for, performed the one good deed of his long sojourn by subscribing for the New York *Tribune*, and we would purloin it from his table, and peruse it regularly. We grew to girlhood under its regular ministrations, and in spite of the hasty denunciation of our honored father, we liked Horace Greeley, and it was not long till our father liked him too.

For a number of years after settling in the Oregon backwoods we were unable to receive the *Tribune*, but when we emerged again into the society of the world, to our great satisfaction, we again found our weekly friend, and recognized, after ten years of separation, the genial visits of Horace Greeley. . . .

We hope to see the day when we shall see him in the flesh, and shall shake the hand that has, all unconsciously to the great brain that guides it, done more to shape our destiny than that of any other living intelligence; and we too shall see the day when Horace Greeley shall espouse the Woman Movement and become its champion, even as he has espoused the cause of the Sunny South, whose enemy for long years he openly proclaimed himself. On behalf of the intellectual suffragists of Oregon we earnestly insist upon an early visit from Horace Greeley.

*(June 30, 1871)*

## Answers to Correspondents

**Farmer's wife:** Ashes from the common ash wood will make soap, but you cannot save enough ashes from a winter's burning to make enough to pay you for your trouble. A good chimney flue draws most of the ashes from the wood through the chimney with the smoke. The oak is the only Oregon wood to be relied upon for ashes to make good soft soap. When we lived on a farm we always made our own soap, and saved the money that would otherwise have gone for that necessary commodity to subscribe for newspapers. Though our soap was always excellent, we had no precise *rule* for making it, but like Mother Mudlaw with her potato pudding, we only wanted necessary "ingrediences." Our ingenuity did the rest.

**Farmer's daughter:** Riding on horseback is or should be considered a very womanly occupation. If girls were taught to hunt the sheep or drive the cows to pasture every day, riding in a free and easy gallop over hill and dale, instead of drumming at the piano with their hair in curl-papers, and their hands in old fingerless gloves through the bright forenoon, they would gain in health and beauty, and would really lose nothing in skill and power as musicians. We love to see young ladies cultivated, polished and intellectual, but we equally love to see them healthy, exuberant and strong.

*Economy:* A copper wash-boiler will cost from ten to fifteen dollars: one for a No. 8 stove can be bought for twelve. Copper boilers will not rust the clothes. They are not liable to leak, and are really more economical than tin boilers, which must be often repaired. We have not had opportunity to test the steam action washing machine, but we like the principle upon which it works and believe it to be excellent.

*(June 30, 1871)*

*An inexperienced housekeeper:* You have no right to be inexperienced. You should have learned your trade most thoroughly before commencing life with it as your only stock in trade. But as you didn't, we will do what we can to assist you, now that you are in perplexity. "Doing up your husband's shirts," which you call the "meanest imaginable job," is not so hard after all if you only know how. We always succeeded best with "cold starch," which is simply one teaspoonful of common starch to one half-pint of cold, clear water. Dissolve the starch, or rather *mix* it thoroughly in the water, catch up the collar, bosom and wristbands of the shirt, and wring them out of this preparation as drily [*sic*] as possible, and roll them up over night. In the morning they will iron smoothly and clearly. If you wish to iron immediately after starching, run the shirts, with the linen parts inside, through your clothes wringer. If you have no wringer, get one. Your husband will not work without convenient tools, and you shouldn't.

*Sallie C.:* The new style shoes, with silver tips, are principally worn by fast women, who live off of the combined earnings of perhaps a dozen of our fast men—those men whom we may remark, *en passant,* already have, or some day expect to have, pure, chaste, economical wives. We would not advise you to wear the silver tips at present.

*(July 7, 1871)*

*A nervous sufferer:* It is folly for you to spend your time and strength in making patchwork quilts. We have known women whose natural genius was of the highest order who crucified it all on the altar of patchwork, tatting, embroidery and crochet. Such work is well enough for occasional pastime, but with many women it has become a mania. We do not very much wonder at this. Women must have something to employ idle thoughts. The best remedy for "nerves" that we ever tried was "lots" of active and absorbing business.

*(July 28, 1871)*

## Visit to the Oregon Insane Asylum

Through the accommodating kindness of Jacob Stitzel, Esq., Mrs. Carrie F. Young and ourself were recently conveyed to the Insane Asylum,[2] where we spent an hour or two in visiting the different wards, under the guidance of the gentlemanly physician in charge, Dr. J. C. Hawthorne.[3]

The buildings are large, clean, well ventilated and commodious, and the unfortunate inmates are well provided for. One noticeable and pleasing feature of the institution is that the patients are all fond of Dr. Hawthorne, and do not exhibit the least symptoms of fear or hatred at his approach.

There is a park adjacent to the buildings where the patients spend much of their time in pleasant recreations. The location is healthy, commanding and beautiful.

One elderly unfortunate stepped up to us as we were promenading in his ward and said as naturally as though his brain had never been unhinged: "We have a very comfortable home here, madam; I had no idea that the accommodations were so good.". . .

Sitting in one of the bed rooms in the women's ward was an old lady whose tidy surroundings were peculiarly refreshing. She was busy making floor-mats, and appeared as happy as a queen. A pile of partico-lored strips of cloth lay beside her, and she braided, sewed and twisted them into shape and comeliness, talking incessantly, and evidently happy as the day. . . .

Then we saw an old negress, the mother of twenty-three children, a hideous monster of mein [sic] sufficient to convert Darwin himself to a life long adherence to his own theories. Twenty-three children! to nurse through measles, whooping cough, mumps, scarlet fever, rash, teething, weaning, jaundice, dysintery [sic]! No wonder she's insane![4]

Then there are the epileptics, idiotics, and deaf, mute and blind.

Oh! The inequities of the parents are indeed visited upon the children! These histories are not unwritten, for they are here stamped legibly upon these blighted lives.

The food for the patients is of excellent quality—consisting of breads, fruits, meats and vegetables, all well cooked, well ordered and clean.

There is but one innovation which the people of Oregon should labor to secure. The asylum needs a woman physician for the care of the women and children. Will not our State authorities see that our request is granted?

*(September 8, 1871)*

## Snails in Portland's Water Supply

The Portland Water Company intend supplying their patrons with meat hereafter, as well as water, in evidence of which they generously sent us two half-grown, slimy, crawling, squirming snails the other morning, through the medium of our water hydrant. We don't know, however, but that the Company will demand pay for them, as charging seems to be its particular forte.

We should judge by their looks that the meat of these snails is very tender, juicy, easy of digestion, and particularly adapted to the tender stomachs of convalescing invalids. Families desiring this article of food left at their residences had better send in their orders at an early day as we apprehend there will be a lively demand for snail meat when it is generally known that it can be obtained so readily. The Company, however, is prepared to supply quite a demand, as there seems to be at present a very large stock on hand in its snail fisheries in this city.

We did not have these snails served up on the table, by-the-way, and cannot therefore vouch for the deliciousness of their esculent qualities. They were handed over to the tender mercies of our obtuse Chinaman, who turned up his nose and rolled his moon eyes as only a Chinaman can, and exclaimed, giving his head a vigorous shake of disgust, "Weh! him vellee muchee no good; him heap nasty. You makee me cookee him, me leave!" And so, to keep on the good side of our Chinaman we had to forego the pleasure of a dish of snail. Oh, dear! those Chinamen are *so* fastidious!

*(September 29, 1871)*

## To the Walla Walla Fair with Miss Anthony

On the morning of the 18th ult. we availed ourself of Captain [John Commingers] Ainsworth's proverbial hospitality and, accompanied by Miss Anthony and others, proceeded to The Dalles [Oregon], where Miss Anthony lectured to an intelligent and deeply interested audience.[5]

The morning was one of those excessively foggy ones that only serve to render darkness visible: A dead calm settled itself over the murky Willamette and the fleecy atmosphere enshrouded the steamer "Oneonta" like an impenetrable pall. It was nine o'clock before we swung loose from the moorings of the dock and guided our steamer's head into the gloomy darkness. Carefully we ploughed the waters and joyfully we at last emerged in bright and balmy sunshine. . . .

Eight o'clock at last, and the town of [The] Dalles is reached. Runners from the two hotels jostle and crowd us in the darkness, disturbing the equanimity of belated lecture goers

*Susan B. Anthony*

and making the evening hideous with their discordant yells.

Getting into the nearest hack we drive to the nearest hotel, to find that our baggage has been left behind, the people congregated and waiting for the coming lecture, and everything in commotion and confusion.

Miss Anthony is capable of composing herself and making a good speech upon any occasion, no matter how adverse may be the circumstances, so the people of The Dalles, who were accommodated in Mr. [Thomas] Condon's well-appointed church,[6] were treated to a lecture of one hour and a half in length, with which they were so intensely gratified that upon our return one week afterwards another delighted audience assembled for another discourse, which was as well appreciated as the first.

(But at the rate we're running we won't reach Walla Walla [W. T.] this week, and we started out to write of Walla Walla rather than The Dalles.)

Taking the morning train past the wild wonders of The Dalles and around Cape Horn, we reached Celilo, where we boarded the steamer "Tenino," and were once more steaming up the Columbia, through a barren-looking region of seemingly interminable undulation, abruptness, boulders and oddity, where, in spite of the forbidding aspect of the country, the fat cattle of a thousand hills come down to drink, bringing in their sleek sides and playful gambols evidence unmistakable that the fat of the land is spread for them in these grand solitudes.

Be patient, reader. We have not forgotten that this article is headed "Walla Walla Fair."

Umatilla [Oregon] is reached, and here we spend the night. What once was known as a thriving commercial town is now a rocky succession of sand hills, and what once were streets and stores and dwellings look now to be abodes of owls and bats. Trade has taken another direction, and this dilapidated town bewails its wind-worn raggedness and weeps o'er days departed. A few prosperous and responsible business men are here, however, and we wish them joy of all they get in Umatilla.

With the early dawn our steamer is off again, and for three or four hours we stem the rapid current, and at last we reach Wallula, [W. T.] which looks like a ragged fragment of poor, tattered Umatilla which the wailing winds had wafted to this barren rock and left in desolation. As this God-forsaken spot is now the head of navigation, we here met the stage, a huge, ungainly omnibus, with six fine horses and a manly driver, who handled the lines with that dexterity for which his class are so particularly famous.

Miss A. mounted the outside of the lumbering vehicle. We tried the seat beside her for a while, but soon yielded to the burning sunshine, exchanged with not an unwilling hombre and seated us beside a placid Chinaman, who seemed oblivious to all surroundings. Oh, that Walla Walla road! Pen cannot paint or picture portray it! Driving up a long and narrow grade upon the rugged hillside, where a careless move would upset our coach and land us in eternity, we suddenly meet a loaded prairie sloop, drawn by four horses with a leader of the *mule* fraternity.

Our driver stops suddenly to give the teamster opportunity to get out of the way of the coach.

"Hold on, good friend; you'll smash my hub to smithereens!" yells the busy teamster.

One of his horses, a piebald, rat-tailed caricature upon well-kept horse-flesh, rears and dodges as if he expects the great stage coach to devour him bodily.

"Your horse is young and skittish," says one of our passengers.

"Young! d__n me! he's seventeen years old."

"Ah! I see; he's quite a colt."

Everybody laughs and we are by this time disentangled from the disagreeable proximity, and on we go, through the stifling dust and over rocks and ridges, down sidelong declivities and up steep ascents, feeling all the while an intense longing to plant our feet upon *terra firma* and trust horse-flesh nevermore. But the long ride of thirty miles is over now, and we drive up to the Walla Walla Inn, looking like pilgrims to some ancient Mecca, or the forlorn hope of a caravan of forty-niners.

"What the creation has all this to do with the Walla Walla Fair?" asks an impertinent type.

"Wait till the next issue and we will tell you," is our meek reply.

We didn't mean to be so garrulous.

*(October 6, 1871)*

## Miss Anthony's Work in the Great Northwest

Miss Anthony's work goes bravely on. Our multitudinous duties connected with traveling, writing for the paper and sending letters to the loved ones at home, have precluded the possibility of preparing such reports as would at all do justice to our illustrious co-worker.

At Walla Walla . . . Miss Anthony held wonderful and enthusiastic meetings, first in the new and commodious district school house which, proving too small to hold the hundreds who flocked to hear her, was reluctantly given up for the only available hall in the place—a hall good enough in its way, but, unfortunately, situated back of a saloon, where the tender-footed preacher who locked his church against us couldn't go in on a complimentary ticket because the hall was in such an unrighteous locality! Miss Anthony made scores of converts, and frightened the few old fogies in the city almost out of their wits. The *New Northwest* gained a larger number of new subscribers, and the women are unanimously resolved to use their right to vote.

At Corvallis and other West Side Oregon towns the lecturer and paper were equally successful. But the crowning success was met at the State Fair [in Salem], where Miss Anthony was invited by the Agricultural Board to lecture on the grounds. She cheerfully complied, and for one hour and a half she held a congregation of three thousand people, who stood, many of them, with a child in arms, spellbound and eager listeners to the glorious new gospel, which captivated every *brain* in the vast audience. She held that every woman was, in common with all other creatures of the good All-Father, brought into existence *primarily* for her own highest personal good, and secondarily for the good of others. Old men and women, young men and maidens, listened to her words of wisdom, believed and were converted. . . .

Miss Anthony has sojourned in the Northwest about thirty-five days, has made thirty speeches, traveled one thousand miles, and, we may safely say, has converted fifteen thousand people. Has any other preacher done as much? . . .

*(October 20, 1871)*

## The Oregon State Fair

Oregonians are disposed to be happy. They are resolved to make the most of circumstances; consequently, when the time for the Annual Fair approaches, every man, woman and child, who can be spared for the occasion, hieth to the Donnybrook of ye land of Webfoot, prepared to make money, spend money, patronize side shows, camp out, eat dirt, breathe smoke, sleep on the ground, race horses and be gay. Among the numbers thus inclined was the redoubtable staff of the *New Northwest*.

On Monday, October 9th, (the same day being the first of the great jubilee), we mustered our forces, rolled up our tent and blankets, and hied us to the depot, resolved to make a week of it. And—we—succeeded.

First, after having run ourselves down to reach the depot in time to catch the train, we found that the time had been changed to a so-called "accommodation" table, which disappointed everybody, so we dropped our feathers and wended our way home, a sadder but wiser people.

Seven o'clock A.M., Tuesday, and we tried it again. Succeeding upon this occasion in getting a seat in an unfinished passenger car, mounted upon trucks, which rocked away like a caution to dyspepsia, we reached the famous Webfoot Donnybrook at ten o'clock, and prepared ourselves to enjoy the many delightful pleasures above enumerated.

As is always the case at these places, horse racing is the principal amusement connected with the agricultural exhibition.

The women here, as in Walla Walla [W. T.] and Albany [Oregon], are getting too financially sagacious to spend much more time and money to make the pavilion attractive, when all the profit is on the outside. So the show, compared to that of former years, was meager in the extreme.

We saw a committee of men busily engaged in examining the embroidery and "tatting" on a lady's *chemise*, and we couldn't help feeling that they were slightly "out of their sphere." But, poor fellows! how could they help it? Where women are not on hand to do the women's work the men must do it, and *vice versa*. These matters regulate themselves in spite of laws or usages.

The general exhibition has been so minutely served up for the public palate in the daily papers that the *New Northwest* will now bring on the "side dishes" and furnish the intellectual feast with such dessert as the opportunities afford.

*Minnie Pixley, acrobatic performer, ca. 1880*

We have the famous and sprightly Pixley Sisters, who always draw crowded houses, and who made a handsome sum of money; we have the world-renowned Madagascar Family and the famous Circassian Beauty, the Vancouver Fat Woman, Madam Forestelle and the women of the Aurora Restaurant. In all these "shows" the women do the work and, with the exception of the first, the men pocket the profits, and then boast that they "support the women." The Pixley Sisters are remarkably successful in their profession. The eldest, Miss Annie, is but eighteen years of age; Minnie is fifteen and Lucy twelve. We learn that their masculine "help," with one exception, struck for higher wages on the last evening, whereupon these heroic young girls "doubled" in the acts and performed without them. To those carping men who boast that women need their "protection," we proudly point to the Pixley Sisters and say, "behold!"

Madam Forestelle, the contortionist, performed her wonderful and dangerous feats every day and evening. The husband who "supports" her by getting men to tie her up on the stage with a fifty feet [*sic*] rope, from which she magically frees herself in a box; by causing her to twist herself in every imaginable contortion for the vulgar gaze of the curious; by taking a sledge hammer and breaking a three hundred pound rock upon her breast; and then squanders the money thus earned at the peril of her life at the saloon or gaming table, cannot keep the "wool over her eyes" much longer. There's just rebellion a-brewing in that kingdom.

Then the Fat Woman, of 417 pounds *avoirdupois*, who resembles "Brother Ike," of the *Herald*, is another example of the capability of man to "support" his wife.[7] This woman is nineteen years old, the mother of two children, and when found by the appreciative showman who has charge of her, was washing by the day to support her family. She is a stolid specimen of phlegmatic obesity, and agrees with "Brother Ike" on the Woman Question.

Well, this description of the Oregon State Fair has the merit of variety if nothing further.

This is only part of our bill of fare.

*(October 20, 1871)*

## Travels with Miss Anthony

The following letter originally appeared in the *Golden Age* of Dec. 21 [1871]. As it will probably interest our readers who do not get Theodore Tilton's wide-awake newspaper, we publish it, although it is out of date.[8]

*To the Editor of The Golden Age:*
Far away on the Pacific slope, beyond the flutter of the stars and stripes, in Victoria's Dominion, Susan B. Anthony and my comparatively unknown self, have strayed in our itinerant occupation. For the last four evenings the unanswerable logic of our feminine Patrick Henry has held the British Colonists as by a spell, and to-day we have them thoroughly convinced of the power of Universal Suffrage, as the only safeguard of universal liberty.

Miss Anthony reached Portland, Oregon, on the first day of September, having parted from Mrs. [Elizabeth Cady] Stanton, her hitherto inseparable companion, in

California, some days previously. Since her arrival in Oregon up to the present time, she has been constantly occupied, having spoken upon forty different occasions, traveled sixteen hundred miles, and converted thousands of people to the principle of Woman Suffrage.

We have together journeyed to the head of navigation on the broad Columbia; gazed with bated breath upon the mighty mountains of the Cascades; stood upon the towering bluffs of black and gray basalt that loom bleak and desolate above the dashing Oregon; crossed weary miles of rocky desert in great lumbering coaches; glided over magnificent waters in elegant modern steamers; dashed through fertile valleys, and over dark deep gorges, behind the iron horse; have traveled for successive days through forests grand and old, some of them green and glorious, as they were for ages ere the white man's foot had pressed the soil, others all bare and black and ghastly, holding their skeleton arms as if in mute appeal, their headless trunks all scarred and shrunken, yet mighty in their wierd [*sic*] magnificence; have watched the brilliant day god as he sunk beneath the rolling billows of the broad Pacific; and again have greeted him as up he rose, refreshed and dazzling, to bathe the snow-capped summits of old Hood, Rainier, and Adams in his limpid glories, and illume the gladdened earth with his most welcome presence, and in these mighty scenes have gathered strength and inspiration.

At Portland Miss Anthony lectured three evenings, always to crowded and appreciative audiences, carrying conviction to the minds of hundreds who flocked eagerly to hear and understand this new gospel of humanity and justice.

From Portland we proceeded to Salem, the capital of Oregon, where success in gratifying form crowned our repeated efforts. From Salem we went to Oregon City, Milwaukie, and then back to Portland, thence up the Columbia to [The] Dalles, Umatilla, Wallula, and Walla Walla; back again up the Willamette to Albany; from thence to Corvallis, Monmouth, Dayton, Lafayette, McMinnville, Forest Grove, and towns of lesser note; then back again to Salem to the annual State Fair, where by special invitation of the Agricultural Board, Miss Anthony addressed three thousand people in the open air; then off by steamer and stage coach to Olympia, the capital of Washington Territory, where by invitation we addressed the Territorial Legislature in joint session assembled, and where one of us at least, acquitted herself right royally; then down the majestic waters of the world-famed Puget Sound to rouse the stolid sons of old Britannia, and to-day we are off again for Madison, Townsend, Ludlow, Gamble, Steilacoom, and Seattle, and are to be back again to Olympia by the 8th proximo, when a Territorial Woman Suffrage Convention will be held over against the walls of the capital where the Legislature sits in state and man's rights doctrine trembles on its tottering throne.

By virtue of the Territorial law and under the Fourteenth and Fifteenth Amendments to the Federal Constitution, the women of Washington are already voters, and the object of the Convention is to insure harmony and concert of action among them at the next June election.

Everywhere I reap rich harvests of subscribers for the *New Northwest*, and send you to-day new subscribers for the *Golden Age*. I hope ere long to send you a large list.

Miss Anthony will proceed from Olympia to Portland, where a farewell reception will be given her in Oro Fino Hall, after which she will depart overland for California and her eastern home.

Mrs. A. J. Duniway
Editor and Proprietor
of *New Northwest*
Portland, Oregon
Victoria, B. C., Oct. 27, 1871.

*(March 29, 1872)*

## In Washington Territory with Miss Anthony

Taking passage on board the steamer "North Pacific" on the afternoon of the 27th ult., we bade good-bye to Victoria in Her Majesty's Dominion, with its legion of saloons, its multitude of "shops"—as English people style what we call *stores*—leaving its wainscotted, dark hotel, its McAdamized streets, its colored population, its awkward barouches and ewe-necked horses; casting farewell glances of admiration at its well-kept gardens, substantial improvements and elegant Government buildings; bidding good-bye to cheerful friends and gladly setting our faces homeward, we steamed out from the docks and up the beautiful inlet, heading for Port Townsend, where, on the evening of the 28th, we were favored with a good audience of intelligent and kindly-disposed people, to whom Miss Anthony delineated the Power of the Ballot.

Then, on Sunday, the 29th, she addressed an audience at Coupeville, a milling point across the Bay, on Whidby's Island, where the people, having already been prepared by the Rev. Mr. Greer to accept the new gospel of reformation, were particularly harmonious and wide awake. Again, on the evening of the 30th, we held a meeting in Port Townsend, which was as well or better attended than the first. . . .

We have rarely seen a more beautiful situation for a city than Port Townsend. Its land-locked bay is a most excellent harbor, and being near the great ocean, offers inducements for the railroad terminus, which are so satisfactory to its land holding inhabitants that they claim high prices for real estate, which are sufficient to retard the growth of any embryo city of almost any species of aspiration. This real estate fever rages all along the Sound, and Portland is not alone in making the great mistake of shutting out real estate buyers who are not large capitalists. Port Townsend gave us a long list of subscribers to the *New Northwest*, and of course we left the busy little town with an agreeable opinion of the intelligence of its people.

Our next appointment was at Seattle, considered one of the most favored places for the terminus. . . . We had the honor of addressing the citizens of Seattle on the subject of Temperance, by invitation of Rev. Mr. Bagley, on Sunday Evening, November 5th. The fact is, that our view of the Temperance work was a novel one to the most of the audience, yet the interest manifested on the occasion showed that they were quite ready to accept the new gospel of woman's moral and pecuniary responsibility and influence. . . .

The Woman Suffragists of Seattle organized a county society during our stay, and a number of delegates are going up to the Territorial Convention at Olympia, on the 8th inst.

Miss Anthony lectured at Port Madison on the 4th and 5th, and joined us yesterday at Port Gamble, where she lectured in the evening.

Port Gamble is one of the many lumbering establishments on the Sound, of which the reader may get a very accurate idea from the description given by Captain Crandall in the *Oregonian* some time since; only the Captain didn't tell that man's idea that he must support woman is practically and not theoretically considered here. The wives of the mill men live in houses by themselves and the men take their meals at the company's cookhouse, leaving the women nothing to do but keep their homes. Yet these women are strong suffragists, who with one accord agree with the slave Tom, that they "would like to have a little *more* that is their own and a little *less* that is master's."

To-night we join the King county delegates to the Woman Suffrage Convention, and will proceed to Olympia to finish the work inaugurated there some two weeks since.

Port Gamble, W. T., November 7, 1871.

*(November 17, 1871)*

## A Lesson of Subjugation at Port Gamble, W.T.

The dear, generous, good-natured, philosophical, philanthropical, free and easy *men*, who think too much of women to allow them liberty of voice, conscience or inclination, got an overdose of their own *regime* the other day at one of the milling points on the Sound.

When the steamer landed [at Port Gamble] a lady [Mrs. John Seany], with whom Miss Anthony and ourself had formed an agreeable acquaintance at another place, met us at the wharf and invited us to her home, saying that our company would be a great pleasure to her and she could make us more comfortable than we would be at the hotel, where there were indifferent accommodations for ladies. We protested, fearing that we might incommode her, but the invitation was repeated and we accepted the hospitality of a very comfortable home.

The lord and master who supports this woman, and who "loves, cherishes and protects her" according to law, came in in the evening and informed us that he had engaged rooms for us at the hotel; that he didn't keep public house and his wife in inviting us to her house had done that which he had not given her permission to do. The wife sat in tearful silence, feebly remonstrating occasionally, but to no purpose, and, of course, we could not dispute the authority of the legal power of her "protector" to order her invited guests to leave the house.

Indignation ran high at the mill, and the men were all ashamed of him, but the poor, boorish niggard, who owns and possesses that woman in fee simple, feels that he has taught her a lesson of subjugation which she will not dare to forget.

*(November 17, 1871)*

## Our Banner Yet Waveth

Home again! thank Heaven! where, with health and strength renewed from the effects of a vigorous campaign, we gather our loved flock around us and, in the gleesome joy of sweet reunion and interchange of words of cheer, we are so befuddled that we cannot hear ourself think. If Congressmen and Senators feel as anxious to get home to the fireside at the end of their terms as we do after a month's absence, we don't see how they can accept office. We wouldn't be President to-day if we could.

Settled again at our little desk, scribbling away at a rapid rate, while the click of falling type is heard within and pattering rain-drops fall without, we feel that we wouldn't exchange our office for a Dukedom or our editorial chair for the sole possession of the Isles of the Sea. And our fingers tingle with an electric glow that longs to burn itself into words of greeting to the many friends of our glorious cause who read the *New Northwest*. To each and all of them we say, "Thank God and take courage! Our cause is marching on!"

*(November 17, 1871)*

## Reply to a Letter from Oregon City

*Charles Pope, Jr.—Sir.*—Your letter of October 20th, which is deemed unfit for publication, was duly received and answered privately by my agent during my absence from home. In reply to your inquiry as to "who the _____ sent" you my "infernal paper," it is necessary, in defense of myself, or rather as an excuse for having made such a stupid blunder, to say that your honored father, lately deceased, whose obituary appeared in these columns, subscribed for the *New Northwest*, probably in the forlorn hope that it might make a gentleman of his degenerate son. Had he lived, the subscription would have been promptly paid. You doubtless know the law regulating newspaper subscriptions. No paper discontinued until all arrearages are paid.

Yours stiffly,

Mrs. A. J. Duniway

*(November 24, 1871)*

## Persecuted Celestials in Portland

Last Sunday, large crowds of ruffianly boys amused themselves by unmercifully pelting every Chinaman they could succeed in waylaying or cornering with snow balls—very hard snow balls, too, we think, from the pitiful manner in which the persecuted Celestials received the punishment; and in many instances the quality of material used in assault consisted more of wood and pebble stones than snow.

Nor were the boys alone in this outrageous persecution. Great, stalwart men, by the half dozen, might be seen vying with the boys in persecuting some poor wayfaring Chinaman, surrounded on every side by his tormentors, with apparently no avenue of escape from the almost blinding storm of projectiles hurled at him.

Now, snow-balling may be a very proper amusement when rightly conducted; but when carried to such an extreme as just indicated, it is certainly anything but fun to the victims. The Portland police permitted these outrages to be committed with impunity—certainly not a very favorable comment.

*(December 1, 1871)*

## Language Above Sex

[To] Sarah J.: Jean Ingelow is an English poet. We do not say "poetess," because art and intelligence have no sex. We do not call Rosa Bonheur an artistess; we call her an artist. So in speaking of an editor, author, lecturer, merchant, milliner, banker, broker, baker, teacher, farmer—no matter whom—there is no discrimination. We never hear anybody say "teacheress," "merchantess," bankeress," "farmeress" and so on, yet women are engaged in all these occupations. Art and intellect are *above* sex.

*(December 15, 1871)*

## Notes for 1871

1. Edward Dickinson Baker (1811-61) was a popular statesman, soldier, and orator. He became a partner in the Springfield, Illinois, law firm of Stephen T. Logan, J. D. Stuart, and Abraham Lincoln; served in the Illinois Legislature, 1837-45; was elected to the House of Representatives in 1845; distinguished himself in the Mexican War; and served again in the Illinois legislature, 1849-51. After gaining a reputation in San Francisco as an outstanding criminal lawyer and orator, he accepted an invitation to move to Oregon in 1859. In the fall of 1860, after fourteen ballots in the Oregon Senate, Baker was selected as Oregon's first Republican United States Senator. During the Civil War, he served as colonel of a regiment of volunteers and was killed at Ball's Bluff, Virginia, in October of 1861, the first Union officer and only U.S. senator to die in the war. The U.S. Senate honored Baker by placing a large statue of him in the Capitol rotunda in 1873.

Baker was an important, inspirational figure in Duniway's life. During economic hard times for the Scott family in Illinois, he helped John Tucker Scott obtain credit in 1846 to import the first circular sawmill west of Ohio, and Scott became Baker's agent to sell portable sawmills in Illinois and Indiana.

In "The Coming Man," *NNW*, 14 Dec. 1877, Duniway told her readers:

> We well remember a conversation we had with Col. E. D. Baker in Lafayette, a short time prior to his election to the United States Senate in Oregon. We were young then, and wholly unalive to the importance of freedom. . . . "Madam, the next great question that will engage the attention of statesmen after the present national difficulties are settled will be the enfranchisement of woman." In our pert ignorance and pitiable inexperience, we only laughed at him in reply.

In the winter of 1886, Duniway was still thinking of Col. Baker and believed she saw his guardian ghost in her photograph (Clyde Duniway notes and photograph in Duniway Papers). For more about Baker, see Harry C. Blair and Rebecca Tarshis, *Colonel Edward D. Baker: Lincoln's Constant Ally* (Portland: Oregon Historical Society, 1960); and G. Thomas Edwards, "Six Oregon Leaders and the Far-Reaching Impact of America's Civil War," *Oregon Historical Quarterly* 100 (Spring 1999): 4-31.

2. Carrie Fisher Young (ca. 1828-1911), a California editor and lecturer, was mentioned frequently in *The NNW*, especially during her early speaking tours in Oregon and Washington Territory. She had a particular interest in women's health, advocated for temperance in all aspects of life, and supported woman suffrage. At the time of this 1871 visit with Duniway to the Oregon insane

asylum, Young was editor of the monthly *Woman's Pacific Coast Journal,* which she began in California in May of 1870. See Sherilyn Cox Bennion, *Equal to the Occasion: Women Editors of the Nineteenth-Century West* (Reno: University of Nevada Press, 1990), 108-112; 117-118.

Young was also apparently associated with the Spiritualist Movement. In 1875, Duniway included Young in her list of "nomadic Spiritualists" from California:

> *The first of these nomadic Spiritualists whom we encountered was Carrie F. Young. She perambulated this State and Washington Territory, professing to be a Methodist temperance lecturer. We, meanwhile, gratuitously advertising her everywhere, and she, requiting the favor by breaking into our business in every possible way, in the hope to break it down by injuring us personally. We were young in our newspaper venture then, and not strong enough to fight, so we considered it wise to pat the head and praise the forked tongue that smote us, knowing that to succeed we must be wise as a serpent and harmless as a dove.* ("A Growl from Our Friends," *NNW,* 9 July 1875)

3. Oregon did not have funds for construction of a state asylum until the early 1880s, when one was established at Salem. Until then, the state contracted with J. C. Hawthorne and A. M. Loryea, who had a private asylum in East Portland. In Sept. of 1870, the asylum had 122 inmates: 87 males and 35 females. See H. H. Bancroft, *History of Oregon,* Vol. II (San Francisco: The History Co., 1888), 646, n. 17.

4. The "old negress" to whom Duniway referred was apparently Polly Holmes, who was brought by Nathaniel Ford from Missouri to Oregon Territory in 1844, with her husband, Robin Holmes. The 1870 census records show Polly Holmes, age 68, as an inmate at the Oregon state insane asylum. Although Polly Holmes was not known to be "the mother of twenty-three children," the circumstances of her life might have created this story in Polly's confused mind. The known children of Polly Holmes were Mary Jane, born ca. 1841 in Missouri, and three children born in Oregon: James, born 1845, Roxanna, born 1847, and Lon, born 1850. Records show that Nathaniel Ford brought Polly and Robin Holmes and their three-year-old daughter, Mary Jane, overland to Oregon and promised their freedom if they worked for five years on his Polk County farm. After the five years were up, Ford insisted that Robin Holmes must go to California, to help his son, Mark Ford, mine for gold. When Robin returned to Oregon, Ford refused to release the three oldest Holmes children, and Robin began a long court battle. After many delays, Robin Holmes won his case in 1853 and gained custody of his children; however, Nathaniel Ford apparently did not fully comply, and Mary Jane Holmes remained at his home. See Martha Anderson, *Black Pioneers of the Northwest, 1800-1918* (n. p., WA: Martha Anderson, 1980), 54-57; Elizabeth McLagan, *A Peculiar Paradise: A History of Blacks in Oregon, 1788-1940* (Portland: The Oregon Black History Project, Georgian Press, 1980), 15, 33-36, 80-81; and K. Keith Richard, "Unwelcome Settlers: Black & Mulatto Oregon Pioneers Part II," *Oregon Historical Quarterly* 84 (Summer 1984): 186. For the claim of one of Ford's descendants that the Ford and Holmes families were always close and that Robin Holmes brought the suit at Ford's request to test the legal status of slavery, see Pauline Burch, "Pioneer Nathaniel Ford and the Negro Family," manuscript collection, Oregon Historical Society.

5. Captain John Commingers Ainsworth (1822-93) was a founder and president of the Oregon Steam Navigation Company, chartered in 1860. The O. S. N. Co. was formed as a coalition of interests that

grew to control transportation on the Columbia, Willamette, and Snake rivers, to Puget Sound, and along the coast to San Francisco. After the company ended in 1880 and Ainsworth sold his shipping interests, he turned to banking.

6. Thomas Condon (1822-1907), a Congregational minister, is best known as Oregon's foremost geologist and paleontologist. In 1862, Condon discovered the fossil beds at John Day, one of the largest in the world, and sent his first specimens to the Smithsonian Institution in 1870. He published *The Two Islands and What Came of Them* in 1902, later revised as *Oregon Geology* (1906). Condon was born in Ireland and came to New York in 1833. After graduation from Auburn Theological Seminary in 1852, he came to Oregon Territory as a home missionary and was a pastor at St. Helens, Forest Grove, Albany, and The Dalles. In 1873, he joined the faculty at Pacific University in Forest Grove and was appointed professor of geology and natural history at the University of Oregon in 1876. Duniway frequently reported on Condon's scientific findings and lectures in *The NNW*. See Rick Harmon, "Thomas Condon and the 'Natural Selection' of Oregon Pioneers," *Oregon Historical Quarterly* 99 (Winter 1998-99): 436-71.

7. Duniway's uncomplimentary reference to "'Brother Ike' of the *Herald*" is typical of her criticisms of Democratic editors, particularly those who were openly sympathetic to the South during the Civil War. In this case the newspaper was probably Portland's *Oregon Herald*, a daily established after the war, in March of 1866, with the avowed mission to serve as "an humble advocate of Democratic principles." Beriah Brown, who became editor in June of 1866, was followed in 1868-69 by owner-editor Sylvester Pennoyer, who later became mayor of Portland and governor of Oregon, and then Eugene Semple in 1869, who became governor of

Washington Territory. In December of 1871, the *Oregon Herald* was sold to a stock company, and the paper ended in May of 1873.

8. Theodore Tilton's *Golden Age*, which he owned and edited, was backed by Henry Ward Beecher, a fact that Tilton supposedly did not know until the famed Beecher-Tilton scandal erupted in the fall of 1872 and captured the attention of the nation. The scandal involved accusations that Beecher, one of the country's best known ministers and first president of the American Woman Suffrage Association, had conducted an adulterous affair with Tilton's wife, Elizabeth ("Lib") Richards Tilton, one of the parishoners at Beecher's Plymouth Church in Brooklyn. Tilton, first president of the National Woman Suffrage Association, was a reform journalist and lecturer, and his own long-term affair with Laura Curtis Bullard became a part of the scandal. Circumstances of the Beecher-Tilton scandal, coupled with years of investigations and trials, brought Tilton to bankruptcy and the *Golden Age* to an end. In 1877, Tilton moved permanently to Paris, leaving behind his wife and four children. For more on Tilton, see Barbara Goldsmith, *Other Powers: The Age of Suffrage, Spiritualism, and the Scandalous Victoria Woodhull* (NY: Knopf, 1998).

# 1872

## At the Oregon State Temperance Alliance Meeting

### We Went

Hearing everywhere that there was going to be a grand temperance gathering in Salem on the 22d of February, and knowing that, as ladies would be present, the crowd thus drawn together would constitute the most numerous, respectable and able legislative body ever convened in Oregon, and having been invited to attend and address the Convention, we redoubled our already over-taxed energies and hurried to the scene of action.

We had come as an independent delegate, and, taking our seat as a member, watched for opportunities to throw hot shot as a representative of the large company of women present, who, accustomed to being choked off from all participation in public debate by their retiring and modest brethren, and being wholly unaccustomed to public speaking, did not dare to raise their voice in behalf of womanhood, and sat watching us with anxious eyes and fluttering hearts.

As we kept our seat in that vast assembly, listening long and earnestly to spirited debates over quibbles about "points of order," hearing men's sarcastic shots, and hugely enjoying the spirited defenses, we inwardly rejoiced that it was not a Woman Suffrage Convention, for, if it had been women who were thus unruly, no power on earth could have prevented our brethren from believing that "the sex" were by nature too combative to be trusted with any governmental responsibility. (Two or three men never try to talk at once, you know.) Reader, the clause in parenthesis is meant to be whispered in your ear; if we should say such a thing out loud, somebody that attended that Convention would believe it to be a sarcasm. We'd regret that.

### We Fought

As the *Oregonian* contains a condensed but very correct account of the proceedings, which we copy, we will not attempt to use the notes which we had gathered, except in some instances where important omissions occur. The Chair [S. C. Adams], in response to our inquiry as to whether ladies who had paid expenses to attend this Convention were expected to submit to gag law, said: "I am sure, if there may be such a thing as stretching the line a little, I shall always endeavor to embrace the ladies."[1] (Loud laughter amid prolonged applause.)

As soon as a few hundred men had each made a speech or two, we managed to get the floor, when we proceeded to apologize for the unlucky witticism of the Chair: "I thank you, gentlemen, for giving your wives, mothers and sisters a seat in this house and a vote on this floor. It is to me an ernest [*sic*] of success. But I want to apologize for the slur which our worthy President inadvertently cast upon womanhood a while ago. Did I not know him to be a gentleman I should feel that every woman who remains in this house tacitly submits to insult; but as I know that his injudicious speech was an error of his tongue instead of his brain, I want you to forgive him. We do not want men's embraces. We want the recognition of equal rights. We want to command respect."

As usual, we were called to order; but as almost every man who spoke was also called to order, we concluded there was something "parliamentary" in the expression, and, being sustained by the chair, we kept the floor a few moments longer, but, as we've forgotten what we said, except that it was vehemently applauded, we guess it isn't worth repeating. At the close of these remarks (whatever they were), the worthy President arose and tendered the large company of ladies present a neat and handsome apology for this thoughtless speech, which was heartily accepted, and the ladies smiled upon him graciously. . . .

Repaired to the hotel after the afternoon session and spent several hours upon "copy" for our boys [at *The New Northwest*]. Heard much applause in the Opera House, and went over at nine o'clock to attend the "sociable" and see what the "fuss" was about. Found that Mrs. [Carrie] Young had been giving a lecture. Paid a half dollar at the door and was admitted. Brilliant throng. Promenades. Elegant toilets. Smiles. Bows. Wit. Fun. Was called upon for a speech. Responded. Applause. More promenades. Supper. More speeches. The whole ended with a general dance, and we repaired to the hotel, where, after one o'clock, we went to sleep, lulled by the dulcet music of a brace of violins and the heavy tramp, tramp, tramp of what some simpleton has styled "the light fantastic toe."

### We Conquered

Since the above was written the *Oregonian* of Monday has made its appearance, in which the report of the second day's proceedings is so correct, full and comprehensive that the wind is taken from our sails, and but little is left for us to do except to confirm the report, clap hands and jubilate.

*(March 1, 1872)*

The *Oregonian* of February 26, 1872, reported that, on the second day of the Convention, Mrs. A. J. Duniway offered the following:

WHEREAS, This Alliance realizes the power of the ballot in all public reforms; and

WHEREAS, Women are everywhere recognized as legitimate auxiliaries in the Temperance movement, and have proven themselves active and efficient members of this Alliance, and have here freely exercised their right to vote; therefore

RESOLVED, That we urge upon the Legislature of the State of Oregon the necessity of passing an act instructing the judges of elections to receive the votes of women upon the subject of Temperance . . . in their various precincts.

After heated debate, the resolution passed by a vote of 119 to 12. Upon the announcement of the vote it was greeted with cheers lasting several minutes.

That evening, Mr. Wooden introduced the following resolution: Resolved, That this Alliance in passing the resolution introduced by Mrs. Duniway, praying the Legislature of Oregon to give women the right to vote on the temperance question, does not mean woman suffrage further than the temperance question. The resolution was adopted. Before adjournment, however, and, after being assured that they should have unlimited time, Mrs. [Carrie] Young and Mrs. Duniway addressed the audience. . . .

## At Brenner's One-Horse Hotel

To give our readers an idea of the delights of an itinerant lecturer we have sharpened our pencil and taken our seat to particularize.

Was going from Albany to Corvallis [Oregon]. Waited twenty-four hours to go by the boat. Went to Brenner's hotel and put up for the night. Asked when the boat would start. Answer, at six. Gave injunction to be called up in time for the boat. Was called at half past three. Hurried; got ready. Halls dark; no fires. Nobody astir but a stupid watchman and a savage dog. Asked for a fire in the parlor. A gentleman from Benton County, whose honest face we would be willing to trust anywhere, built a fire. Sat there listening for the boat and wondering why nobody was on hand to see about anything. After an hour or two the boat whistled. Once; twice. Must be off now, for she'll go in fifteen minutes. Watchman pokes his head in at the door and says, "You'll have to hurry or you won't make it." Thought we must "make it." No lantern; no porter; nobody belonging to the house on hand. Gentleman from Benton kindly shouldered valise and accompanied us through the rain and storm and darkness. Missed the wharf. Stumbled through the mud. Stumbled down some steps. Waded. Hurried. All to no purpose. Missed the boat.

Back to the hotel a madder but wiser woman. Told Brenner he knew how to keep a hotel. Got thanked for the compliment. Land-lord wanted us to know that his was a "one-horse" hotel, without any connection with steamers. Agreed with him. Washed the mud from our shoes; but great rolls of it are still clinging to our skirts with a tenacity more enduring than pleasant. Much obliged to the gentleman from Benton. Concluded the night's lodging at the hotel was a nuisance.

And as we sit here scribbling away at the facts thus fresh in our memory, we warn all women who can beg or hire or accept—we could have done any or all—accommodations among the citizens of Albany to trust not to the delusion that they will be able to make any connection with the boat to Corvallis by taking a night's lodging at the "one-horse hotel."

Albany, March 5, 1872.

*(March 8, 1872)*

## Celebration of the Fifteenth Amendment

The colored citizens of Portland will celebrate the ratification of the Fifteenth Amendment to the Constitution of the United States, at the Washington Grand Armory, on Tuesday, April 9, 1872, at 7:30 P.M., by a literary and musical entertainment, on which occasion Miss Octavia Mercier will sing one of her favorite selections.[2] The Oration will be delivered by Rev. Daniel Jones.[3] We acknowledge receipt of complimentary tickets.

*(April 5, 1872)*

## Trained Dresses

[To] Ellen: Efforts are made to revive the trained dresses for street wear. We honestly doubt any woman's capacity to exercise the prerogatives of an American citizen if she willfully mops up dust, tobacco juice, cigar stumps, and other filth, with her skirts. A trailing dress is an emblem of degradation. It is suggestive of weak brain and back aches; of dependence and incompetency; of frailty and subjugation. Mark the contrast between your tidy, brisk little woman, whose neatly trimmed skirts coquettishly clear the dirty sidewalk, and that would-be stylish dowdy who mops the pavement with several square yards of costly silk, and choose between them for your model of neatness and beauty.

*(April 12, 1872)*

# Ho, Bound for the People's Convention in New York!

[An Appeal to Ben Holladay, Oregon and California R. R. Company]

The Finance Committee, upon whom devolved the duty of raising the requisite funds with which to defray the traveling expenses of the delegate elect were ready to report success.

Being ourself anxious to serve the good cause of Human Rights in every honorable capacity, we concluded to apply to the railroad nabob for a pass, and consequently sent him the following letter, which was returned unanswered:

Portland, Saturday Morning
April 27th, 1872

Mr. Ben Holladay—Dear Sir:—Although the daily papers are silent over the fact that I am Delegate elect to the People's Convention in New York, you have doubtless seen, in your *New Northwest*, a full account of the proceedings.[4] Friends have raised me the sum of $200 towards defraying my expenses. Now, I want a pass. If I go I must be off on the "Oriflamme" this evening. I have cheerfully paid your roads and steamers, in money earned with my sewing machine, the sum of nearly $400 since I began my newspaper enterprise. This visit to the east—if I make it—will be of much pecuniary benefit to you, as I shall lecture in the cities on "Oregon, her climate, developments, resources and people," and I ask this pass to New York if you can give it—and of course I believe you can—but to San Francisco anyway—as a matter of business, in which you are, to say the least, as much interested as myself. Hoping to hear from you before noon to-day,

I am very respectfully, your
obedient servant,
A. J. Duniway

We were not disappointed at the result, for we had before tried the same experiment and failed. But—the steamer was going. Our friends had raised the sum of $200, being half of the least possible amount for which we had agreed to spend six weeks' time, at a pecuniary sacrifice of at least six hundred dollars. Something must be done, and there was no time for dodging. Concluded to start at all hazards and depend upon our tried and zealous friends for funds to bring us back. Can take second rate car and save something. Before Fred Douglass was emancipated he couldn't get passes in his missionary work.[5] *We'll* be a voter, too, some day, Mr. Holladay.

*(May 3, 1872)*

## First Stop:
## San Francisco

San Francisco, thank Heaven! And now that our sadly stirred-up organism is enabled to settle its rebellious bile on solid *terra firma*, we resume the thread of this narrative where it was suddenly snapped short when the steamer was nearing Astoria. . . .

We were steaming slowly forward, in the teeth of a strong sou'wester, which caused the "Oriflamme" to shake its timbers with a constant shiver that raised a sort of tintinabulation in our nerves—the very music of misery—and kept us retching till we almost expected to cast up our boot soles.

On the second day out we met the "Ajax," which kindly lay to, like a great lazy whale, and allowed a number of our men to board her (only we never knew a whale to do anything of the kind; she only looked like that, you know), and all her passengers shot up from her hatches to get a peep at us, looking like ants on an anaconda, and we doubtless looked to them—but then, we can't think of anything else that some of us looked like just then, except vultures on a carcass, and if we'd say the like of that Ben Holladay's Man Friday [James O'Meara] might think we'd slandered the Oregon railroad, so we won't attempt a comparison.[6]

A goodly number of passengers were our companions in misery; and on Tuesday, our last day out, the fickle wind got behind us, filled our main sail, steadied our steamer, and sent us onward with a velocity that was exceedingly gratifying.

Midnight, and we reach the crowded, jammed, crammed, piled-up, running over docks of the Transportation Company, and soon find ourself and friends packed away in a coach and bound for the Russ House. But Mrs. F. F. V. [Frances Fuller Victor] . . . and ourself, after paying two and a half each for the privilege of leaving the vessel, where we at least had shelter, were met at the Russ House door with the announcement that there were no vacant rooms.[7]

Doubtless our readers remember the adventures of Japhet in search of a father. Two ladies, in a strange city, after midnight, driving from one hotel to another, fruitlessly seeking a place to sleep, after having been as worn by seasickness as to be almost unable to sit up, make a picture ludicrously like poor Japhet in his wanderings; but the reader may, of course, make such application of the simile as suits him.

The International, or Webfoot Hotel, at last gave us rooms. Somehow, wherever Oregonians are in the habit of congregating, there is found the very soul of hospitality. . . .

[T]omorrow morning we are to be off for New York, with just two hours' dodging room ahead of us if we make our destination by 9 A. M., May 9th, which the Railroad Company says will be easily done.

*(May 10, 1872)*

## San Francisco Fashions for Ladies

In millinery we noticed hats in windows with high, puffed crowns of lace, crepe and tulle, having slightly drooping brims of gimp and cactus, the whole surmounted by an enormous rose at the back, from which depends a trailing vine and knotted lace and ribbons.

Dolly Varden calicoes, Dolly Varden hats, Dolly Varden collars and Dolly Varden dandies are all the rage.[8] These last are all bare on the chin, with villainous side whiskers if they can raise 'em, which they pet and twist while walking, and at intervals a sort of noisome smoke ascends from an ugly orifice above the naked chin, from which protrudes a machine called a *meerschaum*, or some such horrid name, the Dolly Varden dandy all the while imagining that he is killingly irresistible.

But hold! We headed this article with "Fashions for Ladies." Whither are we tending?

The weather, which made furs a necessity in Portland only four days ago—this is May Day—is here in San Francisco warm to suffocation. White piques, with black overskirts, and linen suits of two shades of brown are very fashionable, the trimming being laid in kilt pleats and broad ruffles. Brown and lavender are much used as contrasts. Guipure lace (real) is in high demand for trimming silks, and mohair guipure for alpaca. Fringes are not so fashionable as formerly.

There! Ladies—yes, and gentlemen—busy as we have been to-day, and many weightier matters as we have had to engage our attention, you see we have not forgotten the "Fashions."

A. J. D.

*(May 10, 1872)*

## In New York: The Woodhull Departure

As long before this reaches our readers they will have heard of another split in the Woman Movement, they will expect me to throw some light on the situation. It is difficult to understand differences thousands of miles from the scene of action, especially for those unacquainted with the person and principles of the leading actors. But with a knowledge of all this, and in their midst, I soon saw division between Victoria Woodhull and the enthusiasts and extremists that surrounded her, and the more moderate women who have led the Woman Suffrage Movement for a quarter of a century, had been, in spite of both, inevitable.[9]

In issuing a call for a Political Convention, it was the intention of such women as Mrs. [Elizabeth Cady] Stanton, [Matilda Joslyn] Gage, [Isabella Beecher] Hooker and Miss [Susan B.] Anthony, taking the ground, as they do, that women are already citizens, possessed of the right to vote, to rouse them to some preparation for their duties as such— to the study of National questions and the consideration of a party platform. . . .[10]

Mrs. Woodhull's plan, however, differed widely from this, and her action defeated the whole purpose of the combination. She proposed an immediate revolution of the Government, a new Constitution, a new party, a new platform that should cover every extreme political and social issue, and all to be crowned with herself for President. This plan was precipitated on the Convention, which had been called for the consideration of the initiatory steps in the formation of a People's Party, and dissolved in a twinkling of an eye the elements that Mrs. Woodhull, on the one side, and Mrs. Stanton, on the other, had been trying for months to bring together.

The result was the withdrawal of Mrs. Woodhull's force to Apollo Hall, leaving the National Woman's Suffrage Association to conduct its deliberations in its own way in Steinway Hall. . . . Now that Wood-hull and her infatuated followers have sloughed and run off from the legitimate work of Woman Suffrage and National Reform, we shall have opportunity to work, untrammeled by the extreme views of avowed free loveists and the ignorant marauds of rabid Internationals.[11]

New York, May 13th, 1872.
A. J. D.

*(May 31, 1872)*

## An Interview with Victoria Woodhull

Sitting here, at the desk of Elizabeth Cady Stanton, in her grand, quiet home in "the blue hills of Jersey," I seize my pen to write of some of the many vicissitudes of my life in the last fortnight.

I reached New York on the morning of Friday, May 10th, one day after the opening of the Convention at Steinway Hall [and after the convention of Radical reformers, led by Victoria Woodhull, had adjourned from Steinway to Apollo Hall]. . . .

At the [Friday] evening session [at Steinway Hall], after several eminent ladies had spoken, I was introduced and spoke but fifteen minutes, promising an Oregonian protracted meeting next week, which idea "took" immensely; and then, seeing there was no political work upon the tapis, I repaired with Mrs. Belva Lockwood, of Washington, D. C.,[12] and Mrs.

Curtis, the California farmer, to Apollo Hall to get a glimpse behind the scenes.

Victoria [Woodhull] had finished her speech. There was a noisy, enthusiastic crowd in the hall. In the ante-room to which Mrs. Lockwood led me were Moses Hull, Stephen Pearl Andrews, Laura Cuppy Smith, Tennie C. Claflin, Col. [James Harvey] Blood, and prominent among them all, Woodhull the victorious, in a furbelowed suit of black, and high hat with broad ribbons, her beautiful face shining with a deep hectic, her eyes fairly starting from their sockets, and her nervous organism in a state of unnatural and evidently unhealthy enthusiasm.[13]

With much *eclat* I was introduced to the "Presidential nominee of the Equal Rights party," and, having an eye to business, spoke then and there for the position of Secretary of War during her Administration—at which she smiled benignly, but I am not sure that the office was promised.

Said I, "Do you have any idea that this thing will succeed?"

Said she, "Of course I do. A legion of spirits are back of it. I knew six months ago that it would terminate in this way. But what do you think of Fred Douglass for Vice President?" she asked abruptly.[14]

"I think he's splendid!" I answered heartily, and then—there being but one step from the sublime to the ridiculous—I could scarcely help

adding, "Go the whole hog or none!" But you know it would have been a pity to mar my overeagerness by such an exclamation.

Mrs. Woodhull spoke freely of the abuse and misrepresentation of which she had been and is yet the victim, but says these persecutions have purified her, and that they would not have been allowed by her spirit guides if they had not been needed. She is a woman of exceedingly fine form and presence, and possesses a sort of magnetic power over the ignorant rabble who flock to the standard. It is not surprising that her winning ways and matchless conversational powers hold wild sway over members of Congress and other notables. . . .

Was urged to take a seat on the platform. Respectfully declined. . . .

Intend calling on Horace Greeley tomorrow. Will write again in a few days.

Tenafly, New Jersey, May 12, 1872.

A. J. D.

*(May 31, 1872)*

## A Visit to Horace Greeley: Syncophant and Political Pigmy

The National Woman Suffrage Association decided at one of its committee meetings that it would be a capital thing for the editor of the *New Northwest* to interview Horace Greeley, the world renowned humanitarian and Cincinnati nominee, in his editorial sanctum.[15] Accompanied by Jane Graham Jones, of Chicago, and Susan B. Anthony, the omnipresent, we proceeded one afternoon through long lines of cars and omnibuses, down among stately rows of rusty brick and stone buildings, where dirt and decomposition run riot, and where men, with furrowed, careworn faces, and boys, with the look of self-important upstarts, are the principal objects of attention. Entering a dirty office door, with a rusty iron grating in the front, we approached a dapper-figured clerk and asked for the sage of Chappaqua.

"He wasn't in. Didn't know when he would be in."

"Tell him," said Susan, "that Mrs. Duniway of Oregon wishes to see him on important business."

An appointment was made for the following afternoon. Promptly at the stated time we were on the spot. Same clerk that met us before said "he wasn't in; didn't know when he would be in."

"Very well, then we will go into the office and wait."

Readers of the *New Northwest,* you should have seen that clerk. His face elongated a yard—more or less—and he said hesitatingly that he "would see about it." Then I knew that, like the fashionable ladies, whom Horace in his better and younger days had [be]rated soundly in the *Tribune* for such prevarication, he had told his servant to lie.

Firmly we stood our ground until, finding that we must give Horace and his clerk some chance to slip (apparently unnoticed), out of the immediate exposure of their joint peccadillo, or fail to obtain an interview, Mrs. Jones and ourself repaired to a dingy stationery store nearby to wait for further orders, and Susan B., disgusted, betook herself to more honest quarters.

Waited half an hour, and were then waited upon by an office boy, who said Horace would see us. Up a narrow dirty flight of winding stairs we went, into a sanctum even less pretentious than our own, and not half so clean or well ventilated, and there, at a high desk, sat the sage "hen," scratching away on a piece of paper, and from the fact that he occasionally dipped a pen in ink, we concluded he was writing, though aside from the fact of the ink, there was nothing to convince us that the marks he was making were other than necessary efforts to discover "chicken feed."

The document finished, he handed it to a waiting man, who proceeded to prepare it for perusal, and the sage-hen looked up and smiled, shook hands and welcomed us. If it hadn't been for the lie down stairs, we might have believed the welcome genuine. As it was we received it with due grains of allowance, and went straight to business.

"I have read your paper, Mr. Greeley, ever since I was a little girl, and need not tell you that I have looked forward to this meeting with much interest. I congratulate you, sir, upon your success at Cincinnati."

Horace smiled radiantly and said, "It was unexpected, was it not?"

"No, nothing surprises me in politics. I think your show for an election is quite as good as [Victoria] Woodhull's."

A slight blush mantled his polished crown, and was faintly visible on the tip of his nose; otherwise he betrayed no embarrassment over the half ironical, half malicious mention of his Presidential antagonist.

"Woodhull," said he, "seems to command money. Consequently she is the only advocate of Woman Suffrage of any political importance."

"Well, Mr. Greeley, the vast army of wives and mothers in this Nation who do not indorse the social views of Mrs. Woodhull, and who are represented in this city to-day by leading women from every State in the Union, are anxious to know if you are going to so far commit the *Tribune* to the cause of our political enfranchisement as to enable them to work for your election without stultifying their own self-respect."

"I don't believe," he answered, with the same sort of self-complacency with which the editor of the *Oregonian* smiles upon his disenfranchised superiors, "that women ought to be men."

"Neither do I, my dear sir," was the indignant reply, and I felt very much like saying something not very complimentary about believing that "men ought not to be women," but a glance at Greeley's weak frame and effeminate appearance evoked my sympathy, and I abstained from the "retort justifiable."

"Mr. Greeley, what shall I say to my constituents about your views on the woman suffrage question?"

"You may say to them that when they do not need my aid, when there is no danger that it will do them any good, they shall have it."

"Very well. We shall not want it then. Remember, we do not ask you for help, even now. I learned the first principles of personal liberty from the New York *Tribune* in its younger and better days. The seeds that you have sowed, my dear sir, are destined, in spite of your present efforts, to bear fruit to the honor and glory and ultimate salvation of this Nation. But what do your daughters think of your present course?"

"One of them is a Roman Catholic," smiling complacently and stroking his chin, "and of course I suppose she would rather confess to a priest than cast a ballot. The other daughter likes the theatre."[16]

"Well," I promptly answered, "if my influence shall amount to nothing more with my children, I shall feel that I have lived in vain."

The interview ended there, and bidding the perturbed old candidate a polite good afternoon, we gained the open air, caught a decent breath, and meditated long upon the difference between the imagination and reality, between preaching and practice, and between a man as a theorist and a man as a political demagogue.

Dear readers, we cannot tell you how our interview dwarfed the humanitarian, progressionist, philanthropist and philosopher of imagination into an infinitesimal political pigmy of reality—one who . . . is willing to disintegrate the great Republican party, whose most truckling syncophant he has been, that he may thereby enhance his own self-aggrandizement; . . . who is ever ready to espouse a principle of justice while it is yet afar off, and yet ever ready to discard it when it becomes a live and tangible issue.

In our heart of hearts we had looked to Horace Greeley for better things; but alas! when you sift out and simmer down the little of genuine goodness that exists in the bosom of the greatest man, it too often vanishes in the sordid smoke of selfishness, and leaves nothing but a reeking odor of almighty dollars and villainous self-aggrandizement, while the ashes of your disappointed good opinion scat-ter themselves to the four winds of Heaven, to be garnered, mayhap, in some younger and purer specimen of humanity, whose life has not been encrusted with the craft of political demoralization.

*(June 7, 1872)*

## Illinois: Memories of Auld Lang Syne

Since leaving Springfield, Ill., I have been visiting and lecturing within the sacred circle of dear childhood associations, with my mind in such a whirl of olden memories and present realities as to totally unfit me for newspaper duties.

Have held large, pleasant and well appreciated meetings in Atlanta, Delevan, Hopedale, Tremont and Groveland, Illinois. On the last evening of my sojourn in my native State, a large company of old time associates assembled at the dear old homestead [at Groveland], where I had the melancholy pleasure of addressing them in the grand old rambling farm house, where once our father's voice and mother's song made melody; where once our aged grandparents on both sides of the genealogic tree, with dear old "Granny" [Chloe Riggs Scott], the great grandmother of a long line of descendants, kept ward and watch over turbulent, impetuous and oftentimes rebellious Young America. . . .

At Atlanta I found aged maternal relatives and their jolly, happy daughters, who knew me at a glance in spite of wrinkles which they had never seen and gray hairs that they knew not of.

It seemed almost wicked to allow my much-changed features to be reflected from the mirror which had been my mother's in her youth, and which I, in long gone years, had so often studied, as is young ladies' wont, but I looked at last, and was startled to see how much more my altered face resembled mother's than my own. I stood expectant, as if waiting to hear her speak, but aunt addressed me by my girlhood's name and broke the sudden spell.

In one corner of the cozy sitting-room sat grandmother's [Mary Smith Roelofson's] vacant chair. She had been for many years a cripple—dear blue-eyed, golden-haired old darling—and her amputated foot yet sleeps in the little garden of the long ago.[17] The chair in question was of the most primitive, substantial pattern, guiltless of paint or polish, but scoured to a severe whiteness, with its plethoric cushion of feathers covered with a snowy case upon which she rested her crippled limb while engaged in her household duties long after every child had married into another home. How severely neat, precise and prim she was! And how I love to think that when she reached the shining shore she found no dirt

to blemish and no grease to tarnish her immaculate surroundings. What a terror to us children was her mania for cleanliness! How good and loving and solicitous she was when one of us grew sick!

Grandfather's [Lawrence Roelofson's] well-worn Bible and hymn book lie near the vacant chair.[18] Tears blind me as I write; but after all, thank Heaven! their work on earth is done, and it is better so! . . .

The trunk is packed now, and the last bundle is ready, so we must leave these reminiscences and start with mine host of the old homestead and his bright-eyed wife to Peoria, where I am to take the cars for Council Bluffs and *home*.

Reached the Bluffs at 9 A. M. on the 24th inst., where my father's sister [Louisa], who had not seen me for twenty-eight years, but who knew me by the "family resemblance," for which we are all noted, met me with a cheery welcome, and in her cool and quiet guest's chamber I sit and scribble, scarce heeding the flying moments.

Have engaged to lecture here two evenings, and will then write again.

Council Bluffs, Iowa, June 23, 1872.

A. J. D.

*(July 12, 1872)*

## Wyoming's Noble Position

I stopped in this place on the 28th and have been lecturing with usual success before the only citizens of the United States who are all such in reality.[19]

Laramie is a perfect gem of a village, with about two thousand inhabitants, five churches and good, enterprising and intelligent society.

I have been stopping at the residence of Dr. Hayford, editor of the Laramie *Sentinel*, and Territorial Auditor of Wyoming Territory, who, with his pretty, bright, young wife, has entertained me like a queen. From him I have learned a detailed history of Woman Suffrage and its effects in Wyoming. . . .

The sensation stories, gotten up by the man's rights press, about the bad workings of the jury system are laughed over by the sensible lady jurors and their equally sensible and well pleased husbands, who not only never did object to their wives fulfilling the duties of citizenship, but who honored them for so doing and sustained them in their sacred obligations to the commonwealth as only freemen can.

The houses of ill-fame that flourished here before the women became voters have betaken themselves to man's rights quarters in Colorado, and but for the support the saloons receive from the traveling public of the man's rights States and Territories, there would not be a doggery sustained in the place.

The people here are especially wide awake, public spirited and liberal; and if they could only realize how famous Wyoming has become all over the United States for her noble position in the van of political progression, they would feel, even more keenly than now, the injustice of being deprived of a voice in the Presidential election.

The idea that an individual who for twenty or forty years has voted for President or Governor in New York or Iowa, becomes partially disfranchised as soon as he removes to a Territory, is beginning to show its absurdity on its face, and when I get to the United States Senate, I shall see if we can't further free the Territories. . . .

I start this evening for Salt Lake, to see what can be done with man suffrage and Brigham Young. Woman Suffrage and Victoria Woodhull have been receiving too much of my political solicitude of late.

It will never do to allow men too much liberty. They'll all become polygamists if the ballot isn't taken from them. Isn't Brigham Young a fit example of the dire consequences of man suffrage?

Laramie City, W. T., July 1st, 1872.

*(July 12, 1872)*

## A Ferocious Spanish Brigand

Leaving Laramie City on the evening of the 2d, I found, to my amazement, that, although I had telegraphed to Cheyenne to secure a sleeping car, there were no accommodations left except the upper berth of a small state-room, the lower half of which had been secured by a Spaniard, who looked up as the conductor showed me the alarming prospect, with a ferocious flash in his eyes and a question of evident annoyance on his tongue, which, after an uncomfortable silence on my part, he concluded with the expression, "no sabe, eh?" on an upward sliding key which almost frightened me out of my wits.

"Can't afford to take lodgings with this brigand," I said in dismay. "Is this really the best accommodation you have?"

"All I can do, madam. Could have sold this berth a half dozen times."

"To ladies?"

"Certainly. There are a number of ladies in the next car, any one of whom will be glad to get it."

This announcement raised the value of my sleeping car investment, and shrinking from the guns and other border ruffian pharaphernalia [*sic*] with which the little box of a room was filled, I retreated to the other end of the car, where a number of tourists, ladies and gentlemen, who are on their way to Oregon, were watching with amusement and evident interest the denouement of the comedy. We were soon all well acquainted and happy—that is, all except myself, and I confess a nervous tremor made me very uncomfortable whenever I thought of the approaching darkness and my anticipated night of terror with a state-room full of blunderbusses and a ferocious Spanish brigand beneath my elevated couch.

A Southern Methodist minister on his way to Albany, Oregon, from Baltimore, an old gentleman who, notwithstanding his clerical dignity, was as full of fun as a boy of fifteen, and an excellent lady whose acquaintance I hope to be able to continue, finally began a conversation with my brigand, who proved to be a cultivated Spanish gentleman, who for twenty years has resided in Sonora, Mexico, and was now on his return from a late visit to his native olive groves. I found— oh, shades of adventure and anticipation!—that my perturbation over his blunderbusses was altogether unnecessary; and all unmindful of the fact that "brigand" and "Corsair" were among the mildest of our half-earnest epithets, the gentleman, in the best English at his command, tendered the "Senorita" the choicest section of the state-room, which I had the audacity to accept, but not without some compunctions of conscience over my unjust judgments.

*(July 19, 1872)*

## Fourth of July in Salt Lake City

Arrived at Salt Lake City on the evening of the 3d, and on the morning of the 4th was called upon by Governor [George L.] Woods, who accompanied me to his pleasant home, where for several days I have been enjoying a delightful visit with his excellent family.[20] On the evening of the Fourth, a large assembly of citizens, headed by the National Brass Band, marched to the residence of the Governor and discoursed the National airs, after which mine host addressed them in an impromptu speech in his peculiarly eloquent and patriotic style, concluding a stirring peroration with an announcement, somewhat to my perturbation, that "an eminent editor and speaker, an old friend, and Oregonian," etc. etc., "was present, and whom he wished to introduce." And, there being no alternative but to retreat or "face the music," I preferred the latter, and made my first Fourth of July address before a dense jam in the gathering darkness standing in the Governor's gateway.

A number of gentlemen came forward at the close of the little speech and tendered me the Liberal Institute

for a lecture, which I accepted, and on Saturday evening a fine audience of intelligent and orderly people filled the spacious hall.

*(July 19, 1872)*

## Salt Lake: The City of Broken Hearts

"President" Brigham Young has tendered me the use of the Tabernacle this evening, and, anxious as I feel to get on homeward, I must stay and talk to the Mormons, who will not enter the [Liberal] Institute because it is owned by the apostate Godbe and others, whom the Latter Day Saints consider infinitely worse, if possible, than the murderous Gentiles. . . .[21]

Rode out with the Governor [George L. Woods] and his family to Prospect Hill, where with a good field glass we swept the city, Salt Lake and the . . . nearby mountains; but the objects of most particular interest to me were the long double and quadruple adobe houses, where victims of polygamy live and propagate, and where the old women are often abandoned, to beg as best they may for a sustenance, while younger wives are installed as favorites of hard-favored Mormon autocrats whose religion—ah, me!

Passed the Mormon burying ground, the city of broken hearts, where the largest class of occupants are "first wives," who died in their heroic efforts to become reconciled to the wonderful beauty of the practical workings of the Mormon faith.

Yet the women are often as zealous advocates of polygamy as the men. They are sustained by a religious zeal which is as enthusiastic as is that of the Hindoo widow who casts herself upon her husband's funeral pire. . . .

Called at the office of Brigham Young, who was not able to "see company." The office walls are adorned with pictures of the Saints, done in oil, and conspicuous among them is a large photograph of Ben Holladay, with his autograph at the bottom, preceded by "respectfully, your friend." Asked if Brigham would accept my picture to adorn his office, and was answered by "of course, and glad to get it." Will think about it when I get home again. . . .

I am to talk to-night on Human Rights and Motherhood.

Later. Have just been visited by apostate Mormons—a lady and her two daughters—who have influential relatives living in Portland. The mother is a remarkably intellectual and engaging conversationalist, whose tale of horror froze my blood. The daughters are bright, beautiful girls, and the one idea of all of them was to borrow means to run away. They have renounced the Mormon faith, have had all their property taken away by Brigham Young, and the husband and the father having found other loves and founded other families, they want to flee like fugitives. The Governor and his wife, of whom as representative Oregonians I am justly proud, ought to have an appropriation from the General Government to use at their discretion to aid these fugitives. Oh, if women were only in Congress as men's associate lawmakers, how much human suffering might be thereby alleviated.

The Mormons have a wholesome fear of the Governor. He has outlawed many of their pet schemes . . . , and commanded their respect by his honorable course, though there is no doubt but that there are many who would delight to destroy him. . . .

Salt Lake City, U. T., July 8, 1872.
A. J. D.

*(July 19, 1872)*

# Back in the Golden City

Leaving Salt Lake City, from which place I last addressed you, after having lectured in Brigham Young's Temple to the Mormon faithful, for which I expect my man's rights brethren to be consistent and accuse me of espousing Mormon doctrine, I hied me onward to this Golden City by the sea, where for one week I have been diligently engaged in necessary preparation to fling my banner to the breeze for Grant and Wilson, as the nearest exponents in the present political field of the doctrine equal rights, humanity and progression.

I was last night greeted by an immense audience, a fine band of music and any amount of enthusiasm at Platt's Hall, where I spoke for nearly two hours upon "What I know about politics and Horace Greeley.". . . I am spoiling for the chances of the Presidential row, and must work out my mission. The chances are that I shall come back to California to stump the State, but will give Oregon the preference if desired.

San Francisco, July 24th, 1872.

A. J. D.

*(July 26, 1872)*

## Cogitations and Conclusions

Well, here we are home again, thank Heaven! And if anybody wants to endure the wear and tear, pleasure and fatigue, fun and anxiety inseparable from such a suddenly projected, hastily completed and expensively extensive journey as ours has been, they may have our credentials for the next Convention.

*(August 30, 1872)*

## Advice to Correspondents

*A vexed housekeeper:* We haven't our cooking harness on, but we distinctly remember our own vexation when "batter cakes would stick to the griddle and men were waiting and the baby cross." In such a case, if we had our young life to live over with our present experience, instead of fretting at the cook stove till we spoiled the baby's food, we should bathe our heated face, take the baby and sit down, and direct the "waiting men" to scour the griddles with salt and bake their own batter cakes.

*Mary:* Your bridal outfit should be in keeping with your expected style of married life. As you are "going over the mountains to help herd a band of cattle," we should advise a substantial suit of waterproof, stout boots and gloves, and plenty of flannel hosiery and underwear. A traveling suit of lavender or drab alpaca, with gloves and veil to match, is the only wedding dress admissible under the circumstances. Receive our congratulations. Take the benefit of the Homestead Act, raise bands of cattle, flocks of poultry, troops of children, and the world will be the better for your struggles.

*(October 11, 1872)*

## At the Republican Rally with Grant's Invincibles

The grand rally at the Court House on Monday evening, November 4th, was the most enthusiastic meeting ever witnessed in Portland. The speakers were Mrs. A. J. Duniway, ex-Gov. Gibbs, Hon. H. W. Scott, Hon. J. H. Caples, Geo. P. Riley, Esq., (colored) and Geo. Venable Smith, Esq.[22] The speeches were all so well received that it seems invidious to particularize, but we cannot forbear a word of comment upon the eloquent and masterly address of "our friend Caples," who espoused the main issue of the day, Woman Suffrage, with a spirit and zeal which is going to immortalize him among the ladies of Multnomah. They're already talking him up for the Congress. . . .

The Grant Invincibles, a colored company, occupied the middle seats, and sitting upon the platform, with a vacant chair of State between them, were two colored men, and as we entered the crowded hall and passed up the aisle, the impression was general that that vacant seat was for the lady speaker. Ladies who were strangers to us caught our attention and whispered, "don't take that seat! It's intended as an insult to the women." But we were calm and determined, and perfectly ready to take the seat,

if it was offered, as we knew a strong point in woman's favor could be made thereby. When the Chairman met us we asked, "Do you intend to seat us between those two darkies?" He quickly answered, "O, no indeed, that chair is for the colored speaker; here is your seat," conducting us among the Honorables.

But those negroes were our inspiration. And the points we made for woman's enfranchisement with those colored voters behind us was one which struck conviction home to everybody, but a few of the "Grant Invincibles," who yelled *no* quite lustily when the question as to whether or not the women should vote on the morrow passed by an otherwise unanimous aye. Mr. Malarky [Chairman of the County Central Committee] decided that the "ayes had it," whereupon the ladies gave him three rousing cheers.

After Mr. Caples' address the spirit moved us "to tell a story," so by consent of the house we arose and said that the last speaker had made us so happy we couldn't keep still. They all remembered a little tilt we had run with Caples on the evening of the ratification reception a few weeks since. Well, our friend went back to the Legislature and voted for Woman Suffrage like a man. . . .

The women were quite as enthusiastic as the men, and had we but succeeded in getting our suffrage bill through the Legislature, the State would have gone Republican by [a] twenty thousand majority.

Our cause is marching on.

*(November 8, 1872)*

## Black Sunday in Portland

Scarcely had the State recovered from the shock of the Oregon City devastation [burning of the Oregon City Woolen Mills] ere Portland was visited by the fire fiend, and the tracks he has left are indeed terrible.

Our citizens were suddenly alarmed on Sunday morning by a dense cloud of smoke which seemed to originate simultaneously, from an American saloon and a Chinese wash house. The daily press with one accord lay the blame upon the Chinamen, who, like the O'Leary cow, have no means of denial, but citizens, living adjacent, have declared to us that the flames were first seen rising from the saloon. Be that as it may, the fiery monster gained so rapidly upon the combustible materials which lay in waiting for it, that our gallant firemen were unable to control it, although they worked with a will that excited wonder and admiration.

For a time it seemed that the whole city was doomed. The wind blew sometimes in fitful gusts, and again in steady currents, scattering the breath of the fire fiend broadcast upon the buildings, where, but for the vigilance of everybody, hundreds of conflagrations would have rekindled from its contact. Our firemen worked to the extreme of exhaustion.

Chinamen were impressed onto the service by means efficacious but reprehensible. White men stood idle by hundreds, unable to find anything to do. Men and women vied with each other in removing and damaging property. And still the insatiate monster gained upon the engines, laughing as he licked the rushing water with his ten thousand tongues, roaring forth his fierce defiance of the shrieking winds and hissing horribly at the fast falling ruins.

Some of the finest fire-proof structures in the city, with all their contents, were in flames. Explosion after explosion rent the air and hope seemed well nigh dead, when the wind, as if in pity of the city's woes, veered suddenly away from the ruins, under which three noble firemen had been almost fatally crushed, and moaning, as if repentant over the desolation he had helped to scatter, sought the river, to which he chanted a solemn requiem. Shortly after this providential change of the wind, a drenching rain began to fall, and our exhausted firemen were relieved by reinforcements from Vancouver, Salem, Oregon City and Albany, and the elements and men combined to quell the fire fiend's reign of devastation. We have not space for full particulars. The whole amount of loss was $411,170. The insurance was $111,000.[23]

*(December 27, 1872)*

# Incidents of the Portland Fire

One of the most soul sickening features of the fire was the brutal manner in which Chinamen were treated by rude, burly boys and a few children of a larger growth. It is well known that these people never shirk a duty when it is required of them if its performance is within their range of possibilities. Throughout the day of the fire and far into the night, no cessation of the labor of individual Chinamen was permitted at the brakes, although hundreds of great large white men stood idly gazing at the famished and weary Mongolians who were met with blows or bayonets whenever they would so much as pause to catch their breath.

We do not say but that Chinamen should have done their full quota of the work, but we do emphatically declare that the inhuman manner in which they were abused was devilish. No milder word will at all express our meaning. This abuse was mostly the work of boys whose mothers "have all the rights they want," so they let these graceless young scamps run riot on the streets, preparing themselves for the penitentiary or gallows, by whetting their appetites with the exercise of that manly (?) supremacy which their mothers consider their sexual prerogative.

Three Chinamen have been missing since the fire, and the belief is general that they were drowned by boys. One poor fellow, a quiet, harmless cook in a private boarding house in the city, was struck by a boy and his leg broken.

Another, who worked with a will until dinner time, started to the house of his employer, promising to come back as soon as he could cook the dinner. His excuse was not taken, and he was unmercifully beaten back to the brakes. One, becoming exhausted, fell back a little, and was caught by two ruffians and hurled back to the engine, and in his attempt to catch the flying brake, was struck under the chin and thrown back in the mud. He was not allowed one second to recover from the shock, but compelled to arise and work right along. We watched two large men beating one poor little image of his Maker, until we grew so faint as to be scarcely able to stand.

We fear a dreadful self-avenging of these creatures' wrongs before the people are aware. As we looked at the panic-stricken citizens whose cheeks blanched at the fiery inroads of their ere-while useful servant, we plainly saw another fearful holocaust in the near future, when these other servants may wreak their cunning vengeance upon the Christians (?) who have persecuted the heathen in their midst.

*(December 27, 1872)*

## Modoc Uprising

The first fight with the Modoc Indians occurred on the Oregon side, a few miles north of the California boundary, and almost all the settlers killed were Oregonians, but the future fighting will no doubt be all in California, south of Tule Lake, unless the Indians leave the lava bed and strike out northeast into Oregon again, toward the Idaho boundary.

The Jacksonville *Sentinel* learns that a subscription has been started for the relief of Mrs. Brotherton, whose husband and elder sons were lately killed by the Indians. In mid-winter, illy provided to meet the task, is thrust upon her the care of the remainder of her family, and her condition should elicit a more substantial evidence of sympathy than words of mere condolence.

*(December 27, 1872)*

## Notes for 1872

1. The "Chair" referred to by Duniway was identified in *The Oregonian* report of the State Temperance Alliance as "S. C. Adams"—Sebastian Cabot Adams (1825-98). His brother was W. L. Adams, the editor of the *Oregon Argus* who published some of Duniway's early writings. Sebastian Adams, born in Ohio, was a teacher after his arrival in Oregon in 1850. He served as a state senator from Yamhill County (1868-69) and, after a move to Salem in 1869, was minister of Salem's Christian Church.

2. Octavia Mercier was the daughter of Charles H. Mercier, a barber listed in the 1870 Portland directory and a leader of Portland's black and mulatto community. Octavia became a teacher of music and also gave public performances, as upon this occasion in 1872.

3. The Rev. Daniel Jones was minister of Portland's African Methodist Episcopal Church, 1872-73. Judge Deady noted in his diary, 5 June 1872:

   > [D]ropped into the "Colored Church Fair" a moment. . . . The pastor of the Church is "Dan Jones" a good looking mulatto who used to shave me when I held court at Jacksonville 18 years ago. Met him there last night and shook hands with him. He was always a favorite with the brush & razor and I suppose he is equally well liked as Preacher.

   See *Pharisee Among Philistines: The Diary of Judge Matthew P. Deady, 1871-1892*, ed. Malcolm Clark, Jr., (Portland: Oregon Historical Society, 1975), 82.

4. The People's Convention in New York was called by Elizabeth Cady Stanton, Isabella Beecher Hooker, and Susan B. Anthony to form a new political party at the NWSA Convention in Steinway Hall, New York City, May 1872. Dissatisfied with both the Republican and Democratic parties, the women invited "all citizens, who believe in the idea of

self-government," to join in the inauguration of "a political revolution, which shall secure justice, liberty and equality to every citizen of the United States" ("People's Convention," *NNW*, 19 April 1872). Duniway reported that she had been "nominated and elected by acclamation" as a delegate to the convention at a Portland meeting of between three hundred and four hundred people ("Independent Political Mass Meeting," *NNW*, 26 April 1872). Although she did not expect the People's Party of Progression and Human Rights to win a national victory in 1872, she thought that, with hard work, they could win in 1876.

Ben Holladay (1819-87), from whom Duniway requested "a pass" for this trip, was a major promoter and financier who could provide stage, steamer, and railroad passes for those he chose to favor. He made his first fortune with stage and express routes in California, which he sold in 1866 to Wells Fargo Express. The native Kentuckian, noted for his aggressive behavior and promotional schemes, invested in weekly steamboats between San Francisco and Portland, and gained stock in the Oregon Central Railroad. In 1870, as head of the Oregon and California Railroad, Holladay supervised construction to link Oregon with California. After the depression of 1873, Holladay gave way to Henry Villard, who eventually joined the Oregon line to the transcontinental Northern Pacific and completed links between Oregon and California to merge with the Southern Pacific system.

5. Frederick Douglass (1818-95), the famed abolitionist, writer, and orator, appears frequently in Duniway's writings as "Fred Douglass." The son of a slave woman and probably her white master, Douglass escaped from slavery at the age of twenty and first told his story in *Narrative of the Life of Frederick Douglass, an American Slave* (1845). A friend of women's rights and woman suffrage, he

attended the Seneca Falls Convention in 1848, the first woman's rights convention in the United States, and reported on the proceedings in his newspaper, *The North Star*. Frederick Douglass, "the great agitator," was a hero in Duniway's eyes, and she often used the metaphor of his struggle against slavery and for black rights to convey the struggle she faced for women's rights.

6. In 1870, James O'Meara (1825-1903) became editor of the Portland *Daily Bulletin*, a paper established by railroad promoter Ben Holladay, hence the label "Ben Holladay's Man Friday." During Susan B. Anthony's visit to Oregon in the fall of 1871, O'Meara covered one of her Portland speeches. He wrote that "this distinguished champion of Women's Rights and Women Suffrage had a very full house last night"; however, he found her "doctrines and arguments" to be "mischievous and revolutionary in a social way," and "capable of causing division in homes, anarchy in families, chaos in society in general" (*Daily Bulletin*, 12 Sept. 1871).

Duniway had known James O'Meara in Albany, when he was editor of the new *State Rights Democrat* for about a year, 1865-66. In *The Presumptuous Dreamers* (Lake Oswego, OR: Smith, 1974), Helen Krebs Smith discusses the O'Meara-Duniway dispute in late 1865. At one of Duniway's school exhibitions in Albany, Willis Duniway, then about age nine, gave a speech on the American flag, which was followed by cheers for the flag from the school children. O'Meara charged Duniway with including politics and "sectional matters" in the school exhibition, and Duniway essentially called O'Meara a "rebel and traitor" (102-4). See also "Women Have More Rights than Men," *NNW*, 25 Oct. 1872.

According to George Turnbull, in *History of Oregon Newspapers* (Portland: Binfords & Mort, 1939), Duniway's brother Harvey Scott was a member of the stock company that bought the *Daily*

*Bulletin* in late 1872, and Scott succeeded O'Meara as editor of the *Bulletin* for a few months in 1873 (154). A story was told by a veteran Portland editor that Harvey Scott once felled O'Meara in a fist fight, but the two editors eventually became friends (131).

7. Frances Auretta Fuller Victor (1826-1902) was a friend of Duniway. During this San Francisco trip, Victor was probably promoting the recent publication of *All Over Oregon and Washington* (San Francisco: John H. Carmany & Co., 1872). She also published pieces in *The NNW* and helped edit the paper while Duniway was on a lecture tour in the spring of 1874. Although Victor and Duniway disagreed on the effectiveness of the Woman's Temperance Crusade of 1874, they agreed on the need for woman suffrage. See Jim Martin, *A Bit of a Blue: The Life and Work of Frances Fuller Victor—Historian* (Salem: Deep Well Pub. Co.), 1992; and Jean M. Ward and Elaine A. Maveety, eds., "Frances Auretta Fuller Victor," *Pacific Northwest Women, 1815-1925: Lives, Memories, and Writings* (Corvallis: Oregon State University Press, 1995), 40-48.

8. The character of Dolly Varden appears as a gaily dressed coquette in Charles Dickens' *Barnaby Rudge* (1841). To help readers understand what was meant by "Dolly Vardens," *The NNW* carried an unsigned piece under that title on 5 July 1872. Supposedly, in the spring of 1870, Napoleon's wife, Empress Eugenie, was making up a party to go to the Longchamp Races and planned with "a man-milliner" named Worth "those rose and sunflower spangled *cretonne* suits, and got up a leghorn 'shoe-fly' hat, with velvet and daisies and dandelions." The effect was that "the dress was the most insane specimen of window curtain, and the hats looked just as coquettish as our Dolly Varden hats do now. It looked as if it had been struck by a whirlwind behind—or, in a word it was a cocked hat just ready to fly, but anchored down with velvet strings." Now, "[t]hey are cutting up their window curtains to make what they call 'Dolly Varden' dresses, and the little forty-five cent palmetto hats made by the darkies in Florida are brought up here cocked on side, ballasted with $10 worth of Paris pansies and poppies and bachelor's buttons, and sold for $26."

9. Victoria Woodhull (1838-1927) first declared herself as a candidate for President of the United States in April of 1870, and soon after the first issue of *Woodhull and Claflin's Weekly* was published in New York City to explain her program. The charismatic Woodhull's unorthodox views on Spiritualism, women's rights, sexual freedom for men and women, and a single sexual standard for all drew considerable attention, including that of Elizabeth Cady Stanton, who agreed with Woodhull on a number of issues. When the beautiful and eloquent Woodhull spoke on women's rights before the Senate Judiciary Committee in January of 1871, she impressed women's rights leaders and was invited to speak at the NWSA Convention in May of 1871. In November of that year, Woodhull spoke on "Principles of Social Freedom" in Steinway Hall, New York City, and announced that she both advocated and practiced free love. She repeated the speech in Boston and other cities, shocking audiences with her beliefs about free love, marriage, divorce, and prostitution. To the dismay of many NWSA members, Stanton defended Woodhull, believed an alliance could be formed with her, and invited her to attend the 1872 NWSA Convention. Stanton and others had intended to form a revolutionary "People's Party of Progression and Human Rights" at the NWSA meeting, but Woodhull formed her own "People's Party," later named the "Equal Rights Party." Sensing that a takeover was likely, Susan B. Anthony firmly opposed Woodhull, who withdrew with her followers to Apollo Hall.

10. The four women named by Duniway—
Stanton, Anthony, Gage, and
Hooker—were connected by their
commitment to woman suffrage yet
differed in style and philosophy.
Elizabeth Cady Stanton (1815-1902),
one of the major organizers of the Seneca
Falls Convention in 1848, was concerned
with all aspects of women's rights, from
suffrage to employment to divorce. Her
avowed goal was to question all that
limited woman's mind and sphere, and
she frequently caused controversy, as with
publication of her two volumes of *The
Woman's Bible* (1895, 1898). Despite the
controversies, "Mrs. Stanton," the
mother of seven children, was better
known and more highly praised during
her lifetime than her co-worker, "Aunt
Susan" B. Anthony.

In 1851, through Amelia Bloomer,
Stanton was introduced to Susan B.
Anthony (1820-1906), and the two
forged a friendship and collaborative
working relationship that drew on
Stanton's talents as a writer and speaker
and on Anthony's strengths as an
organizer. Together they began *The
Revolution* in January of 1868 and
formed the National Woman Suffrage
Association in 1869.

Matilda Joslyn Gage (1826-98) was
better known for her writing and
organizing work than her speaking. She
became a member of the NWSA in 1869,
headed both the NWSA and New York
State suffrage associations in 1875, and
worked with Stanton and Anthony on
the first three volumes of *History of
Woman Suffrage* (1881-86). In *Woman,
Church, and State* (1893), Gage argued
that Christianity systematically degraded
women.

Isabella Beecher Hooker (1822-1907)
was active in the NWSA and drawn to
Spiritualism by Victoria Woodhull. She
was the daughter of the Rev. Lyman
Beecher and sister of the Rev. Henry
Ward Beecher, Catharine Beecher, and
Harriet Beecher Stowe. Although Henry
Ward Beecher was exonerated by his
church and a council of Congregational
ministers in the Beecher-Tilton scandal,
Isabella Hooker believed he was guilty of
an affair with Elizabeth Tilton. As a
result, Isabella was ostracized by her
brothers and sisters, publicly declared
insane by her brother Henry, and barred
from attending his funeral in 1887.

11. The "ignorant marauds of rabid
Internationals" is Duniway's disparaging
reference to Woodhull's followers from
Section Twelve of Marx's International
Workingmen's Association, which was
organized in New York in 1871 and led
by Victoria Woodhull and Tennessee
Claflin until they were expelled in March
of 1872 for their "eccentricities." The
sisters also published the Communist
Manifesto in English in *Woodhull and
Claflin's Weekly*, the first time it appeared
in the United States.

12. Belva Lockwood (1830-1917), who
accompanied Duniway on the visit to
Apollo Hall, supported Woodhull and
spoke in favor of her candidacy for the
presidency at Cooper Union in New York
in 1872; however, she endorsed Horace
Greeley by the fall of that year.
Unorthodox in her own way, Lockwood
graduated from National University Law
School in 1873 and was admitted to the
bar of the District of Columbia. When
denied the right to plead in federal
courts, she successfully lobbied Congress
for a change in the law. In March of
1879, she was the first woman admitted
to practice before the United States
Supreme Court. In 1884, a group of
California women, identifying themselves
as the "National Equal Rights Party,"
nominated Lockwood for the presidency
of the United States. Running on a
platform of equal rights for all, including
blacks, Indians and immigrants, she
gained over four thousand votes in six
states. After another run at the presidency
in 1888, Lockwood devoted her energies
to efforts for world peace.

13. This group surrounding Woodhull included her sister and some of her closest friends and advisors—all Spiritualists. Tennie (Tennessee) C. Claflin (1845-1923), Victoria's sister, had established a relationship with Commodore Cornelius Vanderbilt about 1868 and secured funding from him for financial speculation that led to establishment of the highly successful New York City brokerage firm of Woodhull, Claflin & Company in January of 1870. The sisters also began *Woodhull & Claflin's Weekly* in 1870, which ran intermittently for six years and was edited chiefly by Stephen Pearl Andrews and Colonel James Harvey Blood. Andrews, schooled in both medicine and law, was a Spiritualist, radical reformer, and skilled linguist. His vision of Pantarchy was a perfect state of free love in which children and property were held in common. Col. Blood, a Civil War veteran and "clairvoyant consultant," was the third husband of Victoria Woodhull. Blood introduced Woodhull to reform causes surrounding the nineteenth-century Spiritualist Movement and advocated for socialism and free love. Moses Hull, a Spiritualist author and lecturer, supported woman suffrage and believed in "free marriage," with which his wife agreed. Laura Cuppy Smith, a Spiritualist trance speaker and suffragist, was a loyal friend to Woodhull and testified on her behalf when Woodhull, who published what she knew of the Beecher-Tilton affair in November of 1872, was charged with sending obscene material in the mail, a violation of the Comstock Anti-Obscenity Act.

14. Although Woodhull named Frederick Douglass as her running mate, he evidently knew nothing of her intentions, ignored the honor, and supported the re-election of Grant.

15. Horace Greeley (1811-72) had been nominated at the Cincinnati Convention of "Liberal Republicans" as their candidate for the presidency. He was later endorsed by the Democratic Party at Baltimore as their candidate. With this uneasy coalition of Democrats and Liberal Republicans, Greeley ran for civil service reform, laissez-faire liberalism, and an end to Reconstruction. Woman suffrage was not a part of his platform.

16. Greeley's daughters were Gabrielle and Ida. His wife, Mary Cheney Greeley died a few days before the election, and Greeley died shortly after the election, in December of 1872.

17. Duniway's grandmother, Mary Smith Roelofson (1779-1862), the spirited mother of twelve children, was bitten on the leg by a wild sow, not long after arriving at Groveland in 1821. Gangrene set in, and she survived three separate amputations performed without anesthetic "by an unskilled doctor with crude instruments" (a saw). With her leg finally amputated just below the knee, Mary Smith Roelofson managed to keep an immaculate house by supporting herself with crutches and resting her leg on a wooden chair. For particulars, see "Memoirs of Mrs. Mary Roelofson Gamble," 5, Duniway Papers; *History of Tazewell County, Illinois* (Chicago: Chapman, 1879), 475-76; Letter from Joel Knight, in *Missouri Cumberland Presbyterian*, clipping reprinted in Wylie Wayne Rolofson, "The Rolofson [*sic*] Family Story," photocopied typescript in Duniway Papers.

18. Duniway's grandfather, Lawrence Roelofson (1764-1855), was a self-taught leader in the Cumberland Presbyterian Church and had been cast out by the Conservative Presbyterian Synod for his unorthodox views, including denial of absolute predestination. One of Duniway's cousins recalled that Grandfather Roelofson retained his Bible memory work throughout his life and was "considered a very fine scholar for those days when schools were so few and books a novelty" ("Memoirs of Mrs. Mary Roelofson Gamble," 2).

19. Wyoming Territory approved woman suffrage in 1869.

20. George Lemuel Woods (1832-90) traveled from Missouri to Oregon with his parents in 1847. He was educated in Yamhill County schools and McMinnville College, and became noted as a prominent political speaker and organizer of Republican clubs. He was admitted to the Oregon bar in 1858 and was Wasco County judge in 1863. Woods was elected governor of Oregon in 1866, and President Grant appointed him governor of Utah Territory in 1871, a position he held for four years.

21. British-born William Samuel Godbe (1833-1902) converted to Mormonism in 1849. In the 1860s, Godbe and a group of Mormon intellectuals and businessmen who disagreed with Brigham Young's authoritarianism on economic and religious issues formed a dissident group known as the Godbeites. For his dissent, Godbe was excommunicated from the church in 1869.

22. At the time of this event, Harvey Scott, Duniway's brother, was a junior editor with *The Oregonian* and also collector of customs. John H. Caples and George Venable Smith were Portland attorneys. Addison Crandall Gibbs (1825-86), who had served as governor of Oregon, 1862-66, and raised an Oregon regiment for the Union during the Civil War, was U.S. district attorney.

The "Geo. P. Riley, Esq. (colored)" named by Duniway is evidently the George P. Riley, a black barber from Portland, who was the main speaker at an Emancipation Anniversary Celebration held in Salem, on January 1, 1870. The Salem *Oregon Statesman* described Riley as "a natural orator, whose ability in that respect is scarcely surpassed by any of our most gifted speakers" (4 Jan. 1870). And, the *Statesman* noted, despite some difficulty with pronunciation and grammar, if Riley were white, he would probably hold high political office. Riley was also the principal speaker at the Portland "Ratification Jubilee," April 6, 1870, to celebrate ratification of the

Fifteenth Amendment, and he spoke on "The Colored Citizen and the Ballot" in Portland's Philharmonic Hall on April 26, 1870. According to K. Keith Richard, in "Unwelcome Settlers: Black and Mulatto Oregon Pioneers, Part II," *Oregon Historical Quarterly* 84 (Summer 1983), Riley was a native of Massachusetts, age 37 in 1870, and had worked with Wendell Phillips in the abolition movement (182). Richard adds that Riley's mother, who had been president of the first Female Emancipation Society in the United States, was disappointed that her son never attended college. Instead, Riley left Boston and came west to mine for gold in California and the Northwest Territories. In Portland, he was involved in organizing groups such as the Colored Benevolent Society in 1867 and the Sumner Union Club in 1870. For more on Riley, see Esther Hall Mumford, *Calabash: A Guide to the History, Culture & Art of African Americans in Seattle and King County, Washington* (Seattle: Ananse Press, 1993) and *Seattle's Black Victorians, 1852-1901* (Seattle: Ananse Press, 1980).

23. The Portland fire of December 22, 1872, destroyed several blocks on Front Street and created public demand for more police protection during times of emergency and as regular patrols. Judge Matthew Deady wrote in his diary:

*It is estimated that the loss was about $400,000. A great deal of labor was performed in what was called saving goods, but in many instances the fire could not have done more harm than the savors. The poor Chinamen were cruelly used and abused by the Fenian Guards [Emmet Guard] and the street Arabs upon pretense of making them work the engines. (Pharisee Among Philistines, 104)*

# 1873

## You Need Not Fear the Modocs

[To] Helen H., New York: The Modoc Indians are seemingly as far from Portland as they are from your city. They are few in number, and their present revolt is in consequence of dissatisfaction concerning their reservation. Their depredations were committed upon our extreme border, where the settlements are sparse and remote from each other. You need not fear them if you want to immigrate.

*(January 10, 1873)*

## To Our Patrons

The *New Northwest* is going to have a few months' vacation. Our young and growing sons have stood faithfully at the [printer's] case for twenty-three months, and now, having been prostrated by an attack of *measles*—the prevailing epidemic—they are unable, at once, to resume their work, and the finances of the paper will not justify us in employing other aid, so we now propose to spend a few months in lecturing, organizing suffrage societies, and soliciting financial aid for our paper.

*(March 28, 1873)*

## Salutatory

Again the bright, crisp pages of our "Journal for the People" go out to greet our many readers. . . .

Within a space of about two months we have held thirty-nine public meetings and traveled in Oregon and Washington Territory about twelve hundred miles. . . .

Our principal meetings were held in Astoria, East Portland, Oregon City, Lafayette, Woodburn, Hubbard, Gervais, Forest Grove and Hillsboro, in Oregon, and in Kalama, Olympia, Tumwater and Seattle in Washington Territory.

*(June 20, 1873)*

## Hair Dressing

Molly writes: "How *shall* I wear my hair? I've tried to fix it a dozen times in some new-fangled way, but don't succeed at all to my liking." Well, Molly, you're in the same category with ourself. The prevailing mode of hair dressing brings all the braids, puffs, curls, etc., that you can buy, beg or pilfer high upon the top of your head and pins them there, though by just what sort of a freak of legerdemain we have not yet discovered.

Perhaps some of our lady friends will enlighten us.

*(June 27, 1873)*

## Bustles

[To] Susie, Halsey: If you want to disfigure your form with a bustle you can make one of *Weekly Oregonians*. The steel ones cost from $1.00 to $2.00, but the *Oregonian* is preferable for the purpose, as it is made of substantial paper and ought to be good for something.

*(August 15, 1873)*

## Portland's Great Conflagration

Portland lay asleep. . . . But the incendiary did not sleep.[1] With his fiendish appetite for destruction whetted beyond its ordinary wont, he prowled among the sun-dried buildings wherein yet greater combustibles were stored, and at the silent hour of four, the hour when sleep is soundest and danger and suspicion of danger is supposed to be at rest, he applied the torch that laid a city low. . . . But at last a solitary fire bell rang out its sharp alarm. Portland awoke—awoke and flocked to open windows, with drowsy eyes and disheveled hair, with blanched cheek and fluttering heart and gazed out upon great mountains of smoke, surmounted by slender spires of lurid flame. Another, and yet another fire bell rang.

Men hurried on their clothes and darted pell mell down the erewhile deserted streets. Women, scarcely taking time to clothe themselves, followed at a little distance. Thousands gathered at the scene of disaster and gazed and struggled, till lot after lot and block after block fell before the devouring element, driving back, with the fierce tongues of fire that possessed them, or the great billows of smoke that they sent forth, the frantic owners who fought for longer mastery in vain.

Women, with little children clinging to their clothes, struggled along the streets under all sorts of burdens. Men divested of all thought of self, fought the arch fiend face to face, saving property wherever they could. Brothels emptied the low, vile, horrid life with which they teem into the open streets, and filled the air with curses. Ministers stood upon the steps of costly churches within a stone's throw of these awful dens, and lifting up their hands and voices, besought the God of elements to stay his hand. Men, more practical, enshrouded buildings in wet blankets, and prayed with hose and buckets, and we trust, silently as well. Other men, by dozens, became brutally intoxicated, helplessly leaving their wives and children to bear the burdens of the day.

Our noble firemen did their duty grandly. Assistance came from Salem, Oregon City and Vancouver, and chiefly by the aid of these

*The Fire of 1873 swept through Portland and burned to the brick walls of the St. Charles Hotel, S.W. Front and Morrison.*

reinforcements was the conflagration headed off before it could destroy the St. Charles Hotel, the only brick building that stood between the conflagration and the almost entire remaining front. The loss is computed at $1,185,325, insurance $285,000. It is a greater calamity to the Northwest than the Chicago fire was to the central portion of the Union, for it is a far greater loss in proportion to the age of the country, its wealth and population. But our people are again at work.

*(August 8, 1873)*

## An Outrage Against a Chinaman

A barefoot Chinaman was compelled by a member of the Emmet Guards, on the day of the fire, to run through a burning street at the point of a sabre, although the poor fellow, who could not speak English, protested as well as he could against the outrage.[2] When he got across the street he fell upon the sidewalk, quivering in every nerve with pain. Some gentleman carried him to the shade of a tree, bound up his charred and mutilated feet in oil and flour, and putting him in a wagon with one of his country-men, sent him away to be taken care of.

*(August 8, 1873)*

# Call for Investigation of the Outrage

Portland, August 15, 1873. To-day I accidentally picked up your paper of the 8th ult., and read in its columns that a "member of the Emmet Guards on the day of the fire compelled a barefooted Chinaman to run through a burning street at the point of a sabre." It was news to me, and if it is true (which I doubt much), the witnesses of the act are to a very great extent accomplices if they allow the committer of the deed to go free without paying the penalty of the law for unwarrantable and outrageous cruelty to a human being—even if said person is a Chinaman.

Desiring that the reputation of the Emmets may not be sullied, even by any prejudiced, unfounded and un-proved report of Madam Rumor, I remain, yours truly. Jos. R. Wiley, Captain Emmet Guards.

*The gentleman who gave us the report, and who dressed the Chinaman's mutilated feet, is called upon to explain.—Ed.*

*(August 22, 1873)*

# Reply to Mr. Wiley

Portland, Aug. 27, 1873
*Joseph Wiley, Esq., Captain Emmet Guards—Sir.*—I am pleased to see the spirit manifested in your letter to the *New Northwest* of last week [22 August] in relation to cruelty practiced upon a Chinaman on the day of the fire. I do not know the name of the Guard who did the deed. It was witnessed by the editor-in-chief of the *Oregonian,* Mr. J. Taylor, myself and many others. I, myself, bound up the Chinaman's feet, which were horribly charred, and the poor fellow's agony was simply *awful.* It was not my intention to cast a reflection upon the Emmet Guards as a body. I judged the offender to be an Emmet by his uniform, which was grey, ornamented with green. He probably did not know that the Chinaman was barefoot, but the facts are just as I have related them. I should be very glad to know just who the offender was, and if he was not an Emmet, make the *amende honorable.*

Very respectfully
B. [Benjamin] C. Duniway

*(August 29, 1873)*

## A Spiritualist Camp-Meeting at Zumwalt's Grove

[W]e last week crowded about three days' work into one, and accepting a kindly invitation from a number of Portland friends, visited the Spiritual camp-meeting about eighteen miles from this city at Zumwalt's grove, near Graham's Landing, where "Mrs. [Belle] Chamberlain, the Spiritualist and seer," was to be the chief attraction, and where we could see her for ourself.[3]

We confess that there is much about the Spiritualists that we like to study. One reason that we like to notice them in the *New Northwest* is because no other paper dares to do so upon editorial responsibility; and our sympathy naturally runs with the proscribed classes from the fact that our position as a political nonentity causes us to hold involuntary rank in the same category. . . .

Awaking with the Friday morning dawn, we rubbed our aching eyes, reached languidly for pencil and paper, and while the household was yet asleep, and ourself but half awake, scribbled the partly finished chapter of "Ellen Dowd" which appears, with a very abrupt termination, on our first page. A hurried toilet and more hurried breakfast, and we were off for the train. Took the Yamhill boat at Canemah, and reached Graham's landing at 10 A. M. A walk of three-quarters of a mile through the ferny woods was next in order, and nobody knew the way.

Several "mediums" had by this time joined the party, and at the suggestion of one of our number, we sat down by the wayside to wait for the spirits to direct us. A few moments waiting and munching hard tack, which a lady's sensible forethought had provided, and we got the "revelation." A young lady "medium" had struck the trail mentally! This would have been a splendid "test," only the sequel proved that the *course* indicated was exactly in the wrong direction!

Finally, when all were tired and one of us really ill, a good angel in the material guise of a barefoot boy, with bright eyes and obliging disposition, came to meet us, and, leading the way, soon brought us to a beautiful grove with seats and stands and camps prepared very much after the style of all modern Druidic worshipping places. . . .

One by one and two by two the curious and faithful came, until at eventide we had a congregation of fifty or sixty souls. Braced by a cup of country coffee, we gathered to listen, for the first time, to the teaching of the lady preacher, whose fame had attracted us thither. We had listened to Henry Ward Beecher's magnetic eloquence, had hung, as if entranced, upon the studied utterances of Elizabeth Cady Stanton, and floated off into ethereal ecstasy over the well-committed lecture of Bishop Peek, but we know what we are saying . . . when we declare that Mrs. Chamberlain excelled them all. It was announced from the platform after the lady had made her appearance that a committee, to be named by the audience, should select her subject. This was done, and then Mrs. C., who, by the way, is a fine-looking woman of the Mrs. Stanton type near fifty years of age, jolly, pretty and dumpy, announced that she was under "control."

The subject was then named, and without a second's waiting for prayer or preparation the feast of reason and flow of soul began. But we should not attempt to report the lecture. We'd fail entirely if we should. Besides, Portland shall have an opportunity to hear for herself. . . .

Accompanied by Mrs. Chamberlain, we repaired to an adjacent farm-house and retired for the night. Such a headache! When Satan afflicted Job with the boils, he might have known he couldn't subdue him. Why didn't he try the headache.

Putting our fevered brain a-soaking in a soiled pocket handkerchief, we lay there pressing our throbbing eye-balls, and Mrs. Chamberlain, at our request, began to "see spirits." But her graphic descriptions awoke no recognition, and we gave it up, assigning ourself to sleep, or rather to a futile attempt to woo the drowsy god, who couldn't come because of the headache.

"I see," said our companion, "an oldish man, with a delicate, round face, white whiskers, bald head, gray side locks, short nose and blue eyes."

"I can't recognize him," was our feverish answer, as we returned the hot, wet handkerchief, in the vain hope to find a cool place on it.

"If I should tell you who he looks like you would laugh," said she.

"Tell me, then, for I want to laugh," we answered, dreamily.

"Well, he looks like Horace Greeley."

"If there is anybody on the other side of Jordan who needs to apologize to me before his soul can rest, it's Uncle Horace," said we, a little interested, in spite of the headache.

The seer threw up her hand with a sudden motion and exclaimed, excitedly: "He says that if he had accepted the Woman Movement when you officially tendered it to him he would have been President and alive and well today."

"Are you acquainted with the circumstances?" we asked, by this time quite curious.

"What circumstances?"

"My Steinway Hall speech in *favor* of Mr. Greeley; my amnesty *resolution*; my official visit to his sanctum, tendering him the aid of the Woman Movement in consideration of his official recognition of the same, and so on?"

"No; I had not heard that you were the vessel chosen to do that work; but

Horace says you're right. He says you served him right, too. And he further promises to aid you from the other side."

Mentally saying that we should have better appreciated more tangible aid when he was compassed by a tangible body, we forgave the great Horace and went to sleep, somewhere about the grey dawn of the morning.

*(September 12, 1873)*

## On Spiritualism

[To] M.J.B., Salem: Your first question, relative to the political situation, you will find answered at length in other articles. Your second, "Why are you not a Spiritualist, since you say you believe in the philosophy?" we will try to answer briefly, here and now. We believe in the science of Astronomy, but we are not an Astronomer. We believe in the science of Botany, but we are not a Botanist. We believe in very many other things in the abstract, to which we cannot devote much attention. The sect of Spiritualists look upon their belief as a religion. We simply regard it as a science, and have no more desire to make a religion of it than of the science of Astronomy or Botany. It is yet crude and imperfectly understood, but so are many other revelations of the great laws of Nature that are yet in their infancy.

*(September 19, 1873)*

## Notes for 1873

1. It was widely believed that the December fire of 1872 was the work of anti-Chinese incendiarists. During the next summer, prior to the devastating fire of August 2, 1873, anonymous notes were sent to persons and firms employing Chinese workers, some containing open threats of arson; however, no protective action was taken. See Charles A. Tracy, III, "Police Function in Portland, 1851-74," *Oregon Historical Quarterly* 80 (Fall 1979): 307-9.

2. The Emmet Guard, Company B of the 2nd Brigade of the Oregon Militia, was composed entirely by men of Irish descent. Judge Matthew Deady commented on similar cruelty by the Emmet Guard in the earlier fire of December 1872.

3. Belle Chamberlain was described by Duniway in 1875 as one of the "nomadic Spiritualists" from California:

   *Belle Chamberlain next appeared upon the scenes, the noblest Roman of them all. Never have we heard that woman's equal as a speaker, and she was utterly incapable of the narrow, intriguing selfishness that characterized her forerunners. True, nobody liked her apparent intimacy with her agent; but like Beecher, she escaped all proof of criminal conduct, and like him held her sway, despite the evil suspicions of almost everybody. If she was not chaste, she certainly was not sly and selfish.* ("A Growl from Our Friends," *NNW*, 9 July 1875)

# 1874

## The Colored Folks' Festival

As this paper goes to press Thursdays, we had no opportunity to give a notice of the colored folks' festival held in Nonpareil hall on that evening last week. We therefore take this opportunity to congratulate them upon the success of the entertainment, which was in every way highly creditable to them. The colored minister, Rev. Adam Smith, G. P. Riley, Esq., the renowned colored orator, and Revs. Devore, Dillon and [Thomas Lamb] Eliot, Hon. J. F. Caples and Mrs. A. J. Duniway each made a short address.[1] Songs, recitations, dialogues, readings, etc., etc., were continued to a late hour, the Sunday school children taking prominent parts and acquitting themselves well. A repast of cakes and ice cream was served at half-past-nine, which was quite liberally patronized.

*(January 25, 1874)*

## To Pay an Associate Editor

Friends of the *New Northwest*, a word in your ears. We, as journalist, lecturer and general servant of the Woman Suffrage Movement in the great Northwest, have stood at our post until the enterprise has grown too large for us to manage longer without editorial aid. The paper cannot be sustained without keeping some person continually in the lecture field.

The Executive Committee of the State Association . . . have appointed us as lecturing and organizing agent for the State.

We must employ an associate editor that we may have opportunity to do this work well. This editor must be paid. She [Catherine Scott Coburn] is a widow and is dependent wholly upon her salary for a livelihood for herself and children. If you want the *New Northwest* sustained—and without an organ you are powerless—you must exert yourselves to increase its patronage, and sustain the associate editor, who will soften all the asperities which some of you complain of in us, and thereby please you far better than we alone can do. . . .

What say you, friends? Every one of you can get us five new subscribers if you will. Shall we depend on you, or will you drive us to relinquish this work and engage again in our former occupation, which was lucrative and is again ready to be a source of profit instead of loss?

A. J. D.

*(February 20, 1874)*

## Praying Down Saloons

This exciting topic, being just now the theme of the newspapers, it behooves us to have an editorial word upon it [the Women's Temperance Crusade].

To begin, then, we are rejoiced to see something started which will bring the women to the knowledge that they can deviate from long-established customs without bringing down the heavens upon their heads. Thousands and tens of thousands of them will blockade sidewalks, interfere with municipal ordinances, sing and pray in the most public places to be seen of men, and by this means be awakened to a realizing sense of their political duties, when but for an excitement that originated upon the plane of their religious prejudices they could have never been induced to go before the public at all. . . .

And we see in this uprising among the women, the beginning of the end of a political upheaval which will not stop short of their universal demand for a right to prevent by law that which they now assail by religious anarchy.

We have much faith in the potency of singing and prayer. A concentrated effort of the minds of the majority of the people in any community, to accomplish any one object by this means, was never known to fall as long as the pressure lasted. But, as this constant public praying among the women cannot last, the effect will cease as soon as the cause is with-drawn, unless the law-making power is given into their hands, with which to clinch the pivot of conviction which the arrows of their prayers are sending home.

Again: Hundreds of prejudice-beblinded-editors who would condemn a raid upon the ballot-box and law-making power as unfeminine, are attacked on their vulnerable side by the "cant" of singing and praying, which they dare not attack for bread and butter's sake, and they will laud these women continually, thereby encouraging them to demand, as the outgrowth of their present action, equal rights before the law. The recognition of woman's right to a voice in making the laws, whose effects she cannot avoid, is becoming every day more and more imperative.

We are anxious to see the ladies' crusade begin in Portland.

*(March 6, 1874)*

## Tell Us All About a Sea Voyage

Just before leaving Portland for our present sojourn in San Francisco, a Salem [Oregon] friend forwarded us the following note:

"Dear Mrs. Duniway—Won't you, for the benefit of thousands of your readers who have never taken an ocean trip, and never expect to take one, be considerate and kind enough to give us all the particulars of your forthcoming journey?. . .

*The steamship* COLUMBIA, *O.R.N., ca. 1885.*

As it is our business to serve our patrons, the exacting and often capricious public, to the best of our humble ability, we shall endeavor to give the desired information. . . .

The "Ajax" is like, and yet unlike, all other ocean steamers on the Northwest coast. It is long, narrow, unwieldy and staunch-looking, cramped in its staterooms, capacious in its decks and dining saloon, villainous in its odors, stifling in the confinement of its atmosphere, narrow in its bunks, hard in its beds and pillows, musty in its sheets and towels, mysterious in its cookery, affable in its servants, jolly in its captain, gentlemanly in its pursar, greasy and busy-idle in its crew, mixed in its passengers, uneasy in its movements, creaky in its timbers, and freezing cold in its cabin.

There is more of the "shoddy" element visible on board of an ocean steamer than anywhere else outside of Government barracks. Here cheap army officials, in imaginary titles, or their wives, daughters and—*relicts*, put on airs of pigmy superiority, which causes everybody who is republican enough to stand upon his or her own merits to look with a quiet and pitying disdain upon mock dignity and would-be aristocracy. . . . There are also to be found on every voyage that we have yet made high-toned, dignified gentlemen of worth, title and culture, who take great pleasure in giving you the benefit of their superior experience in journeying, and in every other proper way alleviating the little annoyances of travel and its accompanying curse, the omnipresent and inevitable sea-sickness.

After purchasing your tickets, taking care to secure state-rooms as nearly as possible in the center of the vessel—which we failed in doing this time, and our perch was, therefore, at an angle of forty five degrees from the mizzenmast, whatever that is— you send your trunks down the hatchway, put your checks in your pocket, and with basket or bundle in hand, proceed to ensconce yourself in your narrow domicil, happy indeed if not more than two of you are to have quarters in a state-room seven by five feet in its dimensions, including bunks, wash-stand, chair, band-boxes, baskets and bundles.

The first day on the river is decidedly pleasant. Everybody, not forgetting the omnipresent Israelite, the most migratory of human beings, is ready for breakfast, lunch and dinner. These meals consist of every imaginable and unimaginable style of cookery, ancient and modern. It is beyond our power to describe the bill of fare further than to say we did it justice. . . .

The scenery grows gradually more beautiful as you near Astoria, and by the time you reach this quaint little old town and find your vessel moored for a few moments along the deck, you are lost in amazement at the broad expanse of land-and-water-scape that rolls on and away, through the dim and misty distance, giving you a painful sense of your own personal littleness. . . .

After leaving Astoria you pass rapidly out toward the breakers. Taking the advice of everybody, you go to deck and stay there, fighting the fate of seasickness in store for you; and if you laugh at everybody else, knowing you are getting pale about the mouth the while, yet strangely tempted to believe that you are feel-

ing "splendid." But it's no use trying. You suddenly grow as limp as a frost-bitten tomato vine, and gladly accept the escort of some strong arm, while with your disengaged hand you clutch nervously at this and that to save you from a dangerous fall. The grandeur of the scenery falls upon you and you reach your state-room, sick enough to die. But you can't die, and everybody knows it, and you get little sympathy. For two days you lie at the mercy of the stewardess, who sometimes sips your broth before she gives it to you, which doesn't whet your appetite, and urges you to get up and go on deck, which you attempt only to fall back limply upon your pillow as you give vent to ejaculations in your retchings which some imaginary mortal has likened to crying out "New York" in tones of despair.

But the sea grows smoother and you grow calmer and your appetite becomes voracious after a while, and you gather courage to go on deck and find that you enjoy the change immensely.

The remainder of the voyage proves intensely interesting. You are never out of sight of the distant coast, and sometimes sail very near it. As you approach your journey's end the landscapes become marked by visions of light-houses, fog-whistles, farm-houses and the cattle upon a thousand hills. . . . [A]nd after a while the Golden Gate, guarded by Nature's fortresses, opens to your vision, and soon the Golden City looms before you with Oakland in the distance, and the busy crafts around all buffeting the winds and waves as though sporting with the elements in glee.

An hour later and your vessel lies panting at the dock, and after encountering the usual rush of hotel runners, drays, omnibuses and what not, you enter a coach and drive to your hotel, where your first thought is of home and friends and what your loved ones are doing.

A. J. D.

*(March 27, 1874)*

## Over the Sierras to the Nevada Gold Mines

Leaving Stockton [California] on Monday the 12th inst., after having closed our lectures with a very large audience on Sunday evening . . . , we took the overland train at noonday, by the way of Colfax, for Nevada City, where we had an appointment for the evening. Our road lay through the lonely valley of the Sacramento, whose exquisite verdure of spring-time green was gorgeously variegated with every imaginable shade of floral beauty. . . .

Arriving at Colfax, a little railway station, perched among the foothills of the bold Sierras, we learned to our disappointment that the staging to Nevada city would occupy us till far into the night, and prevent the possibility of our meeting our engagement for the evening. To make the best of circumstances was the only alternative, and we lugged our basket to the nearest hotel and took lodging for the night, speculating upon the uncertainties of mundane calculations in general and ours in particular.

Nine o'clock on Tuesday found us aboard the stage, with the usual crowd of passengers and baggage. We never saw a stage that wasn't capable of holding one or two additional passengers after it was already full. When about twenty feet from the hotel door, the horses plunged into a mud-hole, going down until, but for many similar observations, we should have expected to lose sight of their ears.

But the horses came up and down went the coach, throwing the travelers into a heap upon the forward wheels and righting them again with the next lurch, only the matter was so badly overdone that the cerebellum of the undersigned received the next contusion, thereby through sympathy, restoring a painful equilibrium between the organs of intellect and antagonism. . . .

[W]hen you get your spinal column snugly telescoped, you become in a measure stage-hardened, and you learn to endure everything but the patient suffering of many pairs of rat-tailed, ewe-necked, ring-boned, knock-kneed horses, for whom we humbly hope there is a future life, where cruelty will be unknown forevermore. The lady passengers walked up some of the worst pulls and down some of the deepest gorges through pity for the patient animals and a laudable ambition to preserve their own bones unbroken. . . .

While in Nevada we indulged in a visit to the hydraulic mining works. Steady streams of water with over two hundred feet fall, are brought through large pipes, with six-inch nozzles, to bear upon the solid mountain sides with a force that disembowels the complaining earth, and sends it crashing to the plain below. Occasionally, blasting is resorted to, thereby aiding to loosen the solid mountain wall from its foundation, upon which the ceaseless waters play with such stupendous power as no army with strongest fortifications could long withstand.

The flumes that gather up the debris of the elements extend for many miles through the gulches, and woe to the robber, who, when the waters are turned from their course to allow for the full "cleaning up" of the sluices, shall essay to "prospect" here for "tailings." His life would quickly pay the forfeit of his ill-advised cupidity. These mines yield an immense annual revenue, but are owned by wealthy companies and the laboring man's wages are but two and three dollars a day.

The Temperance meetings in Nevada and Grass Valley were quite largely attended. . . . This evening we are to lecture upon "What will we do with our boys?" in the Methodist church in Grass Valley, and to-morrow night, the twentieth lecture since coming to the State, the subject will be, through request of many of his old friends, "The Life and Times of Col. Baker."

Everywhere we are greeted by the press and pulpit with the utmost courtesy, though in many places we are compelled to fight our way through many obstacles engendered by the "shrieking sisterhood," whose rabid "Woman's Rights" doctrines have thrown the Woman Movement into disrepute. These man-hating fanatics, who in dowdy dress and disheveled hair avail themselves of every opportunity to force themselves before the public to denounce "the tyrant man," are our pet aversion. They have hitherto kept many noble, womanly women from coming to the front in California, but through the Temperance reform another class are now being led into the ranks, and soon a universal shout for suffrage will go up from the people which no interests of office-holders or lawmakers shall be able to withstand. . . .

A. J. D.

*(April 24, 1874)*

# Trial of the Temperance Crusaders

On the afternoon of the 16th inst., between fifteen and twenty ladies assembled at the corner of Morrison and First streets [in Portland], and taking up their position on the outer edge of the sidewalk, began to sing and pray. Only one prayed at a time, and in an ordinary voice. Very few of them can sing, therefore the "noise" of their singing could not be very "loud." As soon as these ladies appeared, Mr. [Walter] Moffett, by blowing a police whistle, and by other means, began making a loud and discordant noise, which very soon brought a large crowd to the side-walk in front of his [Webfoot] saloon. This crowd increased until the street was pretty effectually blockaded. The ladies soon ceased to sing or to pray audibly, because the noise made by the gong-beaters, organ-grinders, bell-ringers, and tin-can and drum-beaters was so overwhelming as to drown every other sound. These were the paid servants of Mr. Moffett. Mr. Moffett's bar-tender, inflamed with drink, and totally regardless of decency, used insulting language and committed insulting and violent acts in the presence of the ladies. All these facts were brought out by the questions and cross-questions of the counsel who conducted the case on either side.

The ladies, surrounded by an excited crowd, remained hour after hour, silently or inaudibly praying, in the hope of quiet being restored, and perhaps also because it was not easy for them to extricate themselves from the crowd. Some of the men congregated there were of a rough and disorderly class, but many also were of a peaceable and right-minded class. Naturally, these latter, and some of the former as well, were indignant at the insults offered the ladies, and, as Mr. Moffett expected, soon got into a quarrel amongst themselves. Two men, according to the evidence, were knocked down, one man stabbed, chairs thrown about, etc. Mr. Moffett himself brandished a pistol. These were the facts elicited at the trial.

But by some unaccountable reasoning the jury agreed in their verdict of guilty, as charged in the complaint, of the City of Portland against Mrs. Shindler, Mrs. Swafford, Mrs. Fletcher, Mrs. H. Stitzel and Mrs. Sparrow for "making a loud noise," and engaging in "violent and disorderly conduct.". . .

After three days' trial, and the above-mentioned verdict, the ladies, attended by many friends, appeared for sentence on Wednesday morning at eleven o'clock, and were fined five dollars each and costs, or, in default of fine, one day's imprisonment in the city jail. The ladies with one accord agreed to spend twenty-four hours in jail rather than submit to be fined and they are there while we write this report. . . .

*(April 24, 1874)*

## Turning Out the Crusaders from Jail

About half-past eight o'clock Wednesday evening, as the lady prisoners were preparing to spend the night with what comfort they could in apartments so unusual, a Captain of Police suddenly appeared upon the scene and turned them all out of doors. They insisted that they wished to comply with the law, and to suffer for their "disorderly conduct" to the full extent of their sentence, which, being the sentence of the Court, was of course just and right. But Captain _____would not permit it. He politely invited them to "get out of this," and contended that he was "boss" in that institution. "Tis ever thus," etc. If the ladies do what they think right, some man (say Moffett) gets them sent to jail. If they then meekly submit, and just as leave be punished as not, to please these captious gentlemen, a policeman turns them out upon the street, amongst a crowd of waiting men. These gentlemen are very hard to please, seems to us?

Well, the ladies, finding they were homeless for that night if they did not go home, asked a young gentleman, a stranger whom they found near, to escort them to the church, where a meeting was being held, and where they knew their friends could be found. Their appearance at the church was the signal for a round of cheers and burst of enthusiasm as never was heard since the war times of '63-4. It was in vain that Mr. [George W.] Izer requested silence and decorum inside the sacred edifice. There are times and occasions when the voice of the people is the voice of God and will be heard; and it was heard on that night. Several of the ladies made addresses, which were very interesting. So the good cause goes marching on. But we don't see how that Police Captain could be so unmindful of justice as to turn those poor prisoners out into the street! "*O Tempora! O Mores.*"

*(April 24, 1874)*

## Mr. Walter Moffett of the Webfoot Saloon

We hope Mr. Moffett is satisfied with the result of his arduous labors in defending his right to do wrong. What with twenty-five cents to one boy for gong-beating, fifty cents to another, a dollar and a half to an organ-grinder, and two hundred and fifty dollars to a strong-minded lawyer for prosecuting five praying women, not to say anything of the valuable time wasted in following the ladies about from place to place, we judge he must by this time be convinced that he is paying dear for his (policeman's) whistle.

The other day the ladies started in the direction of the "Tom Thumb Saloon," followed as usual by Moffett, but as they did not stop there he finally went about his business.[2] Not long after, returning that way, the ladies commenced religious exercises before the "Tom Thumb," and [J. F.] Good, Moffett's creature, ordered them away. One elderly lady, fatigued with much standing, took a seat upon the door stone of the adjoining house, occupied by a Chinaman. Good also ordered her away from here; but refusing to go, she asked permission of the heathen Chinaman to occupy his door-step, to which he politely assented, inviting the ladies to come in, and on their declining brought chairs for them.

Even Chinamen rebuke the coarse and indecent behavior of these two men. Neither policemen nor rabble any longer gather at the sound of that historical whistle, and the hater of prayer, of good morals and gentlemanly conduct, is wounded in the house of his friends, "with none so poor to do him reverence," not even for the drinks.

*(May 8, 1874)*

# Crusaders, What Think You?

Haven't you discovered at last, to your sorrow, that the boy preachers who, in their silly zeal, have commanded you to be content to work as outlaws, instead of demanding your rights, as citizens, to a voice in the legislation which controls the liquor traffic; haven't you at last learned that we were preaching the true temperance gospel, when we were urging you to put on the whole armor of God, that you might be prepared to fight the demon with his own weapons as well as yours?[3]

What think you now of the ten thousand iterations that have been poured in your ears by a few zealots, who, without judgment and common sense, have urged you on to do a work by prayer alone, which can only be accomplished through mortal agencies, after having been properly inspired by prayer? What think you now of the mockery that is made of prayer by the majority of men, who, having the ballot, can laugh your holiest prayers to God to scorn while bandying the braggadocio of your boy preachers on the street as a proof that Christianity cannot and will not do what they have claimed for it, and, therefore, religion is a flaunting lie?

God ever proves himself upon the side of the ballot. And if whisky has the *ballot* and you have it not, your prayers are but a wretched mockery when weighed in the scale against it, and it is time that all preachers who declare to the contrary shall receive the rebuke their declarations merit, that God may not be dishonoured by religious fanaticism, or Christianity be placed in a false light before people of common sense who are out of the fold, because of the vehement clamor of boys who have planned a work for you and God, which everybody can see doesn't meet with the Divine sanction, or it would be successful.

We have all along rejoiced in your work, not because we believed that the saloons of Portland would tremble under it—we knew better all the time, in spite of the declaration of the ministers—but we rejoiced, because we saw that your failure to make a permanent success of the temperance reform through the necessarily spasmodic efforts you were making, would open your eyes to the *power of the ballot.*

Fred Douglass prayed fervently for a dozen years that God would strike the shackles of slavery from the necks of himself and brethren, but the first prayer that God answered was the one he made with heart and heels when he became zealous enough to use the means that God had given him to travel toward the North Star.

So, you are praying earnestly that God will remove the yoke of wickedness from the necks of the intemperate; but the first prayer that will be effectually answered will be made with *ballots in your hands* to keep company with the prayers in your hearts.

*(July 17, 1874)*

## To Lafayette on Horseback

Leaving home in the afternoon of July 16, after having had a short family reunion, which sufficed to make leaving the genial society of home for another brief season a double irksome endeavor, we found ourself at night a welcome and well pleased inmate of the cozy farmhouse of Mr. and Mrs. [Amos] Cook, near Lafayette [Oregon]. . . .[4]

[B]ehold a wagonload of us on the morrow, bound McMinnvilleward, to attend the Woman Suffrage meeting. Mr. [William Jennings] Martin, husband of the President of the Woman Suffrage club, generously tendered his time and team for the occasion, and we filled the wagon so full of Suffragists and their children, that a certain editor took a back seat on the hay, just over the wagon wheels, where "bump-ity-bump" she jolted along, swallowing dust in unknown quantities, and becoming so completely inhumed in the same, as to appear metamorphosed into a mummy from some ancient excavation. . . .

On Saturday evening a good audience greeted us to listen to an address upon temperance. We gathered as usual, a goodly number of new subscribers, and on Sunday afternoon took the stage for Lafayette, where we had an appointment for the evening.

Reaching St. Joe, we found the proprietor of the Lafayette stage line in a fever of disappointment. He had loaned his hack to some camp-meeting frolickers who had failed to come back as they had promised, and he was compelled to carry the mail on horseback. This left us no alternative but to go to our appointment on horseback also.

We hadn't ridden a horse for many a year; our "toggery" was anything but equestrian in style, and the basket, satchel, fan and parasol necessary to our comfort in traveling, made a formidable appearing load for a horse to carry in addition to our own *avoirdupois*. But "mine host" of the hotel at St. Joe kindly risked a favorite equine, which we mounted and went our way—slowly.

When we reached Lafayette, the principal street was thronged with the beauty and chivalry of the place on their way to the lecture, and as we whipped poor, patient Rosinante with the parasol handle, and held on to the cumbrous basket, to keep it steady as we jogged along, we'll venture to assert that Don Quixote couldn't have outdone us in grotesque appearance had he tried.

Tying Rosinante near the residence of a friend, we hurriedly changed our dusty traveling clothes for a fresh suit of platform apparel, and in a few minutes met a large and eagerly expectant throng of auditors in the quaint old Court House.

Amity, July 27, 1874.

A. J. D.

*(July 31, 1874)*

## Oregon House Rejects the Woman Suffrage Bill

We snatch a moment from multitudinous other duties to drop you a line in regard to the last night's debate upon the Suffrage bill.

The House resolved itself into a Committee of the Whole, and met in special session at 7 o'clock. The Bill was introduced by Mr. [Cyrus Adams] Reed of Marion [County], who proclaimed himself proud of the high honor of being permitted to enroll his name among those who favor Human Freedom.[5]

A species of parliamentary filibustering followed, which would be a lasting disgrace to any people. . . .

Mr. Reed was reminded of the story related of Mr. Lincoln, who, when interrogated as to what he'd think if a negro should vote for a certain measure, and a white man should vote against it, replied, "I'd think the negro had a deuced sight the most sense." Everyone saw the point. . . .

Several gentlemen were "constitutionally" obstinate. Johnson of Multnomah got babies and potatoes badly mixed with ballots.

A gentleman from Wasco made a splendid speech.

Another, a Democrat, from somewhere else, is still choked with Mr. Greeley's boots, and mad because the women were too smart to try to swallow them too.

Mr. Johnson's *dignity* was insulted when ladies were invited to speak. He felt smart enough to run the whole concern with the aid of Bradshaw. The House thought differently and Mrs. [Addie L.] Ballou and your humble servant made speeches.[6]

Mr. Reed made one of the finest addresses to which we ever listened.

The House was packed for three and a half hours. The porches, galleries and windows being full also.

The bill was rejected in its present form, but is coming up again.

One or two more such meetings and no man will stake his reputation upon an adverse vote. We already have the *brains* of both Houses.

Salem, Oregon, October 7, 1874.

A. J. D.

*(October 9, 1874)*

## Umatilla, Wallula, and Walla Walla

When last we wrote you we were traveling up the Columbia on board the O. S. N. Company's Steamer "Tenino" where, as a guest of the Company, we were sumptuously entertained . . . aboard the well-ordered craft, bound for Umatilla

[Oregon], Wallula and Walla Walla [W. T.]. . . .

Half-past 8 A. M. found us at "gale-torn Wallula," which has, during the past three years increased in proportion as Umatilla has diminished. . . . Halted for a little while, and then enjoyed the hospitality of the Northwestern Stage Company, who favored us with a ride to Walla Walla. . . .

Would like to tell you something about the staging from Wallula, but we remember the story of the man with the wagon-bed full of shelled corn and forbear. This man, as our readers know, was a very profane individual, and was quite "gifted" in that line when provoked. He was driving up a steep hill with a load of corn one day, when, unbeknown to himself, although seen by others, the gate fell out of the back end of the wagon, allowing all the corn to be spilled on the hillside. Everybody expected an unusual volley of profanity, but to their surprise the farmer surveyed the scene and made no comment.

"Why don't you swear?" queried one with a merry twinkle in his eye.

"I couldn't do the subject justice," was the quiet answer. Our readers can see the point.

Whitman Station is the half-way house and present terminus of the Walla Walla and Wallula railroad.

"How often do you make through trips?" queried a traveler, who sought information from one of the railroad bosses.

"Tri-weekly," was the reply. Then, by way of explanation, he added, "we make a trip one week and then try to get back the next."

Walla Walla, Nov. 12, 1874.

A. J. D.

*(November 20, 1874)*

## Traveling With Master Ralph

Our last hailed from Lafayette, and you will remember that we promised to go from thence to Dayton. Well, we went. Mr. Dale, the gentlemanly and obliging Sheriff of Yamhill, was going over to Dayton to serve a summons on somebody, and, as it is an ill wind that blows nobody any good, we and Master Ralph [age 5], (our "neglected" baby," who sometimes accompanies us on short journeys to "take care of mamma,") were accommodated by the Sheriff with a free ride to Riley's hotel. . . .

The day had been unusually pleasant and balmy, but the evening was ominous of rain. . . . The morning brought a fearful rain; none of your Oregon mists, but a regular drenching outpour from the overcharged heavens.

Steamer started before daylight. Master Ralph grasped the hand of a gentleman and started ahead with the admonition, "Look out for the mud, mamma," which we did—to no purpose. There is a long incline of steps leading from the warehouse to the

*The A.A. MCCULLY at Dayton, Oregon, on the Yamhill River*

river; steps that were made when Oregon was young, and they were horribly slippery, dark and muddy. Had a satchel in one hand and a bundle in the other, of course, (being a woman), and our shoes and skirts attracted so much of the classic soil of Yamhill, that they were literally ruined. Don't know but we had better let them to some enterprising woman-gardener for a potato patch.

Somebody took Ralph by the hand and led him forward to the boat, causing us to lose sight of him in the darkness. We feared that he'd fallen overboard, and for a long time were almost frantic. Then, after looking everywhere else, and calling ourself hoarse in a vain attempt to make him hear, we rushed into the cabin and found the Young American calmly superintending the porter, who was building a fire. If we hadn't been a Christian we might have spanked our embryo "protector." As it was, we admonished him very gently, and received for answer, "Why, mamma, don't you suppose I'm able to take care of myself? I could travel alone to Boston if you'd only give me enough cash."

We sighed for that child's prospects. He's bound to go to Congress or to be Governor or do some other damaging deed yet, if his precocity isn't nipped in the bud.

About noon our steamer, the "Dayton," drifted into the basin at Oregon City. While we were seated upon a bale of brown paper in the warehouse, impatiently awaiting the swinging round of the "Welcome," so we might get aboard, a gentleman who knew us well, came along and said: "Mrs. Duniway, I should think you wouldn't find much pleasure in leading the life of an itinerant missionary. Wouldn't you be a great deal better off at home?"

We looked ruefully at our mud-be-spattered shoes and skirts, answered in this wise: "A man was once aboard an ocean steamer, and when the vessel began to roll fearfully, he grew very pale. He was leaning over the side of the vessel, yelling *Oh, my!* in choking accents when the Captain came along and said, "Halloa there! sick?" The man gasped out spasmodically, "You don't think I'm enduring all this for *fun*, do you?"

Our friend saw the point and promised to subscribe for the *New Northwest* for his wife who had long wanted it, but couldn't get the money.

A. J. D.

*(December 11, 1874)*

# Notes for 1874

1. In 1874, the Rev. Adam B. Smith was minister of Portland's African Methodist Episcopal Church, and George P. Riley continued to hold his reputation as an outstanding speaker.
2. Walter Moffett, a former city councilman and reputed to be a good citizen, owned both the Webfoot and Tom Thumb saloons. Prior to becoming a saloonkeeper, Moffet had been involved in the shipping business. After the Temperance Crusade was over, he sold his saloons, returned to the shipping business, and set off for the South Seas, but died along the way. For an entertaining version of Moffet's story, see Malcolm H. Clark, Jr., "The War on the Webfoot Saloon," *Oregon Historical Quarterly* 58 (March 1957): 48-62.
3. The "boy preachers" who organized the Temperance Crusade in Portland were the Rev. George W. Izer (1839-1917) of the Methodist Church and the Rev. Mr. Medbury of the Baptist Church. They had come from the East to join their newly organized Portland congregations and established headquarters for the Woman's Temperance Crusade in the basement of the Methodist Church. Izer, in particular, drew Duniway's wrath when he organized "a little choir of hostile women" to sing her down whenever she arose to speak at his temperance meetings. He even attempted to ban her from speaking again in his church, but Duniway managed to slip in a speech after standing and calling out: "Let us pray." See ASD, *Path Breaking: An Autobiographical History of the Equal Suffrage Movement in Pacific Coast States*

(Portland: James, Kerns & Abbott Co., 1914), 69-72.

4. Mary Frances Scott Cook (1833-1930), one of Duniway's sisters, resided with her husband Amos Cook near Lafayette.

5. Cyrus Adams Reed (1825-1910), born in New Hampshire, was one of the builders and directors of the Willamette Woolen Mills at Salem. In 1862, Reed was appointed Oregon's first state adjutant general and elected to the state legislature, where he served four terms.

6. Addie L. Ballou was a poet, suffragist, lecturer, socialist, Spiritualist, and trance medium. She supported Victoria Woodhull's candidacy for president of the United States and Woodhull's presidency of the American Association of Spiritualists. In the summer of 1874, after attending a Spiritualist camp-meeting where Mrs. Ballou was the featured speaker and gave two lectures, Duniway reported that "no pen can do the speaker justice." "[W]hile we do not endorse all, or half her doctrines," she wrote, "we've never yet heard two men who could equal her in arguments or eloquence" ("A Trip to the Country," *NNW*, 3 July 1874). Duniway published reports of Ballou's 1874 tour of Oregon, Washington Territory and British Columbia, and the two women spoke before the Oregon legislature on the woman suffrage bill (*NNW*, 9 Oct. 1874).

But Duniway's position on Ballou shifted when it appeared that Calvin B. McDonald, editor of the Salem *Statesman* and unfriendly to Duniway and her cause, was smitten by Ballou, who apparently relished his praise. In the "Yours Truly" column of *The NNW*, supposedly written by a young girl but possibly by Duniway herself, the following appeared: "She [Ballou] may be a good Woman Suffragist, but the Woman Suffragists of Oregon can't afford to countenance her in that kind of company [McDonald]. The Suffragists which we can afford to sustain are those who stand by the women and the

women's paper as Susan B. Anthony does" ("'Yours Truly' Gets a Letter," *NNW*, 30 Oct. 1874).

By the next year, Duniway had had her fill of California's "nomadic Spiritualists," including Ballou. "The Spiritualists of California are a discordant class of people," Duniway wrote, "as narrow as predestinarians and as sectarian as hard-shell Baptists. Of course, there are grand and noble exceptions; but *they* take the *New Northwest* and pay for it." Ballou was on Duniway's black list:

*Then came Addie L. Ballou, a pretty-faced, ready-tongued little lecturer, whom we foolishly thought we might be able to patronize and encourage without any fear of suspicions or intrigues upon her part. But the jealous, sly little body did her puny prettiest to undermine us, putting on a sanctimonious air of injured exaltation when our friends took umbrage at her sly maneuvering, and setting a few of her gentlemen admirers into heroics because they considered we were jealous (?) of the fulminations with which she was being crushed by a certain badly smitten editor [McDonald]. The little woman went her way at last, abusing Oregon in general and us in particular, her exit followed by a volley of blank cartridges, levied at our devoted head, which hurt nobody.* ("A Growl from Our Friends," *NNW*, 9 July 1875)

Judge Matthew P. Deady was not complimentary about Ballou and mentioned her in his diary entry for August, 3, 1878: "During the week my full sized picture by Pebbles was placed on exhibition at Morses. . . . Mrs A L Ballou—a she Bohemian—had a gushing article [about the picture] in the *Oregonian*" (*Pharisee Among Philistines*, 263). Clark adds: "Mrs. A. L. Ballou was a traveling journalist with artistic pretensions" (273).

# 1875

## Life on the Frontier

To the Editor of the *New Northwest*:

I feel a strong desire to address you again, and having nothing of vital importance to write about, I am inclined to tell you of the events of my past week's "house-keeping.". . .

Well, to begin at the beginning, I said to my husband the first of last week, in view of the nearness of the approaching winter, that if he would assist me a little I would take down the house lining, for we don't have hard finished houses out here, our walls are merely covered with canvas, and wash it clean, put it up again, move the family bed by the fire and have things nice and cozy in case of a snowstorm. He assented, and down came our pictures, etc., and in a very short time everything was piled in a heap on a table in the middle of the room, and our log cabin walls showed what they were made of. By the time dinner was over it was too late to wash the lining that day. The next day the boiler was on early, when husband informed me that he would like to have my assistance about killing those "porkers." I made all haste to get my washing out, and then—well, Mrs. D., did you ever help to kill hogs? If not, you have no idea how I spent the day.

I think that in sparsely settled countries where help is scarce, women are more truly co-laborers with men, than anywhere else. And here I think they almost always find that they can accomplish almost anything that they undertake. . . .

With sincerest wishes for your welfare and that of the cause we hold in common, dear Mrs. D. and readers of the *New Northwest*, I make my bow.

Wasco county [Oregon], December 16, 1874.    E. E. S.
[Ellen E. Sommerville]

*(January 8, 1875)*

## Mrs. Duniway's Corroborative Experience

Our Eastern Oregon correspondent, who so truthfully portrays "life on the frontier," is assured that we thoroughly understand and have many a time practically experienced what "hog killing days" mean to a Western farmer's wife. In fact, we can repeat one exploit in that line that throws hers into the shade.

One time our liege had a large pen full of rapidly-fattening porkers, and many of them were very ferocious, having been captured wild in the autumn by well-trained dogs. One day a merchant having ordered one of the fattest for a waiting customer, Mr. D. being for a wonder without hired men, undertook the job with the assistance of his protected and supported spouse. He first shot and killed the hog in the pen, causing all the others to become very furious, as was natural. Then he placed a heavy slab across the top of the pen and directed us to stand upon the slab and help him pull the carcass on it. To say we "hankered" after the job would require a stretch of imagination of which we prefer not to be guilty; but we climbed upon the pen, stood upon the slab, and waited the next move. Mr. D., by some sort of maneuver, managed to elude the vicious monsters while he stooped down and caught the defunct porker by one hind foot. As soon as he raised the animal enough to allow us to reach the other foot, we did so, and both gave a tremendous pull. Mr. D.'s hands were wet, and the foot he was pulling slipped through them suddenly, leaving the whole weight upon our clenched fingers. In much less time than it takes to tell it, we, too, had "let go," and with such a vengeance that we were pitched backwards into the oozy, abominable mud, eight or ten feet away, the back of our cranium having stopped so suddenly when we fell, that apertures were seemingly made in it to admit the light of stars. If we had thought to look backwards, we might possibly have gazed through into China,

but we waived geological and geographical exploration just then, and began to beat the air for breath, a necessary auxiliary to corporeal existence that will not be ignored with impunity.

Our liege wasn't in as big a hurry about the hog for awhile as he thought. . . . Our mud-soaked clothes were ruined, and we were somehow led to the conclusion that a woman's right to butcher hogs was one which we would ever after willingly delegate to the men, and insist upon their sole possession.

*(January 8, 1875)*

## School for Chinese in Portland

The Chinese Mission School, inaugurated in this city by the Baptist Church last November, promises to be a success. It is open every evening of the week, except Thursday evening, and its average attendance is about thirty. The teachers represent their pupils as pleasant, tractable and industrious, and very quick to learn. Several young men and ladies have acted as teachers since the opening of the school until the present time without pay.

*(April 23, 1875)*

## Spelling Mania at Lafayette, Oregon

Forest Grove is just *lovely* in its garb of spring-time green. To get rich enough to retire to such a spot and have a quiet home, where we might cultivate lambs and chickens and babies and "garden ease," is our highest personal ambition. To owe nobody and *dun* nobody, to pay as we go and help others to do likewise, is our pet hobby. But we see no chance for such a prospect till our mission shall be ended and the women of the country are free.

Wednesday's train took us to St. Joe, through a glorious Eden of rolling landscapes and well-tilled fields. . . . One and a half miles of staging and we reached Lafayette, where we had an engagement to lecture upon the "Advantages of the Ballot."

The spelling mania had seized the people, and they were pretty generally busy in preparing for a great contest that was advertised to come off on Thursday, between the Grangers on one side, and the merchants, lawyers, and doctors upon the other.[1] Our lecture was therefore more sparsely attended than usual, though the audience was larger than expected.

But the fun came on Thursday evening. The Court house was crowded with spectators. Ten lawyers, doctors, and merchants, including three ladies, were soon in their places. Upon trial the Grangers only mustered six, three being ladies—one of them a schoolma'am. The Grangers looked upon the array of orthographical talent before them and got frightened. "They hadn't agreed to spell against ladies."

"Then take the ladies out of your ranks," said the spokesman of the three professions.

Arguments, witty and logical upon the "professional" side, and bombastic and dogmatic upon the other, were carried on to a late hour, and resulted in the Grangers of Yamhill backing square down from their own banter, because three of the opposite side were women.

We informed them that we'd often bragged about the Grange because of its recognition of the equal rights of women, and we were *surprised* to see them take their present stand.

The press and the people stood by the professions, women and all, and the battle was won without the firing of a single orthropic columbiad. We have never seen a greater victory for the woman question, which, like Banquo's ghost, will down at the bidding of nobody.

Portland, May 26, 1875.

A. J. D.

*(May 28, 1875)*

## Our Rebellious Cranium

On Wednesday evening of last week, after having lingered in the society of dear ones at home, until compelled to run thoroughly exhausted to reach the ferryboat "on time," we went aboard the south-bound train, on our way to meet a lecture engagement in the Capital city [Salem].

We're disgusted with any mortal who knows better, and will yet suffer himself to get the sick-headache through over-work. We had it. And *such* a headache! None of your quiet, dozing, grumbling affairs, which you might bathe in *eau de cologne* and drowsiness, but a regular bumping, thumping, nauseating, nerve-weakening, soul-sickening sensation, of the kind that sticketh closer than a bur or a brother.

The principal incidents of that journey we shall never remember. Beg your pardon, readers. Let us take that back. The principal incident of that journey was the abominable headache, and we shall never forget it. . . .

Obtained a half hour's rest, including washing, dressing, and combing, for the lecture—if you call such exercise *resting*—and then repaired to the Opera House, where a goodly array of smiling faces greeted us. After an hour and a half we dismissed the multitude, and as we write, we recall a confused commingling of congratulations, invitations to this, that and the other home, pre-scriptions for the headache, etc., etc., to all of which we listened as in a dream, and, then, with thanks, hand-shakings, and promises to see the friends to-morrow, repaired to our room at the hotel, tied up our rebellious cranium in a wet towel, and went to sleep to dream that our brain was being tunneled through for the accommodation of the iron horse, who was plowing his way to Winnemucca. Oh! We're disgusted with sick-headaches, and anybody who will harbor them.

Salem, May 31, 1875.

A. J. D.

*(June 4, 1875)*

## Our Twenty-Two Married Years

After reaching Astoria last Saturday and failing to meet our disappointed liege, as we had confidently expected, we concluded to somewhat change the programme; so on the following Monday we went aboard the "Dixie Thompson" and spent the day in going home, for the anniversary of twenty-two married years had come, and we must needs keep the wedding day. What a joyful evening! . . .

How memory darts back over the dreamy distance that spans the intervening years! And now a vision comes of a hopeful bridegroom and a pale young bride; a household in tears; congratulations, blessings, partings. And there the affectionate

*Benjamin C. Duniway, 1876*

band of brothers and sisters were left with one vacant chair . . . for we were the first to leave the paternal home. . . .

Gray hairs have slightly silvered the head of one of us, and deep furrows long ago traced themselves in the brow of the other; but twenty-two years of toil and pleasure; of trial, disappointment and success; of mistakes, experiences, and hopes, have builded themselves a witness in a large family without one vacant chair, without one missing link. Twenty-two years! . . . What will the next twenty-two years of life's history unfold? . . .

But a truce to all this. What care the strangers, whose eyes may light upon these pages, for the fancies that

are flitting through a dreaming brain?

Astoria, August 9, 1875.

A. J. D.

*(August 13, 1875)*

## Knappton's Slaughtering Saw

When last we jotted of our journeyings, we were on the eve of visiting Knappton [Washington Territory], the well known lumbering point opposite Astoria. . . .[2]

The amount of lumber here manufactured is almost beyond belief. Looking up and down the river at almost any time, you notice a raft of logs in care of a tug that comes snorting toward the wharf like a porpoise in charge of a whale.

Wait an hour and you will see a section of a mighty forest tree, which has occupied ages in growing, gripped tightly between the ravenous fangs of a monster log chain, and obeying the mandate of the motive power in the regions under the mill, drag it torn and bleeding to the slaughtering saw, which goes ripping remorselessly through it, while it screams incessantly as if in pain.

Another hour and the mammoth log, eight feet in diameter, lies at your feet a dissected skeleton, ready to be made into floors which the thoughtless will tread upon without a sigh of regret for the assassinated tree, whose like, it is said by observing lumbermen, will never be produced again upon this earth. Only scrubby, gnarly, knotty, and insignificant pines ever grow again in lieu of the grand, gigantic old ones, which forest fires and mammoth saw mills are destroying year by year in myriads.

Knappton, August 20, 1875.

A. J. D.

*(September 3, 1875)*

## Consequences of a Premature Marriage

Again, after a brief sojourn within the happy shades of our Portland home we find ourself upon the wing. . . .

Salem is leisurely jogging along in her old fashion, getting ready for her annual harvest at the State Fair. . . . A sad case of scandal mars the morals of the place just now, bringing only another evidence that women are never protected, against themselves, by men.

In the case alluded to there is a lesson taught which all men would do well to heed. Nearly twenty years ago a man of forty abducted and married a child of fourteen. Taking her by stealth from the fond embrace of her anguish-rent parents, he tried to atone as best he might for the great wrong through many years of devotion to the childwife and their growing family. But the laws of nature were outraged by the premature marriage of the child, and retribution came.

The perverted child grew to perverted womanhood and—it is the old, old story—became unfaithful. Now she is an outcast from society, her family is broken up, her children are motherless, and she, poor creature, more deserving of pity than censure, is adrift upon the breakers, going—only God knows where.

The [Salem] *Statesman* of this (Saturday) morning contains one of the most sorrowful chapters of life-tragedy (a letter from her pen), that we have ever known. The stricken husband, with motives only meant to be good, publishes the letter and the woman's name, thus revealing a confession of her shame to the world that will follow her everywhere, while around him are the men, equally guilty, who bid open, unblushing defiance to social laws, to whom may be traced her downfall.

We here insert the letter, omitting names, as we wish the dishonored husband had done. We publish it because of the sad, warning lesson it gives and the eloquent appeal it unconsciously makes to woman's forbearance and sympathy.

St. Charles Hotel, Portland, Sept. 9

"DEAR ___ AND MY DEAR CHILDREN: Oh! how bad I do feel, now that the time comes for me to go away; but I will go and be a good woman, and I pray that we may all meet and be happy yet. I will do everything I can to bring it around.

Take good care of the children—they are never out of my mind. . . . I know I have done wrong; I beg your forgiveness. Oh! N__, do be a good girl, and do not follow in your mother's footsteps, for she has done wrong. Let the men alone, for there is no dependence to be put in any of them. I would rather see you all nuns than do as I have done. It will blast my life, and I pray God that it will be a short one. And to think of the trouble I have caused my dear husband—may I be forgiven in the next world, if not in this. . . . If Anna does not receive me this may be the last time you will hear from me. . . . I send back all a kiss and tears from your bad mother and untrue wife."

Verily, "let him who is without sin cast the first stone at her."
Jefferson, September 15.
A. J. D.

*(September 17, 1875)*

## The Husband's Reply

To the Editor of the *New Northwest*:

Permit one, who shall be nameless, (as you have an aversion to publishing names in such cases), to make a few remarks in regard to the early marriage case alluded to by you in your letter of last week [Editorial Correspondence, *NNW*, 17 Sept. 1875] from this place. Perhaps I owe an apology to the good people of Portland for that marriage; and if so,

I claim one from the Government of the United States to me and to many another poor madman in Oregon, for inserting in Sec. 5 of the public land laws the following words: "one quarter-section of land if a single man, or if he shall become married in one year, one half-section of land," etc.[3]

Was not all Oregon demoralized by that law twenty-odd years ago? I recollect of men of fifty marrying girls of twelve, with consent of parents at that; and several men married girls but eleven years of age. All Oregon was married off in 1853, and I had to wait for a new crop, and could not wait long or somebody else would snap them up.

May I remind you of an incident? You were teaching school in Eola. One morning in July a man looking very much like myself rode up to your school-house door, called for the mistress, put a letter of proposal in her hand, waited nearby till noon for an answer, was then very courteously informed that "he was too late," and only two weeks after that, the more fortunate B. C. D. [Benjamin C. Duniway] carried the schoolmistress off to the minister, and from there on to his double land-claim, while I only got a cold quarter-section.

But I was out of luck. That year I rushed around all over Polk and Yamhill counties. I only found eight single marriageable women. I asked them all, and was "too late" with all except one, and with her I was *too early*. She was a widow and I didn't know it, having only heard of her as a single woman. I asked her how it was that she being full grown was a single woman in Oregon. She replied: "Oh, I have been married, but my husband is dead."

"Would you like to marry again?" said I, looking her honestly in the face and meaning that I was the man.

Then her dear blue eyes filled with tears, a shadow came over her sunny face, and she answered: "Oh, it is almost too soon to talk about it yet; my husband has only been dead two weeks."

I felt awfully, apologized, mounted my tall bay riding mule, and went over to—Eola.

I know I became, with the rest of the people of Oregon, utterly demoralized by the land law, or by the climate of Oregon, or something else; for three years before, in the States, I refused to *propose* to a very accomplished, large, fine, lovely blonde who seemed very fond of me, just for the reason that I was thirty-six and she only eighteen. I came to Oregon, saw them marrying without regard to age, got over my prejudices, or discretions, as did everybody else, and gladly got the first one that would have me. I shall bear the consequences, or charge them to Uncle Sam. . . .

[Salem, Oregon]

*(September 24, 1875)*

## Benjamin C. Duniway's Response

"The fortunate B. C. D." begs leave to state for the information of this correspondent, that he owned and held a half-section of land in his own right, and needed not a wife to perfect his title to the same. Consequently, the Eola schoolmistress did not marry for land, and obtained none by the transaction. Twenty years ago, Mrs. D. wrote and published in violent denunciation of the "demoralizing" practice of "marrying for land"; and she will doubtless be very much surprised to discover that any person should be so devoid of judgment as to be such a length of time in finding out that the practice *was* "demoralizing."

*(September 24, 1875)*

## The Women of Junction, Oregon

[We reached] Junction before two o'clock, where we were welcomed, first at Berry's Hotel, and afterwards at the pleasant abode of brilliant little Mrs. Roach, who entertained us hospitably and . . . fed us like any preacher, upon the best of chicken fixings, sweet pickles and cream.

Two fine audiences greeted us here, also a goodly number of new subscribers. Junction is improving rapidly. Many persons are buying corner lots, anticipating the completion of the west-side railroad, and contemplating a fat speculation in real estate. The amount of grain constantly coming in for transportation by rail is surprising. If wheat, at its present price—and so much of it—does not make all the farmers rich, it ought to.

But how the country women toil and drudge. Look upon the street at any hour, and you will see a bowed and careworn object of man's protecting gentleness, in scant calico dress and ample sun-bonnet, lugging a load of butter and eggs from the wagon to the store, to exchange for saleratus, concentrated lye, fruit cans, coffee, denims, calico, bed-bug exterminator, candle molds, bed-quilt materials, crockery, wash-boards, carpet-warp, etc., etc., everything she buys only adding to her means of toil, while her sickly baby frets in the lap of an older child, and her rich husband's favorite brood mare roams at will in the September shades of the great farm pasture, "raising a blooded colt."

Talk to one of these horny-handed, hopeless, weary women about the *New Northwest* and she'll sigh or sneer, owing to her mood, and shake her head and find fault with you, because you appear healthier and more hopeful than herself. Get her out to a lecture though, and you have her. Once let her even dream that there is a balm in Gilead, and her eyes will brighten and lan-

guid step grow quick; and then she'll "wish she *could* get the paper; but he must have tobacco; and *he takes several papers*, and the children need so many things she can't afford it."

But she grasps our hand at parting and says, "God bless and speed you," as she mounts the high seat in the great wagon and takes the baby in her lap and the little girl beside her; and while her husband touches the well-kept horses with an elegant whip, she ties up her sunken jaws to keep her decaying teeth from the draught, and we watch them till the rising dust enshrouds and hides them, and then walk on, repeating to ourself the hollow, mocking words we so often hear, "Women are protected and supported by men."

*(September 24, 1875)*

## The Hungriest Bedbugs Imaginable

Our next destination was Roseburg, which we reached on Friday at 8 P. M., and were ushered into a lumbering coach, among mail-bags, baggage and tourists, and driven to the hotel, where we wrestled through the long hours of the night with the hungriest bed-bugs imaginable— big, voracious, monsters, whose bites—ugh! . . . [O]ur language fails us, and we give it up.

We were sitting in the parlor the next morning, dolorous and forlorn, disgusted with bed-bugs and fleabotomy, when who should call but the little son of our old friend, Mrs. M. J. Hall, with an invitation to one of the coolest, dearest, cosiest suburban suffrage homes you ever saw, reader; and as we sit in her pleasant parlor and look abroad over the glories of the autumn landscape on this balmy Sabbath morning, awaiting the hour of eventide, when we are to address the public, a drowsy restfulness becalms our senses, and our dreams of home and loved ones there are sweet and longing. The pencil drops from our languid fingers, ideal, distant voices reach us, and—and—and—good-bye.

Roseburg [Oregon], September 19, 1875.

A. J. D.

*(September 24, 1875)*

## Spirit Mediums and Flower Manifestations

Arriving at Umatilla on the 29th ult., expecting to hold a meeting and then proceed further up the river, our course was changed by what seemed the merest accident.

A son of our old "Hardscrabble" friend, James Vinson, Esq., was in town with a freight team, and we accepted his invitation to go out in the wagon to the house of an acquaintance of his, fifteen miles distant, where his parents were to come and spend Saturday and Sun-

day. Our load was flour and our road was sand.

For miles we followed the Umatilla, a busy stream that feeds the hungry sands and supplies the thirsty cattle with the sweetest water, where, on its banks, we saw a great eagle fishing for its breakfast, and a mud-hill crane that stared us out of countenance; with sage brush to the right and left of us, through which monster rabbits darted—the only living thing visible away from the little river, while in the distance, long rows of blue-black mountains shook their shivering heads at us in the scintillating light of the hazy autumn, and near-by hills of lesser magnitude loomed up in bleak unsightliness, the scarcity of timber comporting well with the unbroken solitude of a "desert all desolate" that tearlessly gazed at the beclouded sky.

After we had proceeded a mile or two on our journey, we learned that the place of our destination was the home of Mrs. Ewing, a noted "spirit medium," where we were informed that we should be favored with the companionship of John Milton, Dr. Watts, and other distinguished and erewhile supposed-to-be extinguished notables.

The farm-house where this medium lives is rambling and roomy, the inmates are hospitable and pleasant, and but for the fact that the lady medium who entertained the aforesaid visitors is a confirmed invalid, and wholly unable to endure the "supported and protected" condition in which custom has placed her, we should have highly enjoyed the visit.

But John Milton, poet, refused to allow Colonel E. D. Baker, statesman, to "control his medium," although he did have the grace to say the said statesman was present; so your correspondent, forgetting the superstitious awe with which Spiritualists generally accept every revelation of the unseen, began to ask questions in a very material way, and received for answer that said statesman was "Deistical," thereby leading us to infer that sectarian bigotry exists in heaven, although we had always hoped the contrary. . . .

The next evening was very stormy, but nothing daunted, we all collected in the front sitting-room to join in a circle for "flower manifestations." The family had told us of wonders in this line, and we said we should like to behold them, for, like Thomas of old, we were something of a doubter. They said that the rain would spoil the "conditions," but they would *try*. So the doors and windows were fastened, the lamp turned down to a dim flamelet that only made the darkness visible, though we could plainly see the hands and faces of all present.

After a long time spent in singing, . . . a little girl of Mrs. Ewing's, five years old, who does not know the alphabet, became entranced, and wrote many words and some sentences quite plainly. Some of the words were written in an ordinary running hand, some up-side down and some wrong side to, so you could only read them (that is, the last) by reflection in a looking-glass. And while we confess that "John Milton" didn't excite our curiosity much, we freely admit that this child's performances did. Whence came this power? and whither goeth it? Verily, we are led to exclaim with Job, "Man giveth up the ghost, and where is he?"

George Vinson, although a strong opponent of Spiritual belief, went into a comatose, or unconscious trance condition, and spoke, sung, and wrote, while apparently under mesmeric influence.

After several hours thus spent in the circle, the light was turned fully on, and we all drew back from the table, when under it we found, neatly tied with a beautiful silver cord, an immense bouquet of hollyhocks and prince's feathers, fully seven inches across, and weighing half a pound. The same was said to be intended "for the editor," and the laugh we enjoyed over the exquisite taste displayed in its selection was as contagious as enjoyable. The medium said that the flowers were brought from the garden adjacent; that on a clear night they could bring them from long distances, but the rain interfered with the electric currents and limited their power. . . .

Like Bosco, in his magic, we "make no explanation." Indeed, we couldn't if we would. To narrate facts, as we behold them, is our mission. To draw your own conclusion, reader dear, is yours.

November 11th [LaGrande, Oregon].

A. J. D.

*(November 19, 1875)*

## Pendleton Swarms with Indians

Leaving Pendleton on a warm, spring-like afternoon, and climbing one of the many great bald hills that environ it—our seat in an open buggy commanding a fine view of the fertile valley in which the town is situated—we after a while reached the broad alluvial plateau, comprising forty thousand acres of the best and most desirable farming land we ever saw anywhere, but which is wholly given over to the abode of Cayuse horses. This plateau is an Indian [Umatilla] reservation, where a few hundred great, stalwart wards of the government, who are amply able to be self-sustaining—and would be much better off if compelled to be so—claim, although they do not cultivate, this vast area of acres, while industrious white men, and thrifty, thorough-going white women, are driven to the most undesirable tracts of government land to get themselves a foot-hold.

Pendleton swarms with Indians. Great, lazy louts, who stand nearly six feet in their moccasins, while the women perform the drudgery alike of the camp and field, lounge languidly around the fires in the great stoves in the stores; and the younger fry, clad in nondescript undress, of which the fashion has not changed to our certain knowledge in a quarter of a century, practice on the common with bows and arrows as their shiftless fathers did of yore.

We freely confess a lack of fashionable religious enthusiasm over the prospect of civilizing the native Indian according to the white man's idea of enlightenment. The noble red man is at best a wild animal less susceptible of being tamed than the white man's horse or dog. No doubt this declaration will startle somebody; but no matter. The truth must be spoken. Occasionally we find exceptions to the general rule, and would by no means decry the efforts of philanthropists to make the most of such. But the Indian is better off in his own element, and more prosperous in every way when let alone, than he can ever be among white men.

As we rode along over the beautiful reservation with our mind busily occupied with these cogitations, we could not help feeling that, after all, the Indian is much like many white men. There are leagues of unoccupied land in the valleys of the Sacramento, San Joaquin and

Willamette equally as fertile as these acres, which some autocrat of the soil has spread his imaginary wings over, driving humanity back to the mountains, while hogs and sheep enjoy the luxury of the grass-grown common in undisputed serenity.

Uniontown, Oregon. November 17.

A. J. D.

*(November 26, 1875)*

## Close Shave on a Stagecoach

On Wednesday, the 24th inst., accompanied by our good friend Mrs. Hannah, of Uniontown, we mounted the great stagecoach [at Baker City, Oregon], and long before the first glimpses of Old Sol's streaming hair had begun to greet human eyes with a shimmering array of golden tangles a-spread upon the clouds and mountains, we turned our faces Union-ward, well wrapped in veils and nubias to protect our eyes and noses from the frosty, icy, snowy gloom. . . .

We had sighed over being shut up in the coach on our way to Baker City, for we wanted to see the country. To-day, we were to be gratified; for Boreas was holding his breath, and from our perch beside the driver, our vision was only bounded, at a distance of many miles across the level vale, by chains of bleak, white mountains, with here and there a purple ridge of cone-shaped trees, all mantled with the snow.

The ground being frozen, and the ruts filled with snow-drift, the roads were better than when we went over a few days previous; but on many sidelong places, the coach would slide until the danger of upsetting was imminent. We had thumped and rumbled and crashed and glided by turns over the diversified roadway, and had come within a half dozen miles of our day's journey's end, when we met, for the dozenth time that day, one of the immense freight wagons with what teamsters call a "train" behind it—we hope no fashionable train-draggler will imagine it to be like her own. It is simply a common heavy wagon with a stubby "pole" hooked under the running gear of the forward vehicle—to which (we mean the last one named) were hitched at least eight rat-tailed, ewe-necked mules, with spindle legs and shaggy coats and overgrown joints, reminding us strongly of many overworked specimens of motherhood we wot of, who foolishly imagine that they "have all the rights they want."

We were just coming upon a long, narrow grade from which the landscape sloped toward a rocky gulch, when we met the above-mentioned team and train. The team halted, and our driver veered to the right to pass by it, when the great stage adopted a sudden sliding-scale movement, suggestive of immediate dissolution.

"Whoa!" cried the driver.

"Let's dismount," said Mrs. H.

"How can we?" answered we.

"Sit still!" commanded the boss.

"We'll have to," thought we both.

"Say, teamster, take hold of the hind end of the coach and steady it till we get by, won't you?" said the driver, as cool as a cucumber.

Said teamster wasn't in any hurry, but he finally obeyed.

We had three Chinamen inside the coach, but they proposed to fight it out on that line if it killed the whole crowd of us, and they wouldn't budge an inch.

So the teamster clung to the upper and well-locked coach wheel, looking about as big and heavy as a horse-fly clinging to a buffalo; our driver said "get up," cracking a keen "persuader" vigorously as he spoke, and then a sudden jolt took us over the most dangerous rut. Grazing the traces of the forward mules in the freight train with our horses, and slapping the single-trees against the reed-like legs of the hinder ones with our coach wheels, we gained the level ground and went rumbling on.

"*By George!*" that was a mighty close shave!" said the driver earnestly.

"Hope we won't meet another team," we said, tremulously.

"It's nothing, once you get used to it," remarked Mrs. H., dryly.

"Getting used to it's the rub," said we, solemnly.

A. J. D.

*(December 10, 1875)*

## Notes for 1875

1. Public spelling contests between adults had caught on as a fad in Oregon in 1875 and were reported frequently in *The NNW.*
2. Knappton was named after Jabez Burnel Knapp, formerly co-owner of a hardware and agricultural machinery store in Portland. Knapp began an early sawmill at Knappton, originally called "Cementville." By about 1873, there were two mills at Knappton, each producing an average of 37,000 feet of lumber per day.
3. To encourage settlement of the Oregon Territory, the Donation Land Act was approved by Congress in Sept. of 1850. The law provided grants of 320 acres to single men and 640 acres to men and their wives, if they were in the territory

*House at Fifth and Clay streets, Portland, purchased by the Duniways in the mid-1870s. Photo, ca. 1895, shows Abigail Scott Duniway on the right and her housekeeper seated on the left.*

before 1 Dec. 1850. Later settlers, who arrived by 1853, could receive 160 acres if single men and 320 acres if married couples. In all cases of grants to married couples, half of the land was in the husband's name and half in the wife's name. When settlement under this law and its modifications ended in 1855, 7,317 claims had been entered for over 2.5 million acres in Oregon Territory and almost 300,000 acres in Washington Territory. Grants were limited to citizens of the United States, thus excluding blacks and Indians. Settlers were required to live on the land and cultivate it for four years. One of the effects of the Donation Land Act was that women were sought after as wives, sometimes resulting in the hasty marriages of young girls to men several times their age, as in the case of this husband who married a girl of fourteen. For more on the Donation Land Act, see Bancroft, *History of Oregon*, Vol II, 261-75; and James M. Bergquist, "The Oregon Donation Act and the National Land Policy," *Oregon Historical Quarterly* 58 (March 1957): 17-35.

Ben Duniway could claim 320 acres in his own name because he was in Oregon before 1 Dec. 1850 but, since he had not married within a year after arriving, he could claim nothing for his wife.

# 1876

## No Canada for Fugitive Wives

Had business [in Salem] on Thursday [of last week] with a dear, intelligent, but broken-down example of protected and supported womanhood, who at the age of fifty had fled from the protecting gentleness of a husband for whom she had toiled without recompense for a third of a century. Had much difficulty in finding her, for she was hiding with her children from her lawful head, and was in mortal terror lest she should be discovered and robbed of her little ones. Found her at last, ensconced in a dingy, unfurnished building, her children cowering and clinging around her, and the doors and windows securely fastened against intruders.

For the first time in our life we felt like building an underground railroad. There is one obstacle in the way, though, and that is that there's no Canada in all the world to give such fugitives protection.

A woman who is driven in her desperation to defy the law and flee with her little ones . . . ought to have her freedom, and the fruit of the "labor of her hands.". . .

But the children—"ay, there's the rub." Legally, a mother has no children. They belong to the law-maker; and when the mother of such a family goes back to the hated life rather than give them up, the husband may exultantly exclaim: "I told you so! She had no reason to be estranged from me. She comes to her senses when she's thrown upon her own resources for a while.". . .

"You believe in easy divorce, then?" cries somebody, who inwardly chafes under bonds to which he has long been untrue in thought, if not in deed.

"No, sir! We do not believe in divorce at all, we believe in that which will eventually prevent divorce, which is nothing more than equality before the law. This is the panacea that will put both wives and husbands on their good behavior and keep them there."

Salem, March 4th.

A. J. D.

*(March 10, 1876)*

## Chinese in Portland

Over 200 Chinese passengers arrived in this port by the steamer "Idaho." It is said that they came to work upon the railroad which is to be constructed from Tacoma to the Puyallup Coal Mines the coming summer.

Rev. Dong Gong, the Chinese missionary, was violently assaulted by his countrymen on the supposition that he was instrumental in the prosecution of Chinese brothels in this city.[1] Timely interference of others saved his life.

*(March 24, 1876)*

## Visit to Seattle Coal Mines

On Saturday, accompanied by a number of musical friends, we repaired to the Seattle coal mines, some fifteen or twenty miles away [from Seattle]. Our route lay over a primitive railroad to Lake Union, which we crossed on a car-laden steam scow, after which came another railroad portage to Lake Washington. . . . Crossed the lake in about two hours, and then climbed up the hill and into a coal car, in which last we stood like so many cattle, while the little engine bore us to Newcastle, which is the new name of the Seattle coal mine.

A succession of knolls and gulches, all blackened with the fine coal that everywhere abounded, was dotted with rustic houses, around which many children and a few pigs were playing; the dark forest hemmed the village like an amphitheater; the open shafts of three coal mines peeped at us with their great, watchful, black eyes; the hotel, a rough, whitewashed and roomy building, over which Charley Foss presides as steward, invited us to enter, and we were soon struggling in vain with the accumulated coal dust, which, like the headache we were enduring, adhered to us much closer than a bur or a brother.

A local minstrel troupe were making active preparations for a performance, and, much to our relief, the lecture and concert were postponed till Monday evening. . . .

Captain Wilson, . . . the gentlemanly superintendent of the mines, who takes special pride in showing the mines to strangers, kindly lighted us [on Monday] through a long tunnel as black, but for the lamps, as Erebus, where for at least a mile we waded into the very bowels of the earth, under a great arch of sandstone upon the left and bituminous coal upon the right, with here and there an opening through the inky blackness that led to the chambers where the men were excavating the immense caverns from which they garner inexhaustible supplies of coal. . . .

Occasionally the rumble of wheels was heard, causing the girls of our party to scream with fright, and the jolly captain to highly enjoy their trepidation. After the rumbling had been heard for several minutes, a coal-blackened miner, with a lamp on his head, would appear beside a donkey in the dense gloom; the rumbling of wheels would increase to a deafening roar, the girls would scream yet more lustily, and we would all shrink close to the side of the dripping mine till the wierd [*sic*] specter thundered by; then on we would go till a similar experience would induce a similar diversion, and so the long walk through coal dust, clay, and slush, though unpleasant, was not endurably monotonous.

Two of the immense coal veins that crop to the surface many rods apart intersect each other about half a mile from the opening of the mine we are in, the great strata of rock that divides them growing thinner as we proceed, until at last it runs along for several yards not wider than a seam in an army tent or a sailor's tarpaulia. Where the two coal veins become one, the lode is over twelve feet in diameter, the sand rock against which it rested when the whole was in liquid state—whether among fire or water—deponent saith not—being pitched or "dipped" toward the north at an angle of perhaps 38 degrees.

"How far under the surface, are we, Captain," we ask, as we contemplate the situation and shiver with the cold and damp and gloom.

"Oh, quite a distance," is the cheerful and definite answer; "you can get out by climbing the air shaft, almost perpendicular, only five hundred feet. Would you like to try it?"

We respectfully decline, but the girls insist on making the attempt, and almost feel offended because they are not permitted to do so.

Back again over the railway, the same monotonous gloom everywhere; and at length, tired out with the long walk, we emerge into daylight, with our eyes dazzled, stockings soggy, shoes muddy, skirts wet, and appetites sharp.

We are informed that the men at work in the mines number two hundred, about forty of whom have families living in the shanties that dot the hillsides. The remainder board at the hotel, where plenty of good and wholesome food is to be had at reasonable rates at all hours. If humanity everywhere were fed by hundreds on a like scale, thereby apportioning to each worker a regular line of duties, instead of compelling every woman to become mistress of a dozen trades as now, house-keeping would become a grand cooperative science, in which the whole world might take good paying stock. . . .

Tuesday came, and with it a rain that kept us indoors until train time, when a seat in the railway engine was assigned us, . . . [the musicians] riding on a coal car, and a number of other travelers hanging to the brakes. We thought it a hazardous business, especially when a linch-pin broke, leaving the aforementioned members of our party sitting in solitude upon the track, while the engine and its tail of other cars went switching on toward Lake Washington. But the engineer returned for the rear guard, and we reached the lake without further accident. Again we cross Lake Washington; again we make a portage; again we embark upon Lake Union, and again, after another hour's travel by water, make another portage, fetching up at Seattle, tired, travel-soiled, and wet, but blessed with high spirits and appetites like so many ravens. . . .

Seattle, May 1, 1876.

A. J. D.

*(May 12, 1876)*

## Port Blakely's Driven Men and Hopeless Concubines

Did we write you concerning Port Blakely, [W. T.]?

The men in the mills of Port Blakely are driven, day and night, like so many cattle. They take their meals at a "cook house," and the few of them who have wives keep them in a row of harems, where they have nothing to do but cultivate an abnormal growth of sickly sentiment and unholy suspicions of other women, imagining, poor creatures, that because they live as aimless, hopeless concubines, all other women could, and ought to love as they.

Yet they are a most unhappy set, and no wonder. But few of them have children. They are far too nice for the holy office of motherhood; and oft-repeated abortion is written in tell-tale lines upon their faces. That bad women have sometimes come among the bad men at Port Blakely, and thereby given cause to some of these same abnormal women to be unduly suspicious, is not wonderful. But it is sad to see whole communities living

so unnaturally in this life as to retard their spiritual growth in the future state for centuries.

Olympia, May 11, 1876.

A. J. D.

*(May 19, 1876)*

## A Protest from Port Blakely

A gentleman writing us from Port Blakely, states that the *New Northwest* containing our strictures upon its inhabitants has been very freely circulated among the denizens of the place. While he takes us to task for publishing the truth, he gives some excuses for the conduct of the citizens toward us, which we are willing they should have the benefit of. He says they are compelled to live isolated as they do, because the mill company owns everything. The ways of the men are not sufficient to enable them to support themselves; hence, the "cook-house" must feed them. Two-thirds of the men have "cloochmen," or Indian women, and the head proprietor of the mills compels every man in the company's employ to buy provisions and clothing for the "cloochmen" at the company's store. The company have no use for the visits of respectable women—do not want them to visit Port Blakely.

Old Captain Renton and his wife make bargains for certain men to live with certain Indian women, and sell them outfits for housekeeping from the store at fifty per cent premium.[2] If a respectable lady were to be allowed to lecture before such men, they might reform, and then the mill company would not employ them. The legal wives (he scolds us soundly for saying "concubines") are as good women as the average. They only need to mingle with the outside world to get rid of the morbid suspicion of which they are guilty. They are shy of strange ladies because so unaccustomed to see company, etc., etc.,—all of which only the more assures us that our strictures were strictly true. If men will sell the birthright of freedom for a mess of saw-mill pottage, they must not get over-angry when women find fault with their wives for becoming suspicious social monstrosities.

*(June 2, 1876)*

## Mrs. Duniway Heads for the East Coast

In pursuance of plans she has been steadily maturing for the past few months, Mrs. Duniway started on Thursday, the 8th inst., for the East. She proposes to go to Umatilla by the O. S. N. Co.'s boats, and thence take stage to Kelton *via* Baker City and internal points, lecturing and canvassing for the *New Northwest* as she goes, and hoping to be able to reach Philadelphia in time to participate in the women's centennial ceremonies on the Fourth. We think

our readers can scarcely imagine the sacrifice of comfort and the vast amount of labor that the journey thus taken imposes upon Mrs. Duniway, else they would be more prompt in discharging their financial obligations to the journal she has worked so unceasingly during the last five years to establish and maintain.

*(June 9, 1876)*

## The Columbia River Is on a Spree

With the confidence in manifest destiny which astonishes us every time we think of it, behold your correspondent again upon the wing, or rather, *wave*, for the upper Columbia is boiling like the ocean, and even the hotels we sleep in at night rock in the water like the agitated "Ajax" when it enters the river at its mouth. As we sit scribbling, we pause to scratch our pate for an idea, and the only one that assumes very important shape is the astonishing one already alluded to, but not expressed in the beginning of this paragraph, namely: We are off to the Centennial. . . .

But let us not brag too soon. We haven't begun the staging yet, and *such* a water-course! Water to the right and water to the left of us, and water everywhere.

The town of The Dalles, which is usually so dry as to almost choke you with sympathy . . . has succumbed to a decidedly *wet* condition of things, and sits with its nose under water, and the bodies of its streets, hotels, and stores ditto. . . .

The Umatilla House, famous for good dinners and dry surroundings, looks like a swamped steamboat with the smokestack and wheels gone, as it crouches in a great, muddy eddy and stares at you with its windowy, watery eyes, and gasps continually with wheezy waves of watery respiration.

The old omnibus met about forty of us as we emerged from the steamer "Daisy Ainsworth" . . . ; and as we gazed, disconsolate, we considered what the—*deluge* was coming next. Dear reader, don't accuse us of profanity. We're going to the Centennial, but we never swear. "Deluge" is a proper word.

The passengers piled into and onto that omnibus like frightened wharf rats, and the driver took us about fifteen feet away and dumped us into the second story of the old Empire Hotel, where Messrs. Handley & Sinnott, the drowned-out proprietors of the Umatilla House, have temporarily taken refuge; and here we are supplied with good beds, and, by walking a temporary planking for a block or two, through streets filled with boats and boatmen, we get very good—*grub*. What the mischief makes anybody say *grub* for *food*, we wonder? A lady sits near us, in good clothes, whose acquaintance we were anxious to make till we heard her say, when speaking of a certain San Francisco hotel just now, "The traveling public don't go a cent on *style*. They're principally concerned about *good grub*." Is the word a good one? And if so, when, where, and how did it originate? We never think of it but we think involuntarily of a great, brown, lazy tobacco worm.

Supper being over, we wended our way back over the narrow, rickety bridgeway to the hotel. . . .

The mad river, all swollen with its angry flood, lashed the sides of the hotel with a warning vehemence, but only rocked us to sleep with its billows. . . . The water had risen several inches during the night. . . . Boatmen paddled their own canoes right into the emptied store-houses, rats swam for dear life to get somewhere, out of the wet, and cats scrambled for dear existence almost right beside them, while bent on the same mission. If you want the cat and the rat to lie down in peace together, just get the Columbia River on a spree, and you'll see 'em at it.

Up the Columbia, June 10, 1876.
A. J. D.

*(June 16, 1876)*

## Chinese Driven from Seattle Mines

The white miners at the Seattle coal mines have driven off the Chinamen, numbering about thirty, who have been working at those mines. At last account it was understood to be the intention to take the same course at the Renton and Talbot mines.

*(June 16, 1876)*

## Chinese Immigration

The speech of Senator [John] Mitchell [of Oregon], delivered in the Senate chamber of the United States on the 16th of May, upon this question [of Chinese immigration] which is now occupying the thoughts of all classes upon the Pacific Coast, is before us.[3] Following up on the line of argument employed by Senator Sargent of California, in his great speech upon the question, Mr. Mitchell shows in forcible language the evils that have resulted and predicts the dire evils that must necessarily result from the immense influx of Chinese to this coast especially.

*(June 23, 1876)*

## High Water at Midnight

Took stage at night [from La Grande] for Baker City, our fellow-passengers numbering four, two gentlemen and two ladies. The coach was so full of baskets, valises, wraps, knapsacks, and bundles, that a delightfully crowded state of affairs presented itself. Our trunk, without which we are in the Flora McFlimsey condition, was left behind. The water was high, but the driver was careful, and through the long night we bowled along, fetching up once in a while at a damaged bridge or a deep mud hole, and snoozing a little in spite of the baskets that bruised our shins, till we sighed for gentlemen's boots to protect them.

One diversion we must not forget to chronicle. The time was midnight; the situation, owing to high water, doubtful. The southbound stage met us and halted, and the colloquy between the drivers was as follows:

"How's the road?"

"By the holy powers of mud, it's awful! How's the Powder River bridge?"

"Unsafe, I'd say." (Our coach had just crossed it.) "Apron afloat, banks full, mud—by Jiminy!"

"Well, we'll try it. We may give up the ghost, go dead an' busted, pass in our checks, or go to Davy Jones, but we'll ask the Old Man to put us through."

"Have we any more bad bridges?" asks a nervous lady passenger.

"There's a mud-hole on ahead that'll mire a saddle blanket," is the encouraging reply. "The mud'll cover all but your eyelids; but it's good, to what it's been!" and cracking his whip, he disappears in the darkness, and we go on and on, looking anxiously for that mud-hole, and failing to find it, whereof we are glad.

Baker City, [Oregon], June 24, 1876.

A. J. D.

*(June 30, 1876)*

## Remembering the Death Angel

Lectures being over [in Baker City], and good-byes exchanged, we . . . take a room for the two intervening hours between lecture and stage time. . . . [W]e are aroused at 1 A.M. to embark for Boise City.

Away, away, and yet away we journey, our companions the stars of God, that twinkle over the vast expanse of sand and sage and desolation, relieved here and there by a willow-fringed water course. Daylight comes, and we strike Burnt River with its noisy rush of waters, its borders of willow and cottonwood, its bluffs of sand, slate rock and basalt, flanked by the nearby mountains. Strange, primitive, awful, sad, silent, and sere they loom above and around us, their juniper-studded sides peeping in great patches through bald openings, their flora, grand and beautiful, smiling at us. . . .

Yonder, high above the level of the plain, under a lone juniper that, for a quarter of a century, has kept solitary guard above the "silent home of the dead," is the lone grave of our brother Willie!

Oh, God! How like a vast scroll do the long years unroll themselves as we gaze through the dim vista of departed decades! On and on we go. The tedious day's journey of a quarter of a century ago is now made in one hour and a half, and there, under the shadow of the stunted trees, we mark the spot where our childish muse came to us in the awful solitude, when face to face with the Death Angel, we watched the waning breath of the bright little four-year-old, whose mother and ours had been buried in the Black Hills of Wyoming just ten fleeting weeks before.[4] As we gazed, it seemed as though an angel whispered. The spot was holy. We were glad we were alone. . . .

Eight o'clock, and breakfast. . . . [A]nd, in spite of the flood of olden memories that have filled our spirit, the body is half famished.

On we go again. How the long miles unroll, one after another in seemingly endless succession. Snake River is reached long before noon. Again old memories crowd upon us. The river seems to sing a requiem to John McDonald, who lost his life in trying to recover the strayed cattle of our immigrant party a quarter of a century ago.[5] But John knows no desert country now. Like brother Willie, he has long been transplanted from the arid plains of earth to the evergreen gardens of God. With a sigh to his memory, we cross the river in a boat, and find ourselves in Idaho.

*(July 14, 1876)*

## Caught in a Swamp

We must hurry, for the Payette, like the Columbia, is on a spree, and we must cross it before dark. Reach the river at six o'clock. The banks are full to overflowing. The current runs like a mill race. A well-rigged ferry-boat conveys us safely across the swift waters, and here the struggle begins. The horses plunge into a swamp, the stage splashes and labors, and we catch the straps nervously, for there is trouble ahead, the great danger being the possibility of upsetting. Three of the horses swamp and fall down.

"Whoa!" says the driver.

Instantly, a half-dozen brave men [from the ferry] doff their boots, roll up their pantaloons, and plunge into the slough. The horses are loosed from the coach. We'd give the Kohinoor, if we had it, to be ashore. How we'd like to be busy, too. But we must watch and wait. The running-gear of a wagon is brought, drawn by a span of gray mules. They are hitched on with a rope. The men lift the great wheels with herculean labor. The driver whips the team. The rope breaks. Some time is spent in procuring a cable. One is brought at last that could hold the steamer "Ajax." A mighty effort of men, mules and horses, a groaning, splashing resistance of the great coach, some nervous clutching at the side straps from your correspondent, and we are safe on *terra firma*, and the men crack jokes over the occurrence as though it had been fun. . . .

All night long we journeyed, after crossing the swamp. As we were a solitary passenger—something very unusual—we made a bed of the cushions and, curled up like a mammoth dormouse, tried to sleep, and succeeded, despite bumps and bruises, in reaching dreamland once in a while. But, how lonely we were—away out on the wide desert, the driver on the box outside as deferentially reticent as though dumb from babyhood. Often there were no habitations within many leagues, and nothing between us and eternity but the great rumbling coach and the flooded though dusty plain. This last expression may seem paradoxical, but it is literally true. The floods run in channels and the dust upon ridges. One moment you are in water, and the next you cannot breathe for dust.

Toward morning the scene changes. Well-made farms abound upon either hand. Long rows of cultivated trees make graceful obeisance to you in the star-lit breezes. Cattle sleep by the roadside and lights gleam in many windows. At four o'clock we reach Boise City and the Overland Hotel, where a night watch shows us to a cozy room, and we sink upon a downy bed in our travel-soiled garments, and are soon in a dreamless sleep.

June 29, 1876.

A. J. D.

*(July 14, 1876)*

## Independence Day Celebration at Boise

Finding we could not work our way to Philadelphia in time for the celebration of the Independence day of the men, we concluded Boise was the next best place, and so we tarried.

The celebration was a complete success. Bunting and buncombe and fireworks and a liberty car; ice cream soda and strawberries and sandwiches, balls, horse races, and buggy rides, firecrackers, fuses, and fun of every description ruled the day. . . .

On the fifth there was to be a great race at the grounds adjacent to Boise, and we accepted a seat in the carriage with the family of Mr. Jacobs [formerly of Dayton and proprietor of the Boise flouring mill], and repaired hitherto with the multitude. A grand pavilion had been erected, high, airy, and convenient, and, after a pleasant drive, we found ourselves seated on an elevated tier of benches, overlooking the race track, the valley, and

adjacent mountains. Quiet and good humor reigned everywhere.

After long waiting, three excited colts were let loose upon the track, backed by as many excited boys. Neck and neck they rode for an instant, and then, seeing the smallest boy with the black colt holding the impatient steed in the rear, we inwardly "bet on Fred Douglass." Mr. Jacobs took sides for "Horace Greeley," a beautiful chestnut four-year-old, with a white hind foot. We recollected that in [James] Fenimore Cooper's novels we had once read of a failure of a white-footed horse, and so we stood by "Fred Douglass."

At least half way round the track our favorite was behind. Then his rider relaxed his hold and the black colt came out ahead, amid cheering that would have sounded very foolish to us if "Horace Greeley" had beaten. What simpletons we all are! And how animated we'll get over nothing! Verily, man is an anomaly.

*(July 21, 1876)*

## Meeting Mormon Women

Called at the office of the *Woman's Exponent* [in Salt Lake], where Mrs. [Emmeline B.] Wells, sixth wife of Mayor Wells, and a very intelligent and conscientious woman of middle age, met us with hospitality.[6] While here, we were introduced to the foreman in the co-operative store, or "Co-op," as everybody terms it, an enormous building, three hundred feet by fifty, lighted entirely from the roof, and containing three stories and a basement, well stocked with every conceivable merchantable commodity. "Zion's Co-operative Union" is so far practicable in money matters that it hesitates not to deal in everything imaginable, from a needle to a threshing machine, and a nutmeg grater to a quartz mill.

We were next invited to the Mormon ladies' Centennial fair, where we were surprised to note the prevailing evidences of woman's handiwork. Laces of every kind, quite equal to those imported, may be seen here, also cloth, carpets, fancy work, paintings, and, indeed, industries of every class. . . .

Aside from the superstitious belief in latter-day revelations and the plural wife fallacy, nobody can help admiring the energetic and kindly women one meets in the Church. From their standpoint, they are as chaste as ice, though why they cannot see that God never ordained two codes of law, one for man and one for woman, is an inexplicable mystery. Their young people partake of none of the enthusiasm of the older ones, and are especially averse to polygamy, while many of them barely tolerate the Mormon priesthood because they think their parents are crazy on religion. This we have gathered from young Mormon ladies'

own confessions to us, and would give their names right here only that we would not cause them trouble.

The Mormon people are noted for their hospitality to strangers, non-residents of Utah, but they do not like outsiders or Gentiles to live among them, as the association makes apostates of so many of the erewhile faithful. Brigham Young is being "tried" on all sides. "Wife No. 19" [Ann Eliza] has her case for temporary alimony in the courts at this time, Judge McBride, her counsel, making, yesterday, a most efficient appeal in her behalf. . . .

We spent several hours yesterday in the company of Mary Ann Angell, Brigham Young's Kirtland wife, and the mother of his prominent sons. The old lady is quite infirm and occupies one of the grandest palatial residences on the Pacific slope. The mansion is now receiving its finishing touches, and when finished will indeed be a magnificent establishment. Mary Ann lives almost wholly alone. She has the devoutest faith in the Book of Mormon and the latter-day priesthood, and tries hard to believe that polygamy will prove a blessing in the next world, in spite of the suffering it entails in this. Her belief, as we understand it, is a strange admixture of Spiritualism, Solomonism, Davidism, and Abraham-Isaac-and-Jacobism, encrusted in Joseph Smith and Brighamism, and founded upon the natural longing of the human heart for a tangible religion that can lay hold of something it can see and feel, a natural longing which crafty men have taken advantage of among the ignorant of all ages. . . .

We saw "Darwin's missing link" at the court-room the other day, a monkey-ish-looking Saint, with a number of wives, who is interested just now, for pecuniary reasons in Ann Eliza and alimony.

Salt Lake, Utah, August 1, 1876. A. J. D.

*(August 18, 1876)*

## Rights for Mormon Women

The Sunday evening lecture in the M. E. Church [at Salt Lake] was largely attended, despite the intense heat. . . . As elsewhere, our meetings were popular among the masses, but the press, especially the Gentile portion, did not take so kindly to them because of our well known opposition to . . . [disenfranchising] Mormon women. If polygamy is a crime, let the Government have sufficient stamina to so declare it, or else give all women an opportunity to do that which men haven't stamina to undertake, and they will not hesitate to do so. Or, let men ask for an Act disfranchising Mormon men as well as Mormon women, for the violation of the law, and we shall not object; but we shall

fight one-sided legislation and one-sided oligarchy wherever we find it, whether among polygamists or other prostitutionists. . . .

*(August 25, 1876)*

## A Visit to Brigham Young

On Monday, accompanied by H. J. Chapman, of Portland, who is sojourning in Salt Lake for a season, we called upon President Young and chatted for a half-hour. The prophet is almost the exact image of [Henry Ward] Beecher, though a little older and more infirm. He has the same magnetic eye, the same thick neck, a less sensuous mouth, and quite as hearty and social a manner. And, after all, Brigham Young's people are no more attached to him, and obey him no more implicitly, and trust him no more thoroughly, than Beecher's do. The difference between the two is not in their intellect or intelligence, but in their religious views. Both are born leaders, and both are, in spite of themselves, opening humanity's eyes to the necessity of doing their own thinking.

*(August 25, 1876)*

## Thank Heaven for Chinamen

We wish all the opponents of Woman Suffrage could visit the homes of Laramie, where women vote, and thereby get an opportunity to dispel the bogies that haunt them in the shape of unkempt children, neglected homes, masculine women, and general debauchery. . . .

Just now we are quite disturbed. In our desire to aid an ignorant widow who has been left destitute in a land where government claims to protect women, we took her our washing rather than patronize a heathen Chinese, and she scorched and ruined our best traveling dress, charged us two dollars, and made us thank heaven for Chinamen and skilled labor. We hope Chinamen will continue to throng our borders till no washer-woman can get the ghost of a job, and every mother who needs aid to raise a dependent family can draw a pension, as she should. There! We've spoken, and yonder comes the train.

Laramie City, [Wyoming Territory], August 4, 1876.

A. J. D.

*(August 25, 1876)*

## A Grasshopper Blockade

Owing to a break in the Central Pacific road, our train was a half-dozen hours behind time when we left Laramie; so night was on hand, and we retired to a "section" in a sleeping car and wooed the soothing company of Morpheus all in vain. A restless night at home is bad enough, but the long, sleepless hours of darkness in a crowded Pullman, where everybody around you (from whom you are hidden only by a curtain parted in the middle) is snoring and somnolent, are absolutely dreadful.

Morning came—Sunday morning, bright and breezy, but brought no breakfast. The train passed the breakfast station at midnight, and our next stopping place would not be reached till midnoon.

The Rocky Mountains were far in our rear, the snow-sheds became less frequent, the grass was more abundant, and after a while sage brush grew scarce. Countless herds roamed at will over the verdant expanse, bounded only by the bending sky. But for the telegraph poles, which you count for hours in a desperate attempt to beguile the time, there are no objects that give signs of the rapidity of the flight of the iron horse across the plain.

We know nobody, and, for the nonce, have attempted the experiment of traveling *incog*. But how lonesome and tedious the hours are! We're too hungry and weary to read or write, and too restless and nervous to sleep. Breakfast and dinner come together at the hour of twelve, and we get the full benefit of the greenback dollar.

Every car door has the words upon it, in raised letters, "Passengers not allowed on the platform." Perhaps for this reason we enjoy the platform better than any other part of the train, except the engine. (We once bribed an engineer with four bits to get a ride on the engine through Webber Canyon, and we got the best half-dollar ride we ever experienced; but it was stipulated by the second part that we were not to tell on him, so mum's the word, good reader.)

Taking a stool from a wardrobe hook, we sat upon the platform, and rode for hours in the teeth of a breeze like a Washoe zephyr. Now we are in Nebraska's broad prairies, green and undulating, entirely destitute of timber, save here and there a grove of cultivated cottonwood, they roll away into the interminable vastness of seeming infinitude. Corn fields wave in the winds, wheat fields bow their million heads to the breezes, pastures are carpeted with luxuriant sward; the Platte River seems to lie flat upon the bosom of the plain, like a mammoth yellow muslin web laid out to bleach, and the sky above us is as pellucid as ether.

But what causes that cloud that seems to gather forces from the far southeast? Why do we see such mountains of smoke in the distance? Is the prairie on fire? We are not left long in doubt.

The grasshopper is abroad in the land. He darkens the horizon; he fills the zenith with glistening points; he lights upon the railway. The great engine snorts as in anger. The great wheels glide round and round, but not forward; the great train comes to a dead stand.

We have encountered a grasshopper blockade.

"Look!" says a fellow traveler.

We turn in the direction indicated, and behold, a mighty swarm of the hungry, winged nomads hovering above an adjacent corn field. A moment and they are out of sight among the corn.

"Listen!"

The sound as of fire crackling through a dense, dry thicket is heard. Another minute and the great corn leaves fall as though clipped suddenly by millions of shears.

Brushes are placed upon the cowcatcher to clear the way for the train. The track is sanded for a space, the engine snorts again, and—they've raised the blockade. Pity we couldn't say the same for the poor, despoiled farmers. . . .

Through a belt of at least a hundred miles of as beautiful prairie as ever lay upon the bosom of the earth these pests abound in myriads. Then we get out of their range and a sense of thankfulness fills us with a quiet joy.

*(September 1, 1876)*

## Needed: Separate Sleeping Compartments for Women

It is midnight when we reach Omaha. Now we are tired enough to sleep. The porter arouses nobody till morning.

If there is any one thing that is more needed and called for on the trans-continental cars than a separate sleeping apartment for ladies, we don't know what that commodity may be. You are compelled to dress lying prone upon your face, and you run the gauntlet of not over-modest masculine eyes every time anybody squeezes through the narrow passage-way and parts the curtains that form your chamber walls. If the car is crowded you must sleep directly under the berth of some strange traveler who snores, and every time he turns over you tremble lest his bunk will break and fall upon you.

We think we're blest with strong nerves. We can ride beside the stage-driver on a dark night, along the edge of a frightful precipice, without a tremor; but we do shudder at the possibility of being crushed under a loaded Pullman bunk by several hundred pounds of human *avoirdupois*.

Then, it may be education, and it may be fancy, but we can't well get accustomed to exhibiting the mysteries of feminine toilet to bachelors. Such dodging in and out among half-dressed ladies, in their attempt to shy past the gentlemen in undress, who, though sublimely unconscious of their own state of semi-nudity, don't fail to be serenely conscious of feminine *dishabille*, would be excessively amusing if [you] were not one of the dodgers yourself.

*(September 1, 1876)*

## Help from Amelia Bloomer

Mrs. Amelia Bloomer of American costume fame [bloomers], who edited the *Lily* for several years, a paper begun in '49, and the first publication of its kind ever undertaken by ladies, resides here [at Council Bluffs, Iowa] in an elegant home, surrounded in her declining years with everything to be desired to make one happy or wise.

With her assistance we secured the Court-house for a lecture, although it was like cutting eye teeth to get it, some of the voters of Council Bluffs who were clothed in authority being afraid to allow the taxed and unrepresented citizens the right of free speech, lest by so doing somebody's toes might be trodden upon before the fall elections.

Council Bluffs, August 8th.

A. J. D.

*(September 1, 1876)*

## The East Coast at Last!

We have so much to tell you! Since last we wrote, we've been to Philadelphia, attended the Woman Suffrage Convention, the Woman's Congress, and the great Exposition, all within a week, and now we are back again in New York, overseeing the publication of our new epic [*David and Anna Matson*], writing the serial story [*Edna and John: A Romance of Idaho Flat*] and editorial letters, and overhauling our wardrobe to make ready for the coming blasts of King Boreas.

How you'll be surprised at the announcement—but New York is a huge city. None other on the Continent can compare with it. For miles and tens of miles you may traverse its interminable labyrinth of streets and alleys, parks and palaces, hotels and stores, tenements and tabernacles—dodging loaded trucks, rattling omnibuses and ever-abounding street cars, always fetching up where you least expect, and always finding some friendly policeman of elephantine proportion and conspicuous star and buttons ready to set you right when lost. But we can't write that promised New York letter now, for Philadelphia looms up before us and exclaims, "Here I am! Publish *me*!" . . .

On Monday, October 2d, we left the publishing house of S. R. Wells & Company, of New York, who at present preside in magnanimous patience over "David and Anna

*Abigail Scott Duniway, frontispiece for **David and Anna Matson***

Matson's" poetical adornments, . . . bound for the city of Brotherly Love and the Centennial show. . . .

Having secured our [Centennial grounds] press ticket and sat for a "photo" to adorn it—a beautiful thing it is, too, resembling a cider mill as much as ourself—we returned to the city and the [American] Woman Suffrage Convention. . . . In a little while we were on the platform with the Boston suffragists, with stately Mrs. Livermore at the head, facetious Lucy Stone as standard-bearer, positive Henry Blackwell as *fac totum*, earnest Julia Ward Howe as adjutant general, and men and women from twenty-four different States and Territories as reserve corps.[7] And such a meeting! From all parts of the Union the speakers came, ready to work in their own way for the great principle of human freedom. . . .

For two days and evenings the work went on, and then came the Woman's Congress, lasting three days and evenings longer.

Here Prof. Maria Mitchell,[8] of Vassar College, headed a long retinue of heroic retainers, who read papers on every imaginable topic, from co-operative house-keeping to astronomical trigonometry, from stripiculture to the sciences of government, and from the genesis of music to the exegesis of dead languages, the whole supplemented at last by some of the calmest, ablest, and most convincing arguments for Woman Suffrage which have ever been produced upon any platform, always excepting the one whereon brave, indomitable Susan B. Anthony and stately, beautiful and logical Elizabeth Cady Stanton are the inspiration of the work.

How we value the acquaintance of so many good and leading spirits in the great work of woman's emancipation, dear readers, we can never tell you. When we think of the persecution and obloquy we have borne in days gone by because we saw the right and humbly dared to espouse it, and realize that we now have an opportunity to meet and mingle with other women who have also dared and done, we feel that some of the sharpest stings of our present exile from home and the dear ones there are being somewhat compensated.

One day, only, have we given to the [Centennial] Exposition as yet. But what a day! . . . The main building teems with every imaginable work of art of beauty from every land under the sun, while many thousand things that are neither useful nor beautiful abound everywhere. Then the agricultural and horticultural halls, the art gallery and its "annex," machinery hall, woman's pavilion, restaurants of all nations, where people of every clime are fed by tens of thousands; the industries of every people and the fine arts of every land so bewilder you. . . . At present we can only recall playing fountains, superb statuary, glorious paintings, marvelous porcelain, inimitable terra cotta, complicated machinery, bronzes, upholstery, jewelry, flowers, silk embroidery, massive frescoe, fret work, pharmacy, cookery, and— and—we're so tired and sleepy that we must retire, or good Dr. [Clemence] Lozier, with her usual forethought, will be accurately prophesying a headache.[9]

New York, October 7, 1876.

A. J. D.

*(October 27, 1876)*

## In a Fearfully Chaotic State

What have we written, any way, for the People's Paper within the past month? Through some unaccountable dereliction in somebody's duty, the paper does not come to us, and we are too busy to recall what has or has not been chronicled. *[We will answer that whatever "ye chief" may have written, nothing from her has reached the office during the past month or more, but a single chapter of story.—Ed.]*

Did we tell you of a visit to Tenafly, New Jersey, to the home of grand Elizabeth Cady Stanton, where she and our beloved Susan B. Anthony are at work upon the "History of the Suffrage Movement," which is to surprise the world with its wonderful details of woman's struggles for liberty?[10]

The home of Mrs. Stanton is an elegant country villa, with beautiful grounds and pleasant drives, situated in the hills of New Jersey, where, at the time of our visit, the autumn leaves were aglow with a holocaust of glory. . . .

Mrs. Stanton is a trifle stouter, a trifle graver, and even more beautiful than she was four or five years ago. Her husband is jolly and genial, her sons and daughters, ditto. Their home is the abode of hospitality and order. . . .

Then, did we write you about having lectured by invitation before the Liberal Club of New York, of which Horace Greeley was first President, and with which most of the eminent men of the city are in some way connected? There was a fine audience, and an hour's address, followed by a lengthy discussion upon the Woman Question. The Club decided that we "got away with it," and honored us with an invitation to lecture again, which we courteously declined, thinking it better to quit while our credit was good.

Then we visited Orange, New Jersey, Dr. [Clemence] Lozier's country residence. Did we tell you anything about that?

You see, dear sage associate [editor], how badly at sea we are when we don't get the papers. That story [*Edna and John: A Romance of Idaho Flat*] worries us *awfully*. We have no copy of it, can't get the back papers, don't remember the names of the characters, and are going it blind to keep the boys in copy; so we are making bricks with straw. We dreamed the other night that copy failed to reach you in time, too, which isn't strange, seeing mail doesn't come this way regularly. The postal service is in a fearfully chaotic state somewhere.

New York, November 1, 1876.

A. J. D.

*(November 17, 1876)*

## What Cares the World for Our Domestic Sorrows?

Between conflicting emotions of joy and sorrow we again essay to write you. We are glad because our book [*David and Anna Matson*] is done; glad because the critics like it; glad because there is a prospect that it will pay its way; glad, thrice glad, because we're going home! But oh, so sorry that we had to be absent when Willis left the parental roof! It seemed we couldn't live and bear it. The one simple paragraph [*NNW*, 10 Nov. 1876], announcing that the boy who had been for three years foreman on the *New Northwest*, who had set type on every issue thus far, and who had now plumed his pinions and betaken himself to San Francisco, there to carve a career of his own, meant very little to the general reader, but oh, so much to us! Important literary work was before us and we had no time for the luxury of grief. What cares the world for domestic sorrows, and why should we intrude them here?

New York, November 23, 1876.

A. J. D.

P.S.—We don't often add a postscript, but it is necessary to state that the National Woman Suffrage Association has changed our name, or, rather, resumed a part of our maiden one, and with the first of January the *New Northwest* will do likewise.

*(December 15, 1876)*

## New Teeth and Bald Heads

[W]e've patronized the Machesney [McChesney] dentists,[11] three brothers who do the largest business of this kind in Chicago, and they have succeeded in making a partial plate to fill the gaps in our bicuspids, and so forth, which hardship made in them in Oregon before dentists were, *and we can wear the plate.* As this is the fourth experiment of the kind by as many dental firms, and the first that has succeeded, we desire Oregonians in passing through Chicago to always patronize these dentists. They make full sets of teeth for $8.00, and are getting rich, because everybody needs teeth and can afford them at the price. If somebody next door would go into the wig business, and supply the capillary substance equally cheap, that would prevent toothless masculines from looking on the top-head like frost-bitten watermelons, they would soon find themselves equally prosperous, for two-thirds of the men everywhere are as bald as eagles. Toothless people are scarce, thanks to dentists, but bald-headed men are plentiful and no thanks to anybody.

Chicago, December 12, 1876.

A. J. D.

*(December 29, 1876)*

# Notes for 1876

1. The Rev. Dong Gong, the first convert of the San Francisco Baptist Mission, arrived in Portland in November of 1874 to help establish and teach in the Baptist Mission School for Chinese, initially held in rented rooms of the Good Templars Building. *The NNW* reported that this English language school, aided by the volunteer teaching of several young men and women of Portland, promised to be a success. The school was open every evening, except Thursday, with an average attendance of about thirty (*NNW*, 23 April 1875). Later that year, however, when Dong Gong, a regular ordained minister of the Baptist Church, tried to preach on a Portland street corner, his efforts were unappreciated by other Chinese, and police had to protect him from the angry crowd (*NNW*, 13 Aug. 1875). By 1876, Dong Gong was clearly unpopular with some in the Portland Chinese community for his stand against Chinese brothels, and he was running a school for English language instruction in Olympia, Washington Territory. *The NNW* reported that the people of Portland were shocked to learn in 1880 that "Miss Mitchell, a teacher in the Chinese mission school, has married Dong Gong, one of her pupils. The twain have gone to San Francisco, and will proceed to Honolulu" (*NNW*, 23 Dec. 1880). For more about Dong Gong, see Daniel Liestman, "'To Win Redeemed Souls from Heathen Darkness," *Western Historical Quarterly* 24 (May 1993): 181-82; and Robert Edward Wynne, "Reaction to the Chinese in the Pacific Northwest and British Columbia, 1850 to 1910," Ph.D. diss., University of Washington, 1964: 87.

2. Captain William Renton, born in 1818, was hardly "old"—only about 58—when Duniway visited his mill. Renton came to Washington Territory in 1853 and was considered one of the most successful pioneers of the Sound. He began cutting lumber at his sawmill at Port Blakely in 1864. By 1874, the firm was Renton, Holmes & Co., with Renton supervising the mill operations and Charles S. Holmes handling the marketing out of San Francisco. Although the mill was twice destroyed by fire, it grew to be one of the largest mills in the world. Renton's company owned schooners for transporting lumber, held some 80,000 acres of timber, and ran round the clock, with electric lights for the night shift. During the years of 1885-95, the company had about twelve hundred workers. See Ruth Kirk and Carmela Alexander, *Exploring Washington's Past: A Road Guide to History* (Seattle: University of Washington Press, 1989), 370-71; Clinton A. Snowden, *History of Washington*, Vol. IV (NY: Century History Assoc., 1909), 354-56.

3. Despite his reputation as a scalawag and a womaniser, U. S. Senator John Hipple Mitchell (1835-1905) was Duniway's strongest political ally for woman suffrage, and their lasting association was beneficial for both. Mitchell, whose actual surname was Hipple, came from Pennsylvania to Portland in 1860 and was a successful attorney and Republican politician, serving many years in the United States Senate, 1873-79; 1885-97; 1901-05. During his first term, he was charged in the Senate with financial dishonesty and bigamy, while living under an assumed name. In June of 1873, when the charges could not be ignored and public sympathy was clearly with Mitchell's wronged second wife, Duniway continued to support him but suggested that he should atone for his sins ("Repentance and Restitution," *NNW*, 20 June 1873). Judge Matthew Deady noted in his diary for the same month: "Read local papers in Library on Hipple case. They are beginning to speak out on the bigamy question. The *Oregonian* wants to know about Hipples [*sic*] opinions on polygamy in Utah" (*Pharisee Among Philistines*, 129).

When Mitchell had his assumed name (actually his mother's maiden name) legalized and obtained a divorce from the wife he had abandoned in Pennsylvania, the scandal was quieted; however, he was later accused of a relationship with the sister of his second wife and continually charged with corruption in office and mercenary financial dealings, including land fraud and bribery. Harvey Scott of *The Oregonian* attempted to expose and defeat Mitchell, but Duniway remained faithful. Following the return of Mitchell to the Senate in 1885, Duniway wrote: "The *New Northwest* never forgets a favor. It never forgets that when other men who are now its friends turned the cold shoulder to its struggles to secure for women liberty, John. H. Mitchell stood by it with unflinching bravery. He did this, too, at a time when it was a political detriment to him to do so" ("And on Beyond the Railroad," *NNW*, 26 Nov. 1885).

4. Ann Roelofson Scott (1811-52), Duniway's mother, died of "plains cholera" on June 20, 1852. She was married at the age of nineteen to John Tucker Scott and bore twelve children, a case of what Duniway referred to as "excessive maternity." Prior to the Scott family's departure for Oregon in the spring of 1852, three babies—two sons and a daughter—were buried in Illinois graves. Ann's own gravesite was near Laramie Peak on the Platte River, Wyoming Territory. William ("Willie") Neill Scott (1848-52), youngest of the Scott children, died on August 27, 1852, two months following his mother's death, and he was buried in the Burnt River Valley on the Oregon Trail.

5. John McDonald, about age twenty-one and Abigail Scott's "beau," drowned on July 30 1852, in the swift and cold Snake River, in what is now Central Idaho. He had joined the Scott party at St. Joseph, Missouri, and hailed from Mt. Sterling, Brown County, Illinois. On the date of the tragic accident, Abigail recorded in her journal that McDonald had gone into the river after the Scott's stampeding cattle, and "he was carried down the river by the current and drowned!" He was, she added, "a worthy young man; and being sociable affectionate and accommodating he won the esteem of all, and was beloved by all who knew him" ("Journal of a Trip to Oregon," 30 July 1852).

6. When Duniway made this trip to Utah Territory, Emmeline B. Wells was sharing editorial responsibilities with Louisa Lula Greene Richards, who founded the *Woman's Exponent* in 1872 and was editor until 1877. Upon the retirement of Richards, Wells assumed the editorship of this semi-monthly periodical for Mormon women and continued in that position until 1914, when she was eighty-six. See Sherilyn Cox Bennion, "*The New Northwest* and *Woman's Exponent*: Early Voices for Suffrage," *Journalism Quarterly* 54 (Summer 1977): 286-92; and "The *Woman's Exponent*: Forty-two Years of Speaking for Women," *Utah Historical Quarterly* 44 (Summer 1976): 222-39.

7. Mary Ashton Rice Livermore (1820-1905) was active in volunteer work with the Sanitary Commission during the Civil War and later became a leader in both the temperance and woman suffrage movements. She began her own suffrage paper, the *Agitator*, in early 1869, and represented Illinois at the founding of the American Woman Suffrage Association. At the urging of Lucy Stone and other AWSA leaders, she moved to Boston and merged her paper with the new *Woman's Journal*, which she edited until 1872. Livermore then joined Redpath's professional lecture circuit and became one of his most popular speakers, a "Queen of the Platform."

Lucy Stone (1818-93), one of the most impressive speakers of her era, graduated from Oberlin in 1847 and was soon appointed an abolitionist lecturer with the American Anti-Slavery Society.

Her commitment to speaking for women led to Stone's involvement in the women's rights movement, and she lectured on woman suffrage as far west as Missouri, into Canada, and in the South. On one of her lecture tours, Stone met Henry Browne Blackwell, an abolitionist from Cincinatti and brother to pioneer women physicians Elizabeth and Emily Blackwell. The couple married in 1855 and, to signify her full independence, even in a marital relationship, Stone retained her own name, calling herself "Mrs. Stone." In 1869, when the American Equal Rights Association split over how to respond to the Fifteenth Amendment, Stone, Blackwell, Julia Ward Howe, and others formed the American Woman Suffrage Association, with headquarters at Boston. When Mary Livermore resigned as editor of the AWSA's *Woman's Journal*, Stone and Blackwell, and later their daughter Alice Stone Blackwell, assumed editorial responsibility. In her private life, Lucy Stone lived with the knowledge that Henry Ward Beecher was not the only prominent man to be involved in an extramarital affair; Blackwell was involved for years with Abby Hutchinson Patton, wife of Ludlow Patton, a prominent stockbroker (Goldsmith, *Other Powers*, 184-85; 200; 335).

Julia Ward Howe (1819-1910) is best known for the "Battle Hymn of the Republic" (1862), but she was also a leader in the suffrage movement. With Lucy Stone, Howe formed the New England Woman Suffrage Association in 1868, and she was one of the founders of the American Woman Suffrage Association the next year. As a leading spirit in the AWSA, Howe often spoke at conventions and legislative hearings. She, like Duniway, was a member of the 1889 committee that negotiated the merger of the AWSA and the NWSA.

8. Maria Mitchell (1818-89) was the astronomer who discovered a new comet—"Miss Mitchell's Comet"—on Oct. 1, 1847, and the next year she was the first woman elected to the American Academy of Arts and Sciences in Boston. Mitchell was hired in 1865 by Matthew Vassar, a wealthy brewer and founder of Vassar Female College, as a member of the school's first faculty. When Duniway heard Maria Mitchell speak in 1876, the professor had published widely on sunspots and faculae, solar eclipses, and changes on the planetary surfaces, particularly of Jupiter and Saturn. She had also been on two trips abroad to exchange research with European scientists and to visit the Russian observatory at Pulkova.

9. Dr. Clemence Harned Lozier (1813-88) was a medical doctor and an advocate for woman suffrage. After the death of her first husband, Abraham W. Lozier, she pursued her interests in female health and anatomy and graduated with highest honors from Syracuse Medical College in 1853. She established a successful practice in New York City, with a specialty in obstectrics and general surgery for women, and was soon giving lectures on women's physiology and health. With the assistance of Elizabeth Cady Stanton, Lozier convinced the state legislature to charter her New York Medical College and Hospital for Women in 1863. From her substantial income, Lozier made generous contributions to the suffrage movement and was president of the NWSA in 1877-78. In 1878, Lozier went into bankruptcy when her medical college and hospital were moved, against her wishes, to an expensive site.

The doctor was a favorite of Duniway, and she often stayed at Lozier's home when she visited the East. Duniway described Lozier as "a little, plump, pretty, gentle-voiced lady, with short white curls framing a face as classic as the Madonna's," who carried on her "very extensive practice, with the skill and dexterity of a Pasteur, or a Koch" ("Eminent Women I Have Met," Speech to the State Federation of Women's Clubs, Pendleton, OR, 2 June 1900, Duniway Papers). In 1876, Lozier hosted "a literary reception" for Duniway to celebrate publication of *David and Anna Matson*. At this event, Duniway read the poem "to a select circle," including Susan B. Anthony, Matilda Joslyn Gage, Lillie Devereux Blake, and others (*NNW*, 3 Dec. 1876). The next year, Duniway published one of Lozier's lectures ("Lecture Delivered by Dr. Clemence S. Lozier at the Annual Reunion of the New York Medical College for Women, Oct. 14, 1876," *NNW*, 22 June 1877).

10. *The History of Woman Suffrage* grew to be a massive work of six volumes, with Stanton, Anthony, and Matilda Joslyn Gage as editors of the first three volumes; Anthony and Ida Husted Harper as editors of volume 4; and Harper as editor of volumes 5 and 6. In 1881, when the first volume was published, *The NNW* reported that Duniway had received a large shipment of the "handsome royal octavo volume of over 900 pages of rare, racy and valuable reading" (*NNW*, 13 Oct. 1881). The book could be ordered from Duniway for $5.00 in cloth or $6.50 in sheep.

11. The McChesney dentists of Chicago, who appear more than once in *The NNW*, were clearly Duniway's favorite dentists and saved her considerable discomfort. The three brothers were evidently related to Margaret McChesney, sister-in-law of Duniway and the second wife of Harvey Scott. Margaret and Harvey were married on June 28, 1876, at Latrobe, Pennsylvania, six months before Duniway first visited the dentists in Chicago and promoted their dentistry in her newspaper.

# 1877

## Nearly Prostrate

The lecture work at Springfield [Illinois] of which we wrote you left us so nearly prostrate that lying by for repairs was necessarily in order. Now, if there is anything we have no patience with, it's ourself when an invalid. It isn't hard for us to be a friend to other folks when they're unable to be on duty, but when we glance in the mirror at a hundred and fifty pounds of anything but feeble looking *avoirdupois*, and reflect that there is always a demand upon the hands and brain those pounds sustain that requires constant health and active effort, and then we see the overworked machine break down in spite of its ponderous proportions, while the demands upon it never "let up" for an instant, we go so desperate that if we were not a Christian there's no telling what we might try to do. . . .

An appointment was made for a lecture in Chicago on Sunday, the 11th, but the meeting was unfortunately sandwiched between [Henry Ward] Beecher in the morning and [Victoria] Woodhull in the evening, so the audience, through appreciative, was small, as compared to other facilities.

Council Bluffs, Iowa, Feb. 17, 1877.
A. J. D.

*(March 9, 1877)*

## At Salt Lake Again

It was almost night when the long westward-bound train took up its slow line of progression. Laramie, sitting flat upon a sandy pile, surrounded by eternal mountains, smiled a sweet good-bye, and we were soon bumping over the Union Pacific rails in an upper berth, below which were a crying baby, a fretful mother, and a man that snored. What a pity that anybody should travel till the novelty wears off. . . .

It was again night, and we found ourself at Ogden. Here we took train for Salt Lake, where we were soon at home in the Townsend House, a Mormon hotel of quaint construction and interminable corridors, where we remained for a week among Mormons and Gentiles alike. The minister in charge of the Methodist Church kindly tendered us the same for morning and evening services, and we felt like we were getting among Christians again when we got to quarters where men did not deem it necessary to protect God from women with locks and keys. . . .

Such a scramble [in Utah] for tickets and sleeping cars as we had on the Central Pacific Railroad! At last, after a line of men as long as the Pentateuch had given way one by one, each bearing the magic number that entitled him to a lower "section," the women got a draw, and the berth of the undersigned was over the red-hot stove, where she caught a cold through being literally roasted.

The track was icy between Ogden and Corinne, and we were on an upgrade when the iron horse balked. The engineer let the load drag the snorting beast backward for several hundred yards, and then spurred him ahead with steam and flame, but in spite of straining and panting on the part of the beast, and spurring and swearing on the part of the driver, the train remained on a dead lock, till they were compelled to cut her in twain and make two trips to get her to the summit.

This was delay number one. Number two occurred in the foothills of the Sierra Nevada, by a freight train jumping the track, and detaining us seven hours before the blockade could be raised.

This brought us to San Francisco after one o'clock Saturday morning, where, when daylight came and night printers came forth from their lairs, we found a dear member of our own family band, and were soon engaged in gathering up the links that time had dropped during nine [ten] long months of separation.

To-day we start to San Jose, and the next steamer but one will take us to the waiting ones at home.

March 12, 1877.

A. J. D.

*(March 23, 1877)*

## Home in Portland

Home at last! Thank heaven! . . .

The new propeller "City of Chester" was on her trial trip, and made a slow, tedious voyage. She is a nice, well-furnished little boat, about large enough for a good bathtub, and rolls like a log studded with barnacles.

*The Portland waterfront, with Stark Street ferry at right, prior to the construction of bridges in 1887*

To be two days longer than usual in making the voyage, when we were on the "home stretch," was terrific, yet it had to be endured, and all made the best of it.

Home! and such a greeting! Good reader, if we ever get away from home on another journey of ten months' duration you may suspend the *New Northwest* and write us down as a lunatic.

A. J. D.

*(April 6, 1877)*

## A Fall in the Oregon Mud

Saturday morning was ushered in by a drizzling rain. But the clouds coquetted with the sun and gave a half promise to retire before ten o'clock, and sundry picnickers, our liege with Clyde, Ralph, and self included, started by train for New Era, whither the undersigned had been invited to "orate.". . .

But oh, the rain! the rain! True it didn't come down by buckets, as in New York, nor by hogsheads, as in Illinois, nor yet by rivers, as in Nebraska, but it came to *wet*, as the sodden earth and dripping foliage everywhere attested. . . .

[The next day] at four o'clock we embarked in an open boat for Thomas Buckman's farm, three miles up the river, on the Delectable Mountains, where all parties retired at a late hour, with the skies as clear as crystal, giving promise of a nipping frost. But morning brought, instead, another blinding, driving rain. What could be done? We had to go home; but how? A bright idea struck our liege. We would go back to New Era in the small boat and take the morning train, and ourself and boys would hail the "Fannie Patton" at ten o'clock.

Now, good lady reader, if you want more fun than you can ever pay for, just try running down a slippery side hill for a quarter of a mile in a pouring rain, the mud over your shoes at every step, while you clutch your Sunday clothes with both hands and let your best hat catch the storm. Then, when you're over the worst of it, and turn to look after the boat, and find yourself sprawling in the mud, with your head downwards and your body at an angle of forty-five degrees, and you pick yourself up and go blundering on, while your smallest boy in following falls flat also and raises a pitiful cry for the aid you can't give him—if you don't think a circus is tame forever after, you've a poor appreciation for enjoyment, that's all.

But the dear old boat 'hove to, and a slippery plank was made to span a slippery space, and we, with slippery feet, passed over it, while our good friends, the Buckmans, bade us God speed, and we steamed down the river, wet, muddy and jubilant.

*(June 1, 1877)*

### An Apology for Sickness

We have an apology to make, and of all things deplorable upon the face of the earth we do detest apologies, and we are never compelled to make one but we're shamed of it.

Looking back through thirty odd years of active effort, we see the first foundation of all the apologies we've ever been compelled to make for periodical attacks of sickness. . . .

We first "broke down" at the age of seven by gathering flax from a blue grass lawn, under the vigilant eye of an honored grandfather, who kept our youthful spine in a bent position by vigorous reminders of duty from morning till night, one day, under the old-time impression that children never need tools to work with, (if they happen to be girls), and never need rest under any conditions. A common garden rake in our puny hands on that occasion would have saved us years of subsequent suffering.

Then, when we were nine, we sodded the paternal door-yard with blue grass, a job requiring the strength of a man; yet we never knew till many years of womanhood's experience had come to teach us wisdom that our constantly recurring periods of illness through a life of active toil could be traced to early periodic overwork. . . .

The constant effort upon our part in later years to sustain the finances of our mission brings us down with fits of illness every week or two. Then we lay by and rally. . . . [A]nd we're shamed of overwork and all the consequent failure that comes of it.

Portland, June 18, 1877.

A. J. D.

*(June 22, 1877)*

### Travel with Clyde, Age Ten

After returning last week to Astoria, as we had planned, and making a few days' successful canvass in the interest of the People's Paper, we went aboard the little butter firken of a steamer called the "General Canby," and headed for Fort Stevens, Sand Island, Cape Hancock and Baker's Bay. The tide was low when the whistle sounded for "all aboard" at Captain Gray's new dock, and a gang-plank ten inches wide was placed with one end upon the solid piling, and the other at an angle of forty-five degrees upon the roof of the pilot-house, and upon this rocking, rollicking little board, that looked for all the world like a faded, cross-barred ribbon, we tremulously planted our palpitating *avoirdupois*, said our prayers, and descended to the subterranean regions of the tiny craft and took a seat behind the wheel, profoundly astonished that we hadn't departed from the little gang-plank to the briny deep that surged below and around us.

An hour and a half of puffing, whistling, and laboring on the part of the tiny craft, and we had "done" the dock at Fort Stevens, cruised off Sand Island, touched at Cape Hancock, and fetched up at the dock at Baker's Bay. . . . The next day we embarked in one of J. L. Stout's mail coaches for Sea View, three or four miles distant, across the peninsula that connects Cape Hancock with the rest of Washington Territory.

*Such* a road! Bump, thrash, crash, jolt, bang! Corduroy and common sense! Up hill and down hill; over rocks and ridges; through antediluvian forests; amid ferns and brakes and sallal berries; through tangled dells and past purling springlets we go, and after a while, when our spinal columns are telescoped and our back hair all shaken down, behold us (for there are ladies in the coach), forgetting all our miseries as we come face to face with the hoary ocean, as he dashes his tangled head upon the gravelly shore line, and washes for aye the feet of the earth, with her embroidery of drift wood and undulating drapery of eternal green. . . .

We had intended to pursue our journey this time to Oysterville, but circumstances prevented, so we returned to-day to Astoria in the "Varma," a battered little cradle of a steamer, which stems the waves like a cockle-shell.

Clyde was sea-sick, and the undersigned was ditto. The child played on the beach, bathed in the surf, dug clams, and built sand forts till exhausted before embarking, else he thinks he wouldn't have been upset. As it was, the velvet of his ears grew white, his lips turned pale, his great eyes grew luminous as the boat rocked restlessly, and at last he lolled over against his miserable mother like a sick kitten against a jaundiced canine.

But he's all right now. He's sleeping in our quiet chamber at the Parker House, like a weary infant, while we're scribbling these jottings to keep typos in copy, with our weary brain continually dancing attendance upon the bounding billows that seem to surge around us till the hotel transforms itself into a cockle-shell, the bed-room into a pilot-house, and Clyde's regular breathing into the respirations of a laboring engine.[1]

Astoria, August 13, 1877.

A. J. D.

*(August 17, 1877)*

## Back to Portland

Our stay in Astoria was cut short on Thursday of last week by a desire to give "ye sage associate" [Catherine Scott Coburn] a holiday. Yet we remained long enough, after that "sea-sick" epistle of last Monday was written, to canvass several new quarters for the People's Paper, with very satisfactory results. . . .

Six P.M. and home. The serial story must be written, countless buttons must be sewed on the clothing of the small boys, who will persist, boy like, in tearing them off; bills must be sent to delinquents here and there; plums must be made into jelly, or they'll get too ripe to be managed; callers must be met, editorials written, exchanges read and clipped and credited; beds must be made, and rooms swept and dusted—but stay; if we should tell you half we are trying to do, you'd fail to believe any of it, so pray excuse us this time.

We go to Salem to-morrow (Wednesday), to attend the Teachers' Institute, and next week, if we're still alive to carry on our work and "ye associate's," you shall hear again from A. J. D.

Portland, August 21, 1877.

*(August 24, 1877)*


## At the Teachers' Institute in Salem

[B]ehold us, on Wednesday morning, aboard the east-side train, bound Salemward.

Dame Nature has changed her spring-time robe of emerald green for a demi-train of russet-brown, with overskirt and banner of canary and amber color, and a mantle of purple, trimmed profusely with ripened wheat ears. Her head-dress is purple, golden and scarlet fruitage, and she carries a magnificent bouquet of sun flowers, golden rods and china asters. . . .

[T]he Teachers' Institute is in council. Entering [the legislative hall] we behold a fine array of the professional element, the feminine predominating in numbers and intellect, and the masculine bearing the palm of power and pay. . . .

The chairman is a natty little body, about the size of an ordinary popinjay, and as dignified as a bantam rooster. How he came to be elected to the position deponent knoweth not. Certain it is that he presided well when no knowledge of parliamentary law was needed; and when it was needed, Miss Hodgden, the efficient vice-president, was near by to prompt him, and he got along first rate. . . .

We were especially gratified with the number, culture, and intelligence of the lady teachers. The most of them are yet timid about attempting extemporaneous speaking, but a proportion of them, equal, at least, to the men who usually monopolize the speaking on such occasions, will gradually acquire the habit. Readiness in off-hand debate is a requisite qualification for a first-rate teacher of either sex. . . .

Saturday we spent in rest and calls and writing; and when evening came we gladly greeted a goodly multitude in the Opera House, to whom we discoursed, after our own humble fashion, upon "Law and Liberty."

Salem, August 26, 1877.

A. J. D.

*(August 31, 1877)*

## End of Volume VI

Good readers of the *New Northwest*, we make our best bows to you this morning with a happy heart. As a journalist, we are six years old. Though the paper was started the first week in May, 1871, we suffered one delay of two and a half months in '73 through illness in the family. It has always been our custom to give the typos and all other hands a holiday during State Fair week, and, as fifty-two numbers constitute a year's subscription, the changing seasons have glided over gaps enough to bring the anniversary up to the second week in September, in 1877.

In looking back through the departed years, we cannot but wonder that strength has been given us to carry the business over some of the roughest places. We were as ignorant of the details of journalism in the outset as a child. Not a member of our family had ever had a particle of newspaper experience. The boys, upon whom the mechanical department was to depend, were young and wholly untaught; men could charge us what they pleased for labor and material, and teach the typos just such rules as suited them . . . ; the expenses were double what they ought to have been for a couple of years, until we saddled this concern with a nightmare of debt, out of which we have been slowly crawling ever since the tide began to turn, while interest has all the while been eating into our earnings, like a death-watch eating into a shattered wall.

Public opinion was against the idea of our mission; women who wanted to assist us could not, and those who could would not, so our work oftentimes so deflected from the main object, while we "meddled" in politics, that men of all parties became anxious to patronize our efforts; and thus the *New Northwest* grew to be a permanent institution, popular and respected. . . . The paper's indebtedness on the subscription year just closed, as elsewhere stated, is $106. Who will put shoulder to the wheel and help us through this mire?

*(September 7, 1877)*

## Letter from Miss Anthony

To the Editor of the *New Northwest*:

Are you never going to speak to me again? It seems an age since I saw a pen track of yours, but I see the *New Northwest* every Tuesday, A.M., regularly now, and have read "Martha Marblehead" [serial story] thus far to my dear mother, aged almost eighty-four. What a hardheaded old flint you do make of that Senior Marblehead!

Do make the *New Northwest* bristle all over with the Sixteenth Amendment.

I shall give the last four weeks prior to election in Colorado to canvassing there. Can't get out of it. I go without promise of pay, even for traveling expenses, just as I went to Kansas in '67, and Michigan in '74. If women had *money* they might move the world. But they are making this fight with hands tied financially, as well as politically. Now, if Colorado votes No, I shall say to the States Right's plan, *Three times and out.* But we *must* push the national work, and this can be done more effectually by petitions from [*sic*] the Sixteenth Amendment than by any other method. In haste and affection,

Susan B. Anthony
Rochester, N. Y., August 19, 1877.

*(September 7, 1877)*

# Suffrage Work for Everybody

Circulate petitions for a 16th Amendment, to enfranchise the women, *not of one State alone,* but of all the States and Territories. Woman's right to a voice in the government under which she lives is a natural right, and must be guaranteed to her by the Federal Constitution. Now is our time to knock at the doors of Congress and plant this right deep in the fundamental law of the land.

Petitions for a Sixteenth Amendment, for woman's enfranchisement, from 10,000 United States citizens, from twenty-two States, have been presented in open House and Senate by 31 Representatives and 29 Senators since January 19, 1877. . . . Circulate this petition through the autumn and winter up to January 10, 1878. . . .

Cut this out, and paste it at the head of a piece of paper and go to work. Put the names of the men on the right and women on the left of your petition, and trace every name carefully in ink.

## PETITION FOR WOMAN SUFFRAGE

*To the Senate and House of Representatives, in Congress assembled:—*

The undersigned, citizens of the United States, residents of the State of____, county of ____, town of ____, earnestly pray your honorable body to adopt measures for so amending the Constitution as to prohibit the several States from disfranchising United States citizens on account of sex.

*(September 7, 1877)*

# At a Jewish Celebration

The other day, as we were passing the Jewish Synagogue [Beth Israel], opposite the Episcopal Church, between Fifth and Sixth streets, we chanced to meet the Rabbi, Rev. Dr. [Moses] May, and, in response to his invitation, found our way back at ten A.M. on the day following, to witness the celebration of the Jewish New Year.[2]

The little chapel was well filled with an array of worshippers, the men all with hats on, and many with books in their hands, and in the pulpit, flanked on either side by officers of the Synagogue, stood the Rabbi, in a gown of silk and velvet, with a priestly turban upon his shapely head, and a clerical appearance that was vastly becoming.

We were kindly ushered to a front seat, behind a row of well-mannered little boys, with hats on, in imitation of their sires, and were soon lost in the words of the preacher. The discourse was one which we would gladly hear in every Christian pulpit in the city. It was able, well-worded, deep, plain, concise, logical, fearless, progressive, and eloquent, occupying an hour in delivery, followed by an hour's musical and devotional exercises, in which a choir at one end of the church responded at intervals to the melody of the preacher's voice, awakening echoes of patriarchal days which yet linger in our memory, as we shut our eyes and think it all over.

We noted one peculiarity, aside from the wearing of hats by men and boys, we do not see in Christian churches, that is reprehensible. We allude to reading during service by the young people, and occasional irreverent whispering and laughter. This habit should be corrected, as it results from thoughtlessness rather than ill nature on the part of those indulging in it.

The Rabbi is a gentleman of thorough culture, and his rendering of the English tongue is surprisingly accurate, considering the fact that he has not been long in America, and was ignorant of the language when he came to our shores. Evidently he is a close student, and we should like all people who believe nobody to be right but themselves to go and see and hear what he is doing among his people.

*(September 14, 1877)*

## Lecture at Palouse

Palouse City [W. T.] sits on a hill, hard by the river whose name it bears, and presents even a newer appearance than Colfax, with its numerous box-houses, unfinished and yet occupied, not the least being a hotel, where we found primitive accommodations with an obliging landlord and capable landlady, who partitioned us a bed-room with carpets, up-stairs among the starts, and gave us food as nicely cooked as in the Palmer House of Chicago, at the low price of twenty-five cents a meal.

The dining room of the hotel was chosen for the lecture, and the people had gathered in from every direction and filled it densely, and the speech was fairly begun when *crack* went the floor, and *smash* went the benches, and *down* went the people into the cellar below, leaving the under-signed well-braced against a tottering partition to prevent it knocking her on the head. Luckily nobody was hurt, but the confusion was indescribable.

The fallen and frightened crowd after a while emerged from the cellar through the *debris*, somebody lifted the partition from the burdened shoulders of the speaker, and we all repaired to another room, where the lecture was resumed amid a general feeling of thankfulness that nobody had been injured. By morning the break was repaired and everybody was happy.

Lewiston, Idaho, November 15, 1877.

A. J. D.

*(November 30, 1877)*

## Notes for 1877

1. Clyde Duniway (1866-1944) was the fourth of Duniway's five sons and, as indicated in her letters to him, her favorite son—her "Coydie." She wrote to him: "Since you are the only one of my sons who has at all fulfilled my early ambition in regard to a classical education, I naturally feel an absorbing interest in whatever you undertake" (ASD to Clyde Duniway, 31 Jan. 1893, Duniway Papers). Clyde attended the University of Oregon during his freshman year and graduated from Cornell with his younger brother, Ralph, who became a lawyer. Clyde did his graduate work at Harvard, taught there for a year, and was employed by Henry Clay Frick, the Pennsylvania millionaire who was general manager of Carnegie Steel Company. As home secretary to Frick and tutor of Frick's only son, Clyde traveled with the Frick family in the United States and abroad. After completing graduate work at Harvard, Clyde became a professor of American History at Stanford and was made department chair. Later he held university presidencies at the University of Montana at Missoula, the University of Wyoming, and Colorado College at Colorado Springs. His last professorship was at Carleton College.

2. Moses May was rabbi at Portland's Beth Israel, 1872 80. The Congregation Beth Israel was formed in Portland in 1858, and its first building was constructed six years later. In November of 1880, Rabbi May's house burned down while he was away from home. His wife and children barely escaped, and "his valuable library was totally destroyed" (*NNW*, 4 Nov. 1880). May was evidently a physician, and *The NNW* reported in 1881 that "Dr. May, formerly Rabbi of the Synagogue Beth Israel in Portland, is in The Dalles, engaged in the drug business" and advertising "for a lady physician as partner" (*NNW*, 5 May 1881). According to a later news item, "Rev. M. May, formerly rabbi of the Synagogue Beth Israel in this city, became insane in San Francisco last week, and was sent to the asylum at Stockton" (*NNW*, 11 May 1882).

# 1878

## Ladies' Relief Society

The other day a destitute woman came to us, as they do almost every week, in search of employment for herself and a young girl. We promised to see what could be done, and in the meantime directed her to call upon the president of the Ladies' Relief to get her babe, a boy of two years, taken care of at the Orphans' Home. In a few days she returned, and, with the assistance of the matron at the Helpers' Home, a situation was procured for her daughter. But the president of the Orphans' Home would not agree to receive her baby unless she could pay ten dollars per month for its keeping. So, while she has tramped the city in search of wages from day to day, we learn that that little child has been left at home, alone, in a shanty in the suburbs, without fire, and almost without food. Up to the time of going to press we have not learned whether or not the mother has secured a place where she can find work that will enable her to pay the Ladies' Relief, this benevolent institution, for keeping her child, and yet there are hundreds of dollars in its treasury.

We think the matron of the Home should have discretionary power in all such cases. . . . The Ladies Relief Society has done and is doing some good, but it is not doing what ought to be and could be done by one honest woman, untrammeled by the others.

*(January 11, 1878)*

## Ankle Deep in Milwaukie Mud

It was Friday evening, and we took train for Milwaukie, [Oregon]. . . . The ride to Milwaukie station is a short one; fare, two bits. The walk from the station to the village is a long one; fare, mud and water. We lingered a while at the home of good Mrs. Van Rensaeller, at the station, and then, supposing we had ample time to reach the village proper before nightfall, started, valise in hand, to pick our pedestrian way along a road that the speedily falling night soon made as black as Egyptian darkness.

For a while we were enabled to see the muddiest places, and, with care, avoid them, but the short twilight came to an end, and then came a tussle for solid *terra firma* that would have been laughable to a disinterested owl, or any other bird or beast that might see in the dark. We swamped, and pulled a shoe-string in twain;

swamped again, and dropped the valise; groped and found it and floundered on, reassuring ourself by saying audibly, as we thought sympathetically of the restless ocean:

"I, too, am a wave on a stormy sea,
I, too, am a wanderer, driven like thee.
I, too, am seeking a distant land,
To be lost and gone, ere I reach the strand."

Bye-and-bye a glimmer appeared in the darkness here and there, betokening human habitations, but we were as uncertain of our course as we were certain of the mud. A man passed not far off, carrying some hay and a lantern.

"Can you direct me to Miller's boarding-house?" we asked, panting from fatigue and timidity.

"Over yonder, across the street, where you see two lighted windows," said our benefactor.

Ah, that street crossing! Ankle deep, if an inch, and one shoe-string broken! Luckily, we remembered the wife of Sally Dillard's cousin, and imitated her example. "We h'isted coats and waded it," but what of that? Can't you see such a sight at any hour of the day on a street crossing in Portland? . . .

Saturday evening we met a good audience in the district school-house, and broke the bread of the gospel of liberty for a waiting and eager multitude.

A. J. D.

*(January 25, 1878)*

# A Case of Wife-Beating

Last week we expressed our opinion upon the subject of wife-beating, and showed the practical reasons why beaten wives are proverbially averse to testifying against their husbands and getting themselves fined, as well as whipped, through their testimony. We now present a case in point.

A man named John Gately lives out on the canyon road above Portland, whose wife was induced to complain against him for violence. The wife in this case had no money to pay the fine, and the husband was sent to the lock-up for twenty-six days. After being liberated, he procured a bottle of whisky and went home very drunk, and accused her of having him arrested, and swore he would take her life.

In his rage he drove her from the house, and compelled her to pass the night in the woods; and she states that he would since have killed her outright, but for the interference of the neighbors. She is in constant fear of her life, and has been directed to visit the magistrate and have her protector and head bound over to keep the peace. Such a man has no more business running at large than a rabid dog or a wild hyena. Much less business has he to make the laws for sober wives and mothers to abide by and pay taxes to support in the shape of fines for getting whipped.

*(March 29, 1878)*

## Bon Voyage to Yet Another Son

Some eighteen months ago W. [Willis] S. Duniway, for four years foreman in this office, having finished his course at school, took his departure for the Golden City, where he has since been regularly employed as a compositor on the *Morning Call*. And now, his younger brother, Hubert R., follows, intending also to remain an indefinite period. Both have performed their duties in this office faithfully and well, and they go forth in the world's battle armed with a good profession with which to work their way according to their destiny. The loves [*sic*] and prayers of those at home accompany them.

*(April 5, 1878)*

## At the Oregon Penitentiary

[Superintendent Benjamin Franklin] Burch is doing a splendid work among the prisoners, of whom one hundred and thirty-six are men. One solitary woman is there as a prisoner, and she is committed for life, her crime, the murder of her husband. The poor old creature is excessively miserable, and yet the penitentiary is evidently the best place on earth for her. We would suggest a stove in her cell; and several appliances of comfort and luxury could be added at little cost, to enliven her lonely quarters. She was very humble and obsequious with us until we told her plainly that we thought she was better off in the prison, where she could not get liquor, than she would be if allowed to run at large; and then—didn't she rail?

"An' it's the likes of yer that goes gallivantin' round the counthry, lavin' yer pore husban' at the keraydle an' the wash-tub, while yez be's makin' the spayches an' bossin' the payple!" she said, adding much more of the same sort, which was equally laughable.

We record with profound humiliation the not very surprising fact that the one woman convict in the Oregon penitentiary is opposed to Woman Suffrage. But then she has a good deal of company among the would-be popular women outside, and that's some comfort. . . .

Wednesday, and home. Nobody expected us, but everybody professed to be glad, even to the "pore husband," whom our convict sister had mentally burdened with imaginary "keraydles" and "wash tubs." What a blessing that the "pore" gentleman isn't sensible of his misery.

May 4, 1878.

A. J. D.

*(May 10, 1878)*

## Indian Troubles

Indian depredations are again being visited upon hapless settlers in Idaho, and again the few companies of troops at the disposal of the department commander are being urged rapidly over desert and mountain to their relief. Indications show also the possibility that these depredations will not be entirely confined to Idaho.

The governor of Oregon received from Baker City the following dispatch, . . . under date of June 12th: "Indians are massacreing [*sic*] settlers in the southern part of this county, and moving this way. Send one hundred stand of arms and ammunition.". . . . General Brown responded by sending fifty stand of arms from Salem and forty stand from Portland, together with 5,000 cartridges obtained from Vancouver. . . .

Experienced Indian fighters and frontiersmen believe that there is a general uprising of all the tribes and scattered bands in Eastern Oregon and Southern Idaho, and that they will be able to muster at least one thousand warriors. . . . The settlers on the Boise City and Canyon City stage road in Baker county, for a distance of sixty miles, have . . . left their homes and sought places of safety.

*(June 21, 1878)*

## The Indian War

News from the front continues to foreshadow an Indian war that will tax to the utmost the strategy of commanders and the endurance of troops. The *Oregonian*'s dispatches of Wednesday morning furnish the following: "The advance troops of General [Oliver Otis] Howard under Col. Bernard attacked the hostiles on Sunday on Curry Creek, about forty-five miles from Harney. In the engagement Buffalo Horn, the chief of the Bannocks, is reported killed, and also one of the soldiers. After the second charge of the troops the Indians rallied, when Col. Bernard dispatched a courier with a verbal report to General Howard at Harney, asking for reinforcements. . . . The force under Col. Bernard, including scouts, numbered about two hundred men. The number of Indians is unknown."

*(June 28, 1878)*

## A Day of Terror at Walla Walla, W. T.

Saturday, the 13th inst., was the most exciting day ever witnessed in Walla Walla. All sorts of wild rumors were afloat concerning the proximity of the Indians, battles, depredations committed by them, etc., etc., and the roads leading into the city were lined by fleeing settlers, perfectly wild with terror. It is estimated that fully 750 people, mostly women and children, passed through the various avenues leading from the country roads by 12 o'clock.

The appearance of these refugees cannot be described, and the stories told by them were mainly the off-spring of their terror. . . . The cavalry command of Colonel Bernard . . . reached the city on Friday night. A liberal use of whisky intensified the excitement, and, but for the inter-position of the police, a battle in which redskins had no hand might have resulted between half-drunken soldiery and men eager for fight. Governor Ferry was on hand striv-ing to learn from conflicting reports where the most imminent danger rested. Walla Walla will long remem-ber the memorable scenes of this sudden invasion of hostiles.

*(July 19, 1878)*

## Prineville and the Indian Scare

To the Editor of the *New Northwest*:

Not from the seat of war exactly, but from one of the seats of the great Indian scare this letter hails. This scare has not, however, affected your correspondent as yet, though there has been any amount of "scarey" talk, and our little town is crammed full of refugees. Some were so badly frightened as to commence building a stockade. Work upon it has been suspended, however, leaving one side open, and indeed the three sides that were completed were deemed rather insecure after a test. On the arrival of the government guns the other day, a young man, desiring to test the power of one of their balls, as well as the strength of our defenses, took sight at a particular spot on the wall. The result showed that the bullet went clear through, and also through an object *(We are unable to make out what, but to our disgust it was not an Indian.—Ed.)* that was sitting on the Crooked River bridge something less than a quarter of a mile away. I think the Indians had better give us a little warning before they come.

Numerous residents of this county have suddenly bethought themselves of some dear friends or relatives in the valley whom they much desired to visit; others have taken a sudden longing to go to the mountains to gather wild blackber-ries. Some owned themselves scared and hurriedly decamped, and alto-gether very many of them have left the country. We expect the arrival of volunteers to-morrow, but they do not seem to be needed now, as the Indians have gone since they were asked for. This unfortunate uprising, while it devastates portions of the country more luckless than our im-mediate vicinity has been so far, tends to throw a great check upon all en-terprises, and will, we fear affect our prosperity for some time to come. The final result, however, is not doubtful, and we hope the peace when it comes will be made on a sure basis that will throw this magnificent region open to secure and prosperous settlement for all time to come.

Of peaceful arts I might write you, but just now everybody is too intently listening for the baying of the "bloody dogs of war" to care for the rehearsal of quiet peace chronicles, so I will defer items about schools, literary societies, social pleasures and commercial matters until my next.

Prineville, Oregon, July 8, 1878.
E. [Ellen E. Sommerville]

*(July 19, 1878)*

## Reports of the Indian Scare

The excitement in Lake county [Oregon] relative to Indian difficulties has subsided, and settlers have returned to their homes.

A little daughter of Captain S. Smith, of Umatilla county, who was accidentally shot in the ankle by a volunteer some days ago, was taken to Walla Walla, where her limb was amputated. She lies in a critical condition.

A dispatch says relative to the condition of things in the vicinity of Pendleton: "Grain is ripe, but it is not safe to cut it. Fences are thrown down and much grain destroyed. Horses are driven off in large bands, and cattle and sheep are shot down in large numbers, all these by Indians."

Governor [Stephen F.] Chadwick telegraphed to General Effinger, of this city [Portland], on Saturday, to send one hundred men of "courage, activity and endurance" to the front at once. The news spread rapidly, and in the afternoon men were drawn up for inspection on First street, between Washington and Alder, all ready to depart for the scene of conflict. A subsequent dispatch, stating that they were not wanted, caused much disappointment to those who had in imagination already drawn a bead upon the ruthless invader, and were anxious to reduce it to a reality.

*(July 19, 1878)*

## Quick Trip to San Francisco

So thoroughly tired and exhausted are we with the fatigue of a recent voyage and the subsequent endeavor to "do" the Bay City in the shortest possible space of time in order to be ready to retrace our way to Portland on the returning steamer, that we feel wholly incapacitated to make a comprehensive record of our wanderings. But the *New Northwest*, like the horse leech, cries, "Give, give," and we must endeavor to obey.

Our present trip to San Francisco was planned on the spur of the moment, and is to be excessively unsatisfactory on many accounts, chiefly because of its suddenness; but we resolved, with our liege, to visit the former typos of the People's Paper while the fare was down; so behold us, on Sunday, the 7th inst., in company with several hundred fellow-voyagers on board the steamer "Great Republic,". . . [as we] watch the endeavors of the massive ship to follow in the wake of a little river steamer, that, with the agility of a pet poodle that gambols at the end of a towline in the hands of her mistress, frisks hither and thither, till finally she accomplishes her purpose, and leads the greater craft captive at her will.

Once away from the Portland docks, and well on her downward way toward the ocean, the compiler of these chronicles sets about the ever-recurring task of serial writing, which, like washing day, must come every week, and we saw but little of the ship, the Columbia River, or any fellow-travelers till the last line of Chapter XXIV. of "Her Lot" was finished and ready for the Astoria mail. . . .

Once inside the [Golden] Gate, a strong gale rose and disputed our further passage, compelling the noble vessel to double her docks and consume much time in landing. The crowd on the wharves at Portland had been immense, but the jam at San Francisco was prodigious.

"Workingmen" were out in force to abuse the few dozen Chinamen who had dared to visit this Christian city, and also to prevent their being driven quietly in wagons to their quarters. The coach of the International Hotel drove away with the undersigned and hid from view a crowd of lawless hoodlums of the Kearney clique, who had attacked a wagon load of peaceful "heathen."[1] We regretted that we could not see the close of the fray, as we knew the press of San Francisco would not dare to publish the particulars. Oh, what a free country we do live in, to be sure!

The next morning a heavy fire occurred in China quarters, but no newspaper dares to charge the blame upon the foreign rabble that votes and holds office, while the poor peaceful Chinamen do the work they would not touch at any price.

While the fire was raging, we saw from the hotel windows a most sickening sight. A homeless inebriate, made homeless because his sensible wife would no longer support him in drunkenness, stepped into a store opposite our window, bargained for a loaded revolver, and while holding it in his hand under pretense of examining it, suddenly placed the muzzle to his face and settled the whisky problem on his own account. Of course there was great excitement, not omitting coroners' fees and the like, and while we were still gazing, sick and awe-struck, first one cart and then another was driven by, each with several live men and one dead China-man, the latter in both cases brutally mangled in the head and face, from which the life-blood ran in torrents. *Ugh!* Let us change the subject. . . .

Our gracious liege failed to secure tickets for return upon the "Oregon," so he is now absent in search of ac-commodations upon the "Great Republic." If he succeeds, we will soon be at "home again." Certainly, speaking for ourself, we have had enough of San Francisco for this time. And yet we shall carry away some golden memories, for we have spent delightful hours with Willis and Hubert, formerly typos on the People's Paper, and a glorious day in the halcyon retreats of Lone Moun-tain, where even Kearneyism cannot disturb the sweet serenity that perme-ates the flower-laden city of the dead.

San Francisco, July 12, 1878.

A. J. D.

*(July 25, 1878)*

## Death of a Tiny Waif

Our last hailed from the Bay City, where we were making a flying visit—too short by half for our purpose. And now, when we are at home again, pre-paring hurriedly for our next brief journey, and we undertake to recall events of the past fortnight, the whole seems as an unenlightened dream. . . .

In our wanderings we chanced upon a precious little orphaned waif, to which the parental hearts of our liege and self so spontaneously warmed that we decided to adopt and bring it home and rear it as our own.[2] To resolve was to act. There was no time for reflection, and almost before we knew it we found ourselves aboard the "Great Republic," and afloat upon the bosom of the ocean, bearing in our arms the treasure, who was hence-forth to have no earthly home but ours.

The voyage proved a long and try-ing one. A heavy wind and rain storm lashed the ocean to a fury, and the crowded ship was disagreeably cold. We took the best possible care of the tiny waif, and reached home with him in safety; but alas, the change of food and the hardships of the journey proved too much for him, and after a week's waiting at our fireside, during which brief time the entire household had learned to love him more dearly than words can express, the precious little life flickered and went out, and the first funeral in a home that for a quarter of a century has been crowded with life took place on the 26th inst., Rev. Mr. Anthony officiating, and a genial circle of warm-hearted friends assisting with their love and care.

Then the casket was closed over the beautiful gem, the west-side train halted by previous arrangement in front of the house, and our sorrow-ing liege and self bore away the jewel to the dear paternal cemetery near

Forest Grove, and our sweet, short dream was over. We are too sad to dwell upon this theme. A little while ago and death seemed a long way off. Now he is so very near that we can almost feel the edge of his sickle. . . .

Why we should have desired to add the care of an infant to our other duties is a mystery; but why we should have lost him is a greater one, to be solved only in the great Hereafter, whither we are all drifting.

At this writing, July 29th, we are hurriedly preparing for a flying trip to Dayton and Lafayette, intending to return in time to be on hand in Astoria at the coming convention.

A. J. D.

*(August 1, 1878)*

## Of Hatchets and Hummingbirds

[W]e take the hack [from St. Joe] for Lafayette, accompanied by a weary woman with six little children, refugees from the Indian country, whose relatives she is seeking in the land where the noble red men are no longer numerous enough to be troublesome. Years ago, while we were yet a village schoolma'am, her husband, then a very young man, had been numbered among our scores of pupils, and we could hardly believe our senses as we met his tired, anxious little wife, with her interesting brood of dependent ones, three of whom are already large enough to

attend school on their own account. Surely the title of "Mother Duniway" is not inappropriate, and whenever we hear it we accept it as an agreeable omen that we will some day be growing old.[3] To hear this little woman's story of her early married life on the border, and her rehearsal of the Indian outrages which at last compelled her to gather up her children and flee for her life, would naturally inspire any humane listener with a desire to make a "good Indian" of every camas-eater that goes scalp hunting, from the Clear Water to the Skagit.

She told us of one woman, a Mrs. [Blanche] Perkins, whose husband [Lorenzo] had been murdered and herself scalped and buried alive. The poor creature had thrown a great many of the rocks off her prison before death had come to her relief, and when found her arms were outside the ground and her knees drawn up, showing that after the savages had left her she had made a desperate struggle, alone in the solitude of the wilderness, to free herself from her horrid living tomb. It is quite likely she died of starvation.

Then the Indians would make a raid upon a flock of sheep and cut off their fore legs to the knees, and open the skin of their necks to leave an exposed spot for the reception of maggot eggs, and turn them loose to suffer and die. Shame on a government who treats for creatures beside whom coyotes are fairies and hyenas angels. Let us think of something else, or we'll be tempted to shoulder a hatchet and embark for the border, to prove that armed women can fight, whether they're allowed to be voters or not. . . .

A ride of a mile and a half in the dense dust of the dry season, through the familiar scenes of long ago, and we reach the town of Lafayette, and a little farther on the beautiful country home of a beloved sister. . . .

The next day, urged by sheer necessity, we *rest*. Oh, the dreamy, delicious languor of a rest that has never a minute of toil in it! The contented house-flies dance a quadrille in the air for our special benefit, and busy hornets buzz through the room and disperse them for our amusement. Hummingbirds dart in the windows, canaries sing in the cages, kittens purr in the sunshine, chickens cackle in the back yard, and odors of Araby steal in at the open windows from the fine floral array that revels in its luxury of gorgeous colors around and over the front verandah.

Portland, August 4, 1878.

A. J. D.

*(August 8, 1878)*

# The Oregon State Woman Suffrage Association Convention

In the language of good Mrs. [H. A.] Loughary, we have had a grand, grand time at the convention.[4] While the day, or business, sessions have not been as largely attended as desirable, the evening exercises have drawn crowded houses and aroused enthusiastic interest. . . . [T]he speech of Mrs. Loughary, on Wednesday evening, far surpassed the former efforts of even her own able, eloquent and logical self. Mrs. L., though a grandmother, is not old enough to appear venerable. There is just enough of the gleam of glory beaming through her whitening hair to proclaim the frosts of fifty winters. But her cheeks are as rosy and her general complexion as fresh as a maiden's of twenty, while her stately bearing is as kindly as it is captivating. She is not only an able, eloquent speaker and thorough logician, but she possesses that rare accomplishment in woman, parliamentary skill, and the courage and power to enforce it.

Next in order comes Mrs. Martin, who is yet almost young enough to be a girl, in spite of her dozen children and half a dozen grandchildren. This lady, a wife at fourteen, a mother at fifteen, and a pioneer from the beginning, performs the domestic duties of a farmhouse, and the nursery duties of a large family, and makes her money to attend conventions and pay her taxes to support men's government by weaving rag carpets on a hand loom. Her assistance at the convention was most opportune.

Little Mrs. Flora McKinney, an active granger and as pretty as a picture, is a new and valuable addition to the ranks of workers. And it is but justice to Mrs. Dr. [Mary] Thompson to say that she proved as amiable and agreeable at this convention as any of the others.[5] Her speech on Thursday evening was, like all her former speeches, splendid, and we were all proud of her. . . .

One of the most thorough-going of all the Salem suffragists is Mrs. Ramp, who not only refuses to report her property to the Assessor, but declares herself ready to go to prison any time the lawmakers, who deny her representation, may see fit to place her there for refusing to pay her taxes. . . .

A resolution from the suffrage convention was sent to the Senate and House on Wednesday, asking that the two bodies graciously consent to meet in joint session and grant a hearing to the President of the Association, who desired to make an argument on "Constitutional Liberty." The resolution was presented in the House by Mr. D. P. Thompson and agreed to, the time for hearing being fixed at 7:30 P. M., on Friday.

Promptly at the time specified, the ladies assembled, the rain, which fell in torrents, in no way impeding their spirit of determination. But a shock was suddenly placed upon their expectations by the announcement that the Senate had failed to pass the resolution to meet the House in joint session, and, in consequence, the House had assembled to transact its own business.

Nothing daunted, the ladies, assisted by half a score of gentlemen, tried another tack. Several members, well known friends of Woman Suffrage, were summoned to the library, and it was soon arranged that one of them should offer a resolution that the House go into a committee of the whole and invite the ladies within the bar. This was carried without a dissenting voice, and the women got a hearing. . . . Suffice it to say that the House is happy, and the Senate feels that in its august dignity it has made a mistake. There is little doubt but that we shall yet be heard with its consent before the session closes.

Salem, September 28, 1878.

A. J. D.

*(October 3, 1878)*

## Awaiting the Trial of Mary Leonard

We see in the District court calendar for the term that began on Monday of this week at The Dalles, the case of the State vs. Mary Leonard, indicted for murder.[6] This woman has been in jail since last February awaiting her trial on evidence purely circumstantial, for the murder of her husband, a monster whom for his treatment of women, *should* have been slain by a woman, whether he was or not, while one man at least under like indictment has been allowed liberty preceding his trial and a quick decision in his favor. This woman should be tried before a jury of women, her peers, and those who in the very nature of things would be better able to decide justly upon her case than men could possibly be. One of the grand counts in the movement which advocates of equal rights have brought against existing customs is "for extending unwarrantable jurisdiction over us," a count that before the republic was born caused not merely discontent but was deemed, amongst others, just cause for rebellion. . . .

You tell us that men act with wisdom and without class bias in the administration of laws they have made. We merely cite you to the cases in point. The justice of the decision in the case last named we do not question; the injustice in the case of the (supposed) woman offender admits of no question. She may or may not be guilty; that we do not discuss, but in any event she should, months ago, have had a fair and impartial trial before a jury of her peers, who alone have a right to decide whether she has a right to be hanged, imprisoned, or acquitted of all suspicion of guilt.

*(November 14, 1878)*

## After the Indian Scare

Our stay at Umatilla [Oregon] was an agreeable change from the noise and hurry of the State Legislature. . . . The good people, for the most part, keep reasonable hours, and the one saloon in the place is more orderly than many churches. The school-house has a new coat of paint, and is as clean as an old maid's dimity apron. We confess that we shuddered a little when we went there to lecture, bearing our own candles, bought on the way, when, a light being struck, we were shown the bullet-holes in the wall, where, during the Indian scare, when the school-house was the barracks, a venturesome Lo, who had risked himself as a spy among the pale-faces, had paid the penalty for his temerity by receiving the first force of the leaden missiles, which made him a "good Indian" for all time, and left their impress under the black-board as a memento of the prowess of somebody who had protected the whites by a rifle, while the ill-fated Indian was a prisoner and asleep. . . .

Each day, during our visit, the plain was alive with freight teams. . . . As a forwarding point, this town, as ragged and windworn as it looks, possesses immense advantages. The supplies for LaGrande, Union, Cove, Baker, and Boise, that are shipped up the Columbia, are all landed here, and are forwarded by prairie schooners, with mule engines to their place of destination. . . .

The United States signal station is kept here by Mr. Willes; . . . The gentleman instructed us in the use of the barometer, battery, maximum and minimum thermometers, windometer, etc., etc., and we left the office after half an hour's inspection of everything scientific about it, . . . with a decided impression that such positions properly belong to women. . . .

At five o'clock on the morning of the 19th, good Mrs. Wilson aroused us from a dream of a home, and we arose and departed for the steamer "Almota," that lay alongside the wharfboat, but had not yet given warning of her early departure. A gentleman had carried our baggage to the boat "over night," so we had no baggage but a hand-satchel; but the dim gray of the morning was hardly discernible, and our lonely walk to the riverside was the acme of desolation. We thought of Indians and banditti, and trembled a little, and our heart beat audibly when a span of horses trotted by in uncomfortable proximity to the solitary pedestrian. . . .

Nine o'clock, and Wallula. But it is off day on the passenger line, and we must lie by till the morrow; so we take our baggage to the Cummings hotel, and then seek the office of Mr. Peabody, where we visit for a while with the wife and children, and then proceed to scrawl this missive. . . .

As we scribble, an Indian enters, and upon hearing his name, we realize that we are in the august presence of royalty. His majesty's name is Homely [Homily], and he is too impecunious to pay his way to Vancouver, whither he is going, doubtless on official business connected with his realm.[7] Mr. Peabody kindly telegraphs to General Sprague for the required pass, and his Majesty, the Indian Emperor, awaits its coming, with the air of patience of a monument. In half an hour the General responds, and the great chief of the Wallulas is as happy as he is majestic.

Wallula, W. T., November 19, 1878.

A. J. D.

*(November 28, 1878)*

## Of Sewers and House-Maids

Since last we wrote you, we have seen a good deal more of Walla Walla and are more than ever pleased with its growth and prospects. . . .

But Walla Walla is as badly sewered as Albany or Salem, and filth abounds in many places quite equal in quantity to that of the Chinese quarters in Portland, or the alleys of The Dalles. It is little wonder that malaria runs riot in the form of diphtheria and typhoid fever. A thorough-going council with iron-clad ordinances for cleansing the city, backed by a tax sufficient for proper sewerage, would do more to arrest disease and death than all the united prayers of Christendom. And yet, there are soft-fingered clergymen who sniff the abominable odors they encounter on the way to church, and pass them by in silence, and then raise their voices in supplication when in the pulpit, imploring the Infinite One to stay the work of death and devastation, as though our heavenly Father were the author of the pestilence. . . .

[H]ere, as well as elsewhere, there is urgent need of one reform among women, that merits especial mention. Oftentimes the maid-of-all-work in houses where we visit is a matured, intelligent and interesting woman, who sits at the sewing-table during our call, and often brightens under the conversation, as though she would like to engage in it, but she is almost never introduced to a visitor, and when spoken to by any member of the family, no matter if she is gray-haired and in spectacles, is always called "Lucy" or "Kitty" or "Jane" or "Susan."

Ladies cannot reasonably expect skilled and contented labor among domestics, till they have first dignified the office of cook and house-keeper, by respectfully using every respectable and sensible woman who enters their homes to perform necessary household duties for hire. We know of hundreds of capable women, who half starve at their sewing-machines in pitiless, squalid discomfort, who would gladly go out to service in sumptuous homes but for the social disgrace of it. And yet, why should it

be a social disgrace? Ladies, everywhere, think of it.

*(December 12, 1878)*

## How Long, O Men, How Long?

Weston is growing rapidly. . . . The country people come in with their wagons every day in large numbers, and the amount of carpet warp, concentrated lye, wash-boards, tubs, candle-molds, churns, mops, brooms, butter-stamps, flat-irons, calico and stocking yarn the women receive in exchange for eggs, butter, socks, rag-carpets and chickens, gives flattest contradiction possible to the silly assumption of men that such women are supported and protected by anybody, not even excepting their own scantily attired and shrunken-visaged selves. . . .

The landlord and his wife [Mr. and Mrs. Young] were very kind and accommodating, as was everybody else we met, not even excepting the proprietors of the drug-store, Messrs. McCall and Hendrix, who destroyed our posters and who wrote to the Pendleton *Independent*, calling us a "notorious female sufferer, who had swooped down upon them with the graceful dignity of a setting hen, and given the citizens a course of lectures upon women in petticoats." We thank these weak-minded chanticleers for their left-handed compliments, for they have served us in lieu of much advertising, and insured added success in our forth-coming labors at Pendleton. . . .

But we must not omit to mention our obliging landlord's Chinese cooks. "Louie" and "Annie" are their names, and they are thoroughly Americanized. They dress and act like white folks, and Louie is a voter. As a citizen, we should say that he far better deserves the elective franchise than many a white man we wot of, yet he has no more moral right to the ballot than has his good wife, Annie, and we believe the reader will agree with our modest assumption that he is no more justly entitled to the rights of citizenship than our humble self. Yet he can preempt or homestead a claim, which we have no legal right to do; and should we attempt it, he could jump our claim and hold it through his superior rights as a member of the aristocracy of sex.

We are glad the Chinaman can get his rights when he deserves them, but we protest against being left in political subjugation to him, or any other class of men. . . . "How long, O, *men*, how long" are your wives and mothers to wait and petition ere you grant to them the equal protection which you bestow upon law-abiding Indians, negroes and Chinamen?

Weston, December 6, 1878.

A. J. D.

*(December 19, 1878)*

## Indians: The Doomed Race

This [Umatilla] reservation, which comprises many thousands of acres of the very best arable land in America, is to be given over to the whites in another year, under the expiration of the treaty through which the Indians have held it during the past two decades.[8] Then the Indian must be removed to a remoter field; and long ere that time shall have arrived, we may look for Indian troubles, such as we have scarcely thought of hitherto. If the savages would fence and improve the land, the greedy white man would not covet it so strongly; but the red skin is a natural nomad, and will not take kindly to hard work, the average Indian agent or crack-brained philanthropist to the contrary notwithstanding.

By degrees he may be developed from a camas-digger to a herd-raiser, and the possibility is that the progression of ages might ultimately evolve him from pastoral to agricultural pursuits, but the work of engrafting a cultivated nature upon stock as wild and hardy as the specimens before us, is at best a doubtful experiment.

Not only will the Indian avoid all physical drudgery, except that which he can compel the women to perform for him, but his example is contagious, and many a lazy white man has squatted within sight of the

*Train passes by an Indian encampment on the Umatilla Indian Reservation*

red man's rolling and unfenced acres, and is literally doing nothing except waiting for his chance to pounce upon some favorite portion of the reservation as soon as it shall be open for settlement. These things continually stir the doomed race to anger, and incite them to revenge.

Then there are bad white man as well as bad Indians, and the former lose no opportunity to embarrass and enrage the latter, stealing their horses, and occasionally shooting one or more of their number, and when suspected of theft, or other crime, accusing renegade Indians of committing the depredation. As may well be supposed, these turmoils do not tend to the speedy and peaceful solution of the Indian problem, and the many honest white settlers are in a state of constant uncertainty as to what may be their future fate. . . .

Umatilla, December, 18, 1878.
A. J. D.

*(December 26, 1878)*

# Notes for 1878

1. The "Kearney clique" refers to Dennis Kearney's Workingman's Party, which swept through California in 1878 in violent opposition to Chinese immigration and "cheap Chinese labor." Although Kearney's party was mainly limited to California, its political ideas extended to Oregon, where the legislature sent a memorial to Congress, asking for prohibition of "the importation or immigration of Chinese and other Asiatic laborers to this coast" (*The Oregonian*, 4 Oct. 1878). The Burlingame Treaty of 1868 had guaranteed citizens of the United States and China equal rights in each other's country, including the right to immigrate; however, the Oregon legislature's memorial to Congress argued that "the importation of 'coolie slaves' violated the Burlingame Treaty's provision guaranteeing only voluntary immigration" and that " 'Asiatic slave labor' was driving white labor out of the state." See Hugh Clark, *Portland's Chinese: The Early Years* (Portland: Center for Urban Education, 1975; rev. 1978), 15.

2. The "precious little orphaned waif" was actually the son of Hubert Duniway and Ida Lesley, a simple country girl who became pregnant while boarding with the Duniways and attending school in Portland. Duniway insisted that Hubert marry Ida. Their child was born in San Francisco in April of 1878. Abigail and Ben Duniway went to California in July of that year and returned with their three-month-old grandchild, who died within a week of arrival in Portland and was buried at Forest Grove, as the adopted son of B. C. and A. J. Duniway. Hubert and Ida Duniway were kept waiting in San Francisco for a more appropriate time to return to Portland. Ida died of tuberculosis in Portland in 1883, and Hubert married again in 1884. David C. Duniway interviews; Clyde Duniway notes, Duniway Papers. See also

Ruth B. Moynihan, *Rebel for Rights, Abigail Scott Duniway* (New Haven: Yale University Press, 1983), 127; 243, n. 61.

3. The title "Mother Duniway" was commonly applied, even by those older than she. Judge Deady, ten years her elder, wrote in his diary on Feb. 2, 1884: "Friday paid monthly bills to the amount of $201 including a contribution of $20 to Mother Duniway for female suffrage campaign" (*Pharisee Among Philistines*, 441).

4. Hattie A. Loughary, wife of a successful Yamhill farmer, was an important figure in the Oregon State Woman Suffrage Association. She served as OSWSA president for a number of years, traveled extensively as a suffrage lecturer, and was a correspondent and agent for *The NNW*. Lucy Stone of the AWSA recognized Loughary's commitment and endearing style: "Mrs. Loughary's heartfelt devotion to the . . . cause makes one always wish to grasp her hand and give her a fervent 'God Speed'" (*NNW*, 3 May 1878). For a note on Loughary as the mother of ten children and a nurse-midwife, see Moynihan, *Rebel for Rights*, 249, n. 15.

5. Dr. Mary A. Thompson, an early friend of Duniway and a prohibitionist, was a charter member of the OSWSA. But Thompson believed that women were innately more moral than men, and she clashed with Duniway both ideologically and politically about the goals and leadership of the women's rights movement. After Duniway's opposition to prohibition in Washington Territory's Local Option Campaign of 1886, Dr. Thompson and Dr. Bethenia Owens-Adair pushed Duniway to step down from her leadership of the Oregon movement. Duniway did so and worked in Idaho and Washington "intermittently for ten [*sic*] years, and returned again to Oregon in 1894 to find that not a single meeting had been called, and no steps of any kind had been taken for advancing the movement; so I was compelled to begin where I had left off" (*Path Breaking*, 83).

6. Mary Gysin, born in Alsace and later a resident of Basel, Switzerland, arrived in the United States about 1870. She was apparently a domestic in Portland before marrying Daniel G. Leonard in May of 1875. Daniel, who owned a hotel on his homestead east of Wasco in the John Day Valley, had previously lost a suit to Sarah Elrod Leonard, his common-law wife who had borne him four children. Mary suffered abuse from Daniel and wanted the marriage to end with a settlement she claimed had been promised by Daniel before they married; Daniel insisted no settlement had been promised and filed for divorce in the fall of 1877, accusing Mary of adultery with a man named Nathaniel Lindsay. Mary cross-filed, charging Daniel with physical and mental cruelty, and asking for separate maintenance, which was granted by the court in December of 1877 but not honored by Daniel. During the night of Jan. 4, 1878, Daniel was shot in his bed and died on Jan. 26. Mary Leonard was accused of the crime, and Nathaniel Lindsay was charged with inciting and abetting the murder, although he was absent when the crime occurred. The trial of the *State vs. Leonard and Lindsay* was held at The Dalles and resulted in a verdict of not guilty on Nov. 20, 1878.

As noted by Duniway in various issues of *The NNW*, Mary Leonard went on to study law and overcame barriers for women by gaining admission to practice in Washington Territory in 1884, in federal courts in 1885, and in Oregon in 1886. When interviewed by Duniway in 1886, Leonard explained why she had entered the law profession: "I not only had an ambition to help myself, but to help women also—women who are wronged or are in the power of men— and to advise and assist the helpless and defenseless. . . . You just let me get a legal clutch on some of those who wrong and plunder members of my sex, and see if they long escape punishment" (*NNW*, 26 Aug. 1886). Duniway added that, for an hour each day in her Portland office, Leonard was offering free legal advice to women. For more on Leonard, see Malcolm H. Clark, Jr., "The Lady and the Law: A Portrait of Mary Leonard," *Oregon Historical Quarterly* 56 (June 1955): 126-39; Fred W. Decker, "Letter to the Editor: Discovered: A Photo and More Facts about Mary Leonard," *Oregon Historical Quarterly* 78 (June 1977): 174-77.

7. Duniway's reference to "Homely" was intended as "Homily," the Wallawalla chief who is often credited with firing the fatal shot at Egan, the Paiute chief pursued by some Indians of the Umatilla Reservation in the Bannock-Paiute War. See Robert H. Ruby and John A. Brown, *Indians of the Pacific Northwest* (Norman. University of Oklahoma Press, 1981), 253.

8. The Umatilla Reservation was established for the Cayuses, Umatillas, and Wallawallas in May of 1855 at the Walla Walla Council meeting, which involved Indians from various tribes; Joel Palmer, Oregon Territorial Superintendent of Indian Affairs; and Isaac I. Stevens, Washington Territorial Governor and Superintendent of Indian Affairs. Two other major reservations were established at the same meeting: one for the Nez Percés and one for the fourteen tribes under the Yakima standard. Today, the Umatilla Reservation, located in northeastern Oregon, is one of five Oregon reservations.

# 1879

## Indian Scare at Umatilla

We were toasting feet and fingers before the cheerful fire in Mrs. Wilson's hotel at Umatilla, [Oregon], and thinking longingly of home and our proposed departure on the morrow, when a rumor reached the village to the effect that Indian hostilities had commenced in earnest some sixty miles away, and about a dozen miles below Priest's Rapids. To this startling intelligence was added the cheerful information that the new steamer "John Gates," and the only one now in use above Celilo, was ordered to the scene of conduct with a reinforcement of regulars, and there was no telling when we could go home.

All day we were kept in a state of extreme anxiety over the probability of being caught up at last by the dreaded winter freeze-up. We did not particularly dread the Indian scare. Indeed, we believe there is always a sort of numbing of the senses in the immediate presence of actual bodily danger, and we fancy that death, let it come whenever it may, and under whatever circumstances, is a great deal worse in imagination than reality. But it was pitiful to reflect upon the exposed condition of the defenseless Umatillians and the prospect of their being icebound and savage-besieged in mid-winter.

Happily the rumor of an outbreak, though true in part, was greatly exaggerated. Chief Moses and a posse of his equally "good" Indians had exhibited the normal treachery of the savage character by surrounding the sheriff of Yakima and a company of volunteers who had gone with him to arrest the Perkins murderers.[1] But the prompt interference of the military soon put a quietus upon the dusky warriors. . . .

The report that the steamer would not come to Umatilla on time proved a false one; and at an early hour on Thursday, we gladly hurried aboard, leaving behind a score of warm-hearted friends, for whose safety during the forthcoming isolation we involuntarily breathed a fervent prayer.

Portland, December 31, 1878.

A. J. D.

*(January 2, 1879)*

## The Anti-Chinese Bill

The anti-Chinese bill [restricting Chinese immigration] passed the House, with all the Senate amendments intact, by a vote of 140 to 95. It now goes to the President.

*(February 27, 1879)*

The [President's] veto message accompanied by the Chinese bill was returned to the House of Representatives on the 1st inst. An attempt to pass the bill over the veto failed. Yeas, 109; nays, 95.

President Hayes was burned in effigy on Monday evening in this city—a proceeding neither dignified nor calculated to impress thinking people with the importance of the vetoed bill.

*(March 6, 1879)*

## The Chinese Question

The feeling of the people of this city, which upon this question is an index to the sentiment throughout the State upon the Chinese restriction bill and its veto by the President, was expressed by a mass meeting of citizens at the Courthouse on Saturday evening. Governor [William Wallace] Thayer presided and advocated earnest measures against the influx of Chinese to this coast. . . . If the sentiment of the meeting was not that the "Chinese must go," it certainly was the "Chinese must stop coming."

*(March 6, 1879)*

An anti-Chinese meeting was held in the plaza on Sunday afternoon. Agitation on the question of Chinese labor seems to be on the increase.

*(April 17, 1879)*

## Settlement With Chief Moses

Settlers in Eastern Oregon and Washington will be glad to learn that the Indian question, so far as Moses' pledges go, is settled within certain limits, at least. . . . [A]n agreement has been made with the Indians by which they surrender the lands heretofore occupied by them in Washington Territory, and accept a reservation set apart for them by executive order, adjoining and west of Colville reservation, in the northeastern part of the Territory. . . .[2] In connection with the agreement with Moses, it may be mentioned that an arrangement has also been made with the Umatillas that may result in settling the troubles and questions that have arisen between them and the whites.

*(April 24, 1879)*

## A Quilting Bee and Barn Raising at Cornelius

On Wednesday morning we took [the] train for Cornelius, where we found Mrs. Col. Cornelius at home in her flourishing store, busily engaged in counting eggs, weighing bacon and butter, selling dry-goods, groceries, spades, hoes and garden-rakes, and keeping books and entertaining company.[3] Mr. and Mrs. Spencer were going to a combined barn raising and quilting, at the splendid farm of Ben Schofield, Esq., . . . and we gladly accepted their invitation to accompany them to the "bee."

It proved a grand, old-fashioned time. Quilts in the frames were suspended from the ceiling by ropes, and hung just high enough to reach comfortably while sitting, the farmers' wives, dear, tired-looking souls, reminding us of the days agone, their rosy daughters occupying one room, and themselves another.

From the kitchen came savory odors of countless good things over which we knew the hostess was presiding, and out in the barn-yard a small army of farmers wrestled with beam and stanchion, rafter, cross-tie and what not, the great timbers sliding home to their sockets in unquestioning obedience to the mechanics' will.

Then that dinner. Shades of departed missionaries, but it was capital! Cold ham and roast chicken, vegetables in every style, fruit in every shape; butter, honey, home-made bread, coffee, tea, cream, cakes, pies, tarts—there is no use in talking, the traditional twelve baskets of fragments couldn't have been missed had they been stolen from the remains of that ample and hospitable board after everybody had eaten.

By four o'clock, the quilts were out of the frames, the skeleton of the great loom was up, the dinner dishes were washed, and the crowd at leisure. Then, Mr. Schofield, with the genuine hospitality of the true farmer, invited the men into the yard and the women into the verandah, and announced to them and the undersigned that a short speech from ourself was on the *tapis*. We hurriedly left the quilt that a few of us had been binding, and throwing a shawl over our shoulders, went bare-headed into the yard and talked of national affairs and the woman question as long as conscience would permit us to keep the tired crowd upon their feet.

We went there, not knowing we had a friend, save the gentleman and lady to whom we are indebted for the invitation. We came away without being conscious we had an enemy; and we're going back to that neighborhood again some time, Providence permitting. Humanity is a splendid institution in any community when you can get upon its better side.

April 18, 1879.

A. J. D.

*(April 24, 1879)*

## To Our Patrons

We are ready now to take a new departure, but to furl the banner of human rights. With this issue, after eight years of public effort, as sole proprietor, we admit as co-partners in our work, our major sons, Willis S. and Hubert R., who will hereafter carry on the publishing department in all its phases, leaving us more untrammeled than heretofore for field duty. What will the next eight years bring forth? We shall see.

Abigail Scott Duniway

*(May 1, 1879)*

# A Near Calamity at Kalama

Kalama [W. T.], or "Calamity" as the erewhile pretentious city of the Columbia was once prophetically called, which was for a time the headquarters of the Northern Pacific Railroad, the abode of the Kalama *Beacon*, and the general rendezvous for impecunious seekers after corner lots and landlords' bonanzas; Kalama, the disappointed, doomed and dying city of fixed expectation, was the scene of the visit or visitation of the author of these peregrinations on Wednesday of last week. . . .

[A]rrangements were completed, after much delay for securing the M. E. Church for an evening lecture. The church . . . sits . . . in a *cul-de-sac* formed by the intersection of two spurs of the billowy and abounding hills, and opening at its mouth beside a roaring stream, spanned by a slippery foot-bridge, safe enough in daylight, but a very bridge of peril in the dense gloom of a rainy, moonless night. . . .

Mr. Vestal, as janitor, received us kindly, and caused the long-closed church to be opened, warmed and lighted for the use of the public. But the long-unused stove-pipe had rusted so nearly off at its base that a little expansion by fire sent it tumbling with a crash upon the yet fortunately empty benches. Had the accident occurred fifteen minutes later, there would have been a chronicle of broken heads to render this column tragically interesting.

Some gentlemen carried the hot stove outside with ropes, the few citizens gathered themselves together, and the lecture was delivered amidst profound and respectful attention.

We had gone to the church, over the foot-bridge, and through the gulches, by the expiring twilight. On returning, the night was black as Erebus. . . . Nobody had a lantern; the rain beat time with the roaring waterfall, and beat a silent symphony with the waves of darkness. What was to be done? Never did the headlight in a hotel room seem so far away.

We not only have no dread of death, but we have in later years had no desire to escape it; but the idea of broken bones and crippled bodies has long been our pet horror.

A small boy caught an idea. We had with us a few copies of the *New Northwest*, and he said he would make torches if he had a match. Somebody had matches, and both small boy and smoker are hereby blessed for their sagacity and providence.

The agony was soon over; but it was long before your correspondent could forget in sleep the memory of that falling stove-pipe, that slippery foot-bridge, that roaring waterfall, and those blazing newspaper torches.

Portland, May 13, 1879.

A. S. D.

*(May 15, 1879)*

## Staging to Jacksonville, Oregon

On the morning of the 26th ult., . . . we were roused from a couch of restlessness [in Roseburg] to try the realities of a hundred-mile journey by stage coach, our destination Jacksonville.

When you go by rail or steamer you cannot possibly realize one-half the incidents of your journey. The fatigue is too slight, the transit too rapid, the comforts too many. In such cases you grow indolent as you travel, and if your way is long you will unconsciously forget to look about you.

Very different are your sensations when you mount the box above the stage-coach boot, and, seated behind the prancing six-horse team, suffer yourself to be strapped upon your precarious seat beside the obliging driver, your main business for the next twenty-four hours being an attempt to hold your place and ease, as well as may be, the constantly recurring jolts that shake you to a jelly and bruise you to a pulp.

All day long the patient horses pursue their winding way. . . .

After a supper fit for a king, and a change of drivers as well as horses, we journey on and on, into the heart of the night, into the heart of the mountains, over zigzag roads and

*Stagecoach that operated between Roseburg and Myrtle Point, Oregon*

past many winding turns of the busy Rogue River, our companion for miles the beautiful deer that are so unafraid of the coach and team that they amble gracefully up to us in the waning twilight and gaze wistfully into our faces, regardless of the murderous wishes of the driver, who vainly swears for a revolver. . . .

Sometime after midnight, we reached a way station, where we changed horses, and after driving onward for a mile or so, discovered that the whip, that indispensable weapon without which no driver could think of hazarding his reputation as a Jehu, had been lost or left behind. The driver suddenly gave us the lines, and alighting, loosened the off tug of the off wheeler, so that the coach might not run many yards without a complete smash-up if the team should get frightened, and leaving us there alone in the darkness, so securely strapped in the perch behind the apron that we couldn't extricate ourself from the buckles, though we tore our gloves to shreds in the attempt, hurried back with a lamp and was gone a trifle over twenty minutes, though to the solitary wanderer it seemed nearer twenty hours.

Once, . . . [while the driver was gone], we were startled by a sudden "loo" from some awakening cow in ambush, which so frightened the near leader that he danced an equine hornpipe. Maybe we didn't pull the ribbon and say "Whoa, beauties!" and "Oh, mercy!" and "why *did* the driver

cripple the coach before he left it?" and many other things which can't now be remembered.

But that off wheeler proved a veritable *brick*. He acted as though he was fully aware of the situation, and felt that the entire responsibility of the safety of the United States mail was resting on his tug-burdened shoulder.

"Why did you unhitch the tug, throw off the brake, and leave me wholly at the mercy of the horses?" we asked, nervously, as the driver came panting up.

"The horses won't start when one of the wheelers knows a tug's loose and on his back," he said carelessly, as, readjusting the hooks, mounting to his perch, and vigorously damning the socket that wouldn't hold the whip properly, he lashed the team to a tight run, and on we crashed at a fearful rate, obliged to make up for lost time.

*(July 10, 1879)*

## Peculiarities of Jacksonville Men

One peculiarity of the men has amused us greatly. Quite a number of them have run like Turks—or turkeys—at our approach: One, a merchant, who is a commissioned Brigadier-General [Tommy Ream] of the home guards under Governor Thayer, scooted out the back door of his store as we entered, and we could easily have captured the whole

concern with a single blank car-
tridge if his younger brother hadn't
held the fort like a man. In this instance, the Governor, who is usually
correct in his conclusions, gave the
commission to the wrong person.

The deputy sheriff was another
protector of the public interests who
deserted his post at our approach. . . .

Judge [Paine Page] Prim is another
protector of the people's interests who
ducks his head and runs when he sees
us.[4] His protected and supported wife
[Teresa M. Stearns Prim], whom he
once banished from her home and
children for two years because he was
weak enough to permit somebody to
slander her, and who finally allowed
her to come back to him for her
children's sake and his own convenience, is keeping a very nice and
prosperous millinery store. . . . We're
glad we've heard the other side of the
Judge's well known domestic
story. . . .

There are a number of would-be
prominent men in this place who
have tried their best, because of their
ignorance of our position, to snub
and ignore and ridicule us, who, did
they but know what their impudence
will cost them, would bow like mon-
keys and chatter like magpies. It's too
jolly for anything.

July 2d, 1879.

A. S. D.

*(July 10, 1879)*

## Trouble Brewing at Jacksonville

It is Saturday, 4 P.M., July 12th, and
we've come back to Jacksonville [after
lectures at Phoenix and Willow
Springs], and behold! there's a mighty
tempest in the social and political
teapot. The *New Northwest* of
Thursday [July 10] has just come to
hand, containing our letter of the 2d
inst. And Brother [William M.]
Turner of the [Jacksonville *Oregon*]
*Sentinel*, . . . is madder than two
hornets. . . . [H]e is furious to think
we've justified an injured lady [Mrs.
Prim] by vindicating her in the
women's paper. . . . And, as to the
Judge [Paine Page Prim], whose
champion he has suddenly become,
if he can outlive Brother Turner's
defense, he needn't fear any further
notice at our hands.

At this writing, squads of men are
holding indignation meetings on the
street, hard by the store of a certain
Brigadier-General, and it really looks
as though they'd be calling out the
militia pretty soon for the express
purpose of fighting a lone woman
whose offense against them has consisted in simply telling the truth. . . .

The *Standard* of the 10th is also
at hand, and we see that a certain
Major of the militia, or one of his
colleagues, who can't quite hide his
ear-marks, has been calling us a *he
hen*, and otherwise classically
caricaturing us, as becometh self-
constituted "protectors of women."

Let 'em writhe. They'll feel better after their vomit is over. A moral physician don't expect to give humanity a badly needed emetic and see 'em get over it without ejecting putridity by the way of the mouth.

*(July 17, 1879)*

## Egged and Burned in Effigy at Jacksonville

STILL LATER—
The plot thickens. . . .

The "militia's" been and egged us! And they've burnt us in effigy, the image being a fair likeness of George Washington, so we're told, though we didn't see it; and it wore a white apron with the words "Libeller of families" on it in big letters—a fitting name for the cowardly *canaille* who seek, under cover of darkness, to exhibit their true inwardness. Verily, there's no other form of tyranny that dies so hard as man's rights. . . .

Only one egg hit us, and that was fresh and sweet, and it took us square on the scalp and saved a shampooing bill. But what a comment on the morals and manners of an incorporated town! . . .

But to the credit of the better class of men be it spoken, they were not engaged in the mob at all. It was bearded hoodlums and bad whisky that did it, incited no doubt by the silly indignation of a certain editor, who has learned to his confusion that some editors can write sharp sayings for their newspapers as well as some others. The good work will go on and women will be free. *Selah!*

A. S. D.

*(July 17, 1879)*

## An Interlude

Phoenix, July 18.
Sunday morning, the 13th inst., dawned brightly, and discovered a quiet atmosphere and equally quiet street in Jacksonville, the latter disfigured by the picture of George Washington in women's garb, which had been burned in front of Mrs. Vining's hotel the night before as a feeble effigy of our humble self.

At nine o'clock one of friend Plymale's buggies came for us, and a span of spirited horses . . . carried us over the beautiful country to Manzanita, eight miles distant from the scene of the riot, and here we met a splendid audience. . . .

[After several lectures at Phoenix and Ashland], our last lecture at Ashland was finished, and amid the enthusiastic good-byes of scores of excellent Christian ladies, we took our departure this (Friday) morning for Phoenix, . . . and are now ready to take our departure for the city of the Philistines, where we are appointed to speak to-night, and thereby beard the Jacksonville mob in its den. You shall hear more anon.

A. S. D.

*(July 24, 1879)*

## Through the Howling Rabble

[Five Miles Outside]
Jacksonville, July 19.
Dear reader, we know you are anxious to hear the result, so this morning (Saturday) at five o'clock we are awake and ready to try, though we know we cannot do the subject justice.

At good Mrs. Vining's hospitable boarding-house [in Jacksonville] we were warmly welcomed, the brave woman being all undaunted by the threatening man's rights mob, which was waiting for the coming darkness to begin its raid. But we declined to risk exposing her home to the violence of the rabble by remaining in it, and gathering up our baggage, we entered the carriage, accompanied by Mr. Colver and Mr. Casto, from Phoenix, and drove through the crowded street and howling rabble to the home of Mr. and Mrs. Plymale, who, like all the other respectable citizens of Jacksonville, were afraid to venture out after nightfall, for fear of the mob and the eggs. Here our baggage was considered safe, and we left it till after the lecture, which was given in the Courthouse, the gentlemanly Sheriff, Mr. Bybee, having, at the risk of his life, lighted it up for our use.

But, so far as we know, not one resident of Jacksonville dared to attend the meeting. They bowed before the press and the mob like reeds, so thoroughly intimidated that, but for the presence of about fifty brave persons from the country, of whom a dozen or so were ladies, we should have had nobody for audience except the county Sheriff.

The lecture over, we explained that we scorned to remain over night as a guest in a city that dared not protect a truth-telling missionary of human rights from a howling mob. We would spend the night in the country among the good people who could not be over-ruled by prostitutes, man's rights and whisky. . . .

[W]e were not disturbed except by yells and threats, as after the lecture, the country carriages drove through the principal streets, on the way to Mrs. Wright's pleasant home, five miles from the corporation, where we have spent the night in sweet serenity, enjoying the sleep of the righteous. To-day (Saturday) we go to Willow Springs and from thence to-morrow to Foot's Creek, from which place you shall hear from us again.

The mail is going, and we must stop.

A. S. D.

*(July 24, 1879)*

## Return to the City of the Philistines

Willow Springs, July 21, 1879. [W]e wish we hadn't made our appointments to lecture in other places in such a way before the riot. . . . But we're not done with Jacksonville. We're going back there to-day to defy our defamers, and, if possible, to shame them into decency. . . . Kind friends, everywhere, do not worry. There is a higher Power than men or mobs that overrules this Woman Movement.

A. S. D.

Willows Springs, July 22, 1879. Again, as we are well aware that anxious friends by thousands are awaiting a truthful version of the closing scenes of our sojourn in Jacksonville, we hurriedly seize our oft-offending, though truth-telling, pencil to portray facts as they have occurred during the interim since last we wrote you.

On Monday, the 21st, we returned to the city of the Philistines as we had promised, though we were careful to enter and depart during day light, as the "militia" and other protectors of women with whom we have had to deal in that modern Sodom are of the kind that are only to be feared in the darkness.

At Mrs. Vining's we again found hospitable welcome, and . . .

we scribbled an open letter to the men of Jacksonville, which, after a little elimination, the editors [Charles Nickell and William M. Turner] of the [*Democratic*] *Times* and the [*Oregon*] *Sentinel* agreed to publish, the former in his issue of the 24th, and the latter, whose paper was already full for this week, on his next publication day. . . .

In the afternoon of Monday we made an address on the street, right in the midst of the crowd where we had been threatened with eggs and publicly howled at on the Friday before, and there was the most respectful silence and attention while we spoke.

We defended the boys who had been accused of instigating the riot. We charged the whole cause of the disturbance upon older heads—voters and lawmakers. . . . The boys are not to blame. It was bearded and beardless hoodlums, and bad whisky and voters and lawmakers, that did it. . . .

We've got away with Jacksonville. We've defied its eggs, its whisky, and its thugs. . . . We've left every intelligent woman sorrowing because she did not dare, for fear of her protectors, to attend our closing lecture. But we're coming back again, good ladies. . . .

A. S. D.

*(July 31, 1879)*

## Oh! The Ochoco Road!

Were you ever caught in a storm, in the beginning of an all-night ride, on an open buck-board, after having already traveled all day in the same bobbing vehicle, without a possible halting place until morning except at the bottom of a gulch or river? the night so black with intense darkness that you couldn't see horses or driver, or hardly imagine yourself a visible entity because of the impenetrable gloom?

Such, in brief, was our situation on the night after leaving Prineville to return to The Dalles, on the 5th inst., only the above paragraph is too tame to convey more than a ghost of an idea of the affair as it really existed.

The stage stations on the Ochoco road are thirty miles apart, and the relays of horses consist in each case of a single span of trusty equines, varied only, on the night drive, by an ebony-colored mule as trustworthy and wise as to redeem the character of the much-abused animal. . . . [N]othing but the superior sight, sagacity and endurance of her muleship served the double purpose of postponing the epitaph and continuing the jottings and journeyings of the undersigned.

The day had been an alternate gloomy, windy, rainy and sunshiny one, and at night the great clouds rose like a dense blanket of fog from the depths of the Cascade gorges. . . .

There ought to have been lamps on the buck-board, but there were none. The moon was off duty until near midnight. We should gladly have waited till daylight, but there was no chance for a choice of evils. . . . But the driver knew every inch of the road, and could tell where all the biggest precipices were, which was a great consolation, inasmuch as it kept us in momentary mental preparation for an unceremonious launching into physical oblivion. There was an old black horse on the off side, but true to the instincts of the genus masculine, he depended in his extremity upon the superior foresight of the species whose gender was feminine.

Once, when we were—so the driver said—half way down the Warm Springs Hill, and in direct range of a projecting rock which he was specially anxious to avoid, he pulled a little "haw." The mule reluctantly obeyed, and we were *out of the road.* He was afraid to go forward, it was impossible to go further to the left, fatal to go to the right, and impracticable to go backwards.

In our dilemma we wanted to sit there in the rain till morning . . . , but the driver lighted his way for a minute with an ephemeral match, and, by the exercise of skill which the most expert mariner might envy, steered back into the narrow road, and again depended upon the sagacity of the mule.

Before starting on the night ride we had enjoyed a bountiful supper at the Warm Spring Agency, and been treated to a rare exhibition of vocalism from Mr. C. H. [Cyrus Hamlin] Walker and his Indian pupils;[5] and now, that we were in the extremest peril of our life, we couldn't help humming snatches of their songs to a limping improvisation which ended in every refrain with, "Oh! the Ochoco road."

"How did you feel when the danger was at its height?" asked the driver, after we had descended the precipice and forded the river in safety. . . .

"Felt glad that my life was insured, and realized a hearty admiration for that invisible yet tangible mule," we answered, unable to think of a more appropriate reply. . . .

Four A.M., and a home station. How the wind *whizzed* about us! and how our teeth chattered! . . . [W]e sat and shivered till the driver housed the faithful mule and dependent horse in the barn, and then accompanied the lone traveler to the cabin, where he struck a light and proceeded to build a fire. Nobody stirred about the house, and there was no kindling wood; but there gaped the cavernous chimney, and yonder were the bunks, against the wind-riven walls, that contained the improvident sleepers whose duty it was to have a fire in readiness.

Everything disagreeable must end some time. The dark and cold gave way at last before a ruddy blaze, a hostler was called by the driver from one of the bunks, and we, wrapped from head to foot in shawls and blankets of our own, crept into a dirty bed and fell asleep from sheer exhaustion.

Half past five, and called to breakfast. A weary woman, with a solitary eye tooth, two fretful babies and neuralgia in the head, had ready a meal of boiled cabbage warmed over (very greasy), fried potatoes and bacon (yet greasier), Chili beans (didn't taste 'em), black coffee without milk or cream, saleratus biscuit, and no butter. But the *pay* was first class, and we paid her cheerfully. . . .

November 15, 1879.

A. S. D.

*(November 20, 1879)*

## Mexican Woman Committed

A Mexican woman named Margurita Arnads has been committed to the insane asylum. She is the same woman which the *Standard* referred to some weeks ago since as being brought up by the keeper of a house of ill-fame, and because she refused to ply the vocation of a prostitute, was turned out into the streets.

*(November 20, 1879)*

## Robbery on the Lewiston Stage

The morning after the lecture at Pataha, the weather had sensibly moderated, and the snow by noon was melting rapidly under the influence of brilliant sunshine.

At 1 P.M. we started for Lewiston [I. T.]. By three o'clock we were out beyond the snow, and bowling up and down the dusty roads. Later, and we descended a long, steep, and winding grade, on the "rough lock" and at anything but "double quick." Then we came into the valley of the Alpowa, a little river, along which reside several Indian farmers, who have renounced their tribal relations and builded themselves comfortable homes. The stage road crosses the Alpowa eleven times within a few miles, and the scenery on either hand is decidedly picturesque and wild.

Our stage had crossed the river for the last time, and we had come within four miles of the Snake River ferry, when we saw, to the right, and running along a bend in the creek, a man carrying a gun. The thought of robbers crossed our brain for an instant, but there were two wagons near with drivers, and two Indians farther on, and so we supposed the man was only after a bird or other small game. The fellow came up in front of the stage and crossed the road, and still we thought nothing of it. But when he came up to the team, and pointing a needle-gun at the driver and the undersigned, so close that we both looked down the barrel and almost into eternity, and when he ordered a halt, as though the institution belonged to him, we saw at once that the game he was after was of considerable proportions.

"Stop!" he cried earnestly, and what his word didn't accomplish was finished up by that glittering "persuader."

We stopped.

"Put out that box!" he exclaimed, with a feint at taking aim.

The driver, an honest and worthy denizen of Dayton, W. R. Dixon by name, put on the brake, gave the lines a twist, and went for the express box with alacrity. But it was not under the front seat, and he had to dismount and fish it out from under the back seat, on which a frightened Chinaman and his asthmatic wife sat like statues. The robber followed the driver with his "persuader" and kept him covered with it so closely that there was no chance for dodging.

Once the fellow looked at us with a sort of comical expression, as though the situation was ludicrous, and we should have begun a sparring conversation then and there, only there was too much cash in our side pocket for us to risk a joke with a highwayman. He taught us one lesson, however. We'll never go staging again with cash about us in any quantity worth stealing.

While the driver was getting the box for the bandit, we took another square look at the fellow, and are sure we'd know him anywhere. He was about five feet eight inches in height, would weigh about 150 pounds, was square-featured, intelligent, smooth-shaven, comfortably dressed and handsome. He had partly covered his face with dust from the roadside, but did not conceal his features nor try to avoid detection.

The men in the wagons sat by in a sort of daze while the robbery was going on.

The box once in the robber's possession, he demanded the express packet, but took the driver's word that there was none along unless it was in the box.

"All right," said the robber. "I have three pals on the road above, and if they try to stop you, say 'Skookum chuck,' and they'll understand it and let you off."

When the driver mounted the stage again and took the ribbons to "travel," he was panting like a quarter horse at the end of a mile heat. He drove on a few yards, when we said, laughingly:

"That fellow'll get caught. I've marked him so well that I'd know him if I was coasting and should meet him in Kamtschatka."

"Schse—se—se! Don't talk!" he exclaimed, in a nervous whisper, and we then realized that we ought to have been frightened a little, too. We had some curiosity to see what the robber would do with the express box, and what the men in the wagons would do with him, but couldn't afford to delay the United States mail for such a trifle; and, to tell the truth, we were not sorry to make rapid tracks for Lewiston; nine miles away.

Lewiston, November 27.

A. S. D.

*(December 4, 1879)*

## Notes for 1879

1. In July of 1878, Lorenzo (or Alonzo) Perkins and his wife Blanche, called by the Indians "the pregnant one," were killed by a small band of Umatillas while trying to flee from the mid-Columbia to Yakima. According to Kirk and Alexander, "Blanche and Lorenzo Perkins were killed by Umatilla men who were avenging a wanton gunboat attack on Columbia River fishing camps. The murder of the young couple greatly alarmed all whites in Washington Territory; the shelling of two villages distressed all native people" (*Exploring Washington's Past*, 146-47). Chief Moses was accused of complicity in the crime, and he was captured and jailed for a time in Yakima, an action that satisfied settlers and ranchers who wanted to appropriate his lands. See Ruby and Brown, *Indians of the Pacific Northwest*, 252.

2. During a visit in 1879 to Washington, D. C., Chief Moses was promised the "Columbia Reservation," which was to be located between Lake Chelan and the Canadian border, and from the summit of the Cascade Mountains east to the Okanogan River.

3. This Mrs. Cornelius was probably Missouri Smith, second wife of Col. Thomas R. Cornelius (1827-99), an Indian fighter and farmer after whom the town of Cornelius was named. He served

*Abigail Scott Duniway , ca. 1876*

on the Oregon Territorial Council, was a state senator, and moved to Cornelius in 1872, where he had three large farms and established his general store, sawmill, and warehouse.

4. Judge Paige Prim (1822-99) was born in Tennessee and came to Oregon in 1851. He practiced law in Linn County; was Jackson County representative at the state constitutional convention in 1857; served as a state supreme court justice, 1859-80; and was chief justice for three two-year terms ending in 1878. After serving on the Oregon supreme court, he returned to his Jacksonville law practice and was elected state senator in 1882. Prim married Teresa M. Stearns in 1857, and they had two children.

5. Cyrus Hamlin Walker (1838-1921), son of pioneer missionary Elkanah Walker and Mary Richardson Walker, was born at the Whitman Mission at Wailatpu. He was educated in Forest Grove at Tualatin Academy and Pacific University, and served as clerk, teacher and superintendent at the Warm Springs Indian Agency, 1877-92.

# 1880

## Child of a Prostitute

[W]e've been stirred up by an event [at Forest Grove] that has almost made us resolve to turn theological evangelist. The facts, in brief, are as follows: A fallen woman of Portland [Bridget Gallagher], whose downfall was the result of our so called Christian system that *"Stones the woman, let's the man go free,"* is the mother of a bright, well-mannered little boy, the illegitimate offspring of her devoted but mistaken girlhood's love and trust and a wealthy and respectable villain's false promises. This man's perfidy and the world's scorn years ago converted this woman into an outcast. For years she has kept a house of ill-repute on Second street, an occupation into which she drifted because all other doors were closed against her when her betrayer left her, heart-broken and degraded, at the mercy of the pitiless world, with this little helpless child of shame as her only heritage.

Loathsome as her calling is, we doubt not that her soul is infinitely whiter in the eyes of God than that of any man who would dare to hinder her from placing this tender child in a Christian home, away from the slums of Second street, and under the influence of a Christian school. And yet the acting Faculty of Pacific University has dared to do this wicked thing. The child's mother, anxious to bring him up under Christian influences, last week placed him here [at Forest Grove] in a Christian home, where the kindly sympathy of every member of the household was at once enlisted in his behalf; and, with never a thought but he would be admitted into the [preparatory] school, the kindly host who had taken charge of him spoke to a Professor about the tuition, and was coolly informed that the child of such a mother could not be received in their ranks!

And yet, this school is a noted asylum for Alaskan, Japanese and Chinese pupils, and is just now preparing to receive in its Christian fold a heathen reinforcement of fifty little Indians of both sexes. Oh, that this little boy were a Kanaka, a cannibal, a Jap, or a heathen Chinese! Oh, that Ethiopia or Turkey or India had sent him to the Forest Grove school to be trained as a witness for Jesus! Then would these canting relics of a Pharisaical dynasty receive him with open arms. Then could they solicit added funds from the missionary board to aid them in their arduous work of carrying the gospel to the ends of this earth. . . .

The Faculty that claims to be Christian, and will exclude from its fold one of the least of the sons of man for whom Jesus died, for no other reasons than those for which the child is in no way responsible, is a blot upon . . . Christianity. The school that follows such a proscriptive course will die. . . .

One grand old Christian lady, whose grandchildren are in the school, said to us, in presence of the pupils of the household, "I wonder if the Faculty will ascertain the antecedents of the little Indians who are coming, and exclude all of them from the school whose mothers are not chaste?". . .

Indeed, the general verdict is one of strong and utter condemnation of the Faculty's conduct. In palliation they have trumped up a charge that the child's friends attempted to smuggle him into the school, a charge which we have sifted to the bottom, and in which we find *no truth*.

No wonder there are infidels in the land. No wonder they are multiplying in Forest Grove. Ah, me!

[Forest Grove] January 29, 1880. A. S. D.

*(February 5, 1880)*

## To Right the Wrong

Since the publication, in our last issue, of the account of the refusal, by the Faculty of Pacific University, Forest Grove, to admit into the preparatory department of the school an illegitimate child [son of Bridget Gallagher], we have been in constant receipt of written and oral commendatory remarks on our course in holding the professors up to public obloquy. The school is well known to be under the control of the Congregational Church, and it is with much pleasure that we are able to state that most of the condemnatory remarks on the course of the Faculty come from members of the denomination named. . . . An Oregon City gentleman hopes that the Trustees will have the wrong righted, and that the Faculty "will see their error and take the back track."

*(February 12, 1880)*

## Women's Handiwork at the Oregon State Fair

Now that the State Fair is over, a few thoughts in reference to its management will probably be in order. . . .

It would be vastly amusing, were it not so suggestive of woman's impecuniosity, as well as her inborn acquisitiveness, to note the many little expedients the sex will resort to in order to obtain a premium of a few dollars. Many of the articles they enter for competition are wholly useless, and certainly possess not the slightest claim to being beautiful. One little rocking chair, that we have noticed every year for a long time in a conspicuous position, has become so old and worn that the bits of silk that form its upholstered covering cannot last many decades longer. . . .

Some of the quaint devices of women suggest a struggling genius for invention that makes us fairly tremble with eager desire to strike the shackles from their hampered lives and permit them to indulge their wonderful gifts in Edisonian enterprises, where money could aid their efforts in a practical direction.

One of the greatest curiosities of the fair was a pair of landscape pictures made of the hair from the heads of the Oregon pioneers. Judged merely as pictures, these landscapes were nothing remarkable; but the material of which they were made will startle any beholder into an exclamation of surprise and wonder. Houses, windows, trees, rocks, mountains, flowers, rivers, boats and boatmen are all made of human hair, in every hue and shade, ingenuously interwoven according to its color. The author of this unique specimen of handiwork is Mrs. Ross, of Monmouth, who designs it for the State House when another landscape is completed.

Our hobby is (and we've said before that everybody has a hobby) to offer premiums to women's handiwork a little more on a par with those offered for horse-racing. Let these extra premiums be for babies, butter, starch, soap, candles, cookery, etc., etc., not omitting any one of the thousand femininities already named, unless it be the ever obtruding and always ugly patchwork quilt. Any fool can make a quilt, and, after we had made a couple dozen over twenty years ago, we quit the business with the conviction that nobody but a fool would spend so much time in cutting bits of dry goods into yet smaller bits and sewing them together again, just for the sake of making believe they were busy at practical work.[1] A dozen such quilts as we saw at the fair would be needed to keep one comfortable through an Oregon Summer night, and any one of the dozen would require two months' labor to complete it.

Portland, July 14, 1880.

A. S. D.

*(July 15, 1880)*

# Visit to the Multnomah County Poor Farm

On Wednesday, the 21st inst., the undersigned, accompanied by liege and heir, forsook the heat and dust of the busy city and wended our way over the hill to the poor-house.... The easy-going horses jogged leisurely through and up the canyon for three miles or more, carrying us past the city's laundry and steam carpet-cleaner, the Canyon Gardens, a milk ranch, a mill and a poultry yard, and at last to the foot of a picturesque hillside, where a gate was opened that led the way around the hill to the summit, upon which we halted before the imposing paupers' quarters that mock at destitution amid their emerald surroundings of gardens, fruit trees and wheat fields. Near by is the little white cottage occupied by the Superintendent and his wife, Mr. and Mrs. J. C. Cleghorn, who welcomed the trio to their cheerful home. . . .

The County Farm comprises 205 acres of hillside, forest, crag and canyon, nearly half of which . . . has been cleared off, and much of it brought to a high state of cultivation.

The inmates of the farm now number twenty five—sixteen white men, seven Chinamen, and only two women (one a Chinese and the other a Mexican). The apartments are roomy, clean and well ventilated, and the food healthy, well cooked and plentiful.

Mr. Cleghorn says that nine-tenths of the inmates were brought to pauperism by whisky and licentiousness; and certainly no one can doubt it who sees the mental and physical wrecks as they file in to their meals, some of them hardly knowing enough to eat when food is placed before them. . . .

In addition to the present large building, with its barn, granary, laundry, woodshed and water-tanks, there is soon to be erected a building for paupers of the protected sex, a convenience which is much needed, and would be a help to the county as a measure of economy, as well as a haven of refuge for many a destitute mother and her little ones, who are now cared for in the city when thrown upon the public for support.

Portland, July 27, 1880.

A. S. D.

*(July 29, 1880)*

## Visit to the Indian School at Forest Grove

[T]he crowning feature of Forest Grove just now is its Indian school, which we visited by invitation of Mrs. Huff, the efficient matron, who has a mother's charge over some forty or more children of the forest. . . .

The buildings consist of two large two-story frame structures, in advanced stages of completion—one for the schools and the dormitories and play-rooms of the boys, and the other for the dining-room, kitchen, laundry, sewing-room, matron's rooms, and the dormitories of the girls. Professor Boynton, who has had much experience in Indian schools, is the teacher in charge.

Indian children, like negroes, excel in singing. Some of them are from the Warm Spring reservation, and were formerly under the excellent training of Mr. Cyrus Walker. These singers naturally lead the rest, and the music is a pleasing feature of all their exercises.

Mrs. Huff, who is evidently the right woman in the right place, informs us that the . . . [children] under her care are quite as orderly and obedient as so many white children. There is no quarreling among them, and apparently no disposition to shirk their duties. Like the negro or the Chinaman, they are easily impressed with the Christian faith, and many of the older boys and girls can "speak in meeting" and "tell their experiences" as well as mature white folks. . . . Everybody who doubts the wisdom of Captain [Melville] Wilkinson's latest Indian exploit should visit the school.[2]

While it is well known that we have never been sanguine of the success of engrafting the Christian religion upon Indians, yet we do believe it possible to engraft the young of any tribe upon our civilization whenever, as in this case, the tap roots are cut that formerly connected them with the associations of their kind. We have great faith in this experiment, especially since we have seen it in its primary form. But we could not but wish, as we gazed about us, that the Government and the missionaries would act as wisely and humanely with Mrs. Nobody's white children as with the half-breeds here of whom some are red-haired, blue-eyed, and freckled, and all are passably well looking.

If only the "Gallagher boy" were a half-breed Indian now! But he's only a half-Irish lad, and is consequently beyond the pale of Christian reformation.

We were told by a worthy lady of the Grove that the above-named boy's mother [Bridget Gallagher] sent word that she would give five hundred dollars to know the Professor's name who refused her boy a place in the college [preparatory program]. Without fee or reward we are ready to give the first letter of the surname, which, in connection with its fellows, spells *Marsh*. . . .[3]

*Group of sixty-three children posed for photo at the Indian Training School, Forest Grove, Oregon, ca. 1882*

We had heard much while in Tacoma and Steilacoom about the kidnapping of three young Indians by Captain Wilkinson, under an order from General Milroy, and took occasion to ask the children, while all together, to state the facts from their own standpoint. All who were pleased with their present quarters were asked to raise their hands. Forty hands went up. All who wanted to return were asked to signify it. Not a hand was raised.

Peter Stancup, a young Indian, and evidently the spokesman of the school, stood at the end of our address and stated that all the Puyallup Indians were ready to send such of their children as the Captain wanted, until by some mistake among the white folks it was proclaimed that General Milroy had sent an order to take them by force, at which, very naturally, the parents resisted. But, he said, none of the children were taken without the parents' consent, and several that the Captain wanted he did not bring because their fathers were not willing. . . . The principal fuss, he said, had been made by the white folks who had not believed in the Captain's experiment, and so had opposed it. So far as he knew, there was no dissatisfaction now.

The girls of the school are taught to cook, wash, iron, sew, wash dishes, do chamber work, and all other duties which the supported sex are expected to perform, and the boys are to be taught farming, horticulture and trades. We personally know some thousands of white children whom we'd be glad to see as well provided for and as practically taught in the ways of honest work as these wards of the Nation.

North Yamhill, August 30, 1880.
A. S. D.

*(September 2, 1880)*

## Frontier Marriage and Charivari at Mitchell

After mailing the editorial letter of last week from the Saltzman House, in the John Day Valley, we retired early to rest. After a dreamless sleep, we were ready to mount the Thursday morning buck-board, bound for the village of Mitchell [Oregon], seventeen Cayuse miles away. . . . [T]he village . . . consists of half a dozen new, unpainted frame houses, with the post office, hotel and store in one of them, and all cuddled cosily down upon the bosom of a friendly valley. . . .

Mr. I. N. Sargent, the leading man of the village, and proprietor of the aforesaid hotel, post office and store, welcomed us in the hospitable manner peculiar to the country, and ushered us into the cheery presence of his amiable wife, who informed us that a wedding was in progress, and our help was needed to arrange the drapery of the bride.

In a little while all was ready, and the groom-elect, an honest young ranchman from Baker county, led forth the bride, who was lovely to look upon in her floating veil and snowy orange blossoms, and Elder Rowe, who had halted by the way for the purpose, proceeded to pronounce Frank Hundsaker and Fanny Sargent husband and wife. The wedding was a private affair, only the parents of the high contracting parties and half a dozen invited guests besides ourself and the stage driver being present. But the occasion was all the more enjoyable because of its simplicity. In a little while we all sat down to a sumptuous feast, and the afternoon was spent in neighborly chit-chat. . . .

After the lecture [in the evening], the "boys," as men of all ages are called on the road, to the number of a couple of dozen, began to tune themselves up around the freight wagons and camp-fires for the dulcet harmonies of a grand *charivari*. The newly-married couple took the hint, and disguising themselves, departed in a hack for the house of a neighbor, several miles away.

It was hardly nine o'clock before the fun began. And *such* fun! The "boys" threw stones at the house, and fired blank cartridges at the windows, and rang discordant bells, and drummed on dry goods boxes, and frightened a baby, and made good Mrs. Sargent nervous and angry— all for nothing. The married couple had "vamosed the ranche."

We thought the musicians had enjoyed about fun enough after half an hour, and the elder Mrs. Hundsaker accompanied us out to the teamsters' camp-fire, around which the serenaders had assembled for a few minutes' consultation; and when we graciously informed the amateurs that their victims had "skedaddled," it was our turn to enjoy the fun. Some of them held their guns awkwardly in their hands and gazed straight down their noses in silence, others toyed idly with the discordant bells and said nothing, and others asked questions incredulously.

After being repeatedly assured that their game was gone, they felt that their music had been made in vain; but we begged them to believe it was all right. It was a grand serenade, we said, in honor of Mrs. Hundsaker and ourself in particular, and woman's rights in general. We were very thankful and complimentary, and bowed ourselves away at the close of the little speech accompanied by "Three cheers for the *New Northwest*" and a grand "hurrah for Hardscrabble."

The revelers then suspected the whereabouts of the bride and groom, and, after further consultation, departed for their place of entertainment. But the groom, anticipating such a visit, and determined to mislead them, had hidden his hack in a ravine over an adjoining hill, and, as they could not find it on the premises, they supposed he had gone in some other direction; and they returned, crestfallen but jolly, and consoled themselves by giving another outdoor concert in honor of their own discomfiture.

Canyon City, November 8, 1880. A. S. D.

*(November 18, 1880)*

# Notes for 1880

1. Quilting was neither Duniway's forte nor her recommended activity for already overworked, subjugated women. She intended to complete a silk hexagon pattern quilt, which she began piecing after Ralph's birth in November of 1869, and donate it to the 1899 New York World's Fair as an example of Oregon women's work and accomplishments. The Portland Woman's Club quickly raised a fund and purchased Duniway's roughly stitched, brightly colored quilt for the Oregon Historical Society, where it was safely tucked away. Duniway gave the money to Oregon's 1900 suffrage campaign. The typewritten inscription stitched to the quilt states that it was intended for "the First National Woman Suffrage Bazaar in honor of Theodore Roosevelt, the first champion of the equal Suffrage movement ever elected to a National office by popular vote" (quilt #1721 at the Oregon Historical Society). See ASD to Clyde Duniway, 5 Dec. 1900, Duniway Papers; Moynihan, *Rebel for Rights*, 154; 247, n. 19. For colored photos of Duniway's quilt, see Mary Bywater Cross, *Treasures in the Trunk: Quilts of the Oregon Trail* (Nashville: Rutledge Hill Press, 1993), 84-85.
2. The Indian Training School was founded at Forest Grove in 1880 by Captain Melville Wilkinson, Third Infantry, U. S. Army, and it was later moved to Chemewa, near Salem. This was a government-sponsored school, with Wilkinson as superintendent, and the goal was total assimilation into American culture. The children received English names and were not allowed to speak their native languages. One white observer called the school a "Christian nursery" for "wigwam babies," and Wilkinson was known to scour the Pacific Northwest to find his young pupils. First at Forest Grove, and later at Chemewa, the mortality rate was high, and Indians feared sending their children off "to die." See Bancroft, *History of Oregon*, Vol II, 690; Ruby and Brown, *Indians of the Pacific Northwest*, 237.
3. This may be Dr. Sidney H. Marsh. In 1854, Marsh became the first president of Tualatin Academy and Pacific University.

# 1881

## Reflections on the Indian Question

The dreaded raids of the noble red men have deterred many stock men from coming to Camas Valley [Idaho] to settle with their families. Evidences of the late war abound on all sides. Remnants of stockades remain in Mt. Idaho and at Grangeville around the largest buildings, in which the defenseless whites were corralled like cattle for their own scalps' sake for months in '77, while their honorable foes, over whom the pseudo-philanthropy of the East is still gushing, maimed their stock, destroyed their houses, barns and fences, and killed every white person they could find unarmed; and then, after being routed by volunteers and regulars, these wily heathen held a grand pow-wow with the far less wily heathen at Washington, and are even now being double rationed, clothed and armed, while recruiting on reservations for a future onslaught upon the white settlers, who, unlike themselves, cannot hold

*"New recruits"—children from the Spokane tribe recently recruited for the Indian Training School at Forest Grove, ca. 1882*

their lands unless they "reside upon and cultivate them."

But your average philanthropist must have something to pet, and, now that the negro is free and left to shift for himself, and the industrious Chinaman takes care of himself, the Indian, being a savage, must be kept in idleness. But for the Indian Superintendencies and the political machinery growing out of their manipulation, the noble red man of the United States reserves would find himself no better off as a raider than the Chinaman or the negro; no better off, in fact, than his dusky brother of British Columbia, who, being compelled to take care of himself like other folks, finds it vastly more convenient for his tribe to be peaceable than murderous. The present policy of the Government means extermination to the Indian through his own helpless laziness in time. . . .

Let no one think that we would dispossess the Indians of their homes. Like every other child of Earth, they should be entitled to the use of the soil for a home and sustenance. But we believe that equality of rights is the best of rights, and are sick to chronic nausea of the maudlin sentimentality that provides for the Indian as though he were a child, and treats with him after a battle of his own creating as though he were a sovereign to whom a debt is due whenever he murders a white woman or child or steals or destroys a white person's property.

We confess that we turn from the contemplation of this governmental anomaly to the thought of Captain Wilkinson's Indian school [at Forest Grove, Oregon] with the greatest relief. There, we believe, is something practical being done. And if, after their educations and trades are completed, the students, as fast as their majority is reached, are endowed with citizenship and its accompanying responsibilities, and given homesteads upon the same terms as whites, the Indian Bureau will be of no longer use—on their account at least. But the like of this will ruin the trade of the politicians, so it is almost too good to hope for.

Grangeville, Idaho, May 27th.
A. S. D.

*(June 9, 1881)*

## Trial of Nannie Thomas at Colfax, W.T.

The trial of Nannie Thomas for the murder of Lizzie Shanks was in prospect [at Colfax], and was the talk of the town. In the company of a large number of other sight-seers, we visited the jail where the prisoner was in durance, and found her in the front apartment directly opposite two grated cells, in one of which an Indian and a Chinaman were confined, and in the other three white men. We were told that the woman was locked up at first in the cell with the Chinaman! but we hope the report is untrue.

She was certainly situated badly enough when we saw her, with no furniture but a straw bed on the floor, and no privacy of any kind—no chance, even for a minute, to obscure herself from the gaze of five imprisoned men. She was more self-possessed than any of us when the bolt shot back and we were admitted to her presence. She was neatly attired in mourning, and was easy in her manner and evidently pleased to see the faces of women. She has been confined in damp and dreary cells for fourteen months in Walla Walla, awaiting the tardy progress of that lumbering imperfection of masculine mismanagement inappropriately styled the law. She has grown thin and anxious, and has suffered much from cold and filth and dampness. . . .

The court-room was crowded during the trial—women and lawyers around the bar, and men standing everywhere else. We could only attend for a little while on the 9th, as we had begun to recover from that twisting ride [on a buckboard from Palouse], and had renewed an engagement to lecture at Palouse, but we improved the time we had, and must say that the eagerness of some of the witnesses to convict the defendant was plain enough to be strong presumptive evidence in her favor. . . .

Brumfield had eloped from Kansas with Lizzie Shanks, and in the company of [Bud] Thomas and his wife [Nannie] had come westward. They had swapped names at Walla Walla to quiet the fears of the old Lothario [Brumfield] who feared that his step-son would follow him. This exchange of names enabled the real Thomas to draw Brumfield's money from the Walla Walla banks. . . .

On Tuesday, we came back to Colfax. . . . The murder trial was over, and Mrs. Thomas was acquitted. . . . The jury had been burdened with an interminable array of irrelevant testimony, not one word of which went to prove that Mrs. Thomas had committed the murder, or had even witnessed it. Yet the excited populace demanded blood, and the prisoner's fate hung upon a thread. With the decision of the jury, however, came a reaction. Only here and there a man or woman could be found who indulged in bitter denunciation of the accused and her jury. . . .

Charley Hopkins [grandson of Col. E. D. Baker] is making a lively paper of the *Gazette*. He ran it as a daily during the murder trial, and it gained a wide patronage. Immediately after the trial, Charley called upon Mrs. Thomas and obtained the following explanation, which, unfortunately for the acquitted woman, was published with some inaccuracies that do her great injustice. The interpolations authorized by herself and acquiesced in by the editor are in italics, and all friends of justice are asked to judge of the matter upon its merits.

***

Old Mr. Brumfield was not married to Lizzie. She was his second wife's daughter. He eloped with her. *My husband told me at Sheffer's* (in the Palouse country) that he [Bud Thomas] and she [Lizzie Shanks] had entered into a conspiracy to decoy the old man out to California and kill him for his money. When we got there, no suitable place was found for the purpose, and we then started for the Palouse country. On the steamer the old gentleman became alarmed lest Lizzie's husband should follow and kill him, and he suggested a change of names, which was agreed to, but we did not change them until we left Walla Walla. The night we encamped on the Touchet, Bud, my husband, said that was a good place to do the deed, but Lizzie objected, and Bud decoyed him out of camp, killed him, took his money, undressed him, and threw his body in the creek. We then proceeded to Sheffer's as indicated in the testimony. One day, while there, my husband *told me the whole story about killing Brumfield,* and said Lizzie must be killed or she might betray them. I remonstrated with him, and thought I had persuaded him not to do it. Soon after our experience with the last witness before the killing, we encamped at the place indicated in the evidence, and while I was at the wagon getting some articles for supper, and Lizzie was bending over the fire preparing the evening meal, my husband approached her from behind and shot her through the head. When I heard the report, I knew what had happened, and rushed to the scene in frantic despair, crying, "Bud, for God's sake, what have you done?" He answered, "Shut your mouth!" and picked up the body, which he carried some feet and then dropped. He again picked it up and carried it up the hill some forty feet, when he again dropped it, and called to me, saying, "Nannie, G—d d—n you! come and help me carry this." I assisted him to the top of the hill, and he dragged it the remainder of the way. You ask me why I kept the secret, but if you are a married man you can realize my position. I loved my husband, and would have died rather than betray him.

***

Thus one of the most horrible mysteries that has ever hung upon the hearts of a people has been partially solved. The suspicion that Thomas had intended to murder his wife instead of Lizzie Shanks is forced upon us. That Mrs. Thomas was fearfully jealous of the two is apparent. That they were enamored of each other, was generally believed. If he killed the dead man's paramour on purpose, it must have been because of a recent misunderstanding between them. His confession to his wife would indicate this.

But it is more probable that he mistook the one for the other in the gathering darkness, and, like Laura

Fair [San Francisco case of 1871], made a mistake in the killing. The women were dressed very nearly alike, and the villain shot at the victim in the dusk of the evening through a sun-bonnet that concealed her features.

Of the truth of this we shall never know; but one cannot but admire the heroism of the child-wife (she was but seventeen when the deed was done), who held her peace even to the risk of encountering the fatal halter rather than betray the brute of a husband who had committed the blackest crime in the catalogue. She is now in the motherly care of Mrs. Potter at the Colfax Restaurant, where she will remain until remittances from her own mother will enable her to return to Kansas.

What a bitter experience for such a mere child! No wonder a jury would not convict her.

Colfax, June 15, 1881.
A. S. D.
*(June 23, 1881)*

# Reactions to the Attempted Assassination of President Garfield

The morning of July 3d was accompanied by a pouring rain, which fell all day in copious tears, as though in lamentation over the nation's recent tragedy. The news of the attempted assassination of the President [Garfield] reached Cheney [W. T.] by a round-about way, the telegraph not yet connecting from Spokane, and by 10 o'clock A.M. every cheek was blanched and every voice awestricken, while over all hearts the weeping heavens presided with severest dignity. Great preparations had been made for a celebration on the Fourth, but the committee was appalled by the national disaster, and for lack of communication with the outside, or rather inside, world—for this certainly is the outer border—they could not decide whether to proceed with the festivities or turn the people's rejoicing into a general lamentation.

The rain ceased at nightfall, and the morning [of the Fourth] rose clear, placid dustless, and gloriously, radiantly beautiful. The electric air was fairly resonant with life. Country people began to arrive in crowds [for the festivities and a free ride on an excursion train to Spokane.]

Ainsworth, [W. T.]. July 8, 1881.
A. S. D.
*(July 14, 1881)*

# Bridget Gallagher Speaks for Her Child

The illegitimate son of a prominent and respectable voter and protector of women was sent some time ago to the Pacific University at Forest

Grove by his wronged, betrayed and abandoned mother [Bridget Gallagher], who desired to bring up her son in the ways of Christianity, education and honor. It is well known to our readers that the Pharisees of that University, who compass sea and land to make one proselyte from the ranks of degraded Kanaka, Indian or Chinese mothers, refused to receive this innocent son of a Christian gentleman into their ranks, in direct defiance of the heavenly injunction, "Whosoever will, let him come," for fear the gospel grace of the Divine Teacher would be inadequate for his salvation. It was not charged that the child was bad. They were only afraid he would become bad. So he remanded back to Second street.

His mother, in her strong desire to bring him up properly, recently tried to place him in the Catholic school in this city, but met with no better success than at Forest Grove. We ask the professed followers of the Son of Mary to pause and inquire. What would have been the conduct of the Master under like conditions? Do they not believe that the blood of Jesus Christ cleanseth from all sin? We have no words of excuse for the present life of the wronged and outraged mother of a respectable Christian's illegitimate son. But we cannot refrain from severest censure of the hollow bigotry that respects and honors the father, but condemns the

child, because of the mother's sin, to a life of ignorance and dissipation.

The mother's card is published in the interest of humanity, Christianity, and justice. It speaks for itself.

## A Card

Prejudice against me having closed the avenues to an honorable and useful career against my innocent child, I shall soon start East to place him in a school where he may receive the training which has been denied him in Oregon by men who, while claiming to be followers of Jesus, violate every principle which He taught, and under the cloak of religion exercise the hypocrisy of Judas Iscariot and the malignity of the devil.

When I had secured a good home for my boy in Forest Grove, and tried to get him into the school there, my enemies prevented me; and not thinking that Father Fierens, who stood as my boy's God-father at his baptism, would be so recreant to the doctrines of mercy and justice which he preached, I sought to place him in St. Michael's College in this city. But no! His mother was a denizen of Second street, and every effort of hers to make an honorable and useful man of her son must be thwarted, though no one could say a single word against the conduct of the child. With a heart that not all the holy water which the Pacific Ocean could hold would wash clean, this reverend (?) priest drove the lad away from the doors of the schoolroom, though this same priest had no scruple against eating and drinking in high society with the child's father, L. M. Starr.

I make no claim on the world's charity for myself; I am independent, and care not for its smiles or frowns; but I appeal to all honest people, whether church members or not, to say who deserves more censure—the father of the boy, rolling in his wealth, but unwilling to give a crumb to his son; the priest, who as sponsor for the child promised before God he should be trained in the paths of righteousness, but who casts him out as everything vile; the mother, driven to a life which casts her out of society in order to provide means for his support, or the innocent boy himself. Satisfied that the answer of true Christians and honest men everywhere will be against the seducer and unnatural father and the hypocritical priest, and in favor of the mother and the child, I hope soon to place my boy in school in some community where such men as Father Fierens carry hods instead of preaching, and where such men as Lew Starr do not associate with decent people.

Portland, July 25, 1881.

Bridget Gallagher.

*(July 28, 1881)*

# Death of President Garfield

President Garfield died on Monday evening at Long Branch, surrounded by his wife, physicians and attendants. He had been slowly sinking for several days, and his death was not unexpected. . . . The nation mourns this great sorrow with no loud lamentations, but the deepest grief . . . that once more its chosen head has fallen a victim to the atrocious crime of assassination. . . . Vice-President Arthur took the oath of office as the nation's Chief Magistrate soon after the announcement of President Garfield's death.

*(September 22, 1881)*

# Mrs. Duniway's Religious Views

A subscriber writes from Goldendale [W. T.], asking the senior editor to state her religious views in the *New Northwest*. This was her verbal answer, which we print to gratify the confessed curiosity of our subscriber: "I believe in churches, but not in bigotry; in Christ, but not in creeds; in religion, but not in self-righteousness; in God, but not in the devil."

To this it may be added that the *New Northwest* is not sectarian in any sense. Its motto, "Free Speech, Free Press, Free People," expresses its toleration of all religions or none.

Everybody's inherent right to think and act for himself in religious matters is as inalienable as the right to "life, liberty, and the pursuit of happiness."

*(November 17, 1881)*

## Chinamen Arrested

Forty Chinamen were arrested and fined $5 each last Saturday for violating the cubic air ordinance. They were sleeping in a room 28 feet long and 18 feet wide.

*(December 1, 1881)*

## Plight of Russian Immigrants

Quite a number of the company of Russian immigrants who arrived two months ago are sick with scarlet fever at the old Occidental Hotel building in East Portland, and seven children have died in three weeks. They are almost without furniture, and have little food. The City Marshal, who is also the health officer, has taken them in charge, secured a physician to attend them, and will provide proper food. The members of the company will probably be kept indoors, to prevent the disease from spreading.

*(December 15, 1881)*

# 1882

## A Defamer Punished by Mrs. Duniway's Sons

### THE EDITOR OF THE *SUNDAY WELCOME* BEATEN BY TWO SONS OF MRS. DUNIWAY

Yesterday afternoon about three o'clock, Willis S. and Hubert R. Duniway, the elder sons of Mrs. A. S. Duniway, senior editor of the *New Northwest*, walked into the real estate office of J. D. Wilcox & Co., on Stark street near First, which is also the business office of the *Sunday Welcome*, to punish Wm. M. Simpson, editor of that paper for an article it contained yesterday. They beat him roughly over the head with canes till he fell to the floor crying for quarter. Simpson received several scalp wounds, which bled freely; but his injuries are not considered dangerous. The Duniways walked to police headquarters and surrendered themselves to Captain Belcher, who released them on their own recognizance. Simpson was taken home in a carriage. The affair was witnessed by Dr. Howe, who came in at the same time the Duniways entered, and by two friends of Simpson, who were in the office.

*The sons of Abigail and Ben Duniway. Left to right: Clyde, Ralph, Willis, Wilkie, and Hubert*

The affair grew out of the recent investigation under Postal Agent Ben Simpson at Independence, in which the publishers of the *New Northwest* charged Postmaster Hodgin of that place with having overstepped his authority with regard to a package of the complainants' papers.[1] The *Welcome* of the 14th published a communication abusing Mrs. Duniway. Her sons say they were led to believe that the letter was written or inspired by Ben Simpson, father of William. . . . The [*New*] *Northwest* of last Thursday published an editorial charging the elder Simpson with bias and neglect of duty in the investigation and spoke of him as an "ex-preacher." The *Welcome* of yesterday published what purported to be a communication from Independence, signed "Haroun," in which vile epithets—more unclean than ever appears in the *Police Gazette*—were applied to Mrs. Duniway.[2] Her sons read the letter about 2:30 o'clock, and immediately started out to punish their mother's defamer.

While the affair is to be regretted, yet there can be no possible justification for the vile and defamatory article whose publication by the hoodlum Sunday journal was thus justly punished; and it is well to set a limit, by effective castigation when necessary, to defamatory, scurrilous and irresponsible journalism.

(From the *Daily Oregonian*, Jan. 22, 1882; rpt. *NNW*, Jan. 26, 1882)

## The State vs. W. S. and H. R. Duniway

The Grand Jury, as a matter of course, returned "not a true bill" in the case of the State vs. W. S. and H. R. Duniway, who caned Wm. M. Simpson for slander and were subsequently arrested for "assault with a dangerous weapon," on a warrant sworn out by one of his associates, Charles A. Cole, who was not present and knew nothing of the affair. No other ending to the farcical prosecution was expected.

(March 9, 1882)

## A Portland Tragedy: Annie Murray

On last Friday afternoon, Henry Prang, a saloon-keeper, was shot and killed by Annie Murray, keeper of a bagnio, and she was fatally wounded. She had been his mistress for years, and he had made his home at her house; but he deserted her for another woman of like character, and after seeking in vain to induce him to return, she followed him to his new abode for the purpose of taking the life of the faithless lover whom she had so long befriended. He wrenched the revolver from her, shot her, and as she sank back, mechanically dropped the weapon by her side, when she seized it and instantly sent a ball through his breast near the heart, causing death in a few moments. . . . It is said that he was engaged to be married soon to a respectable girl of this city.

*(March 9, 1882)*

## Chapters of Horror: Annie Murray

The fearful tragedies that have filled the pages of the daily press with tales of crime and horror during the past month are but the outgrowth of a system of laxity in morals at once alarming, degrading and abominable—a system that is itself an outgrowth of the subjugation of woman to the baser passions of men under a code of ethics that estimates the nature of the sin by the sex of the sinner. . . .

The senior editor, inspired by a desire to see something concerning the women's side of these chapters of horror, entered a cab on Tuesday and drove to St. Vincent's Hospital. A Sister of Charity met her at the threshold, and after some delay in the quiet waiting-room, the door was opened, and the weary face of Annie Murray's mother—a chastened, sorrowing woman—darkened the entrance. With thankful sobs the heart-broken mother exclaimed that her wayward child was dying.

We closed our eyes . . . in silent reverie among the scenes of bygone years. We well remembered Annie Murray as a child—a dainty, pretty, piquant creature, who grew up like a rare exotic amid the smoke and grime of a boardinghouse kitchen, a lily upon compost, a rose amid brambles. We also well remembered her ripening young womanhood, when, with her head full of a pardonable desire for the pretty trifles of the toilet which goes so far to fill a maiden's life with happiness, . . . she listened to the wile of the tempter, and fleeing her mother's roof, made the rash and fatal plunge into disgrace from which there was no returning.

From that time forward the young girl's course was downward. A man first sought and accomplished her ruin; other men contributed, God knows how largely, to the general wreck, and then—pure women passed her by on the other side of the street, or spoke her name with scorn and loathing, and every avenue of life, except through the very gates of hell, was closed against her wayward, inexperienced feet.

Time passed, and Annie Murray made the acquaintance of Henry Prang, a young and dashing fellow, whose love, though soiled, was deep and tender, and was returned with ardor by the young girl, then fully budded, despite her life of shame, into attractive womanhood. Annie Murray was no more impure than Henry Prang; her life, bad as it was, was no more a blot upon the fair pages of purity than his; and by every law of morality and justice he should have made her his wife. Then they could have arisen together from the mire of ruin and disgrace, and putting the past behind them, could have walked life's thorny road in union, each forgiving the other's sins and bearing the other's burdens. Annie Murray would have made Henry Prang a faithful wife. God pity her, she proved only too faithful as his mistress. The road of return to a life of respectability was open wide to him; it was closed forever against her.

No wonder the poor girl grew desperate when he separated himself from her, and closing the portal behind him, left her to her fate of hopeless disgrace, while he sought the hand of a pure girl in marriage with every prospect of success. A girl with sensibilities less highly strung than Annie Murray's, however fallen, would have died and made no sign; not so this ardent exotic, with all her senses stimulated by intoxicating beverages.

The rest is easily told. The girl arms herself and pursues her faithless lover; in self-defense he snatches the revolver from her excited grasp and fires a murderous charge into the white bosom that, soiled as it was with sin and shame, throbbed only with love for him. The girl sinks back, and he mechanically drops the revolver and impulsively bends over her. Fired by frenzy, the girl clutches the weapon, and with the deadly aim of desperation returns a fatal shot, and Henry Prang expires.

The girl is carried to St. Vincent's, where the angelic sisterhood of self-sacrificing nuns [Sisters of Charity] administer care and comfort, unheeding the world's accord or blame, and her heart-broken mother is summoned to her tragic death-bed, to weep out her humiliation and wretchedness in loneliness and despair, while the great town turns out in costly equipage to honor the final obsequies of the man who ought to have been her husband.

With these reflections we turn away, carrying in our heart the eye-spoken blessing of the speechless girl as she struggles, death-stricken with the mortal pain of her wounds.

FINIS.—Annie Murray is dead. No bells are tolled at her obsequies, no dress parades are indulged in as her still white body goes unheralded to its tomb. A cyprian has gone to her final home, unhonored by all and unwept by everybody save the suffering mother who alone was true. Let the poor wanderer sleep; and let us hope that in the great awakening of the hereafter she will find no one-sided code of morals to "stone the woman, let the man go free."

*(March 9, 1882)*

## Victory in the Oregon Legislature

The Woman Suffrage constitutional amendment proposed by the Legislature of 1880 has been ratified by the Legislature of 1882, and the measure is now in shape to be submitted to the voters of Oregon. The vote in the

Senate (Tuesday) was 21 yeas to 7 nays, and in the House (yesterday) 47 yeas to 9 nays. . . .

This is a proud and happy day for the *New Northwest*, and with unbounded satisfaction it informs not only the Woman Suffragists of the West, but those in the East, of the decisive victory in the Oregon Legislature. But in the hour of its rejoicing it remembers that the final triumph is yet to be won, and it resolves to labor with renewed energy until the amendment is adopted at the polls.

*(October 5, 1882)*

## Woman Suffrage Fails in Nebraska

The equal suffrage amendment was defeated in Nebraska by the "foreign and colored vote," but in some localities its best friends were foreigners. For instance, in Wayne county, it was given a good support by the Germans. In Oregon there are many foreigners who favor the amendment, and the *New Northwest* is proud to be able to state that a fair percentage of its staunchest patrons and supporters are Germans and Irishmen.

*(December 7, 1882)*

## On a Sleeping-Car From Walla Walla to Portland

What an improvement on the old style of stage-coaching, not to mention the ox-team days of our childhood, is the palatial sleeper into which we are ushered by Conductor Barnes and left in the charge of an affable porter, who proves an adept at making sections up into beds bedecked in showy sheets and pure-white pillow-cases. If we've ever thought a man was out of his sphere when officiating as chamber-maid, we hereby change our mind.

But there's one regulation in the sleeping-car that is far too obtuse for the feminine mind to fathom. The section, which, when closed and curtained, is but little larger than a Saratoga trunk, is also nearly airtight; and when, after an hour's laborious breathing in the pent atmosphere, we raised the double window and began to inhale the delicious outside air, the reader who has never tried a similar experiment with a like result will be surprised to learn that we were firmly but respectfully ordered by the sleeping-car conductor to close the sash, giving as a reason therefor that they would forfeit their insurance if the window remained open!

We reluctantly obeyed orders, but were compelled an hour later to seek the platform for breath, wondering the while as to what possible harm a little fresh air in the car could have brought to the insurance company. The conductor, though extremely obliging, couldn't enlighten us, but the porter explained the next morning that if the window were open and the passenger should catch cold the company could be sued for damages!

We caught a cold because the window was not opened, but guess we won't try to sue the Pullman company for a while yet.

Portland, December 24, 1882.

A. S. D.

*(December 28, 1882)*

## Notes for 1882

1. For Duniway's account of these events, see "Who Then Is Safe from Derelict Officials?" *NNW*, 26 Jan. 1882.
2. On Jan. 21, 1882, the *Sunday Welcome* carried a piece of malicious gossip about Duniway and James Willis Nesmith (1820-85) of Polk County. For Duniway's brief autobiographical account of the event, see *Path Breaking*, 33-34.

Nesmith was a former U. S. Senator (1861-65) and Representative (1873-75) from Oregon, and an anti-Mitchell Democrat. About nine months earlier, Duniway had encountered such gossip in Independence, Oregon, and told her readers:

*Relics of obscene stories, which he [Nesmith] is charged with having related as parts of conversation between him and ourself, are still sniffed as a choice relish by some of his filthy admirers, and we would not allude to them at all save for the purpose of informing the wives of some of these foul-minded beings that kind Providence has aways furnished us with better company than J. W.*

*Nesmith; that we never conversed with him on any topic in our life, and never rode in a stage-coach where he was; that we never spoke to him but once, and that was about a year ago, and by the merest accident; that he never introduced us to an audience in The Dalles or anywhere else; and we doubt that he ever claimed that he did. He may be and probably is a vulgar babbler; but he is not a fool, nor could he afford to make declarations of a libelous nature concerning ourself or anybody else.* ("The West Side," *NNW*, 24 Mar. 1881)

The gossip was probably stirred up by Postal Inspector Ben Simpson of Independence, who was no friend of Duniway. Simpson, born in 1819 in Tennessee, grew up in Missouri, came to Oregon in 1846, and became a merchandiser. He served from Marion County on the Oregon Territorial Council, 1851-54, and as a representative from Polk County in the Oregon legislature, 1862-63. With others, he purchased the Salem *Oregon Statesman* in 1863, gained full ownership in August of 1866, and placed two of his sons— Sylvester Confucius and Samuel Leonidas—as editors and managers. (Sam L. Simpson is best known as poet of "The Beautiful Willamette.") Ben Simpson sold his failing *Oregon Statesman* at the end of 1866. William M. Simpson, yet another son of Ben Simpson, became editor of the Portland *Sunday Welcome*, started in 1875 by J. F. Atkinson and published weekly on Saturday (Turnbull, *History of Oregon Newspapers*, 133-34; 482). Although William Simpson later claimed that the story about Duniway and Nesmith in the *Sunday Welcome* was a mistake, and no case was found against Willis and Hubert Duniway by the grand jury, damage was done. News of the gossip and caning gave more fodder to those who sought to destroy Duniway's reputation.

# 1883

## Speaking at the Emancipation Ball

The colored people gave an emancipation ball in Masonic Temple [Portland] in the evening of New Year's day, which was prefaced by music, reading of the Emancipation Proclamation of President Lincoln, and speeches by ex-Governor [Addison Crandall] Gibbs, Hon. John F. Caples, Mr. W. M. Gregory, Mr. Geo. P. Riley, and the undersigned.[1] Mr. Gibbs gave a comprehensive description of the geographical, agricultural and climatic condition of Africa, showing from unquestioned authority that the Dark Continent of the maps was only a reflection of human ignorance. The grandest possibilities lie before the ambitious colored people who have come up out of bondage to a state of freedom and civil responsibility, and they may now, if they choose, become heroes of a new era, the era that is dawning for their people in the land of their forefathers.

Your correspondent supplemented the Governor's remarks with a brief review of the mighty changes that have during the past few centuries brought the young child Liberty out from the repressing power of ancient and modern dynasties, and planting its feet on the American continent, permitted it to grow strong and brave, and started it forth a century ago with the clarion cry upon its tongue that "all men are created equal." This cry was not at that time thought to have reference to the colored man; but the years rolled on, and a nation that had been born in storms, baptized in tears, nursed by war and cradled in blood was carried through another terrible ordeal, which resulted in striking the shackles from four millions of slaves. Even now there is pending before the people of Oregon a proposition to so amend the constitution that "all men" may be understood to include not only men, whether black or white, but all women as well. . . .

Portland, January 3, 1883.
A. S. D.

*(January 4, 1883)*

## Women, Don't Fail to Vote

The school election next Monday will be one of much importance. The district limits have been extended to keep pace with the city's growth, and as a consequence three Directors are to be chosen, instead of one, as usual. . . . [T]he *New Northwest* hopes that the women of the district . . . will vote in larger numbers at the coming election than at any previous one. . . .

That there may be no doubt as to the right of women tax-payers, whether married or single, to vote at the election, we print that part of the school law which defines the qualifications of election:

*Any citizen of the State shall be entitled to vote at a school meeting who is twenty-one years of age, and has resided in the district thirty days immediately preceding the meeting, and has property in the district upon which he or she pays a tax.*

(*March 8, 1883*)

## A Return to Port Gamble, W.T.

[A]lthough our work [at Port Townsend] was not nearly completed, we departed for Port Gamble, the well-remembered scene of our visit with Miss Anthony twelve years ago, and a place hitherto avoided since, because of an incident connected with the man's rights ideas of the village that could not be forgotten. But there was no danger of inhospitable treatment this time. The obliging landlord of the Tekalet House, Mr. James McGrath, made us welcome in his quiet, well-kept hotel, and the husbands we met respected their wives too highly to order away their invited guests. The memory of that episode [in 1871] still lingers among the

people, all of whom are doubtless ashamed of it, and none more so than John Seavy, the perpetrator of the long since forgiven insult.

Through the kindly courtesy of the Walker brothers, of the far-famed Puget Sound Mill Company, we were favored with a good hall for lectures, and before leaving the pretty and picturesque spit upon which the town is located, we were . . . conducted through their mills and lumber yards, which cover an area of several acres.[2]

The mills were founded in 1853, and have been a source of constant revenue to many persons from their comparatively small beginning until now. Everything about the premises is in the best of order, from the great fire on the spit that constantly sends forth its beacon lights into the air and consumes the slabs and other refuse lumber, to the great fires in the furnaces that lick up tons of saw-dust with their fiery tongues as it goes crawling to its doom along the busy elevators that cheerfully carry their burdens to the jaws of death.

Every appurtenance of the mill machinery performs its labor with a skill that seems superhuman. Yonder is a monster engine driving a monster wheel to which is attached a monster belt, and this to smaller wheels, and these to cogs, screws, wheels, belts, pulleys, and what not— all moving in harmonious obedience to the engine's throbs, and tearing their way like unchained madness through their allotted tasks.

A machine for filing saws, the first of the kind that we have seen, consists of an emery wheel, revolving with the velocity of a planet through its allotted orbit, and tearing away at the saw teeth that dare to cross its path with a ferocity that fills a chimney-like draught with a mass of burning iron particles that look like comets' tails. The operator must look at his work through glass, or lose his eyes by collision with the meteoric showers that refuse to enter the draught, and so assume eccentric orbits ere they flicker and die.

Now we see a great cedar log lying helplessly upon the carriage way, awaiting the action of the screaming saws. . . . [W]ithout visible assistance it lazily rolls over, as if inviting the frantic saw to "scratch its other side." A queer device is this machine for rolling saw-logs over. You cannot see it, for its motive power is beneath the floor, but the effect is here, and you turn away, rejoicing anew over the triumphs of inventive genius that have blessed men's work with so many wonderful contrivances for saving human muscles through the power of human minds.

The usual planers, lathers, ripsaw, gang-saws, gauge-saws and the great electric light next merit attention, as also do the lumber yards, the pile-drivers, and last, but by no means least, the vessels lading at the docks, patiently awaiting orders sometimes, for the demand is greater than the supply.

The cottages occupied by the mill men's families are neat and tasty, and the health of the place is excellent. . . . But, though the houses of Port Gamble are neat and orderly, there is a lack of the home element among the men that is seriously to be regretted. The man who gets his meals at the "cook-house" all his life cannot wholly enjoy his family nor look upon his wife and children except as an expensive luxury; and the woman who only prepares for herself and children the food which her husband has provided does not bear her full share of life's burdens nor become one with him in the truest and grandest sense. Many of the ladies here, and all the more sensible ones, realize these facts; but there are others, not so sensible, who will get . . . angry with us for speaking the truth.

Our lectures were well-attended by the best elements of the town, the larger proportion being young, well-behaved and intellectual men. . . .

April 9, 1883.

A. S. D.

*(April 12, 1883)*

## Editorial Note

A hoodlum "journalist" makes the startling announcement that Mrs. Duniway's younger children were brought up by hand, as it were, on cow's milk, and considers this a weighty argument against the right of women to the ballot. If the said hoodlum is a specimen of what human milk will do for a child, we are devoutly thankful for the cow.

*(April 12, 1883)*

## Bustling Seattle

How busy and bustling the city seems, and how like things of life the Sound steamers deport themselves, as they lazily loll alongside the docks and receive and discharge their streams of human life and loads of insensate freight. Vessels from native and foreign ports lie at anchor in the bay. . . .

Seattle needs cabs, or rather, streets for cabs to run upon. Such grading, leveling and general overhauling of city thoroughfares as are witnessed here and at New Tacoma suggest many difficulties in the way of perambulation. . . . The bus belonging to the New England Hotel is chartered at last, and, as it goes rumbling through the business part of the city, or careening, jolting and jerking along the grades, encountering imaginary dangers, we look with satisfaction upon the scenes unfolding upon all sides and enjoy the prospect until we reach once more the home of our friends, the Georges, in whose genial company we enjoy the afternoon's surcease of toil and travel. . . .

A shock fell upon the city during the week because of a terrible accident, to which we cannot revert without a shudder. The only son of Mr. and Mrs. Le Ballister, of Bell Town [a part of Seattle], who was at work at the barrel factory, stepped into a vat of boiling water and was literally cooked before he could be rescued. The blow is a telling one upon the parents, and the casualty calls loudly for more rigid legal enactments to preserve life in dangerous places. Less than six months ago a similar horror befell a man at the same place. Such vats should be protected by railings, and inside of these should be ledges or network to break a fall should any one at work lose his balance. . . .

We were much indebted to Mr. H. L. Yesler for the courtesy of a free hall for four lectures (no inconsiderable item in these days of gaslight and high taxes), and also to Mrs. Yesler for the pleasure of her company and the assistance afforded by it in finding the places of business of many . . . gentlemen [on whom we called]. . . .[3]

The Woman's Christian Temperance Union has lately organized a little force in Seattle, and when the members get ready . . . to make their demands respected by law-makers, they may hope to accomplish good. At present their work hurts nobody, and so accomplishes nothing further than to exhibit their own weakness. Prayer is all right when backed by practicalities, but "faith without works is dead.". . .

There are three newspapers in Seattle, the *Post-Intelligencer* and the

*Chronicle* appearing every morning, and the *Herald* every afternoon, Sundays excepted. These papers have each caught the spirit of the age, their columns being open to discussions upon the woman question, *pro* and *con*, and their editors are committed to the issue and brave and outspoken in defending it.

But the greatest interest just now centers upon real estate, which is changing hands so rapidly that large fortunes are being made continually by speculators, who talk of tens of thousands with a volubility that they once could not have thought of in connection with paltry hundreds. One very wealthy man, who has grown rich in Seattle within the past twelve years, informed us that he had known what it was to go hungry because unable to purchase food, and at one time he had heard his children cry for bread when he was prostrate with fever and his family helpless and destitute. "And now," he said, huskily, "whenever I see any one in need of food, I never ask any questions. I always feed him."

Great expectations are hinging upon Mr. [Henry] Villard's proposed visit to Seattle, not a few persons exulting loudly over the news that he is to slight Portland by coming here first. (But he is now in Portland.)

Portland, April 14, 1883.

A. S. D.

*(April 19, 1883)*

# Frances E. Willard in Portland

Tuesday A. M., June 12.—If anybody had a doubt, prior to last evening, that woman's hour for liberty is almost here, and she quite prepared to take possession of her kingdom, the display . . . last night would surely have dispelled it. For weeks and months the women of the Pacific Northwest have been . . . engaged in active preparation for Miss Willard's advent.[4] And when the hour for her public reception came, and it found the largest church in the city profusely decorated with flowers, and all the prominent men of the metropolis ready to greet and welcome the distinguished herald of woman's kingdom, the women who were there by many hundreds realized as never before their place as an integer in the fact of human life and responsibility.

Miss Willard is by no means a fanatical agitator of some impracticable idea. She is a womanly, practical, kindly and earnest realization of the womanhood of the future. The Woman Suffragists have broken the way for her advent, and she is now among us, not to antagonize elements already discordant, but to harmonize and blend the public pulse till it shall beat in time and tune to the eternal spirit of progress. A Christian without cant, a temperance advocate without bitterness, a Woman Suffragist without acrimony, she molds into expression the opinions of those already secretly convinced to her liking, and awakens in a wonderful degree the enthusiastic action of women who before were passive, cowardly or apathetic.

All this the pageant in Miss Willard's honor proves most clearly. But it proves more than this. It proves that the agitation of the past half century has not been wasted. . . .

It was odd that men monopolized all the proceedings in the lady's honor; but women were glad, for they well remembered how difficult it had formerly been for them to be recognized at all by prominent politicians and clergymen unless they came before the public as suppliants, with no display of personal individuality except as their self-appointed judges dictated. . . .

While we do not agree with Miss Willard as to the common sense of the [temperance] crusade movement, we recognize it as the one absurd thing needed to shock the women of the nation into the proper recognition of their political status under a yoke of disfranchisement which they had borne so long that they were unconscious of its power till it tested its strength with their weakness at the ballot-box.

To-morrow (Wednesday) we are off for Hillsboro, where a suffrage rally will be held . . . , and will return on Thursday evening to attend the women's temperance convention, which meets here on Friday.

Portland, June 12, 1883. A. S. D.
*(June 14, 1883)*

## The Woman's Christian Temperance Union Convention

[W]e return to Portland to attend the convention of the Woman's Christian Temperance Union, of which Miss Frances E. Willard is the guiding star.

Many women delegates are in attendance, and the administrative and parliamentary ability they display is a matter of wonder to the men who visit the convention, most of whom are beginning to realize the force and magnitude among their loyal wives and sisters, who have come to the front in all moral reforms, and have come to stay. . . .

Miss Willard presided over the convention with wonderful skill, and supplemented her day's labor on each evening by a speech of great length, wonderful power and surprising eloquence. This lady's versatility of genius is as marvelous as her strength is enduring. She models her audience to her ways of thinking with a skill akin to magic. . . .

No woman who labors in the W. C. T. U. can claim to be an opponent of Woman Suffrage after this. They have swallowed the ballot, as administered by Miss Willard, without sugar, and are left to digest it without dilution. That they may all become sufficiently consistent to work for the full and free possession of all the liberties and responsibilities the word implies, and thus do their part to insure the success of the pending suffrage amendment, is our earnest hope. . . .

While we do not believe that prohibition will in our day become the accomplished fact that the ardent women of the W. C. T. U. are working for, we do believe that with woman's added power, as expressed through the ballot, will come her opportunity to demand that no son or husband shall be drunken or unchaste. . . .

Portland, June 18, 1883.
A. S. D.

*(June 21, 1883)*

### News of the Northern Pacific Railroad

The Northern Pacific Railroad will be completed by September 1st. The actual distance from St. Paul to Portland will be 1916 miles. Passengers will take Pullman palace sleepers and go through without change. First-class fare will be $100; emigrant rate, $45. Principal interior points will be placed on a distributive basis, reductions being made according to distance. A large tourist business is expected.

The last spike of the Northern Pacific Railroad is of solid gold, and will be driven with a silver sledge—probably during the last week of August. Many persons have been invited to be present on the occasion.

President Villard will strike the first blow. The place selected is ten miles from Helena.

*(June 28, 1883)*

### Chinese Workers Strike

The Chinese laborers at the front of the California & Oregon Railroad extension are on a strike, and there is little prospect of its speedy termination. The Chinese have a month's provisions on hand, and are very independent. The railroad company has turned . . . [the] cart horses out to pasture, and, as the long days and good weather are gliding by, the road may not be completed this year.

*(July 5, 1883)*

### Visit to the Siletz Indian Reservation

On Tuesday morning we looked longingly toward Cape Foulweather and the famous lighthouse. . . . But the time was not right for a ride on the beach, and the fog was too thick for sight-seeing. . . .

In the afternoon, our esteemed friend, "Uncle" Bart Allen brought round a team, and loading up a three-seated wagon with ladies, proceeded to the Indian reservation, fifteen miles distant [from Newport, Oregon], through and over the mountains, amid an interminable array of scenery. . . . [5]

The mountains receded at last, the brow of the last hill was reached, and a charming valley burst upon the view, green with waving grain, and dotted here and there with comfortable houses belonging to Indians, through whose fertile lands the Siletz River (literally "Celestial") courses on its rocky way. . . .

The boarding house and school buildings belonging to the reservation were burned last Winter, leaving the hospitable officers of the agency to the mercy of visitors like ourselves; but they proved themselves equal to the emergency. . . .

The Siletz Indians, who a quarter of a century ago numbered three thousand souls, have been reduced by death to less than one-third of that number. Lately, so Dr. Carter [resident physician] informs us, the increase and death rates run more nearly parallel, with a slight balance in favor of increase. But it is everywhere apparent that the favorable outlook is only temporary. The diseases of the Christian white race overcome the heathen, whether Indian or Kanaka, and, at the regular rate of decadence, it will not be many years till the "bad Indian" and the leper will alike become creatures of the past.

Accompanied by the doctor and his wife and Rev. Mr. White, the Indian teacher, we paid a visit to one of the many Indian burying grounds, a high, level spot, overlooking the valley that the silent sleepers loved. Some of the graves are left as white men leave them, the occupants having died in the Christian faith; but most of them are covered by the slowly rotting garments of the former owners, while all around and over them are laid the dishes, cooking utensils and trinkets which the coffins would not hold.

The Indians honor their dead far above the living. They are all, whether Christian or not, believers in Spiritualism, and imagine that their dead take cognizance of all their fond attentions. They will deny themselves needed comforts to deposit the money in the coffins of their dead. We reverently named the place Memaloose Acre, and left it alone with the eternal Mystery— a haunting secret that follows mortal life, but a secret no longer to the great majority.

The reservation comprises an area of 350 square miles, and is composed in part of level valleys in a high state of cultivation, with ample timber facilities on the adjacent mountains, and the Siletz River affording splendid water privileges. We saw nothing to criticize under the present management but the public highway, and are pleased to note that this is soon to be put in better order.

But it does seem that the time has come for these Indians to be clothed with citizenship and released from their dependent state as wards of the government. To give them the lands in severalty and turn them out to do their own struggling for subsistence, as whites must, or starve, would be to them an untold blessing, since it would stimulate their self-respect and either restore their emasculated independence or make short work of the present process of decimation, and leave the earth free to the "survival of the fittest."[6]

The experiment is well worth trying, and this reservation is an excellent field for it. The Indians would, no doubt, retain the present officers and pay them better salaries than the government allows. And the officers would then discard the red tape and all the circumlocution that muddles the Indian brain at present, and make their work vastly superior to what it now can be.

[Summit Station, Oregon] July 14, 1883.

A. S. D.

*(July 19, 1883)*

## Henry Ward Beecher to Lecture

Henry Ward Beecher will lecture in this city at New Market Theater on the evenings of August 21st and 23d, and possibly in Salem on the 22d. Manager Stechhan has the entire control of the eloquent divine's Northwest tour, and as it costs $7000 for seven lectures by him, it is necessary that a guaranty be given of a fine audience in each place in which he may appear.

*(August 2, 1883)*

## A Brief Interview With Henry Ward Beecher

Last Friday morning your correspondent, after an almost sleepless night, arose before the dawn and hastened out in the fog and smoke to board the steamer "R. R. Thompson" for the purpose of interviewing Manager Stechhan and completing arrangements for holding a Woman Suffrage rally at the Mechanics' Pavilion, with Mr. Beecher as the speaker. . . .

It was late before the steamer left the dock, later before breakfast was served, and latest before Mr. and Mrs. Stechhan were up. But the desired interview was had at a last, and in a very few minutes we were ready to stop at St. Helens for a return steamer, bearing written instructions to the agent in Portland, authorizing the Woman Suffrage Association to take charge of the Thursday evening meeting and carry it forward under its auspices.

An interview with Mr. Beecher resulted in securing his cordial consent to the arrangements made. He said he had hardly dared to hope, before coming to Oregon, that he would live to see the enfranchisement of woman made a practical issue, but Oregon was stealing a march on the East, and the signs were favorable that we *would win*. He was much interested in our hurried account of the growth of the movement in the Far

West, and heartily seconded our hope that Oregon might be made "the banner State of the new dispensation."

Mrs. Dr. Caples and ourself were in the midst of a recital of our pioneer experiences in crossing the plains, in which Mr. Beecher manifested the liveliest interest, when the steamer landed at St. Helens and cut the conversation short. A hurried good-bye and an equally hurried walk up the slip . . . was followed by a hurried visit among a score of friends in St. Helens, all of whom were fired with the idea of the forthcoming rally. . . .

And now, on the morning preceding the rally, as we hurry these jottings to the printer, the indications for a jam at the Pavilion are most favorable. The city press has taken kindly to the idea, the country press has done likewise, and the great transportation companies by land and water have issued commutation tickets at a discount of 40 per cent from all points within a day's travel, for the accommodation of those who wish to attend.

Portland, August 30, 1883.
A. S. D.

*(August 30, 1883)*

## "Reign of the Common People," Henry Ward Beecher's Lecture

Rev. Henry Ward Beecher's lecture at the Mechanics' Pavilion last Thursday evening attracted an audience of more than 2000 people, several hundred of them coming from the valley towns. . . . The orator was introduced by Mrs. A. S. Duniway, Vice-President-at-Large of the Suffrage Association, whose earnest remarks elicited applause. Mr. Beecher was given a cordial reception, and spoke for two hours, holding the close attention of his auditors. . . .

Henry Ward Beecher's plea for recognition of woman's right to the ballot, made last Thursday evening . . . is a valuable contribution to equal suffrage literature. The thunderous applause which greeted his vehement denunciation of the injustice of disfranchising the wife and mother, showed how completely he carried his hearers with him, and how deeply they felt the wrong which he so vividly portrayed. There can be little doubt that he won many votes for the pending Amendment [in Oregon].

Mr. Beecher's remarks on the very common misconception of St. Paul's commands in reference to woman ought to be read by every person who is troubled about the Pauline declarations. Interpretations similar to his have often been given by scholars and students who have read the Bible intelligently, but we fail to remember another writer or speaker who has so concisely stated the historical facts and so effectually cleared away the mists around St. Paul's commands.

The two salient points of Mr. Beecher's lecture which we have mentioned will be of value to the Woman Suffrage movement in the next few months, and every woman in Oregon owes him a debt of gratitude for the earnest and truthful words which he so eloquently uttered last Thursday evening.

*(September 6, 1883)*

## Portland's Jubilee: Completion of the Transcontinental Railroad

Never before in the history of this great Northwestern country has there been such universal rejoicing and elaborateness of preparation to commemorate any event as that which has marked the ceremonies in honor of the completion of the Northern Pacific Railroad, which now unites us with iron bands to the Eastern portion of this mighty continent. . . . [T]he demonstrations of thankfulness and rejoicing that have everywhere greeted Mr. Villard and his guests but faintly express the gratification that pervades all classes at the consummation of this vast enterprise.[7]

The excursion party from the East and Europe was met late last Saturday afternoon by the invited guests from Portland at Last Spike Station, a point on the banks of the Deer Lodge River, in Montana, about sixty miles west of Helena, when the golden spike was driven by Mr. Villard amid the booming of cannon and the deafening cheers of the assembled multitude. At the conclusion of the exercises the excursion party started for this city, where they arrived during Monday night, in time to witness the grand parade on Tuesday and participate in the ceremonies at the Mechanics' Pavilion. . . .[8]

[A]ll our most important avenues of industry and enterprise were grandly represented [in the parade]; and the procession, commanded by General Morrow, and formed in six divisions, each under the direction of alert and experienced officers, all marching to the inspiring strains of martial music, the whole resplendent in gorgeous regalia and everybody wearing a holiday look, formed a scene that never can be forgotten.

Four emigrant wagons, excellent representations of the ships of the desert that used to occupy six months in their transit across the continent, were drawn by oxen, driven by men in shirt sleeves and slouched hats, with crowds of children peeping from the raised covers, a startling reminder of the days when transcontinental railroads were slumbering, undreamed of, in the brain of the foreign-born boy who, as a man, has wrought the wonderful change which the procession was formed to celebrate. A woman in a cavernous sun-bonnet rode on horseback in advance of the emigrant train, slapping her horse with her bridle rein and forming a vivid picture of the days forever gone. This picture was heightened by a display of wild Indians, painted and clad in fantastic fashion, and mounted in their native style. The Indian school at Forest Grove was also represented; and to complete the picture of progress there was but one thing lacking—a concourse of Chinese railroad builders in bamboo hats, carrying picks and shovels.

*(September 13, 1883)*

## Objections to Woman Suffrage Refuted

A correspondent says "there are ten alleged reasons why some men yet object to Woman Suffrage," and asks that the *New Northwest* "consider and answer them, all and severally." They are:

1. Women don't want to vote.
2. Women's sphere is the home.
3. She would neglect her home if allowed to vote.
4. Men love women better when wholly dependent upon them than they would if the sex were self-sustaining.
5. Women's ballot would weaken the family tie and make trouble in the home.

6. The political pool is too filthy for women to dabble in.
7. Bad women would vote.
8. Women are frivolous and unreliable about business affairs, and too fond of dress, fashion and parade to take interest in the affairs of state.
9. If they vote, they must fight.
10. They ought not to sit on juries.

A formidable array of objections, truly! And yet, let us see how easily they can "all and severally" be reasoned down.

First—If "women don't want to vote," they needn't. There will be no law to compel them to vote. . . .

Second—If God or man has made a particular "sphere" for woman, how does it happen that she often fails to find it? We know thousands of women who have no "sphere" or place whatever, if the allegation be true, for they have no homes to keep unless they go out and earn them. The great majority of women will always find their sphere in the home, but what about those whose God-given impulses lead them elsewhere?

Third—How do you know they would neglect their homes if they should vote? Are all the *men* who vote vagabonds? Do you not know that on an average it requires less than thirty minutes a year to vote—a small part of the time they devote to shopping and visiting?

Fourth—Men love women because they can't help it. They loved them before the right to vote was thought of. There are no wholly "dependent" women but courtesans. If men "love" such better than the self-supporting wives and mothers upon whom they "depend" to make home happy and rear the children, they are victims of depraved tastes. We don't believe it.

Fifth—*Why* should "woman's ballot weaken the family tie"? Does *man's*? *Who* would "make the trouble"? The *woman*? Surely the man who is so willing to "protect" her that he would deny her the right to express her own opinion (which is all the ballot means) wouldn't "make trouble"? And if the woman would, *why* would she?

Sixth—How came the "political pool" so filthy? Isn't the fact that it is filthy a proof that a change is necessary? Do you think the grand good men who gave their lives for liberty imagined that they were dying to create a "filthy pool" in which husbands might dabble and never clean up, while wives were to be deterred from trying?

Seventh—Bad *men* vote, and why shouldn't bad *women*? Woman Suffragists believe in disfranchising all bad men and women; but they fail to see the wisdom of disfranchising the many good women on account of the few bad ones.

Eighth—We have not found women more unreliable in business affairs than men.[9] It is about an even stand-off. And, as to "dress, fashion and parade," what do you say of men's display of "weakness" in that line, as exhibited on the streets last week? Would you take away their right to vote because they looked "pretty" and enjoyed it? Will not enfranchising women decrease "frivolity," by giving them serious matters to think about? Is not the ballot an educator, and will not women reap benefits from it?

Ninth—All men do not fight. A great many are too small in stature to be ever in any danger of the draft; but they all vote! Some day, when woman has been a voter long enough to understand herself, she'll teach men how to change their swords into sad irons and their guns into water pipes, and settle their difficulties by arbitration. Woman *produces* men, and that's a bigger business for the country, by long odds, than *killing* them.

Tenth—Women ought to sit on juries in all cases where women are on trial, and "not to be allowed to do so is an outrage before God and ought to be before man."

*(September 20, 1883)*

## Sad Case of a Violated Daughter

Ophelia Calkins, a girl 14 years old, is confined in a damp, cold cell in the County Jail as a witness against her father, E. S. Calkins, who is charged with a dastardly outrage upon her. The girl is soon to become a mother, and, although every comfort that the jail affords has been placed at her disposal, she sits and weeps for hours at a time, and begs the jailer to either send her home or to a hospital. She reiterates the charge against her father, and characterizes him as a fiend in human form.—*Oregonian.*

Sad indeed is this case. What must a child become that is to enter the world under such fearful pre-natal conditions as have fallen to this poor creature's lot? It is barbarous that this wronged, outraged, suffering girl should rest in a cold, cheerless cell because of a crime of which she is the victim. The case is another proof of one sex's inability to provide for the government or protection of both. Does any one believe that, if woman had always filled her rightful place as man's equal, such added cruelty would be suffered by this child? And does any one believe that it would much longer be possible if the mothers of this nation were to have their rights restored to them?

Talk of "the protection of women from the rude blasts of the world"! Every day the news columns of our press contain the stories of cruel wrongs and infamous crimes against women. And then the press—the majority of it—talks of the "cruelty of the world." Let us have done with this sentimental nonsense. It is not "the world," but alleged "protectors," who commit these crimes. And, as we have seen, even a father may so far forget the bombast about protection

as to become his innocent daughter's worst enemy. Woman demands her rights and is offered senseless sentiments; "asks for bread and is given a stone." Let Oregon voters be honorable and do justice to their helpmeets next June.

*(October 4, 1883)*

## Boy Murders Grandmother

Charles Finlayson, the boy who murdered his grandmother on a farm near Albany, was arrested on Tuesday in Eastern Oregon by Sheriff Humphrey, of Linn county, and brought to this city. The boy confessed the crime to a relative while in the city jail. The murdered woman (his grandfather's second wife) told him to go out to plow; he refused to go; sharp words ensued; she struck him with a stick; he picked up an axe and knocked her down; she crawled to a bed-room; he followed her, and in his frenzy repeatedly stabbed her with a knife. When she was dead he covered her with the bed-clothes, ransacked the house for money, and then disappeared. The prisoner was taken to Albany yesterday.

*(November 15, 1883)*

# VICTORY!
# WASHINGTON TERRITORY'S WOMEN ENFRANCHISED.

## THE COUNCIL PASSES THE HOUSE BILL BY TWO MAJORITY.

The forms of the *New Northwest* are lifted from the press to-day (Thursday) at 11:50 A.M., to insert the following dispatch:

Olympia, W. T., November 15, 1883.

W. S. DUNIWAY, No. 5 Washington street:—

*Suffrage bill passed the Council. Ayes—Burke, Edmiston, Hale, Harper, Kerr, Power, Smith—7. There is great rejoicing.*
A. S. Duniway.

Governor Newell, being a Woman Suffragist, will without doubt sign the bill.

"WASHINGTON AGAINST THE WORLD!"

*(November 15, 1883)*

# The Governor Signs the Bill

The following dispatch is received to-day at 2 o'clock P.M. (after half our edition is printed):

Olympia, W. T., November 22, 1883.
W. S. Duniway:—Governor [William A.] Newell signed Woman Suffrage bill at 11:10 A.M. with gold pen given him for the purpose by ladies of Olympia.
A. S. Duniway.

*(November 22, 1883)*

# A Visit to Verona ("Fanny") Baldwin at the W. T. Insane Asylum

Two hours' ride by steamer brings us to Steilacoom, the oldest town on Puget Sound. . . . Sunday morning dawns in peace upon a white-robed world. But the air is balmy, and at 11 A.M. we accompany Mr. and Mrs. E. R. Rogers and a lady guest to the insane asylum, where, after a brief visit at the pleasant home of Superintendent Waughop and wife, we were admitted to the women's wards, where those unfortunates whose "Thoughts are combinations of disjointed things" are being cared for, whenever necessary, at the public charge.

A pleasant matron met us in a cozy sitting-room, where a peculiar growl from behind a door was followed by the presentation of an epileptic Indian child which had been picked up a few days before on the beach, where it had been abandoned by its tribe to die. Poor little ill-formed waif! It was covered from head to foot with bruises when found, but soap and water had accomplished great changes, and the little darkened life will spend its few remaining days in comparative physical comfort.

The rooms were scrupulously clean, and the pale-faced, weary women who huddled around the grated, red-hot stove were as comfortable, evidently as their diseased mental and physical conditions would permit.

In one of the clean apartments, separated from the more dangerous patients, we found Fanny Baldwin, whose sad case has appealed of late to so many humane hearts and awakened much human sympathy. [She was accused of shooting her "false" friend and supposed uncle, Lucky Baldwin, in San Francisco.] Miss Baldwin is strikingly handsome in form and by no means homely in feature, and no one, to look at her, can feel content to see her immured for life within an asylum's walls.

But the sensational stories afloat in regard to her sanity are the merest nonsense. Miss Baldwin is not yet incurable, but she will be if she does not soon submit to the only medical treatment that in our opinion will so far restore her that it will be safe for her to be at large.

Her mania takes on many variations. At times she is as natural, civil, sensible, and polite as any one, but a half hour's conversation will show the visitor that she is inordinately ambitious for notoriety. She wants to appeal continually to governors, judges, and the President for help. She longed to appear before the Legislature, and, when denied the fancied honor, raved till it was necessary to put her in a straight-jacket, which she tore to ribbons. In a recent frenzy she kicked the matron and compelled her to take to her bed. When she pleads sanity and is reminded of these things, she says she does them to feign insanity for a purpose, but she does not try to define her purpose, so it fails in its object, whatever it may be.

We found it impossible to hold her mind in the consideration of any plan for her release upon any terms not wholly dictated by herself. Physicians say she can be cured, or at least made harmless, by surgical treatment, but she will not consent to receive the assistance anywhere within the limits of the territory. If she leaves the asylum, she declares she will go with none of its officers. She will have nothing to do with her relatives, and rejects all their overtures which tend to the possibility of her recovery. Her mania is homicidal at times, but never suicidal.

After more than an hour's vain attempt to make arrangements with her whereby she might be cured, we arose to go, and she said, arising to her full height and assuming an air of expectancy that pierced us like a knife,

"Are you not going to take me with you?"

"Not yet," we answered, as composedly as possible; "but after you consent to be treated and cured, I'll set to work to get you out."

"Then," she cried, assuming an intensely tragic air, while tears rolled down her cheeks, "I'll rave! *I'll tear*! I'LL BURN! I'LL KILL!"

The door closed behind her, and we went our way with a heavy heart.

Poor girl! The man who had first wrought her downfall, who was the original cause of all her subsequent wrongs, and who refused to honor his vows of fealty after she, by years of hard endeavor, had proved worthy of a better fate than has befallen her, is a successful businessman, with a young wife who knows the facts, occupying an honored position in society, smiled upon by women who condemn the girl utterly. How long shall these things be?

Dr. Waughop says that Miss Baldwin is more rational when kept more quiet, and he will be compelled to prevent her from seeing so much company in future, as it will be for her good to deny her so much opportunity for notoriety.

Steamer "Emma Hayward," Nov. 26, 1883.

A. S. D.

*(November 29, 1883)*

## Verona Baldwin Released

Verona ["Fanny"] Baldwin has been discharged from the Steilacoom Insane Asylum, and is now with relatives and friends in Olympia. We sincerely hope that in the future this grievously wronged girl will find a smoother road than it has been her misfortune to tread in the past.

*(December 27, 1883)*

## Notes for 1883

1. Duniway no longer identifies Mr. George P. Riley, the renowned orator, as "(colored)" in her list of speakers.
2. The Puget Sound Mill Company of Port Gamble, also called the Pope and Talbot Mill, was one of the largest mills in the Pacific Northwest; it boasted the largest foreign sales and held large tracts of timber. By 1870, Washington Territory had over forty mills, most of which were located in the Puget Sound area.
3. Henry L. Yesler was an early pioneer in Oregon Territory and became one of Seattle's leading citizens. He gained the backing of San Francisco investors and established a steam sawmill, the first of its kind on Puget Sound. In 1862, he was part of the newly incorporated Puget Sound and Columbia Railroad Company, which completed the route from Steilacoom to Vancouver in ten years. He also served as mayor of Seattle during the anti-Chinese troubles of 1886.
4. Frances E. Willard (1839-98) was elected president of the National Woman's Christian Temperance Union in 1878 and held that position until her death. For Willard, the causes of prohibition and woman suffrage were joined.

5. When Duniway visited the Siletz Reservation in 1883, many changes had taken place since its establishment in 1855. The Coast Reservation, which included the Siletz Agency and the Alsea Subagency, was created under Indian Superintendent Joel Palmer and opened in 1857. It was a supposedly "useless" area estimated at 1,382,400 acres located along the Oregon coast. The central portion was opened to white settlement by presidential order in December 1865; the far northern and southern sections were opened by Congress in March of 1875, as part of Senator John Mitchell's plan for removal of the Indians from the Oregon coast, thereby opening up more land for white settlement, logging, transportation, etc. Ben Simpson, agent at Siletz (1863-71), became federal surveyor general for Oregon and joined with Mitchell in the Indian removal scheme. See E. A. Schwartz, "Sick Hearts: Indian Removal on the Oregon Coast, 1875-1881," *Oregon Historical Quarterly* 92 (Fall 1991): 229-64.

6. Here Duniway endorsed the Social Darwinist tenet of "survival of the fittest" and foreshadowed the Dawes General Allotment (Severalty) Act of 1887, which converted all Indian tribal lands to individual ownership, with the intent of cutting off ties to tribal cultures and assimilating the Indians into the white culture.

7. Henry Villard (1835-1900), the son-in-law of abolitionist William Lloyd Garrison, was born in Germany and became a major figure in Oregon's economy during the 1870s and 1880s. He took over management of the Oregon and California R. R. in 1876 and then gained control of the Northern Pacific R. R. Under Villard, the first transcontinental line to the Pacific Northwest was completed in the fall of 1883. That spring, Villard visited Portland, and Duniway attended and reported on the grand reception for "the railway king" at the home of U. S.

Senator Joseph N. Dolph (*NNW*, 3 May 1883).

During the panic of 1884, Villard lost control of the Northern Pacific and most of his money, but he later returned to the N. P. board and amassed another fortune. Duniway had anticipated that Villard would regain power, and she hoped he would learn a lesson from his losses and speak out for human rights, including equal suffrage ("Editorial Correspondence," *NNW*, 17 Jan. 1884).

8. Judge Matthew Deady, a member of the excursion party to Montana, recorded the ceremony of driving the golden spike and noted: "Villards [*sic*] 3 months baby taking hold of the handle of the hammer, when the crowd hailed him as 'Henry the Second'—a pretty and for the moment a not inappropriate conceit" (*Pharisee Among Philistines*, 420). Deady added that the jubilee procession in Portland "exceeded anything I ever saw."

9. Through a series of legislative acts, married women in Oregon were legally protected to conduct business on their own. Duniway appreciated this fact but was concerned that anti-suffrage forces would argue even louder that women were "protected and supported" with all the rights they wanted or needed.

In 1872, the legislature passed a Sole Trader Bill, which allowed a wife to carry on business in the absence of her husband and to keep her "property, real or personal, acquired by her own labor," without liability for her husband's debts or contracts (*NNW*, 27 Sept. 1872). In 1878, the Married Woman's Property Act gave a wife the right to own, manage, sell, convey, and devise her property ("Equal Property Rights," *NNW*, 7 Nov. 1878). And, under an act in 1880, wives were given the right to sue in court on their own, and a mother was "as fully entitled to custody and control of children and their earnings as their father." Upon the husband's death, the wife came into full and complete control of the estate and children ("Married Women's Rights," *NNW*, 28 Oct. 1880).

# 1884

## Mrs. Duniway Does Not Seek W. T. Governorship

It had been the purpose of this journal to pay no attention to the importunities which have from time to time reached the ears of its publishers from friends, urging Mrs. Duniway to allow them to present a petition to President Arthur, requesting him to appoint her Governor of Washington Territory. But as the fact is going the rounds of the reading world through the Associated Press dispatches, and petitions are in circulation to that effect, and are, we learn, being numerously signed in Washington Territory and also in California, it becomes our duty to say for Mrs. D., and at her request, that she is not seeking office for herself, but liberty, equality and justice for all womanhood. She does not want the office, has no use for it, and would not accept it if it were tendered her, if the present incumbent, Governor Wm. A. Newell, who signed the Woman Suffrage bill, would thereby be deprived of the reappointment his services merit. She thanks her friends for their good intentions, but feels that she can serve the cause of equal rights in a much more effective way as a private citizen than as a public office-holder.

*(January 3, 1884)*

## Lucy Stone's Congratulations

Office of "The Woman's Journal," Boston, Mass., December 13, 1883.

My Dear Mrs. Duniway:—If I have not before written it, I have nevertheless rejoiced with great joy over the result in Washington Territory, and in my heart congratulated *you*, who have so long and with such persistent fidelity borne the heat and burden of this great strife which has set the women of that rich Territory free.

What an epoch it marks! What beneficent changes are involved in it! What endless good is come to men, as well as to women, by it!

You, and your husband, who aids you so nobly, and all the others who have been instrumental in bringing about this great event, are to be congratulated that the privilege was given you to help the work of establishing a government that represent the *people*, and not merely the men.

Oregon, next June, will be sure to feel the effect of this action in Washington Territory. At that time we hope to chronicle one *State* redeemed from the grave injustice which disfranchises the women of every State, and to unite with you in the great rejoicing that will then come.

Meantime, we are working on. Our present intent is to organize the suffrage sentiment as fast as possible, that it may be felt politically. The West is ahead of us. We have to be content to follow. But we follow in the sure belief of final success.

With pride in the Oregon Woman Suffragists, I am truly yours and theirs,—Lucy Stone.

*(January 10, 1884)*

## Duniway to Speak at NWSA Convention

Mrs. A. S. Duniway left on Saturday evening last to attend the National Woman Suffrage Association's convention at Washington on March 4th, 5th and 6th. Her name leads the list of speakers invited to address the annual convention of the New York Woman Suffrage Association, which will be held at Albany on March 11th and 12th.

*(February 21, 1884)*

## Travel With the Pullman Monopoly and the Baker Heater

How strange it all seems! Only four days ago your humble servant was in Portland-on-the-Willamette, surrounded by familiar faces and enjoying the delights of home. Now we are abroad on the bleak plains of Dakota, nearly 1500 miles from the land of webbed feet and rosy apples, traveling day and night behind the iron horse, and gazing everywhere upon the seemingly interminable wastes of snow that shroud the earth in robes as soft as eider-down, as cold as Greenland, and as white as alabaster. . . .

The journey on the O. R. & N. Co.'s division has been so often described in these columns that repetition would be useless. It was mostly made in the night-time, and much of the sublimity of grandeur that otherwise would delight the tourist as he passes through the wild and picturesque gorges of the Columbia is lost to sight. But we raise the window-blind in the midnight hours and gaze abroad in the moonlight catching familiar glimpses here and there of the old landmarks past which we have many a time gone shivering and jolting in the stage-coaches, and again enjoying the pure river air from the wheelhouses of the steamers "Mountain Queen" and "Anna Paxon," of the past era.

Now we are in a sweatbox (literal fact), with the thermometer away below zero outside and away in the nineties within. The box where we try in vain to keep cool is a six-by-four half-section, lower berth, in a Pullman sleeper, with the upper half-section chained down over our head by a—a—a patent white wire clothes-line. We toss the covers and raise up to catch a breath of fresh air, when our cranium goes thumpity-bump against the upper half or lid of the curtained section, reminding us of Horace Greeley's experience in a stage-coach, and making us almost savage enough to repeat the whole of the stage-driver's story about him as an infliction upon our readers— to get even. "Keep your seat, Horace; I'll get you there on time," said the driver. No need of anybody saying "Keep your seat" to us. We had to.

Morning, and Wallula Junction.... We wade awhile through the snow-drifts for exercise, and then enter the car again and resume the sweating process inaugurated at the beginning of the journey by a new-fangled machine called a Baker Heater, though either name would do the subject ample justice, as the thing both bakes and heats to perfection. A tank, in a sort of cupola on the top of the car, is filled with brine made as strong as possible by dissolving common salt in fresh water, and this brine, heated to the boiling point by a furnace in the corner just opposite the ice water tank, is conveyed boiling hot through pipes that circulate through and through the car, heating the beds and blankets, and keeping the air inside as tropical as it is polar without. Flannels are a superfluity, and fans would be a benison. . . .

How it snows and snows, and blows and blows! The storm is visible from our windows, and but little else can be seen. . . . If the weather were only mild! but it isn't, and we can't endure the glaring white of the scenery long enough to do the subject justice. . . .

Monday night almost "cooks the crowd." The genteel porter has orders to keep the fire-box of the Baker Heater filled with hard coal, and faithfully he performs his duty. We'd be more comfortable if the white wire clothes-line would unlock and let us slide the upper berth out of the way; but when we ask permission to put it up, we find that the Pullman company will make us stand the suffocation unless we pay an extra fee of $2.00 per night for the privilege of sliding it out of the way, where it would annoy nobody. Several voters in the car pay this bonus readily to abate the nuisance, but a disfranchised citizen can't afford it.

There never was a wickeder swindle. If anybody wanted the berth, we, not having paid for it, and not meaning to, couldn't object; but to keep it down and reduce our breathing space to a few enclosed and heated cubic feet of poisoned air, simply because of the Pullman monopoly—on which nobody should ever have had a patent in the first place, since sleeping cars are the necessary result of long railroad lines—and thus do nobody any good, not even the dog-in-the-manger who controls them in Chicago, is simply outrageous.

A fellow passenger, who evidently speaks by authority, says the porter is only paid $15 per month for all the work he does in the car—leaving him dependent upon the liberality of the travelers to make the deficit in his wages good—while a portly "Pullman conductor" at a salary of $75 per month is employed to sit around and watch him to prevent his exercise of a little of the common sense that would injure nobody.

Say what you please about the railway corporations, they are as nothing compared to this Pullman perpetration, which ought never to have been permitted for a day by any government. . . . We are not accusing him of breaking the laws, nor of anything worse than taking the full benefit of all the law allows him. But we have watched the end of more than one monopolist, and the result was never satisfactory. . . .

And now we are in Montana. We pass with little note the young and tiny towns that dot the railroad line at intervals. . . .

There! We've written up the scenes of the past four days from memory, living them over again and again as we have scribbled, and here we are at Dickenson, Dakota, halting for nobody knows what, twelve hours behind time. . . .

[T]here is no time to revise, as this letter must be ready for the next westbound train, which may meet us now at almost any time. . . . [We must not] close this hasty scrawl without mentioning the well-conducted

dining car that accompanies the train, over which no Pullman monopoly is hanging, and consequently the managers of the road can give excellent meals to hungry travelers for the reasonable price of 75 cents—a boon to tourists in the heart of the wilderness for which they are correspondingly grateful.

[en route] February 20th.

A. S. D.

On and on and still on we go toward the land of the rising sun, measuring the ever-lengthening distance by the easy gait of the iron horse, which, equipped for a long journey, accepts the situation like a veteran of the road, pausing now and then to take a drink at a great fire-heated water tank, or replenish his carbonated food from an ice-coated coal bin.

The thermometer goes down, down, and the fires up, up. You can scarcely realize the fact that the mercury is forty degrees below zero as you sit in the heated Pullman, begging the porter (sometimes in vain) to open a ventilator and give you fresh air. But when the train stops at Fargo, we are permitted to alight in the teeth of a blizzard and take a brisk run on the snow-cleared platform alongside, and after a few minutes' keen enjoyment of the bracing atmosphere are advised to go inside and rescue our rapidly freezing ears, and we obey the injunction just in the nick of time to avoid being literally "frost-bitten.". . . [W]e bless the Baker Heater, and wouldn't care if it were called "roaster" also.

Chicago, Ill., February 25, 1884.
A. S. D.

*(March 6, 1884)*

## On to Washington, D. C., and the National Convention

[B]ehold us seated in a horrid Pullman car once more, going by way of the Baltimore and Ohio road to Washington. Oh, that road! It is as crooked as the stage road that used to run by Mt. Shasta, and as rough as the corduroy bridge that crosses Lake Labish. Everybody in the car is sea-sick from the rolling and rocking of the train, and the pentup atmosphere of the chained-down sweat-box in which we pass the night is worse than Pandemonium. That portion of the traveling public than needs pure air must get legislation against the Pullman horror or die. . . .

Midnight, and Washington City. The obliging porter conducts us to a 'bus, in which we are trundled and trundled till at last we reach the Riggs House, a commodious and elegant hotel, in which we soar away into dream-land to the silent music of a slow coal fire, consoled by the fancy that when morning comes there will be letters and copies of the *New Northwest* awaiting us from home. Vain hope, deluded fancy!

The snow blockade on the Northern Pacific has delayed the mail trains, and not a letter or paper has come. . . .

We swallow disappointment with breakfast, and seek Miss Anthony, brave soldier of liberty, whom we find surrounded as is usual, with scores of admiring friends of both sexes, her great brain filled with law, logic and plans of work, and her big heart reaching out, as ever, to all womanhood. . . .

Scarcely are we settled till we hear news of a grand reception to Mrs. Stanton, Miss Anthony and the long line of delegates, representing twenty-two of the States and Territories of the Union, with quite a number from over the sea. The reception, which took place on Monday evening, comprised several hundred guests, who paid their respects first to the hospitable hostess and Miss Anthony, and then to the long row of delegates, arranged and introduced by States. The elegant parlors blazed with light and beauty; and the women delegates were an interesting and pleasing study, as, radiant in their evening dresses, they stood there, chatting pleasantly with everybody, exchanging wit and repartee on all sides.

To the great regret of all, Mrs. Stanton was absent on account of the severe illness of a beloved sister. Among the more distinguished of the guests were May Wright Sewall of Indiana, a most executive, pleasing and able woman;[1] Helen M. Gougar, also of the Hoosier State, editor of *Our Herald*, a fine speaker with a magnetic presence, and truly handsome; Mary B. Clay of Kentucky, a proud descendant of a noble lineage; Dr. Clemence S. Lozier of New York, with her sweet face wreathed in the same benevolent smiles that endeared her to us in the long ago; Mary Seymour Howell of Massachusetts, tall, dignified and amiable; Harriet R. Shattuck, her colleague, short, plump and piquant; Elizabeth Boynton Harbert of Illinois, editor of "Woman's Kingdom" in the *Inter-Ocean*, gray-haired, gentle and womanly; Lillie Devereux Blake of New York, tall, vivacious and stylish; Phoebe Couzins, the famous lawyer of Missouri, and Belva A. Lockwood, the noted lawyer of the District of Columbia; Rev. Phoebe A. Hanaford, the sweet-voiced preacher of New Jersey, and many, many others whom we'd gladly name if it were possible. . . .

The convention met yesterday morning (Tuesday) in Lincoln Hall, and was presided over at the opening session by May Wright Sewall. . . . This (Wednesday) morning's session was devoted chiefly to the plans for Oregon work, all of which will be duly submitted to our constituents as soon as they are properly matured. Suffice it to say we are to have help from headquarters, and our visit to Washington will not be in vain. . . .

To-morrow the President receives our delegation at the Executive Mansion. . . .

The weather is worse than the worst in Oregon. More anon.

Washington, D. C., March 11, 1884.

A. S. D.

*(March 20, 1884)*

## A Call at the White House and a Senate Hearing

On Thursday the officers and delegates of the convention were received at the Executive Mansion, by invitation of President [Chester] Arthur, who met us all in the blue room, and looked as badly frightened at receiving us in his bachelor home as though he knew it was out of order, but couldn't help it. We felt, as we looked upon his pompous form and elegant though unkempt surroundings, that after all there was precious little more glory in being a chief magistrate of the nation than a governor of a Territory, and rejoiced that we were neither. . . .

Susan B. Anthony, with her well-known upright life and glorious devotion to humanity, took the President's proffered hand and looked earnestly into his eyes while she plead [*sic*] for his semi-official recognition of the rights of the delegates from the twenty-six states and Territories of the Union who stood before him, all through her asking in their representative capacity for a word of encouragement for the benefit of their unrepresented constituency, and the President, hoping to secure a renomination from voters for reelection to the office, was too cowardly to express an opinion for or against our united plea, we felt that to be a Susan B. Anthony was a thousand times more glorious than to be a chief magistrate who dared not speak his mind. We all pitied Chester and exulted in Susan. . . .

On Friday a delegation, led by Miss Anthony, appeared before the Woman Suffrage Committee of the Senate and made arguments for a Sixteenth Amendment, in presence of a full committee and a crowd of spectators that filled the spacious room almost to suffocation. The first speaker was Mrs. Shattuck of Massachusetts, whose argument was received with marked attention. The next was Mrs. Sewall of Indiana, and her logic was irresistible. Then came Mrs. Gougar of Indiana, Mrs. Seymour Howell and Mrs. Gilkey Rogers of New York, each excellent in her way, and Mrs. Harbert of Illinois, who made an equally good impression. Your correspondent was the next speaker, and after her came Lillie Devereux Blake of New York, who closed her admirable address with happy allusions to the decorations on the walls and ceiling of the room, all of which represented womanhood as the embodiment of all the virtues. . . . Miss Anthony closed the hearing, which occupied over two hours, and held every member of the committee in an attitude of respectful listening to the end. . . .

*(March 27, 1884)*

## A Visit with Lucy Stone and Henry Blackwell

[After the convention, the next week was spent in New York, with visits in New York City and speeches in Albany.]

Saturday, and Boston. We had telegraphed Lucy Stone that we were coming, and a six hours' ride of 200 miles through a beautiful and populous region landed us at the depot, where we were met by Mr. H. B. Blackwell, the loyal husband of the one devoted wife of America who retains her maiden name, and are conveyed to their beautiful home on Dorchester Heights—overlooking Massachusetts Bay.

Our friends, who have for fourteen years carried forward the Woman Suffrage work, editing and publishing the *Woman's Journal*, holding conventions everywhere [for the American Woman Suffrage Association], and getting annual hearings before Legislative committees, have recently met with a temporary set-back in their work for municipal suffrage, through the action of a few remonstrants of Boston—men and women of enormous wealth—the Tories of the present—who shirk their own public duties and seek to compel others to do likewise. But Lucy Stone and Henry Blackwell never say die; and with a spirit of pluck and perseverance that would do honor to the Daniel Boones of Oregon, they are already "picking flints to try again."

On Saturday, accompanied by our gentlemanly host, who obligingly gives the day to us, we "do" Boston in a carriage, and meet a number of wealthy and philanthropic business men. . . . Then we visit the *Woman's Journal* office, elegantly and pleasantly situated on Park street, overlooking Boston Commons, with lasting mementoes of Revolutionary and anti-slavery struggles hard by on every hand, and not far away the ancient burying ground of the Bostonians, in which the grave of Wendell Phillips catches our longing eyes. All hail, brave heart! all hail! . . .

We are glad to note that the *Woman's Journal* is prospering. Throngs of ladies are flitting in and out, and the cheery office is made doubly radiant by the presence of Alice Stone Blackwell, daughter of our host and hostess, one of the *Journal* editors, and a most able and accomplished young lady.[2]

To-morrow, the 16th, just one month after leaving home, we are to speak in Tremont Temple; then on to Hartford [the] next day, to address the Connecticut Woman Suffrage Convention, under the leadership of Isabella Beecher Hooker.

Boston, Mass., March 15, 1884.

A. S. D.

*(March 27, 1884)*

## Homeward Bound

On Tuesday morning we bade good-bye to Miss Anthony at the Baltimore and Ohio depot, and were soon whirling away to the west-ward, [for suffrage meetings in Lafayette, Indiana, and visits in Chicago].

The annoying face-ache that had been troubling us through all our travels grew insubordinate [in Chicago] . . . and drove us to a seat in the dental parlors of the Mechesneys [McChesneys], from which we arose, after an hour's alternate endurance and flinching, with an upper jaw full of sound teeth which couldn't be purchased with the Kohinoor. . . . [W]e repaired in Dr. A. B. McChesney's company to the Grand Union depot, and very soon were homeward bound.

The journey was a tedious one. First a six-hour stop because of a broken axle, then a two days' detention in St. Paul to secure a Pullman sleeper, and then twenty-four hours' lost time on the Northern Pacific, made the time seem interminable. But it wasn't; for here we are at home at last, adding the closing paragraphs to this letter, and getting ready for an abundance of work in the State before the June election.

[Portland], April 11, 1884.

A. S. D.

*(April 17, 1884)*

## Twenty-Eight Miles in Ten Hours

We left Pendleton on Tuesday morning at 6 o'clock, boarding the train bound for Meacham's station, in blissful ignorance of the afternoon's staging awaiting us at the other end of the line. . . . We had been told at Pendleton that breakfast would await us at Meacham's at 8 o'clock. Maybe it did, but we didn't get there, nor did we ever know before, by sad experience, how hard it was to be deprived of food for a whole forenoon, beginning with the morning. A lady in a construction car passed us a cup of coffee at 11 o'clock, but hunger was not appeased till after noon-time, when the train halted in the edge of a swamp, over which the passengers picked their way on a layer of boards, and thence over a rustic bridge to the great log hotel in the heart of the Blue Range, the present terminus of the railroad, and a place of considerable temporary activity and trade.

A good dinner and an agreeable thaw-out before a huge log fire fortified us—in imagination—for the afternoon's adventure, after which behold us in a great thoroughbrace mud-wagon, seated on the edge of a trunk beside another lady, with the brass knobs on the trunk for cushions, and nothing to brace our feet against but the rarefied air of the mountains. The prospect wasn't inviting, but we stuck to it, reconciled to the situation, as was the Dutchman's wife who was dying, because we "had to be."

But all the reconciliation of the direst imaginable necessity couldn't make us stick to that seat, try as we might; so we attempted to exchange places with John Haily, Jr., who occupied the front seat beside the driver, only to find a vacuum when we tried to dispose of our *avoirdupois*; for we sat down between the seats, on the aforesaid mountain air, and can't remember how we got picked up.

But there was a lot of fun in it all—for everybody except the victim of misplaced confidence. Luckily, we were not seriously hurt by the fall.

But oh! those roads! Imagine the rough and rugged mountain tops, with the snow and ice melting rapidly; rushing rivulets, coursing their way down the wagon ruts and deepening the impending danger; mud as deep as it was slippery, and sticky as it was treacherous; side-long ridges, full of chuck-holes on the lower edges; with rocks, boulders, stumps, logs and ruts *ad infinitum*, with horses straining their strong muscles, and the great wagon rolling, plunging and creaking; imagine it all, and a hundred times as much that was terrifying, and then you couldn't picture the situation unless you'd been there. And they say the roads are good compared to what they have been! Heaven help the worst!

The wagon came at last to a sudden turn in a better part of the road, when the lady on the trunk, who had relaxed her vigilance, alighted on her head, half a rod away from the wagon, falling over Mr. Haily, who had tumbled out also, though striking upon his feet, while a bright boy of eight years landed on all fours a little to the left of them.

Nobody was hurt, but it was a close call. The coach was saved from upsetting by a friendly tree, and on we went again—roll, bump, crash, slam, bang, thump—bruising bones and muscles, and sighing often, as the tedious hours crept on, "Oh, for a lodge in some vast wilderness!"

That ride of twenty-eight miles occupied ten hours, including a stop-over for supper at Pelican Station, and it was nearly 11 P. M. when we reached La Grande, where we stopped at Mahaffey's Hotel and crept shivering into bed, more nearly dead than alive, blessing anew the progressing era of railroads, and eulogizing as never before the enterprising spirit of stage men and the faithfulness of stage horses.

Island City [Oregon], April 27, 1884.

A. S. D.

*(May 8, 1884)*

## A Word to Oregon Women

Women of Oregon be on the alert. You are not asked to engage in arguments with men; on the contrary, you are earnestly urged to avoid all heated discussions pertaining to the pending Amendment [to give Oregon women the vote]. It is too late now to convince any man by arguments. All reasonable and reasoning men who have given the measure mature deliberation will vote for the Amendment, and a man who will not reflect or reason would better be let alone.

But there is a work that you can do which will tell most effectually in a quiet way in your own homes, with the men you love and honor most. Say to them, in the same sweet winning way that you long ago learned to use when asking for a new bonnet for yourself, or new shoes for the children, or new furniture for the parlor, "You will make me very happy to-day, dear, if you will vote for Woman Suffrage. Remember me at the ballot-box, and I will be a better wife and mother through all the coming years because your vote has made me free.". . . [P]ocket your pride for one brief morning and enlist your husband on the side of right and justice. . . .

Young ladies can also do much to stimulate public sentiment between this time and Monday. An old man or a young lover will often listen to a girl's opinions and be guided by them far more than by the sage counsel of a mature woman.

We know there are hundreds and thousands of men who will make woman's cause their own next Monday. They are the very best men of the land, and if they are properly sustained by women in the home and voters at the ballot-box there will be no such word as fail.

A. S. D.

*(May 29, 1884)*

## The Defeat in Oregon

The conflict is over. It is the morning after the battle, and although the returns as yet are quite meager, enough is known to make it morally certain that the Woman Suffrage Amendment is defeated. It is useless to complain of what might have been. . . . [I]t is now in order to review the situation and explain the methods of procedure, concerning which, before election, I was not at liberty to speak.

Immediately after my return from the National Convention, the working force of the [Oregon] Woman Suffrage Association began a silent but vigorous plan of organization [a "still hunt"] throughout the state. Four States [Michigan, Kansas, Colorado, and Nebraska] had previously submitted a Woman Suffrage Amendment to their voters. . . . [I]t was decided that the methods of the beaten States be not repeated, but instead of an open campaign with local and imported speakers, the funds usually expended in that way should be used to organize, as men often do to win in cases where nothing is to be overcome but ignorance, hatred, vice and prejudice. Had the funds expected for the work been anywhere nearly provided as promised, the outcome would have been vastly different. But the majority of the women of the East were unwilling—or unable—to keep their pledges. . . .

It would be idle to call the outlook encouraging, and yet I am not disheartened. I have learned anew, and by sad experience, that the power of the home is the only redeeming possibility in store for the salvation of this government. . . .

We are preparing to renew the conflict even now. Before the smoke of the battle has cleared away, we are reorganizing for the fight, and we will press on as never before, more keenly resolved than ever to halt not until victory is achieved.

A. S. Duniway

*(June 5, 1884)*

## No Lights in Portland

The electric lights in this city are not in operation, as the man sent out with the plant from New York has run away. Another electrician will be here in a few days to remedy the trouble.

*(September 11, 1884)*

## Letter From
## Susan B. Anthony

Rochester, N.Y., September 1, 1884.

To the Editor of the *New Northwest*:

Yours of recent date is here, forwarded from Johnstown, whence I came to this city, utterly tired out with work on the third volume of the Woman Suffrage History—poking over the past like a caged lion. I paw against the gratings, so I must be free to roam for a little while on my native wilds. . . .

I like your decisions as to new plans of work; that is, let the men and women pour in their petitions for a re-submission of the [Oregon] Amendment at a special election. Then have all your lawyers, judges and legislators armed and equipped with the legal and constitutional authorities for the passage of a bill forbidding the disfranchisement of the women of your State. Your Constitution says "all male citizens over 21 years," etc., may vote, but it nowhere prohibits women from voting. In that you are fortunate. Then, you have so many grand, progressive, brilliant men in Oregon, who may yet make her the "banner State."

So close to Washington Territory, too! And the reports from that quarter are indeed gratifying. All honor to the men and women of the far, free West! Your way is clear for a legislative enactment that shall open the doors as wide for Oregon's women as for Washington's. Let your Legislature be made to see it, and "the land of the sundown seas" will be the New England of the new century.

You ask my opinion of a convention of the National Association in Oregon this Fall. Really, the leaving you alone with your Legislature, the State Woman Suffrage Association and the *New Northwest* this year seems to me to be the better course. You are doing splendidly. Considering all the disadvantages under which women labored—with their hands tied—at a general election, when every conflicting interest among men who wanted office in county and precinct was naturally in the ascendant, it is surprising that you should have had so large a relative vote.

I note that the usual secret, underhand opposition of the envious and jealous, which always has to be encountered by the faithful public servant who is engaged in conquering prejudice, has already assailed you. But 'tis nothing. It will soon exhaust itself. All you have to do is to work right along—as the moon did when it was barked at. You shouldn't even stop to brush off the flies that light on the ox's horn. They can't stay there, try they ever so hard and long.

Won't your Legislature pass a resolution requesting the national Congress to submit a Sixteenth Amendment enfranchising women? This is an important move, and needs only to be agitated among the thinking men of the mighty West to induce them to act.

If your Legislature re-submits the Amendment to a special election, we will have plenty of work for all hands in getting ready for it. And should you get a suffrage bill we'll wake the echoes in Oregon, that shall reverberate everywhere with our national jubilee!

Susan B. Anthony.

*(September 25, 1884)*

## A Further Warning to Women of Washington Territory

More than once the *New Northwest* has warned the women of Washington Territory that a conspiracy is on foot to attempt the repeal of the Woman Suffrage Law. It has been informed that the headquarters of the schemers [the liquor interests] is in San Francisco, and that they are aided and abetted by interests in this city and the Eastern States. . . . [W]e warn friends of Woman Suffrage to learn the views of candidates for the Legislature and vote accordingly. The party platforms are all right, but remember that many opponents are so dishonorable that they would sneak into power under any plank that would afford them a covering. Equal suffrage is an existing fact in the Territory; there is no occasion for timidity on the part of anybody in espousing it; the rule to follow is that the man who is not for it is against it.

*(October 2, 1884)*

## Last Call to Women of Washington Territory

To the Women of Washington Territory:

Threats have been made that the next Legislature will be induced to repeal the suffrage law, and it is a generally accepted fact—a fact which is not denied—that the Liquor Dealers' Associations of San Francisco, Portland and St. Paul will furnish money to accomplish this result, because they fear the power of women in the jury-box when law-breaking whisky-sellers are up for trial, and at the polls in case a law affecting the liquor traffic should go to a popular vote. . . .

We have warned women to be on the alert, to learn the views of candidates, and to vote for friends of Woman Suffrage without regard to party. The consequences of a repeal of the law cannot be over-estimated. Not only would the blow be a most severe one to the cause of woman's equality in the Pacific Northwest, but throughout the country.

The election comes next Tuesday, the 4th prox., and the *New Northwest* makes a last call upon the women of Washington Territory to protect their interests and the interests of their families and homes by voting for known Woman Suffragists for the Legislature.

*(October 30, 1884)*

# Washington Women Vote

The number of women who voted in Washington Territory is about 12,000—as large as the total vote of both men and women in Wyoming.

*(November 13, 1884)*

# Notes for 1884

1. May Wright Sewall (1844-1920), who heads Duniway's list of NWSA faithfuls, became widely known as an ardent and capable suffrage organizer. She was chair of the NWSA executive committee, 1882-90, and spoke frequently before Congressional comittees. She helped found and lead the National Council of Women and headed the World's Congress of Representative Women, held during the Columbian Exposition in 1893. Duniway was one of the 333 women who read papers at the Congress.

2. Alice Stone Blackwell (1857-1950) was the only child of Lucy Stone and Henry Blackwell, major figures in the suffrage movement. Two of Alice's aunts also pioneered for women's rights: Elizabeth Blackwell, the first woman in America to earn a medical degree, and Antoinette Brown Blackwell, the first woman in America ordained as a minister. Alice graduated with honors from Boston University and then gave the next thirty-five years of her life to editing *The Woman's Journal*, which her parents had founded. She also became involved in a variety of other reform movements after her mother's death in 1893.

# 1885

## Defeat in the Oregon Senate

The Woman Suffrage bill was beaten in the [Oregon] Senate yesterday. A full report is furnished in Mrs. Duniway's correspondence. Several of the Senators apologized for their negative votes, and not one of them attempted to disprove the justice of the bill; but eighteen of them doggedly voted against a measure which they know to be the most important and beneficent ever before them, all because an ignorant rabble was guided by custom and slander last June. Oh, for men of principle and the courage to do right!

*(February 19, 1885)*

## What of the Future for Woman Suffrage in Oregon?

Sitting here for the last time this year in the Senate chamber, surrounded by the discarded paraphernalia of a protracted siege, our table loaded with the thousands of petitions . . . of disappointed women for whom our heart aches because of their deferred expectations, the question as to the proper course to be mapped out for future Woman Suffrage work comes up for immediate consideration.

Not only are we not discouraged in the cause, good friends, but we are far more hopeful than when the Legislature met. It was a most irksome task to bring together the scattered lines after a bitter defeat at the polls and bravely face discouraging circumstances before.

A. S. D.

*(February 26, 1885)*

## Mary Leonard Admitted to Practice in the U. S. Courts

Mrs. Mary A. Leonard, the woman lawyer of Seattle, W. T., whose application for admission to the bar of this State was refused by the Oregon Supreme Court, was last Friday admitted to practice in the United States District and Circuit Courts for Oregon by Judge [Matthew P.] Deady.[1] Lawyers M. F. Mulkey and J. M. Bower certified to the applicant's good moral character. . . .

*(April 2, 1885)*

## Washington Territory: A New Canada for Women?

The disappointed thousands of Oregon's women who asked for freedom at the ballot-box last June and were answered with invective, ridicule and tyranny may find much comfort in the important announcement that Washington Territory is a new Canada big enough to hold the whole of them. All they have to do to secure their freedom is to cross the line and leave the land of the fossilized Oregonians, where men have denied them liberty, and, taking up their abode in this home of the brave, become clothed with citizenship as with a garment.

Then, too, what a glorious country is this Territory of Washington anyhow. Her area is large enough and her resources amply sufficient to support the population of an empire; her fertility is inexhaustible; her scenery is as varied as that of a mighty continent, combining as it does the accommodations of coast, mountain, river, plain, hill and valley, . . . her climate is as varied as the scenery, being exceedingly temperate on Puget Sound, breezy on the Pacific Coast, dry and arid on the eastern uplands, where the heat of Summer is counterbalanced by the rigors of Winter. . . .

With thoughts like these for company, we sit or half recline in the caboose of the Dayton-bound train and gaze abroad upon the treeless, billowy, grain-laded hills of Walla Walla and Columbia counties. . . .

It is sundown when we reach Dayton, where we take refuge in an express wagon, . . . and take our good friends Mr. and Mrs. Eckler unawares. [S]oon [we] are seated at a cheery tea-table and learning all about jury duty among women, who prize their newly acquired liberties as only sensible women can.

The ladies tell us that every conceivable "bluff" was aimed at them to make their duties as jurors odious. The panel was in one case composed very largely of women; and one man, the foreman of the jury, hung them night and day, while he and others befogged the room with tobacco smoke and often made contemptuous remarks, which the women did not condescend to reply to. Such remarks as, "We'll make 'em sick o' the business," "We'll give 'em enough o' jury service," etc., were often overheard.

But the laugh was turned against the aforesaid foreman when, one of the ladies having been made ill by tobacco smoke, he was compelled to succumb to the same intolerable nuisance and get excused himself, thereby losing the point he had hoped to make—that women were unable to endure . . . jury service. In the other jury the . . . men, being advocates of equality and justice, deported themselves like gentlemen.

But the triumph came when each woman, having faithfully discharged her duty as juror, was herself discharged, bearing in her hands the glittering prize of three dollars per day, and, going rested and recruited to her home, found that the domestic machinery had run smoothly in her absence, and her husband and children had neither starved nor run away.

"It was better than a trip to San Francisco," said Mrs. W. M. Wait, an estimable lady of whose record we heard high praise. "It saved the expense of a journey, gave me needed respite from the long monotony of home duties, enabled me to be an instrument of good, and netted me quite a convenient sum in the bargain.". . .

*(May 14, 1885)*

## Earthquake at Dayton, W.T.

Our lecture on the evening of May 4th in the Congregational Church, and in presence of a very large audience, was nearing its close, when suddenly the shades at the half-open windows began an ominous flapping, suggestive of an approaching wind-storm. There was an instant's pause, as there was danger that the lights might go out; but the flapping ceased and the talk when on for another minute. Then came a second shock or manifestation, more singular than the first; for, after a second instant's flapping of the window shades, a crackling noise,

like the sudden firing of a great brush-heap or the instantaneous lighting of a theater's candelabra by electric currents, so alarmed the multitude that all rose to their feet as by one common impulse, as if to flee from some unseen peril.

We quieted the tumult by assurances of safety, and succeeded in preventing a dangerous stampede; but we wouldn't like to risk the repetition of such a scene. Although the crowd was in motion, the panic was over, and as group after group passed by us at the pulpit stairs near the door, so many urged the need of a second meeting that we consented to remain over and speak the following evening. . . .

The second evening brought another fine audience, and, though everybody was nervous, all remained to the close, and left the church completely mystified as to the cause of the phenomenon of the previous evening. Mrs. Eckler, who was not well and had remained at home the previous evening, reported a slight vibration through the house after retiring; but the great mass of the people felt no symptoms of an earthquake. . . .

A quiet, restful and glorious Sunday at the beautiful home of a beloved daughter [Clara Duniway Stearns], on the vernal banks of the silvery Lake LaCamas, is followed by a return to Portland on Monday.

Portland, May 12, 1885. A. S. D.

*(May 14, 1885)*

## July Fourth in the Land of the Free

For several months past, the good citizens of Vancouver [W. T.] have been in correspondence with their less fortunate friends of equal rights in Oregon, to whom they had magnanimously tendered the free use of their city park for a celebration on the Fourth of July upon the temporary footing of absolute equality with themselves. . . .

The good citizens of Vancouver had many difficulties to encounter, for the spirit of tyranny dies hard; and when it was known among certain elements that the celebration was to be one of absolute equality between men and the newly enfranchised people of the commonwealth, certain local societies refused to parade or otherwise participate in the festivities to which they would have gladly joined if gotten up in the sole interest of the erewhile aristocracy of sex. But the sequel proved that they were neither missed nor needed; for certainly a more successful celebration was never enjoyed by any people.

The steamers "Lurline" and "Fleetwood," the latter towing a barge, left Portland at 8:30 A. M., having first met steamers from Oregon City and other points, whose Vancouver-bound passengers were transferred to their keeping, paddled gaily out upon the water and bore proudly away with banners flying and handkerchiefs waving, leaving behind many a long-ing and loyal woman, who but for her domestic duties (which no equal suffragist ever neglects), would have gladly joined the multitude.

Upon arriving at Vancouver, the excursionists from abroad were met by the various committees, headed by the United States Fourteenth Infantry Band, and those who chose were conveyed in carriages, or permitted to go on foot, if they preferred, to the public park a few blocks away, while many others joined the parade. The gay procession . . . was headed by a magnificent ship of state on wheels . . . decorated with banners and evergreens. With sails furled and flag floating at the masthead, loaded to the guards with a bevy of beautifully attired boys and girls, ninety-four in number, the whole drawn by six splendidly matched horses, . . . she looked the splendid thing of life she was.

Next came the band in elegant uniform, followed by soldiers and citizens, the whole presenting a scene that, once witnessed, can never be forgotten. The chariot drawing the ship of state halted in front of the speakers' stand, the procession disbanded, the musicians marched to their designated seats, and such soul-stirring harmonies as only that well-known military band can create thrilled the ears of the assembled thousands, hushing the multitude into rapt attention, which broke forth at the grand *finale* into loud and prolonged applause. . . .

Dr. [M. Ella] Whipple announced that, owing to the unavoidable absence through ill health of Mrs. H. A. Loughary, President-elect of the Day, Mrs. A. S. Duniway had been chosen to lead the exercises.

After an eloquent and appropriate prayer, . . . the choir led the national anthem, the vast multitude joining in the singing with spirit and understanding.

Reading of the New Declaration of Independence, by Mrs. J. DeVore Johnson, was next in order. . . .

After an extended and excellent interlude of music by the band, Mrs. Duniway made [a] brief opening address, . . . followed by [an address] by Mrs. Mattie A. Bridge [and] a rendition of the "Star Spangled Banner" [by] Miss Louise Lester. . . . Men threw up their hats, and women waved their handkerchiefs. And when, in response to an *encore,* the little lady, who is not yet allowed to vote, sang the closing stanza, the people went fairly wild with enthusiasm. . . .

And when, as the sun slowly descended the fiery West, the good boats stopped at the docks and took aboard the visitors from Oregon, all were emphatic in their praises of the citizens of Vancouver, under whose auspices they had enjoyed one day of perfect equality before the law.

*(July 9, 1885)*

## Illness of Mrs. Duniway's Daughter

Mrs. Clara D. Stearns, of La Camas [W. T.], who recently suffered several severe hemorrhages of the lungs, and whose condition became so critical that she was last week brought to this city to the home of her parents, Mr. and Mrs. Duniway, is slowly but steadily improving. Word had been sent to Mrs. Duniway at Astoria summoning her home, but before she could come the pleasant message was forwarded that her daughter had rallied sufficiently to be considered out of danger.

*(July 23, 1885)*

## Court Week in Oysterville, W.T.

It is court week in Oysterville, and we arrive on time. . . .

[In the] saddest case in the Oysterville court . . . [a] man, a dozen years his young wife's senior, who had always kept her, the mother of his children, in poverty, drudgery and destitution, conceived a plan for raising money by making infamous charges against a man of means, whom he sued for heavy cash damages for alleged criminality with his wife. He did not want a divorce; he desired still to keep his body servant in legal thrall, but he wanted "damages" for the alleged appropriation of his property.

The wife, heretofore accustomed to accepting all indignities and yielding in obedience to all behests, rebelled against this last and greatest outrage, and fled, taking her youngest child with her and temporarily leaving the eldest, because in her destitution she could provide for but one. But when the court met she appeared in defense of her honor, only to be informed, upon taking the witness seat that her husband who had made the most damaging charges against her, through implication, of course, *objected to her testimony on her own behalf,* alleging as a reason therefor that *he didn't want his wife to appear in public before so many men!*

Gentlemen of unimpeachable standing in the community came to us in the church before the lecture began and indignantly complained of the outrage, asking us to denounce it. Seeing His Honor Judge Hoyt in the audience, we went to him for information, and learned that he was obliged to omit the woman's testimony on account of the statute, not yet repealed, although the women are voters, which permits a husband to prohibit his wife from giving testimony against himself in court, no matter how deeply he may wrong her by his own charges. . . .

Portland, August 18, 1885.

A. S. D.

*(August 20, 1885)*

## Anti-Chinese Sentiment

Several carloads of Chinamen have arrived in town from Puget Sound, seeking safety from the violence with which they were threatened there.

*(October 1, 1885)*

Anti-Chinese meetings were held in North Portland on Saturday and Tuesday evenings, and were addressed by Nat. L. Baker, S. B. Pettingill, Thomas Bates, and others.[2] The resolutions are unlike those adopted at Seattle, and simply pledge the men to do all in their power to legally enforce the Chinese restriction act.

*(October 8, 1885)*

*Chinese laborer, Portland, Oregon*

Anti-Chinese societies have been formed this week in East Portland and Albina.

*(October 22, 1885)*

Governor [Watson C.] Squire, of Washington Territory, has sent the Secretary of the Interior a report on the anti-Chinese agitation. After stating the facts about the recent meetings and the intimidation of some Chinese, he says there have been no riots or outbreaks, and he believes none will occur. He hopes to maintain order without troops, and says a strong organization of the best citizens of Seattle has been formed for the purpose. However, should troops be needed, they can be had from Vancouver Barracks on a few hours' notice.

*(October 22, 1885)*

## Off for Minneapolis

"Mother, see; it's almost three o'clock," exclaimed a beloved voice, as we hurriedly scrawled the closing sentences of our last week's letter, preparatory to starting for the American Woman Suffrage Convention at Minneapolis. The reminder hurried us still more; and the sudden announcement that our good sister was waiting at the door with a phaeton added another impulse to overtaxed brain and nerves. But we had ample time to wait till the hurry was over, when, after bidding loved ones good-bye and rushing at a rattling rate along the streets, we reached the dock and hied aboard the transfer boat and found that nobody save ourself seemed in any hurry at all.

Once settled in the Pullman, with "traps" around us and many unfinished chapters of the serial story staring us in the face, we delved into our work, scarcely noting passing moments or receding scenery, and only intent upon catching up with work that, in spite of constant hurry, was lagging ominously.

The short afternoon wore rapidly away, and the long night passed without incident. We awoke at Ritzville, in Washington Territory, the cry of "Last call for breakfast in the dining car!". . . bringing us *vis-a-vis* at table with Miss Bessie Isaacs [of W. T.], our genial companion in travel, with whom at this writing we are snugly settled in a "section," and spending the day (Sunday) amid a perfect maze of Autumnal glories. . . .

It is lazy work, this all-day riding through these mighty solitudes, where scenery grander than on the Hudson and air purer than the perfumed breath of Araby have already tempted many a hardy pioneer to pitch a tent and rear a cabin.

October 12, 1885.
A. S. D.

The incessant traveling for four days and nights, over mountain, river, hill and plain, the long-drawn monotony of sleepless nights in sleeping cars, and the usual incidents of travel connected with a journey overland, were inter-crowded in our own case during the days by spasmodic scribbling at the "DeLauncy Curse," [serial story] which has literally been written thus far "on a fly.". . .

We start from [our] reveries and find ourself, with Miss Bessie Isaacs, under the shadows of the minarets and domes of Minneapolis. The usual rush and confusion attendant upon packing traps and feeing porter and entering a cab is followed by a rapid drive through the stony streets to the commodious and beautiful Church of the Redeemer, where we are made at home among a perfect host of friends. Lucy Stone and Henry R. Blackwell, of Boston, dear honored pioneers of human rights, whom snows of many Winters have bleached white in work for Liberty; Julia Ward Howe, cultured patrician, white-haired and motherly, the disfranchised citizen who wrote the "Battle Hymn of the Republic" for an ungrateful country which yet denies her liberty; Mrs. Campbell of Iowa, Mrs. Cutler of Illinois, Judge Foulke of Indiana, Dr. Spaulding of Wisconsin, Mrs. Lusk of Minnesota, Miss Young of Nebraska—and—and shades of the land of red apples! whom see we here among the nation's notables but our old friend S. A. Clarke, of the *Willamette Farmer*.[3]

We haven't time to more than get a handshake with the persons named and glimpses at a perfect host of others who are ready to greet us cordially till we are met by Dr. Martha G. Ripley, a most thorough-going equal suffragist, a first-class physician, and withal as pleasant and womanly as our own women doctors in Portland.[4] Dr. Ripley welcomes self and Miss Isaacs—famous here and extremely popular as the one "genuine, live woman voter of the convention"—and we are whirled away to her hospitable home to rest till evening, preparatory to engagement on the rostrum.

The Convention had met and organized on the 13th, and all the papers were full of the sayings and doings of the wise men and women of the East. . . . [W]e are absolutely too busy to write out particulars of the proceedings in time for the mails.

A. S. D.

*(October 22, 1885)*

## Tributes to Henry Blackwell and Lucy Stone

The women of America owe a debt of gratitude to Henry B. Blackwell, of Boston, which they can never hope to repay. This gentleman, now hoary white with honored years, began his work for woman's liberty in his younger days, and has from that time forward devoted himself to it with a rarity of judgment seldom equaled.

In the palmy days of the Republican party, ere it became so sated with the lust of power that it could no longer afford to express justice for women and achieve wondrous victories under its grand assertions of right, it was Henry B. Blackwell who wrote the famous resolution that proved Horace Greeley's death-warrant, by committing the party to equal rights, hailing women's demands "with satisfaction," and declaring that the "earnest demands of any class of citizens for additional rights should be treated with respectful consideration."

But for that peaceful battle-cry, the party would have been crowded to the wall in '72, although the purblind politicians failed to see and comprehend the fact. In '76 everybody knows how near it came to defeat, and that it was only kept in power through the 8 to 7 commission.[5] In 1880 the Republican party showed signs of growing weak and disorderly. It forgot women, or rather, feared them, and the tragedy that foreshadowed its future fate is one that never can be forgotten.

Then, in 1884, wholly forgetful of the high destiny that called it into being, and while its faithful allies, the women of the nation, still hoped against hope it would yet return to first principles and prove worthy of its trust, its perversity led to its downfall and its selfishness to its dire confusion. All this was foreseen by Mr. Blackwell, Wendell Phillips and Wm. Lloyd Garrison senior, and expressed by them to us personally on more than one occasion during the early years of the party's declining and decaying power. . . .

Contrary to orders from the person most deeply interested, we must again speak of Miss Bessie Isaacs [of Washington Territory], whose appearance among the disfranchised hosts as "a genuine live woman voter" was of itself a complete refutation of all the silly bluster in opposition to woman's right to vote at all. And we frankly confess to a degree of pride, that we think our readers will consider pardonable under the circumstances, when we reflect that of all the hosts of workers present the undersigned was the only delegate who was able to introduce a living trophy of work accomplished. . . .

We omitted in the proper place to make mention of a reception given at her residence by Dr. Ripley on Friday evening, to the leading suffragists, who, with Lucy Stone at their head, passed a most delightful evening. . . . We also omitted the newsboys' and bootblacks' picnic at the falls of Minnehaha, at which Lucy Stone and ourself made speeches to the delighted ragamuffins. . . .

Nor can we close this long, hurried and rambling letter without referring to a beautiful tribute of respect and affection presented Lucy Stone . . . by ladies of Minneapolis, who, with Dr. Ripley at their head, completed a grand surprise for the gifted lady. . . . The tribute was an elaborate basket of flowers, ornamented with satin ribbons in the national colors, the red bearing the inscription, "Minnesota, October 19, 1885"; the white "Lucy Stone" and "Innocence," and the blue "Woman Suffrage." Speeches of presentation were made by Dr. Ripley and the writer, and a feeling response by Lucy Stone that touched all hearts.

October 21st., 1885.

A. S. D.

*(October 29, 1885)*

## Home on the Northern Pacific

We fall asleep in Montana and awake in Idaho. Here is another magnificent Territory, where friends assure us that the legislature only needs one more season's work to secure the elective franchise for women. Men also say if the right of suffrage is not speedily granted to their wives and mothers they will petition Congress to separate the Pan Handle District, through which the train passes, from the Territory proper and attach the same to Washington.

Passing over the Autumnal glories of the charming region through which the great lake or lakes of Pen d'Oreille are nestled like mighty mirrors between the mountain gorges, we enter, on the third day out from Minneapolis, the beautiful prairies of the Spokane, and at 2:40 P. M. the city of Spokane Falls glides into view. Here we part company with Miss Isaacs and

entering a bus are driven to a hotel, in the midst of a sudden rain which seemed to have gotten up a show in honor of the slowly approaching land of Webfoot. . . .

A. S. D.

*(November 5, 1885)*

## Chinese Troubles in Washington Territory

A serious trouble threatens the men who have been engaged in intimidating Chinese on Puget Sound. They have been violating plain federal laws as well as the treaty with China, and the grand jury has been reconvened at Seattle to consider their offense. The conduct of several prominent citizens of Whatcom, including Mayor Marcy, Rev. Jos. Wolfe, and Editor Nicklin, of the *Reveille*, is to be investigated, and the doings of many other men will also receive attention.

Tuesday was the day set for driving the Chinese out of Tacoma, W. T., and on the morning of that day their houses were visited by whites and they were told to "go." The dispatches say that no violence was offered them, as they promptly complied, and soon many of the celestials were on the march with their personal effects to Lakeview, nine miles distant.

The goods were packed on drays, wagons and trucks, and citizens escorted them away. The Chinese were supplied by citizens with provisions to last till the next morning. The merchants were given a day to pack their goods, and each was allowed three assistants. In a day or two the seven hundred Chinese who formerly lived in Tacoma will have gone nobody knows where—possibly to different localities, but Portland will get the most of them.

*(November 5, 1885)*

## Chinese Agitation at Puget Sound

In consequence of the expulsion of the Chinese from Tacoma, and the threatening attitude of the agitators at Seattle, six companies of U. S. troops were ordered from Vancouver to those cities last Saturday. The fierceness of the anti-Chinese agitation has since subsided. The U. S. Grand Jury at Vancouver has also been investigating the Tacoma expulsion affair, and has returned indictments for intimidating Chinese. . . . More arrests are to follow. Several agitators, among them one woman, have also been indicted and arrested in Seattle.

What the end will be, and whether convictions can be obtained for the offenses charged, remains to be seen. At any rate, the backbone of the lawless movement has been broken; but the vital principle of self-protection and antipathy to the Chinese still lives, and will not [go] down until the people are relieved from the burden of their presence. But this must be accomplished by peaceable and lawful means.

*(November 12, 1885)*

## Dirty Linen in Tacoma, W. T.

It is said that many of the public-spirited and patriotic women of Tacoma who were going to do their own washing have weakened and sent the dirty family linen to Chinamen in this city. But who can blame them? Bending over the washtub is a back-breaking diversion in which no mother of a family should be allowed to indulge. It is work eminently suited for masculine muscles, and if those who wish to get rid of the Chinese would volunteer to take up this portion of the mongolian's steady work, instead of thrusting it upon the "weaker sex," there would be both sense and consistency in their cry that "the Chinese must go to make room for white workingmen."

*(November 18, 1885)*

## Washington Women Flog Wife-Beater

A report comes from Tampico, W. T., that Harry Roberts, who has the unenviable reputation of being a wife-beater, was taken from his residence by a dozen women a few nights ago and tied to a fence and deservedly flogged. Roberts' repeated abuse of his wife had aroused considerable indignation, and the women of the place and vicinity determined to teach him some humanity in true Delaware style. Each woman took the lash in her hand and laid it on Roberts' bare back until exhausted. When the ordeal was gone through with, Roberts was warned never again to ill-treat his wife, on penalty of a repetition of the flogging, which he solemnly promised never to do again, and went his way meekly.

Good for the women! This is the proper medicine for fellows of his stripe.

*(November 26, 1885)*

## Catching Ranch Fever

We never visit the mighty uplands of Eastern Washington, . . . but we get the ranch fever so badly that the newspaper business cloys upon our over-taxed endurance, and the applause of listening audiences falls with a dull, flat sound upon our weary ears.

But for the gratifying results of work thus far accomplished in the great battle for human freedom, we fear we'd be so tempted to desert our destiny-appointed post that we'd give up the prosecution of the suffrage work, get hayseed in our hair, don a liberty cap, and turn granger and grow rich along with the rest of the free people of the glorious Inland Empire.

Thoughts like these stir our tired spirit as we sit in restless expectancy in the railway coach, taking a mental inventory of the alluvial hills and peaceful flats of the great Palouse country, through which the iron horse goes snorting, awakening the echoes as he runs, with steam in his breath and fire in his eye, bearing a train of merchandise and men in strange contrast to the pigmy loads once carried on the crashing stage or splashing buckboard by unwilling horses, driven by the cruel lash of the driver's whip.

November 26, 1885.

A. S. D.

*(December 3, 1885)*

## Floggers of Wife-Beater Rewarded

Mrs. Clark, a merchant of Yakima City, did a graceful deed when she presented a new dress pattern to each of the women who recently thrashed wife-beater Roberts, of Tampico, W.T. Besides encouraging women to protect each other, the effect of such an endorsement will not be lost upon wifebeaters in general.

*(December 10, 1885)*

# Hazards of Winter Staging

Our work [in Lewiston, I. T.] was not half accomplished, but our time was up and on Wednesday, at 1 P. M., we entered the uninviting stage and started for Pomeroy [W. T.], thirty miles distant, the way leading across the Clearwater, and, a few miles further on, across the Snake River. Then the road turned toward the hills, following the ragged cañon of the creek Alpowai for quite a distance.

The seat inside the coach had proved unendurable . . . and we had climbed to the boot beside the driver at an early moment, only to find the old vehicle incapable of doing any better, even there. But at our request the obliging Jehu ballasted its rear with a few hundred pounds of basaltic boulders, and the effect was magical.

But the night was coming on apace, the constant climbing led us on to colder and loftier heights, and soon vast billowy snow fields rose and rolled away in the illimitable distance upon every hand. We had left the balminess of Lewiston far behind and had encountered a fair illustration of a polar world, including its indispensable darkness.

How the wind blew! The driving snow sought crevices in veil and mittens, and the white frost from our breath enveloped head and face in a coat of rigid mail. To add to the discomfort, the road was blind, slippery, sidelong, and often precipitous; but the faithful horses and sagacious driver proved equal to all emergencies, and we reached Pomeroy in safety, having passed Pataha in the darkness, stifling many a longing wish to stop over, and only compromising with conscience by making a firm resolve to come again when the weather is better.

December 18, 1885.

A. S. D.

*(December 24, 1885)*

# Notes for 1885

1. Judge Matthew P. Deady (1824–93) was born in Maryland, attended school in West Virginia and Ohio, and was admitted to the Ohio bar in 1847. He arrived in Oregon in 1849 and taught school and practiced law at Lafayette. Deady was elected to the territorial legislature in 1851, served as associate judge of the Territorial Supreme Court, and presided over the State Constitutional Convention in 1857. When he was appointed U. S. District Judge for Oregon in 1859, Deady moved to Portland where he was a founder of the Multnomah Public Library and a leading citizen. He also served for twenty years on the Board of Regents of the University of Oregon and was a supporter of woman suffrage and a friend to Duniway's cause. Deady simply noted in his diary: "Friday [Apr. 27] decided three cases in C C and admitted Mary A. Leonard to the bar" (*Pharisee Among Philistines*, 465).

2. According to Turnbull, Nat L. Baker started the Portland *Evening Post* in March of 1882, but the paper was soon discontinued (*History of Oregon Newspapers*, 168). A radical journalist, Baker was editor of the *Daily News* in 1885, and became owner-editor of the *Oregon Alarm*. He participated in formation of an Anti-Coolie Club at Portland's New Market Theatre on Jan. 27, 1886 (Malcolm Clark, Jr., "Appendix A, 1886," *Pharisee Among Philistines*, 508).

Sam B. Pettingill, also a newspaper man, purchased the *Standard*, advertised as the "largest Democratic paper in the state, only Democratic weekly published in Portland," in June of 1885. As owner-editor, Pettingill suspended the *Standard* in February of 1886.

3. Samuel Asahel Clarke (1828-1909) was born in Cuba, educated in New York City, and arrived in Oregon in 1850. He operated a sawmill at Portland and later settled in Salem, where he was legislative clerk in 1862. He was editor of *The Oregonian*, 1864-65, participated in organizing the Oregon and California Railroad Co., owned and edited the Salem *Statesman*, 1867-72, and was half-owner of the *Willamette Farmer*, 1872-78. Clarke moved to Portland and served as head of the literary bureau of Villard's railroad syndicate from 1878 to 1883. He was librarian of the General Land Office in Washington, D. C., (1898-1908) and published his two-volume history of Oregon, *Pioneer Days of Oregon History*, in 1905.

4. Dr. Martha George Rogers Ripley (1843-1912) was from Vermont and moved to Massachusetts following her marriage. After the birth of three daughters, Ripley pursued her wish to become a medical doctor and graduated from the Boston University Medical School in 1883. That same year, her husband suffered a severe accident, and the family moved to Minneapolis, where Ripley supported them with her specialty in obstetrics and children's diseases. Committed to woman suffrage since 1875, Ripley became president of the Minnesota Suffrage Association and was active in the AWSA.

5. The "8 to 7 commission" of the 1876 presidential election is Duniway's reference to the fifteen-member commission, composed of ten congressmen and five Supreme Court Justices who were given the responsibility of sorting out the authenticity of two sets of election returns—one from the Republicans and one from the Democrats. The Republican candidate was Rutherford B. Hayes, and the Democratic candidate was Samuel Tilden. Tilden won the popular vote as well as the electoral college vote (184 to 165); both parties claimed the remaining twenty electoral votes. Tilden needed only one more electoral vote, and Hayes needed all twenty, nineteen of which came from South Carolina, Louisiana, and Florida—states still controlled by the Republicans as a part of Reconstruction. The commission, which included eight Republicans and seven Democrats, accepted the Republican vote in all the states. Although the House disagreed, the Senate concurred with the commission, and Hayes became president.

# 1886-87

## Letters From the Fireside, Number One: The Mother Heart

If the undersigned could have voluntarily given up traveling for an indefinite period for the purpose of a prolonged visit with the loved ones at home; were there no pain-racked body among the blessed number, and no precious life lingering under the shadow of the trailing wing of the Death Angel; if, in short, an unexpected boom in business had permitted, rather than the exigencies of illness compelled the present public inactivity of your humble correspondent, how happily would we accept the situation, and how hopefully could we plan for the work of the newly born year.

Ah, me!

We awaken from a reverie that had carried us back to a lone cabin in the wilds of Hardscrabble, where was born the precious invalid whose waning days now fill alike our waking and sleeping thoughts. It was over thirty years ago when she first saw the light, in the early dawn of a beautiful May morning. The chickens crowed in exultation, and the morning star hung low in the pellucid heavens—

"Copy!" cry the printers, and the treadmill work of the People's Paper brings us forward with a painful start to duty and—to-day.

What will you have, kind readers? Must the mother-heart, that beats in unison with the loving, gentle sufferer, whose distressing cough no walls can shut from our sympathetic ears, steel itself to surrounding conditions, while we talk to you of—say—the proposed "demonetization of silver"? Must we attempt a discourse upon political reform, or an argument on Woman Suffrage? Must we talk of tariff, or co-operative house-keeping, or coolie labor, or the servant girl problem? Would you have us devote this chapter to theology or philosophy? or, descending to every-day topics, must we talk to you of the news of the week, or of the other journalists of the period?

None of these things move us, friends. We cannot write of them to-day. Rather let us reason together concerning the life that is to come— a life in which we will all be interested more and more as the years roll on, and our loved ones, one after another, obeying the call of the "boatman pale," shall hear the dip of his golden oar and watch the flash of the rising tide. . . .

"First the blade, then the ear, and after that full corn in the ear," saith the Scriptures. And, as day by day we watch the progress of the insidious

*Clara Belle Duniway Stearns,
ca. 1878*

microbes that find in the decaying lungs of our patient darling the material upon which their countless myriads of invisible hordes are feeding—hordes that Science, handmaiden of Nature, has recently discovered, though their existence was doubtless coeval with the disease itself—as hour by hour we wait in dread anticipation of the birth of her pure spirit into realms of paradise, "where there shall be no more pain, neither sorrow nor sighing," we mentally exclaim, in the words of our Lord to Nicodemus: "The wind bloweth where it listeth, and thou hearest the sound thereof, but canst not tell when it cometh or whither it goeth. So is every one that is born of the spirit."

Blow gently, Winter winds; sigh softly, Winter rains; let the breath of thy coming be tempered with mercy and the balm of thy presence bring solace to the sweet lingerer by the wayside of suffering. Soon, ah, soon must she join the choir invisible; and while our hearts are rent with anguish 'twill then be her blessed lot to sing:

"O grave, where is thy victory? O Death, where is thy sting?"

And while we who are alive and remain shall be compelled to bear earth's burdens yet a little longer, there is solace in the thought that every revolution of this mundane planet enables us to

"Nightly pitch our moving tent A Day's march nearer home."

Ah, me!

Portland, January 5, 1886.

A. S. D.

*(January 7, 1886)*

## Dead

Dear Readers of the *New Northwest*:

The forms are held to give us chance to say that our precious firstborn is no more. She passed peacefully away at 8 o'clock this morning, and at 8:15 we pen this tear-blurred notice, with the hand that closed the darling's eyes. Dear friends everywhere, we know your hearts will beat in unison with ours in this overwhelming sorrow.

Portland, January 21, 1886.

A. S. D.

*(January 21, 1886)*

## Letters From the Fireside, Number Four: It is Finished

The fond vigil is over, dear friends. The sad, funereal rites are ended. And we can only say of the precious earth-life that has throbbed in unison with ours since the days of our earliest womanhood, It is finished!

Bear with us just a little, friends—just a little—while the troubled heart that to-day is throbbing in sore bereavement turns back the pages of the decades gone, to live over again—just for a moment—the opening months of our twentieth year. The same heart is beating yet—not as then in glad anticipation, registering day by day the maturing months of the dear child's initial year. Its throbbings are painful now; and there is a dull, dead ache at its core—an ache that the broad daylight cannot dissipate nor the gloom of night dispel.

"I wish I could go with you, darling," we said, with choking utterance, just five days ago, as the dear one, struggling for breath, looked with an unspoken appeal into our tear-dimmed eyes. And as she fought feebly against her impending fate, she painfully gasped in answer, "You must finish your work, Ma!"

Her words have a deep significance as we resume our labors; and as we turn from the moment of retrospection that you, good reader, have so kindly indulged. . . .

[S]ome day—possibly less than a decade hence—this long-drawn campaign will be ended. Aye, some day—God speed the time—we too shall cross the mystic river; and when we join our darling *over there*, she will have no more need to say, "You must finish your work, Ma!"

Ah, me!

Portland, January 25, 1886.

A. S. D.

*(January 28, 1886)*

## Editorial Note on Equal Suffrage Plans

It was the opinion of the ladies at the conference at Mrs. Duniway's residence last Saturday afternoon that it would be inexpedient to hold an equal suffrage mass meeting at this time in Portland, owing to the prevalent religious revival meetings, the agitation by the anti-Coolie League, and the near approach of the working-man's congress. The *New Northwest* assures its readers that when equal suffrage meetings are again held in this city they will be agreeably surprised at the amount of new and first-class talent that is ready and waiting to come to the front in its advocacy.

*(February 11, 1886)*

## Letters From the Fireside, Number Six: The Chinese Question

The recent disturbances in Seattle, backed as they are by the continued anti-Chinese agitation in this city and its suburbs, indicating everywhere a smoldering riot, that is ready to break into an open rupture at the most unguarded moment, make us pause to wonder whether or not anybody's fireside is safe.

It is well known that the undersigned values labor far above every other accompaniment of physical life. Not only is there no excellence without labor, but there is no possible existence without it. Labor creates capital; and labor, intelligently organized and conscientiously cooperated, can easily control its creature, capital. . . .

Mrs. Sue R. Keenan [sponsored by the Knights of Labor] says that the "prevailing discontent among the laboring classes means something."[1] But she does not go far enough in stating what it means. Let us turn back for a time and try to see if there is not a "cause of causes" which needs investigation during the present crisis; a cause far ante-dating the Chinese labor question, and having its root in foreign immigration that throngs our shores, brought here from over the Atlantic seas.

Who are the men that drink the most whisky, guzzle the most beer, use the most tobacco, and cry loudest against Asiatic labor? Who are they that assume to run this government? who oppose equal rights for native-born American women? who make beasts of burden of their own wives, if they have any? who "labor" chiefly as war politicians? or, failing to get occupation of this character, harangue public assemblies in season and out of season about subjects of which they have little knowledge?

And the answer is, the European foreigners who are menacing our country's peace with the proclamation that the Chinese must go, and threatening every law-abiding citizen, who by industry and frugality has obtained footing in his own country with dire consequences if he does not at once, at the behest of the foreign-born lip-laborers from across the Atlantic seas, dismiss from his employ, however insignificant or menial, his foreign-born hand-toilers from over the Pacific seas.

We do not charge that these disturbances are instigated by native Europeans only. Sad to say, there are many American rioters to keep them company—serf-born sons of slave-born mothers. Nor would we be understood as making an onslaught upon any European-born man simply as a foreigner. The Pacific Northwest boasts thousands of progressive, intelligent, liberty-loving German, French, English and Irish citizens. . . .

Nor would we have the reader fancy that we are not in favor of the Chinese restriction bill. We know as

well as any one the evils of slave labor, having seen it perpetuated
among women . . . ; and we know
that coolie labor is slave labor, pure
and simple, and it ought to be abol-
ished. The Chinese Six Companies
comprise a syndicate of slave-own-
ers who are just as much to be
despised, and ought as surely to be
prohibited from operating in
America, as were the African slave-
dealers of a bygone era.

But there is a peculiar difference
between the by-gone agitation to free
the African slave and the present
determination of pseudophilan-
thropists to remand the Asiatic coolie
back to contract-bondage. If the
African race is human, so is the
Mongolian; and a little less hatred
of the poor coolie, and a great deal
more determination to free him from
the domination of the Six
Companies, would certainly be in
order. With the restriction act rigidly
enforced, thus preventing the
Chinese from over-running the
United States and draining our
money from the country, we can see
no danger from the presence of a
limited number of the barbarians to
do menial service among us; that is,
no danger to the frugal, industrious
and temperate classes of white men.
The danger is imminent, however,
to the drinking and squandering
classes—not that they will be ruined
by Chinese cheap labor, but by their
own unthrift, intemperance and
improvidence.

We were at a so-called "labor"
meeting the other night, and the only
genuine laborer among the speakers
was the woman [Keenan] before
quoted; and she had come from the
kitchen to the platform, and right
glad were we to see her there as an
example to the idlers. The pseudo-
laborers on the platform all wore
shirts which had probably been
laundried by Chinamen, and in the
crowd and jam of noisy listeners were
many hundreds of laboring men yelling lustily that the "Chinese must
go," whose ready-made clothing,
from flannel shirts to denim overalls,
was mainly the product of coolie
manufactories.

Keep it before the people that it
is the laboring classes that maintain
the Chinese factories. They spend a
good part of their money for whisky
and tobacco, and then buy cheap
boots, cheap shoes, cheap shirts, cheap
coats, cheap overalls, cheap trousers,
and cheap vegetables; but when they
come in competition with these same
coolies in unskilled labor, having neglected meanwhile to fit themselves
for any line of skillful work, they rise
up in rebellion against the law-and-
order classes who do not buy Chinese
cheap products, and threaten to boycott them, that is, destroy their
possessions, because, forsooth, now
and then they hire a Chinaman to
cook or wash; and this, too, when it
is well known that not one of these
same noisy insurrectionists could or
would wash or cook for hire. . . .

If the "Chinese must go," this is a good way to get rid of them: Boycott their manufactories, buy American-made clothing, boots and shoes; lease garden lands, raise vegetables, and peddle them on the streets; drive swill wagons yourselves; learn to wash and cook; stop getting drunk, and cease loitering on the street-corners and filling the air with sickening odors of villainous tobacco, while you stare women out of countenance, or puff your foul breath in their faces as they pass you on the crossings. The Six Companies will not maintain the coolies here if you do not buy the products of their labor.

If you were as willing to pay a living price for what you purchase as you are anxious to compel others to pay your demands for your own work, you would soon end this difficulty by boycotting Chinese products. But as long as you wear clothing of their manufacture because it is cheap, and make no effort to supply the trade with the superior results of your own workmanship, you need not hope for a better outcome than that at Seattle, wherein the laboring classes are the principal sufferers from riots of their own instigation. . . .

Portland, February 8, 1886.

A. S. D.

*(February 11, 1886)*

## More on the Chinese Question in Portland and Oregon City

The Emmet Guard, which has been organized something over twenty years, and has drawn allowances from the State to the amount of over $10,000, was the only militia company in the city which refused to perform its duty when preparations were being made to meet the riot which was expected to follow last Saturday's ["Anti-Coolie"] "Congress." Ten men, including the Captain and two of his officers, wished to be loyal; but they were voted down. The company has been disarmed, and it should be permanently disbanded. This was the first time it had ever been called upon for real duty, and its refusal is disgraceful.

*(February 18, 1886)*

A large anti-Chinese demonstration was held in this city on Monday evening. There were probably 1000 persons in the procession, which was quite orderly. Speeches were made by several agitators at the plaza, and a committee of fifteen was appointed to notify the Chinamen to leave the city by March 24th.

Oregon City has been the scene of the latest anti-Chinese outrage. About 1 o'clock on Monday morning, a gang of men broke into the houses in which about forty Chinamen, mostly employees of the woolen mills, were asleep, and compelled them to go aboard the steamer "Latons," when they were brought to this city. Some of the Chinamen were also roughly treated and robbed. Nat L. Baker of this city, and Al. White, of Oregon City, who are alleged to have led the crowd, were arrested on complaint of one of the Chinamen yesterday, charged with intimidation and conspiracy. Their bonds of $600 each were furnished by M. Batelbach.

*(February 25, 1886)*

Albina and East Portland kukluxers, as well as those of Oregon City, are finding it a serious matter to terrorize even defenseless Chinamen. Besides the arrests reported last week, four have been made at Albina and one at Mount Tabor, the exoduster from the latter place having also been held to answer a charge of burglary. The Oregon City men are all out of jail, ten on bail and two because of a lack of evidence against them. . . .

*(March 11, 1886)*

On Tuesday evening, a package of either dynamite or giant powder was placed under the steps of a Chinese wash-house at No. 248 Sixth street, near Madison, and an explosion took place about 8 o'clock. The steps, windows and front door of the house were wrecked, the Chinamen were badly scared and shaken up, and all the dwellings in the neighborhood were considerably jarred. Of course, it is not known who perpetrated the outrage, and many of the agitating

*Chinatown, Second and Alder, Portland, Oregon, mid-1880s*

element affect to believe the Chinamen did it themselves!

The 24th of March, which the "anti-Chinese congress" designated as the date for the expulsion of the coolies from Portland, has come and gone—but the Chinese have not. They are still with us, and, much as the fact may be regretted, will remain until the existing treaty expires—or the working people quit patronizing them.

*(March 25, 1886)*

# The Local Option Excitement in Washington Territory

Walla Walla is quiet in all else save the pending excitement over local option. The question as to whether prohibition shall prevail in the city after the coming June election is the all-absorbing theme, concerning which the people are about equally divided. . . .

We need not tell our readers that we are opposed to the liquor business. The fact that for several years past we have sustained the *New Northwest* against a practical boycott by the liquor-dealers is evidence enough that we have worried the business through temperance teachings. But we have never advocated the confiscation of liquor-dealers' property, nor do we believe the local option act will stand in the courts, because a part of the fundamental code of the nation says *no person shall be deprived of life, liberty or property without due process of law.*

In making preliminary arrangements for lectures in Walla Walla, we found the good temperance people overshadowed largely by "Colonel" Hawkins, of peculiar Oregon notoriety; and encouragement for our regular work in organized channels was so small in consequence thereof, that we concluded we'd manage our own affairs. So we advertised for a Sunday evening lecture, subject, "Religion and Liberty," and one for Monday evening, subject, "Causes of Political Upheavals," with a nominal admission fee to pay expenses.

It was necessary to engage a public hall, so we called upon Mrs. Stahl, owner of the Opera House, and widow of the great Walla Walla brewer. We found her peculiarly excited over the prohibition problem. She said in substance (and we're sorry we can't give expression to her peculiar accent in this recital): "My husband and I worked eight years in Canyon City, he at butchering and I at the wash-tub. We made money by hard, honest work. When we came to Walla Walla, we brought twenty-five thousand dollars. The town was new, but it was dead already. My husband started a brewery under the United States laws, and made a market for the people's barley. He gave fifty dollars or more to every church, and he helped build the bridges.

There was no hall, and he built one. And after while we moved out here and he built these brick houses. They cost forty thousand dollars. By and by he die, and there was a debt of twenty-two thousand dollars left on the property. I got to work, I make a slave of myself, I keep the business together to raise my children. Now, they say I sha'n't sell beer any more. Then comes the taxes. If I don't pay them—and I can't when my business is gone—they take everything to pay execution and turn me in the street. Why don't you teach people to let the beer alone? If they don't buy I can't sell. I never in my life ask a man to buy beer." She stopped, out of breath, and we engaged her hall and departed, mentally resolving to give the public the benefit of the story from her stand-point, and let everybody draw his own conclusions. . . .

[T]he worst of . . . [the local option act] is that it will throw vendors and manufacturers out of a business that has long made them a livelihood, and turn them loose among the anti-coolie agitators, whose strength has been developed to such alarming proportions recently in Seattle, Tacoma and Portland, whose methods are pillage and plunder, and their weapons guns and bludgeons—if not worse. . . .

We have no compromise to make with whisky or its votaries. We don't blame them for hating us, for we will always hit them hard, whether they be drinkers or venders. But we do insist that it is wrong in principle, and cannot be made to stand in law, that a town, county or precinct which deprives an individual of the means of livelihood shall be exempt from paying damages. Look to this, friends of temperance. Be careful, lest in going too fast you cut loose from the great train of practical possibilities, and injure the cause so dear to every mother's ear, the cause of peace and soberness.

[Walla Walla, W. T.].
A. S. D.
*(March 25, 1886)*

## Oregon Victory for Mary A. Leonard

Mrs. Mary A. Leonard, of this city, enjoys the distinction of being the first woman who is admitted to practice law in this State. A year or so ago she came here from Washington Territory, where she had been a practicing attorney, and applied for admission, but was denied by the Supreme Court, on the ground that it had no authority under the laws of the State to recognize a woman as a member of the legal profession. Nothing daunted, Mrs. Leonard and a number of her friends induced the last Legislature to pass a bill placing women upon equal footing with men before the courts of the State. She was formally admitted by the Supreme Court last Tuesday, and, having been long ago recognized by Judge Deady, of the U. S. Circuit

Court, she is now a full-fledged practicing attorney. All lovers of justice will rejoice at her victory. Mrs. Leonard will soon open an office in this city, and, if she displays the same energy, intelligence and perseverance in looking after the interests of her clients that has marked her efforts in her own behalf, she will make a permanent success in her chosen profession.

*(April 15, 1886)*

## Willis Duniway Catches Idaho Land Fever

The site of Mountain Home is not, as its name would indicate, a mountainous or even a hilly one. It lies in a level valley, of the usual magnitude peculiar to Idaho's plains, and is well watered by a creek which the people tap for irrigating ditches. The adjacent lands are fertile, sage-grown, and in some spots natural meadow from which the fortunate ranchmen are already cutting heavy crops or rank rye grass for hay. . . .

Before this [trip, Willis] had caught the Idaho land fever on general principles, and we look every day to see him desert his mother's itinerant destiny and settle himself in this country, like a vaquero born. Already he can talk learnedly of "round-ups," "slick ears," "bronchos," and the like; and were you to hear his schemes for raising the waste waters of the Snake (why don't the maps say *Lewis* River?)

and putting them where they would, like a politician's money, do the most good, you'd think there might be "millions in it." Seriously, we think he talks sense, and we mean to back his theories with our own practical endeavors soon.

Shoshone, Idaho, May 19, 1886. A. S. D.

*(May 27, 1886)*

## The Wood River Valley of Idaho Territory

Monday afternoon, and off for Ketchum, thirteen miles up the river. The railway runs through the beautiful valley of Wood River, that steadily narrows as it climbs the hills, breaking out into broader little valleys now and then. . . . Wood River, densely bordered here with cottonwood and balm of Gilead, is a roaring torrent now, from which little irrigating ditches are taken at intervals to supply the Chinese gardens, that even in this altitude are thriving nicely.

Speaking of Chinamen reminds us that the lip-laborers of Hailey have succeeded in chasing out the Asiatic laundrymen; and, as white men can't be had to take their places, the washing here, or part of it, like that of Tacoma, must go elsewhere to be done by Chinamen, or the people must do without clean linen. Of all the "reformers" that ever have annoyed a long-suffering people, the "dirty clothes brigade" are entitled to the cap and bells.

There is one "agitator" here, a pompous and condescending negro, who gave us polite occasion to inform him that if he were not a voter, the average "agitator" would make it as hot for him as he was trying to make it for the dozen Asiatics in the place whom he hates so heartily. He wanted to know "where the women were who did the washing thirty years ago." "In the graveyard," was our prompt reply; and the citizen of African descent subsided into silence. . . .

Bellevue, like Hailey and Ketchum, is orderly and free from drunkenness. Indeed, we have seen but one drunken man on Wood River; and he, poor fellow, incited a team to run away one day in Hailey and badly hurt himself, the general verdict being that "'twas a wonder and a thousand pities it didn't kill him." Maybe it will cure him, though, and that is some comfort.

There isn't a screened saloon on the river. Every drinking resort is entirely open to the street, and we are told that all drinks, including a glass of lemonade, are "two bits." Drunkenness is considered disreputable, mainly, as we could not help concluding, because the vice of liquor drinking is so palpably uncovered and open that men are restrained by the publicity of intemperate indulgence.

Here is a nut for prohibitionists to crack, as well as a hint to Portland's city officers. Let the Common Council order every screen removed from every doggery door, let every cover device for hiding men's iniquity be torn down, and let the nuisance of the dram-shop be made as public as possible by law. This will bring the evil to the surface, and help the disease of drunkenness, like a malignant ulcer, to slough and run off.

With these thoughts, . . . we return to Hailey, where we lecture in the evening for the benefit of the M. E. Church organ fund, and meet a goodly, kindly and attentive audience. . . . Dinner [the next evening] with the esteemed M. E. pastor and his estimable wife at the cozy parsonage, was followed by a hurried walk to the train, pursuant to orders in shape of a dispatch from home, asking us to return at once, as the free women of Washington Territory were continually writing and demanding that in the pending crisis in their local affairs we "Come over into Macedonia and help." Just what is wanted we scarcely know; but we hear of a combination to break the law that grants them liberty, and that is enough; so we are homeward bound.

O. R. & N. train, Saturday, May 29, 1886.

A. S. D.

*(June 3, 1886)*

## Slandered in Washington Territory

We found the good people of Yakima in a tremendous flutter of excitement. Mrs. Switzer of Cheney, and Mrs. Reese, of Ohio, members of the W. C. T. U., had recently been among them in the interest of the local option craze, and, echoing the villainous slanders of "Col." Hawkins, whom the frenzied advocates of the bill had accepted as a welcome ally in an insane and ineffective crusade that cannot possibly injure whisky, though there is great danger that its reaction will destroy woman's ballots, they had told the women that "Mrs. Duniway had sold out to whisky. She had received one thousand dollars from the whisky men of Walla Walla and ten thousand from the whisky men of Portland to boom the whisky interest!"

So long as Hawkins only had spread this vile and characteristic falsehood, we had not thought it worth our while to stoop to contradict it. But when Christian women, taking to their homes and hearts an irresponsible vagabond, a dead-beat, a drunkard, and a habitué of bruisers' resorts and vile dens, take up the refrain of his calumny and industriously circulate the slander in their insane zeal to accomplish they know not what, the case becomes serious.

And it was this slander that had so alarmed the Woman Suffragists of Washington Territory that they had sent an appeal for us to return post haste from Idaho and resume work in their Territory.

To give our readers an idea of the depths of villainy to which the local-option craze has led it votaries, we will mention a single circumstance. On the "dodgers" announcing our speech in North Yakima were the words: "Mrs. Duniway comes at this time in response to the earnest request of many friends of Woman Suffrage who desire to hear her opinions on the present crisis in this Territory." No sooner were the "dodgers" out than they were industriously gathered up by man's rights advocates and a "paster" put over the words "Woman Suffrage," making the "dodgers" read, "many friends of the wholesale liquor dealers."

We were ready to go to the lecture-room when some of the mutilated bills were placed in our hands, with the information that they had been circulated and posted by one Charles Lillie, who, we were told, was a gambler, an ex-gin-slinger, an opponent of Woman Suffrage, of course, and a notorious ward striker, who makes it his business at elections to act the bully in challenging the votes of women. We read one of the bills at the evening lecture, and in the presence of the mighty multitude pronounced the name of the perpetrator, as it had been given us.

The next day, after we had departed for Ellensburg, some of the citizens, we did not learn who or how many, had the fellow arrested, upon just what charge we do not know, but it was in reference to this outrage. . . .

One-ideaed croakers may as well hold their peace in Yakima hereafter. The dear women are too wary, too wise, and too thoroughly in earnest in the great temperance reform. . . . to be driven blindfold over their weak little equal suffrage bridge and made to break it down, carrying with it not only their own enfranchisement, but the fond hopes of the millions of women in other States and Territories. . . . They see, because they are wise women, that it is not the ballot, *per se*, but the power that the ballot represents, that is destined to do their work for temperance in coming years; and they know better, now that they see the situation clearly, than to make their fire too hot, lest they cook their own as well as other women's ballot yeast.

Colfax, W. T., June 12, 1886.
A. S. D.

*(June 17, 1886)*

## The Local Option Campaign Comes to a Close

[U]pon reaching Olympia by train, . . . we learned that arrangements were made for a joint discussion between ourself and Dr. Watts in the evening in the plaza, with His Honor Judge Hoyt as moderator. A very fine assembly convened at an early hour. Fifty minutes were assigned to us for the opening speech. Then the doctor had an hour straight and we were given ten minutes for a final summing up.

Our argument was devoted largely to the unjust and therefore inefficient phases of the local option bill, and more especially to the fact that women's little leaven of ballots was not yet matured enough to cope with the votes of men in a great contest like the one in question. . . . [The women] were exhorted to *wait*, to let their little army grow; to let Territorial uncertainty resolve itself into Statehood, that their votes be made secure before they sought to hurl them in defiance at the men. . . .

Dr. Watts replied with a very unsavory introduction, in which he threatened us with "polecats" and "perfumery." . . . [H]e dodged every point we had made, and launched into the same stereotyped intemperate political harangue that every school-boy has long since learned from him by heart in Oregon.

In the course of his remarks Watts took occasion to read a little paragraph from the *Oregonian* to the effect that "if women in Washington Territory do not vote to hurt the liquor traffic it will be proof that they ought never to have the right of suffrage at all."

"Who is the editor of the *Oregonian*?" he asked, in tones of thunder.

"*Harvey Scott!*" he cried, in a still higher key. "And who is *Harvey Scott?*" he yelled, still higher. "MRS. DUNIWAY'S BROTHER!" he screeched through his liquor-red proboscis, with a sibilant hiss like pouring raw whisky down a soaker's gullet.

To this we answered that Mr. Scott knew as well as we that women could only hurt themselves and help the liquor traffic by voting for free intoxicating liquors for sacramental purposes [from drug stores]; that a certain cheap boy whom the paper employed to do its scrub work was notoriously opposed to Woman Suffrage, and the fellow never lost an opportunity to give the women's cause a treacherous blow at a critical moment, if the editor's back was

*Harvey W. Scott*

turned. Mr. Scott had never seen that cowardly stab till after it was scattered everywhere through the *Oregonian,* and none knew it better than Watts himself. (Mr. Scott was on a trip to Ashland at the time.—Jun. Ed.) Of course the old trickster will not hesitate to repeat the lie, but it doesn't matter. Verily, he and Hawkins are a glorious pair!

We had ten minutes in which to finish our review of him at the last, though, and he got enough. . . .

The polls were open on Monday morning at six o'clock, and men and women were voting in large numbers long before the undersigned was up. At nine o'clock we went upon the street. Good order and apparent good humor reigned everywhere. But the dear W. C. T. U., as if fated to indulge in suicidal blundering, rang a church bell every hour, and every tone of the bell added largely to the vote against them. Temperance people who do not believe in the dominion of the church in state affairs voted against prohibition unanimously; and their vote, added to that of the whisky element, won the day against both fanaticism and free whisky. . . .

[W]e attended the women's prayer meeting for an hour. Oh, it was pitiful! To see the seamed faces of the dear mothers in Israel, who trustingly sought, not divine guidance, but divine support in what they had obstinately assumed to be the only right way, and to know all the time how heavy were the odds against them, while in their blind intolerance they would not have permitted us to say one word if we had tried, almost melted us to tears. But we inwardly rejoiced that they were voters; and we know that their daughters and their daughters' children will, under the inspiration of liberty, outgrow the impractical zeal they now exhibit. . . .

As we write, the battle is over and we are homeward bound. At first, as the returns began to come in, it appeared that "prohibition" had failed to carry in any important town. But the dispatches received at different stations soon settled that question. . . . [W]hile enough of the important towns have carried the law to justify testing it in the courts, women have shunned the trap in sufficient numbers to prevent their ark of liberty from betrayal into the hands of the enemy.

N. P. R. R., June 29, 1886.
A. S. D.

*(July 1, 1886)*

# Results of the Local Option Election in Washington Territory

The local option election held in Washington Territory on Monday resulted in a partial victory for both sides of the question. This was not a Territorial election, but merely a contest held under the new local option law, which allows each incorporated town or precinct to decide for itself every two years between prohibition (so-called) and high license. An election was not held in all the precincts, but only in those wherein not less than fifteen electors had petitioned the County Commissioners to order an election.

The result shows that "no license" will prevail in a majority of the country districts, just as it practically did before, and in many of the smaller towns; but that "license" is preferred in nearly all the important towns and business centers.

The women's vote was wisely divided on the question, enough of them adopting a level-headed, conservative policy to exempt them from the charge of carrying a measure all over the Territory that, wherever adopted, will simply transfer the whisky traffic from the saloons to the drug stores, will deprive the towns of the license money without checking the evils of intemperance, will keep the people in an endless domestic broil, and will increase taxation.

["Prohibition" was defeated at Walla Walla, Spokane Falls, Sprague, Tacoma, Olympia, Seattle, Port Townsend, Port Discovery, Dungeness, Vancouver, Pataha, Ellensburg, Whatcom, Steilacoom, Port Gamble, and Cheney. "Prohibition" was carried at Colfax, Dayton, Waitsburg, Chehalis, Prescott, Winlock, Pomeroy, Huntsville, North Yakima, Wenas, Centralia, Sehome, Puyallup, La Conner, Snohomish, and Goldendale.]

*(July 1, 1886)*

## News of the Duniways

Messrs. W. S. [Willis] Duniway and W. C. [Wilkie ] Duniway retired on the 5th inst. from the *New Northwest*, owing to impaired health from constant office work, and will go to Idaho Territory. They hope to thoroughly recuperate in the fine climate of the Lost River country. The paper will be published as heretofore by the remaining partners, A. S. and H. R. [Hubert] Duniway.

*(July 8, 1886)*

Mr. B. C. [Benjamin] Duniway returned on Sunday from a trip through the Wood and Lost River countries in Idaho. He was well pleased with his journey, and expects to locate in Idaho in the Spring.

*(July 29, 1886)*

Mr. W. C. Duniway returned from Idaho on Saturday. He and W. S. Duniway have secured a 1280-acre ranch in the Lost River Valley, but will not put cattle on their range until Spring. In the meantime, W. C. will remain in Portland, while W. S. will spend the Winter in Hailey.

*(August 5, 1886)*

## Astoria, The Venice of America

Astoria displays commendable activity in keeping up with the times. And this, too, in spite of her many crazy wooden structures, her constantly decaying sidewalks, and the combination of offensive smells that in a less healthy climate would certainly engender pestilence.

These smells come chiefly from Chinatown, since the canning season is over now, and the erewhile decay of fish offal no longer offends sensitive olfactories. Chinatown is a densely populated section of the most public street (being opposite the post office), where the Mongolians gather in groups at the witching hour when crowds are going for their mail, for which there is no postal delivery, and consequently everybody visits the "Custom House block" on an average of twice daily.

Swilltown is another unpleasant adjunct of the Venice of America, to which we earnestly invite the attention of the prohibitionists. If they will put a prohibition plaster over Swilltown, making it large enough to overlap its morally diseased edges, and strong enough to smother out the barnacles of prostitution that protrude here and there through the sour swamp of the perverted appetites that feed the said barnacles; if they can do this and prevent the disease from breaking out in some other place, and, if possible, in more malignant form than that which now menaces decadency and soberness, we shall be inclined to cherish a little more faith in the scheme they are working up with the intent to accomplish greater things.

But we were going to speak of something entirely different and more attractive a while ago, from which our attention was diverted by the sights and smells that for the moment switched our thoughts from the track.

We were speaking of Astoria's progress, which is in nothing else more noticeable than her new electric light plant, which illuminates the city with a white, steady, persistent glow, as palpable as the clearest moonlight and as steady as sunshine. This plant is the property of J. C. Trullinger,[2] present Mayor of Astoria, and proprietor of the extensive sawmill, lumber-yard and box factory in the midst of which the pair of dynamo-electric machines for light and power, manufactured by the Pacific Coast Electrical Company, are set up and operated under the Kleth System.

A close personal inspection of the electrical works reveals much that to the eye of a novice is both inexplicable and marvelous. Mr. Gough, the young and gentlemanly electrician who has charge of the works, talks learnedly, but without ostentation, of "motors," "magnets," "insulated copper wires," "armatures," "commutators," "circuits," "arc," "incandescence," and so forth; and we wander in and out and around among the intricate machinery, feeling like an elephant in a toy shop, and half afraid to turn lest we unchain the lighting somewhere.

We study the carbon burners, and watch in vain for the mysterious, invisible force that generates the glowing light that dazzles eyesight like the sun; we mentally measure the many thousands of feet of coiled copper wire that kinks and curls in curious combinations everywhere; we gaze in happy contemplation at the cute little air-tight incandescent crystal burners designed for lighting dwellings by means of a minute platinum wire; and we turn from these and gaze with a sigh of retrospection at the familiar brick furnace where the heat is generated which forms the power to set the whole in motion.

We left the machinery and sallied forth in the brilliant glare of the mysterious illumination it had set free, devoutly prepared for the next great invention, which we are ready to believe will be the scientific and successful navigation of the air.

Ilwaco, W. T.

A. S. D.

*(August 19, 1886)*

## Local Option Declared Unconstitutional

As our senior editor has predicted from the day she first read the local option bill of Washington Territory, the law has been declared unconstitutional [in the decision of the court of the First Judicial District in the case of the *Territory of Washington vs. Jacob Schumann*, a saloon-keeper of Dayton], and therefore a nullity, upon the very first opportunity.

If the women of the Temperance Union, in their jealous endeavor to wrest from Woman Suffrage the prestige of its own victories, had conferred with its leaders, whom long experience had taught wisdom, they would have been informed in the outset that a Territorial Legislature has no power to pass a law contingent upon the votes of localities, nor even contingent upon the votes of the Territory at large. In other words, it cannot shirk a responsibility to the shoulders of the voters over which it has full jurisdiction within itself.

It was Mrs. Duniway's clear conception of this point, and the fact that she was able to make it plain to Governor Newell at a critical moment when secret enemies conspired to defeat the suffrage bill by sending it to the ballot-box, that enabled her to secure the enfranchisement of women [in Washington Territory] by unequivocal legislative enactment, rather than see the cause defeated at the polls; or, succeeding there, fall at judicial tribunals because not passed in harmony with the organic law. . . .

Maybe some of the ambitious leaders of the W. C. T. U. will get it through their noodles by and by that they are "not the only people on the earth, and neither wisdom nor honor will die with them." After their prohibition craze is over, we hope to see a genuine revival of temperance work again.

*(September 9, 1886)*

## One Faithful Worker: Lucy Stone Honors Mrs. A. S. Duniway

Mrs. Abigail Scott Duniway is the pioneer Woman Suffragist of the great Northwest. It is directly due to her efforts that the women of Washington Territory have had an opportunity to vote on the temperance question, or on any other. She has gone through more toil and drudgery for the Woman Suffrage cause than any other woman we know. For fifteen years she has been constantly in the field, not deterred by the cold of Winter or heat of Summer. She earned her own printing office, had her five sons taught to print, and inspired her husband and sons to join her in the great work of securing equal rights for women.

Under the name of "The Duniway Publishing Co.," they have carried on the *New Northwest*, bearing its expense and its risks, and sharing the hard conditions which must ever attend the advocacy of any unpopular reform. She has always been an able and earnest advocate of temperance, often lecturing for it on the same platform with its most pronounced friends. But when the late special election on local option on the liquor question was held in Washington Territory, Mrs. Duniway thought that it was a trap set with the belief that women would vote solid for local option, and that the fact would be used to exclude women from the suffrage when the Territory comes in as a State. Mrs. Duniway also believed that if local option were carried under the provisions of the existing law, drug-stores, in every precinct where license was not granted, could and would sell, that they would multiply, and that free rum would result. It seemed to her a choice between taxed or free whisky, and she chose the former.

Now, we do not say that Mrs. Duniway was right, or that she was wrong. But a woman who has proved her fidelity to the temperance cause by such service as she has for years rendered to it, should not be held its enemy because she differed in opinion from other advocates in regard to the best method to advance its interests. Temperance societies work in different ways. Individuals must be free to do the same.

(Lucy Stone in *The Woman's Journal*; rpt. *NNW* Sept. 23, 1886)

## A Vigorous Growl from the Senior Editor

And now, to all believers in the great principle of human rights who read this journal and are anxious to see its aim accomplished, we have a word to say: *If you only would exert yourselves a little to keep the paper afloat*, the aggregate efforts of you all, though very trifling to each, would amount to a sum of sufficient importance to the paper itself to meet its regular expenses and leave us free to do missionary work among the enemy, rather than compel us to remain, as now, so much of the time in the grooves already open, gathering up the meager dollars to pay paper, press, printers, postage and rental dues to keep the *New Northwest* afloat, that the years go by with unsatisfactory results. . . .

We hereby tell you frankly that we mean business, and if you do not more promptly attend to your part of the great work, which is nothing more nor less than meeting your own subscriptions and helping to secure others, we'll sell the paper—to the anti-suffragists, if to none else—and move to Washington Territory, where we can be free. So there! . . .

We've been computing our labors lately, and we find that in collecting your dues alone we walk on an average five miles every day of the year, not including Sundays. In writing for the paper, including letters to patrons, editorial correspondence and serial stories, our average is one hundred pages of manuscript per week; and our public lectures average three or four per week, with nearly all the preliminaries, such as securing halls and churches, "filling out" dodgers, etc., etc., thrown in. Add to all this the fact that we will have climbed to the top round of our fifty-second year on the twenty-second of this month, and you will readily see whether we are overtaxing the strength of waning years in your service. Those of you who realize the situation will, we know, excuse this growl.

A.S.D.

*(October 7, 1886)*

## By Stage in Oregon: Ashland to Linkville

On Tuesday morning in the cold gray of the coming twilight, behold us mounting the boot of a great lumbering Concord coach, drawn by four patient, powerful horses, and pulling out from the pretty town [of Ashland], holding for dear life to the straps, and buckles. The stage leaves the town and goes laboring up the mountain side, straining, careening, crashing and bumping, almost whipping bones and muscles to a jelly, and bruising flesh and blood into a compound pulp suggestive of speedy dissolution. . . .

Oh! that Siskiyou Mountain! It was only a "spur," they tell us, but it had double-heeled "gaffs" on, and— and—we'd like to forget it. From the mountain itself may the good Lord deliver us!

By noon we were too weary to walk, stand, ride or recline. So we stopped over at a wayside inn, and literally languished till the next day's ship of the mountain came along, when we reembarked and encountered more bruises. But we stood the ride better than the day before, and managed to reach Linkville with life enough left in us to climb stiffly and creakingly away to a snug room at Smith's Hotel, where we ruminated over the evanescence of every earthly thing but mountains, rocks, gullies, big trees, more rocks, bleak winds, beautiful scenery, more rocks, winding rivers, smiling valleys, placid lakes, tule swamps, more rocks—but we believe we've mentioned the rocks before.

Linkville, October 24, 1886.

A. S. D.

*(October 24, 1886)*

## Staging From Lakeview to Ashland

A heavy snow fell on Friday night, and when we awoke on the morrow and peeping through the muslin curtains, beheld the seemingly boundless landscape clothed in a blanket of eider down, and listening to the winds sweeping through the mountain gorges, remembered that we were 180 miles from the railroad, we felt that we had indeed reached a "lodge in a vast wilderness."

But by Monday at 4 o'clock, the deepest of the snow had vanished in exposed places, and the glittering stars beamed down from the pellucid heavens that, like an inverted sea bespangled with diamonds, gazed at us. . . . [W]rapped like an Esquimaux, we climbed to a perch on the stage beside the driver and went rattling away over the frozen ground toward "the slash," with horses' heads turned homeward and our own face smothered in blankets, leaving only an aperture for breath and eyesight.

Oh, that "slash"! It was just wide enough to make a wagon track, which alternate thaws and freezes had made into a road that was anything but velvety. And then, the bridges! There were about a dozen, and some architect who doubtless meant to earn his money, had made them so steep at the aprons that teams, after successfully hauling loads of lumber from the mountains, were obliged to "stall" here and leave their freight by the wayside.

But this letter is growing too long, and we must postpone further description of that memorable journey till next week.

Ashland, November 6, 1886.
A. S. D.

*(November 11, 1886)*

## Staging From Lakeview to Ashland Continued

We had the Sheriff of Jackson county for company all the way from Lakeview to Linkville, and in his charge was a prisoner in manacles, accused of horse-stealing, on his way to the lock-up. The crime of horse- or cattle-stealing is considered a much greater one in all border countries than girl-stealing, or even seduction or rape. In the latter cases, the perpetrator frequently gets off with a fine or reprimand, a marriage or a joke; but woe to the miscreant who is caught on the back of a "borrowed" horse or in the act of branding a stray "slick-ear.". . .

Late in the afternoon, when coyotes in quest of the jack rabbits that frequently bounded across our way came ambling saucily around the stage, evoking shots that hit not one of them, and sage hens flitted through rabbit brush to serene security from revolver balls, we descended a long incline and came once more to Bly

Valley, where we stopped for the night, and were again invited to speak. But we pleaded weariness and were excused. . . . [L]ong before daylight we were off again, the prisoner's chains clanking as he climbed to the seat, the Sheriff vigilant, the driver obliging, and ourself wrapped as before in borrowed blankets. . . .

During that day's ride we passed a deserted mountain ranch, and the driver related a tragedy connected with the place that made the Sheriff of Jackson county fairly boil with honest indignation, while the prisoner gritted his teeth and clanked his chains, and your correspondent listened, shivering.

A family of Germans, husband, wife and seven children had settled there; and after building a cabin, that had only a dirt floor, and fencing in a few acres with logs and sowing it to barley, the husband wandered off aimlessly somewhere, leaving the wife to manage as best she could without him. The wife harvested the barley by pulling it up with her hands. She did the family washing in a leaky box, and cooked their food in the most primitive way.

One day the husband came home and saw a cow stealing from the barley stack, a fact which so enraged him because his wife had not prevented the theft, although she did not see it, that he knocked out her front teeth and then whipped her with a knotted rope. The act of "ruling over her"

accomplished, the husband went away again and remained three weeks.

The wife took to her poor miserable bed, not to leave it again till after the birth of a dead child, which the husband returned in time to bury. There was no action taken against the man, though the driver said there was much indignation over the affair, and he would have been glad indeed to have joined a company to treat him to tar and feathers.

"What a pity 'twas that, instead of maltreating his wife and murdering his baby, he hadn't stolen a horse or branded a 'slick-ear,'" we couldn't help exclaiming as the prisoner clanked his chains.

The German in question removed shortly to another locality, and all trace of him is lost in the precinct, save his wife's abandoned barley field and his own recorded vote against the equal suffrage amendment. . . .

Upon returning to Linkville . . . we accepted an invitation to repair to the court-house and make another speech. Although the notice was too brief to bring out a very large crowd, it was a very appreciative one; and, although our long and arduous ride had made us too weary to endure the fatigue of standing up to talk, we got along first rate by accepting the permission of the audience to reverse the action of the Dutchman's hen ["and set"].

The next morning at 4 o'clock we were off again, wrapped in more borrowed blankets, and enjoying, in spite of extreme weariness, the invigorating air and sparkling starlight, mute heralds of another magnificent day. Sunrise in the mountains! . . .

Upon reaching the breakfast station, we attempted to alight and encountered an eight-foot fall which surely would have disfigured our countenance if nature hadn't kindly located it in the front of the cranium. Luckily the wheel horse, at whose feet we fell, was neither skittish nor curious, else our epitaph had been in order instead of these jottings.

Oh! That wearisome day! It seemed that it would never end! Not even the diversion of meeting a woman tramp, who dodged by us like a deer and refused to answer all questions, nor the ever-varying scenery of the mountains, could beguile the tedium of the journey, or direct our thoughts from the jolting and the bruises. . . .

[But] a hot bath, bountiful supper, sound sleep and subsequent day of rest so far refreshed us that when evening brought the daily stage again we were quite ready for the pleasant moonlight ride of a dozen miles to Ashland and the railroad. The man who invented railroads was almost as great a benefactor to the human race as the women who invented clothes.

Portland, November 15, 1886.

A. S. D.

*(November 18, 1886)*

## Record of a Year's Work

We have delivered in the past year one hundred and eighty one lectures, as against two hundred and nineteen the previous year. In delivering these lectures, we have traveled, in season and out of season, over three thousand miles, going by stage, steamer, buggy, buckboard, and afoot. We have encountered more than the usual quota of persecution, hypocrisy, malice, gossip and hate from that very sweet and remarkably exemplary association which struggles everywhere to theoretically sustain God and practically to keep its rent paid, under the name of the Woman's Christian Temperance Union. . . .

In the fifty-two weeks past, we have written the MSS. for over four hundred original columns of printed matter for this and other papers, and have personally canvassed every town we have visited for subscriptions and renewals to the *New Northwest*, this last labor requiring more irksome and fatiguing effort than all the rest of the work put together. . . .

[Portland], December 14, 1886.

A. S. D.

*(December 16, 1886)*

## Change of Proprietors

The undersigned, members of the Duniway Publishing Company, have this day sold the *New Northwest,* its plant, title, business and good will, to Oliver Perry Mason, Maggie Allen and Lucea Mason, who assume charge with the next issue. All unexpired subscriptions and advertising contracts will be filled by the new managers, and all subscription accounts from January 1, 1886, are payable to them. All bills against the Duniway Publishing Company to January 7th, 1887, will be paid by the undersigned.

Bespeaking for our successors the same liberal patronage that has been accorded us in the past, and wishing them a successful and pleasant journalistic career, we bid our old friends and patrons cordial farewell

A. S. Duniway.

H. R. Duniway.

Portland, Oregon, January 6, 1887.

*(January 6, 1887)*

## Personal Announcement

TO WOMAN SUFFRAGISTS:—

Over and over again during the past few years I have warned the readers of this journal that I would sever my business relations with it unless they would more promptly remit their maturing subscriptions and relieve me of the compulsory labor of regularly visiting their many

*Yours for Liberty,*
*Abigail Scott Duniway.*

different localities in order to collect its dues. Advancing years and increasing calls in the lecture field have made the financial load heavy that I once carried with comparative ease.

In surrendering the paper it seems like parting with a loved and trusted child whose destinies are so interwoven with my own that I could not disregard them if I would. But I shall not lose interest in it or its career, nor abate one iota of my work for equal rights.

The new proprietors proffer me what space I ask for advocating and agitating the question; and as long as Woman Suffragists do their duty they will not be without an organ. But they intend to run the *New Northwest* on strict business principles—in other words, to make money. And, just as surely as you are remiss in your duty about supporting it, just so surely you will cease to possess a Gatling gun that will fight your battles for freedom, as we have done for sixteen years, regardless of fear, favor, expense or labor.

When this page meets your eye I shall be gone to Idaho, in response to the invitation of many citizens, whom I have promised to assist in representing their protest before the Legislature against taxation without representation and government without consent. I shall return in time to visit the Oregon Legislature before the session is far advanced; and I am not without hope that the spirit of liberty and justice may so stir the hearts of our Solons that they may this Winter pronounce the manly proclamation that shall make their wives and mothers free. . . .

Yours for Liberty,
Abigail Scott Duniway

*(January 6, 1887)*

## Notes for 1886-87

1. Mrs. Sue R. Keenan, from East Portland, also spoke "under the auspices of the Knights of Labor" at Pendleton, Oregon, in early April of 1886. Duniway observed: "This lady is successfully inoculating the laboring classes with the spirit of the equal suffrage movement. Since the mountain will not come to Mahomet, she wisely sees that Mahomet must go to the mountain. The laboring classes welcome her as their chosen evangel, and we most earnestly wish her success" (*NNW*, 15 Apr. 1886). Terence Powderly, leader of California's Knights of Labor, wanted total elimination of the Chinese from the United States, and agitators in Oregon and Washington were following the same line; however, Duniway noted that Pendleton Knights

of Labor were working for the future: "Labor has much to learn ere it can successfuly cope with its competitor, capital, but it will learn its power by and by, through effective organization, as it can learn it in no other way." For more on Keenan, see Margaret K. Holden, "Gender and Protest Ideology: Sue Ross Keenan and the Oregon Anti-Chinese Movement," *Western Legal History* 7 (1994): 223-43.

2. John Course Trullinger (1827-1901) was born in Indiana and came overland to the California mines in 1849. He later lived at several places in Oregon, including Forest Grove, where he built a flour mill in 1870. Trullinger bought forty acres of the Astoria townsite in 1875, where he established his sawmill, box factory and lumber yard, and raised cattle on the logged-off land. As an inventor, Trullinger received patents on seven inventions, including a turbine water wheel and duplex axe. In 1885, he built and operated Astoria's first electric light plant.

# Chronology

## Abigail Jane Scott Duniway

### 1834

Abigail Jane Scott is born October 22, 1834, near Groveland, Tazewell County, Illinois. She is the third of twelve children born to John Tucker Scott and Ann Roelofson Scott.

### 1852

The Scotts make the overland trip from Illinois to Oregon Territory with their nine surviving children. Mary Frances (Fanny) is 18; Abigail Jane (Jenny) is 17; Margaret Ann (Maggie) is 15; Harvey Whitefield (Harve) is 14; Catherine Amanda (Kitty) is 13; Harriet Louisa (Etty) is 11; John Henry is 8; Sarah Maria is 5; and William Neill (Willie) is 3. The family leaves on April 2 and arrives at Oregon City on September 30th.

Abigail keeps the "Overland Diary" for the Scott family. Abigail's mother dies on June 20, 1852, near Fort Laramie, Wyoming. Willie Scott dies August 27, 1852, near Durkee, Oregon. Both deaths are probably due to "plains cholera."

John Tucker Scott takes over management of the Oregon Temperance House Hotel in Lafayette, and Scott daughters help in the hotel.

### 1853

John Tucker Scott marries Ruth Eckler Stevenson on March 15.

Abigail teaches school for about three months in a one-room log cabin at Eola (then known as Cincinnati, Oregon Territory). Abigail uses a blue-backed speller she brought from Illinois.

Abigail marries Benjamin Charles Duniway in Lafayette on August 2. He is 23, and Abigail is 18. Ben came from Illinois in 1850 and worked as a cooper, tried a season of mining, and took up a donation claim.

Abigail and Ben live on Ben's donation land claim located about 18 miles south of Oregon City. The ranch-farm of 320 acres is in the "Hardscrabble" or "Needy" section.

### 1854

Clara Belle Duniway, Abigail's first child, is born May 26.

### 1856

Willis Scott Duniway, Abigail's second child, is born February 2.

The Duniway cabin and furnishings are lost in a fire. The family is taken in by relatives who live nearby. Abigail teaches a subscription school while Ben works to establish a home.

### 1857

September 12—Abigail's poem, "To a Burning Forest Tree," is published in the Oregon City *Argus*.

Late 1857—Abigail and Ben are established on Sunny Hill Side Farm in Yamhill County, two miles from Lafayette.

### 1858 to 1860

Abigail writes poetry and letters for the *Oregon Farmer* and the *Argus*, signing her work "A Farmer's Wife" or "Jenny Glen."

### 1859

Oregon becomes a state, February 14.

Hubert Ray Duniway, Abigail's third child, is born March 24.

*Captain Gray's Company, or; Crossing the Plains and Living in Oregon,* by Mrs. Abigail J. Duniway, is published at Portland.

## 1860

Abigail attends her first political meeting in Oregon and hears Colonel Edward Dickinson Baker speak.

## 1861

Wilkie Collins Duniway, Abigail's fourth child, is born February 13.

December—a flood sweeps away the local grain warehouse, taking with it the year's harvest. Debts on notes signed by Ben grow higher, and he goes north to Walla Walla, W. T., to mine for gold. Abigail remains on the Sunny Hill Side Farm with the children.

## 1862

May 1—John Henry Scott, Abigail's brother, dies at the age of 18 in Forest Grove.

Abigail and Ben lose Sunny Hill Side Farm when they cannot pay the accrued interest on notes signed by Ben.

## 1863

The family moves to Lafayette, and Abigail begins a private school in the Duniway home.

Ben goes with Harvey Scott to the Walla Walla mines. Harvey has recently graduated from Pacific University in Forest Grove, the first student to finish the "classical course."

Ben returns to Lafayette and trains horses, hauls farm supplies, and helps with crop harvests. He is seriously injured when one of his teams bolts and he is thrown under the wheel. He is unable to return to heavy work.

## 1864

Abigail and Ben return to Clackamas County so that Ben can try farming again while Abigail teaches school at Needy. The physical labor is too difficult for Ben, and the Duniways move to Albany.

## 1865

Ben purchases a house in Albany. He has a shop where he makes washing machines, and Abigail opens a private school.

Harvey Scott is admitted to the Oregon Bar, and he is a junior editor of *The Oregonian* from 1865 to 1872.

## 1866

Abigail moves her school house to property on Broad Albin Street in Albany and converts it to a millinery shop.

Clyde Augustus Duniway, Abigail's fifth child, is born November 2.

Abigail buys out her partner, Mrs. Jackson and, with the assistance of Jacob Mayer, a Portland wholesaler, obtains a stock of goods for her shop.

## 1869

Ralph Roelofson Duniway, Abigail's sixth and last child, is born November 7.

## 1870

November—Abigail and two friends, Martha A. Dalton and Martha J. Foster, form a society for equal suffrage in Albany.

December—Abigail travels to San Francisco for a millinery buying trip and woman suffrage meetings. She is offered a salary to remain in California and lecture for equal suffrage, but is called home.

Harvey Scott is Portland's Collector of Customs, 1870-76.

## 1871

The Duniway family moves to Portland.

Abigail publishes the first issue of *The New Northwest* on May 5.

Susan B. Anthony arrives in Portland for a lecture tour of the Pacific Northwest. From September through mid-November, Abigail travels with Anthony through Oregon, Washington, and into British Columbia.

## 1872

Abigail attends meetings of the Oregon State Temperance Alliance and lectures widely in Oregon and Washington Territory.

Abigail attends the People's Convention called by the National Woman Suffrage Association in New York and later attends the American Woman Suffrage Convention in Boston.

Abigail and three other women attempt to vote in Portland.

Abigail speaks before the Oregon State Legislature on women's rights.

## 1873

The Oregon State Woman Suffrage Association is formed at a February convention in Portland.

## 1874

Catherine Scott Coburn, Abigail's widowed sister, becomes associate editor for *The New Northwest*.

Abigail again speaks before the Oregon State Legislature on women's rights.

## 1875

Abigail publishes a small book of her poems, *My Musings*, at Portland.

## 1876

Abigail attends the Centennial Exposition in Philadelphia, the Woman's Congress, and the AWSA Convention. In New York, Abigail publishes an epic poem entitled *David and Anna Matson*.

In December, while Abigail is in the East, Clara Belle Duniway, age 22, is secretly married to Doran ("Don") H. Stearns.

## 1877

Abigail addresses the Illinois State Legislature on "Constitutional Liberty." She returns to Portland in April, after an absence of ten months.

Harvey Scott returns to *The Oregonian* as part owner and chief editor, a position he holds until his death in 1910.

## 1879

Catherine Scott Coburn leaves *The New Northwest*, and two of Abigail's sons, Willis and Hubert, join the paper as part of the Duniway Publishing Company.

## 1880

John Tucker Scott, Abigail's father, dies at the age of 71, at Forest Grove, Oregon.

Abigail again speaks before the Oregon State Legislature on women's rights.

## 1881

Abigail speaks before a joint session of the Washington Territorial legislature and calls for acceptance of a woman suffrage bill.

## 1883

Abigail campaigns in Washington and serves as Washington Territory correspondent for *The New Northwest* and for *The Oregonian*.

November—The woman suffrage bill passes in the Washington Territorial legislature and is signed by the governor.

## 1884

Abigail attends the NWSA Convention and is elected one of five vice-presidents. She calls on President Chester Arthur at the White House and addresses the U. S. Senate Committee regarding the proposed woman suffrage amendment.

June—The equal suffrage amendment is defeated in Oregon by a vote of 28,176 to 11,223.

December —Abigail travels to Minneapolis, St. Paul, and Chicago to lecture and have lithographers complete an historic picture, "The Coronation of Womanhood."

## 1885

July—Clara Duniway Stearns is brought to the Duniway home due to serious illness.

October—Abigail attends the AWSA Convention in Minneapolis.

# 1886

January 21—Clara Duniway Stearns dies of tuberculosis at her parents' home.

In Washington Territory, Abigail argues against local option, which is voted on in June and declared unconstitutional in September.

# 1887

January—*The New Northwest* is sold to O. P. Mason *et al.*

Woman suffrage is revoked in Washington Territory.

Ben, Wilkie, Ralph, and Clyde Duniway move to Idaho, where Willis and Wilkie have secured 1,280 acres. Abigail maintains the Portland house, makes visits to the Idaho ranch, and campaigns in Idaho.

# 1889

Abigail attends the NWSA Convention in Washington, D. C., and presents a speech entitled "Ballots and Bullets."

Abigail serves on a committee to negotiate the 1890 merger of the NWSA and the AWSA as the National American Woman Suffrage Association (NAWSA).

Abigail addresses the Idaho Constitutional Convention on equal suffrage.

# 1891 to 1892

Abigail edits *The Coming Century* in Portland.

# 1893

Abigail attends the Columbian Exposition in Chicago and presents an address entitled "The Pacific Northwest" to the World's Auxiliary Congress of Women.

# 1894

Ben Duniway's health is poor, and he returns to Portland.

# 1895 to 1897

Abigail serves as editor of *The Pacific Empire*, published by Frances Gotshall in Portland.

# 1896

Abigail campaigns in California, where woman suffrage is defeated. Idaho adopts woman suffrage. Utah is admitted as a state and adopts woman suffrage.

June and July—The Woman's Congress convention is held in Portland with Abigail as honorary president. Susan B. Anthony attends and presents three addresses. Anna Howard Shaw is a participant and is honored with "Anna Howard Shaw Day."

August 4—Ben Duniway dies at Portland.

# 1897 to 1898

Abigail continues to help lead the Oregon State Woman Suffrage Association and is active in the Woman's Club movement. She serves as president of the executive board for the Second Woman's Congress in Portland, 1898.

Washington State's referendum for woman suffrage fails.

# 1899

Abigail addresses the Oregon State Legislature, which agrees to submit the equal suffrage amendment to the people in 1900.

Abigail is selected valedictorian to speak on the occasion of the 40th anniversary of Oregon statehood. Her topic is "Women in Oregon History."

Abigail attends the NAWSA convention in Grand Rapids, Michigan, and presents "How to Win the Ballot."

# 1900

February—Abigail attends the NAWSA convention in Washington, D.C., and gives an address entitled "Success in Sight."

June—Oregon voters defeat woman suffrage by 28,402 to 26,265.

# 1905

Abigail publishes F*rom the West to the West: Across the Plains to Oregon*, a novel based on her overland trip to Oregon.

The 37th annual convention of the NAWSA is held in Portland to coincide with the Lewis and Clark Centennial Exposition. Anna Howard Shaw is president of NAWSA, which chooses new management for the Oregon campaign. Abigail withdraws from the 1906 campaign.

Abigail speaks at the unveiling of the statue of Sacajawea at the Lewis and Clark Centennial and presents her poem, "Centennial Ode," on opening day. The exposition declares October 6th as "Abigail Scott Duniway Day."

## 1906

Oregon defeats equal suffrage by a vote of 47,075 to 36,902.

Abigail, at the age of 72, is elected president of the Oregon State Woman Suffrage Association.

## 1908

The Oregon Campaign for woman suffrage is based on plans for an initiative petition and referendum. NAWSA funds are cut off following disputes between Abigail and Anna Howard Shaw.

Oregon defeats woman suffrage by a vote of 58,670 to 36,858.

## 1910

January—Abigail is appointed by Governor F. W. Benson of Oregon as delegate to the Conservation Congress of Governors, where she calls for equal rights for women.

August 7—Harvey W. Scott, brother of Abigail, dies.

Washington approves woman suffrage, but Oregon defeats it by a vote of 58,065 to 35,270.

## 1911

California approves woman suffrage.

Abigail becomes honorary president of the National Council of Women Voters.

## 1912

Abigail is too ill to campaign. She writes the Woman Suffrage Proclamation for Oregon at the request of Governor Oswald West.

Oregon adopts woman suffrage by a vote of 61,265 to 57,104. Governor West arranges for Abigail to be the first woman to register to vote in Oregon.

## 1913

Abigail serves on the Interstate Bridge Project, the first jury to include women in Oregon, and the Ports of Columbia Commission. At the Federation of Women's Clubs Convention in Hood River, she denounces Anna Howard Shaw as the cause of defeat in Oregon in 1906 and accuses her of "confiscation of our fund" for the 1912 campaign.

August 5—Willis Scott Duniway, Oregon State Printer and Abigail's eldest son, dies at the age of 57.

## 1914

Abigail opposes prohibition through her writing and lectures. Oregon adopts prohibition.

Abigail publishes her autobiography—*Path Breaking: An Autobiographical History of the Equal Suffrage Movement in Pacific Coast States.*

## 1915

October 11—Abigail dies in Portland just before her 81st birthday. She is survived by four sons: Hubert, a wholesale lumber dealer in New York; Wilkie, superintendent of the Portland *Evening Telegram*; Clyde, a professor of history and president of the University of Wyoming; and Ralph, an attorney in Portland.

# Bibliography

## Duniway Manuscripts and Special Collections

**Duniway Family Papers. David C. Duniway Private Collection now housed in Special Collections, Knight Library, University of Oregon, Eugene.**

Duniway, Abigail Scott. "Journal of a Trip to Oregon," 1852.
———. Business papers.
———. Correspondence, 1862-1915.
———. Manuscripts of revised novels.
———. Miscellaneous speeches, poems, short stories.
———. Scrapbooks #1 and #2 with news clippings, speech manuscripts, letters-to-editors, and correspondence, 1880-1915.
Duniway, Clyde. Unpublished notes and typescript for "Journal of a Trip to Oregon," 1924; rev. 1930.
———. "My Memories of Abigail Scott Duniway." Unpublished essay, 1929; rev. 1932.
Duniway, David C., comp. Scott, Roelofson and Duniway Genealogical Files, rev. 1985.
Duniway, Hubert, Ralph, Wilkie, and Willis. Letters to Clyde Duniway. 1890-1915.
Scott and Roelofson family letters, memoirs, pamphlets, photographs, and news clippings.

**Oregon Historical Society, Portland, Oregon.**

Duniway Publishing Company Ledgers.
Oregon State Woman Suffrage Association Papers.

## Newspapers Edited by Abigail Scott Duniway

*The Coming Century*, Portland, 1891-92. Ed. Abigail Scott Duniway. One copy in Oregon Collection, Knight Library, University of Oregon, Eugene. 2 Dec. 1891.
*The New Northwest*, Portland, 1871-87. Ed. Abigail Scott Duniway. Oregon Historical Society, Portland. Microfilm.
*The Pacific Empire*, Portland, 1895-98. Ed. Abigail Scott Duniway, 1895-97. Multnomah County Library, Portland. Bound volumes contain: 16 Aug. 1895; 3 Oct. 1895 to 11 Feb. 1897; 10 March 1898 to 23 June 1898. Oregon Historical Society, Portland. Unbound issues include: 3 Oct. 1895 to 11 Feb. 1897; 2 Sept. 1897 to July 7 1898.

## Selected Published Works by Abigail Scott Duniway

Duniway, Abigail Scott. *Captain Gray's Company; or, Crossing the Plains and Living in Oregon.* Portland: S. J. McCormick, 1859.
———. *David and Anna Matson.* NY: Wells, 1876. Rpt. Portland: Duniway Publishing Co., 1882.

————. "A Few Recollections of a Busy Life." *The Souvenir of Western Women.* Ed. Mary Osborn Douthit. Portland: Anderson & Duniway, 1905. 9-12.

————. "From Oregon." A Letter from A. J. Duniway, Albany, Oregon, July 12, 1870. *The Revolution,* NY. 6 Oct. 1870.

————. *From the West to the West: Across the Plains to Oregon.* Chicago: A. C. McClurg, 1905.

————. "How I Became a Literary Woman." *The Western Lady.* Portland: n.p., 1904. 3.

————. Interview by Fred Lockley. *Oregon Journal.* 22 June 1913.

————. "Journal of a Trip to Oregon." Ed. David C. Duniway. *Covered Wagon Women: Diaries and Letters from the Western Trails, 1840-1890.* Vol. V. Ed. Kenneth L. Holmes and David C. Duniway. Glendale, CA: Arthur H. Clark Co., 1986. 21-172. Rpt. with intro. by Ruth Barnes Moynihan. Lincoln: University of Nebraska Press, 1997.

————. "Letter from Mrs. Duniway." *The Woman's Journal,* Boston. 16 June 1900.

————. "Mrs. Duniway in Idaho." A Letter from Abigail Scott Duniway, Blackford Idaho." 8 March 1895. *The Woman's Journal,* Boston. 30 March 1895.

————. "Mrs. Duniway's Reminiscences: How I Became a Suffragist." *The Woman's Journal,* Boston. 31 Dec. 1898.

————. *My Musings; or, a Few Fancies in Verse.* Portland: Duniway Publishing Co., 1875.

————. "Narrative by Abigail Jane Scott Duniway." *The Oregonian.* 7 Oct. 1900. Rpt. *History of the Oregon Country,* Vol. III, Appendix. Ed. Harvey W. Scott; comp. Leslie M. Scott. Cambridge: Riverside Press, 1924. 246-49.

————. Narrative by Mrs. Duniway. In Chapter 54, "The Pacific Northwest." *History of Woman Suffrage,* Vol. III. Ed. Elizabeth Cady Stanton, Susan B. Anthony, and Matilda Joslyn Gage. 1886. Rpt. NY: Arno and *The New York Times,* 1969. 767-80.

————. "Odors Not of Araby." *So Much to Be Done: Women Settlers on the Mining and Ranching Frontier.* 2nd ed. Ed. Ruth Barnes Moynihan, Susan Armitage, and Christiane Fischer. Lincoln: University of Nebraska Press, 1998. 118-25.

————. "Our Editorial Bow." San Francisco Pi*oneer,* 5 Jan. 1871.

————. *Path Breaking: An Autobiographical History of the Equal Suffrage Movement in Pacific Coast States.* Portland: James, Kerns & Abbott Co., 1914. Rpt. New York: Schocken Books, 1971.

————. "Personal Reminiscences of a Pioneer." *Portland: Its History and Builders,* Vol. III. Ed. Joseph Gaston. Chicago: Clarke, 1911. 52-60.

————. "A Psychic Experience." *Religio-Philosophical Journal.* 10 Dec. 1892.

————. "The Stage-Driver's Story." *Phrenological Journal.* Aug. 1879. 85-90.

————. "State Correspondence—Oregon." Letter from Abigail Scott Duniway, Portland, Oregon, Dec. 1, 1902. *The Woman's Journal,* Boston. 13 Dec. 1902.

————. "Susan B. Anthony's Visit to Oregon." *The Souvenir of Western Women.* Ed. Mary Osborn Douthit. Portland: Anderson & Duniway, 1905. 36-37.

————. "Victoria Woodhull and the Woman's Rights Convention of 1872." *Second to None: A Documentary History of American Women,* Vol. II. Ed. Ruth Barnes Moynihan, Cynthia Russett, and Laurie Crumpacker. Lincoln: University of Nebraska Press, 1993. 20-25.

————. "A Woman's Lot Is So Hard!" *Second to None: A Documentary History of American Women,* Vol. I. Ed. Ruth Barnes Moynihan, Cynthia Russett, and Laurie Crumpacker. Lincoln: University of Nebraska Press, 1993. 215-17.

## Serialized novels by Abigail Scott Duniway in *The New Northwest*:

*Judith Reid: A Plain Story of a Plain Woman,* NNW, 12 May 1871 to 22 Dec. 1871.
*Ellen Dowd the Farmer's Wife,* part one, NNW, 5 Jan. 1872 to 26 April 1872, and part two, NNW, 1 July 1873 to 26 Sept. 1873.

*Amie and Henry Lee; or, The Spheres of the Sexes, NNW,* 29 May 1874 to 13 Nov. 1874.
*The Happy Home; or, the Husband's Triumph, NNW,* 20 Nov. 1874 to 14 May 1875.
*Captain Gray's Company; or, Crossing the Plains and Living in Oregon, NNW,* 21 May 1875 to 29 Oct. 1875.
*One Woman's Sphere; or, The Mystery of Eagle Cove, NNW,* 4 June 1875 to 3 Dec. 1875.
*Madge Morrison, the Molalla Maid and Matron, NNW,* 10 Dec. 1875 to 28 July 1876.
*Edna and John: A Romance of Idaho Flat, NNW,* 29 Sept. 1876 to 15 June 1877.
*Martha Marblehead: The Maid and Matron of Chehalem, NNW,* 29 June 1877 to 8 Feb. 1878.
*Her Lot; or, How She Was Protected, NNW,* 1 Feb. 1878 to 19 Sept. 1878.
*Fact, Fate and Fancy; or, More Ways of Living than One, NNW,* 26 Sept. 1878 to 15 May 1879.
*Mrs. Hardine's Will, NNW,* 20 Nov. 1879 to 26 Aug. 1880.
*The Mystery of Castle Rock; a Story of the Pacific Northwest, NNW,* 2 March 1882 to 7 Sept. 1882.
*Judge Dunson's Secret: An Oregon Story, NNW,* 15 March 1883 to 6 Sept. 1883.
*Laban McShane: A Frontier Story, NNW,* 13 Sept. 1883 to 6 March 1884.
*Dux: A Maiden Who Dared, NNW,* 11 Sept. 1884 to 5 March 1885.
*The De Launcy Curse; or, The Law of Heredity—a Tale of Three Generations, NNW,* 10 Sept. 1885 to 4 March 1886.
*Blanche Le Clerq: A Tale of the Mountain Mines, NNW,* 2 Sept. 1886 to 24 Feb. 1887.

**Serialized novels by Abigail Scott Duniway in *The Pacific Empire*:**

*Shack-Locks: A Story of the Times, PE,* 3 Oct. 1895 to 26 March 1896.
*'Bijah's Surprises,* book one, *PE,* 2 April 1896 to 26 Sept. 1896, and book two, *PE,* 1 Oct. 1896 to 31 Dec. 1896.
*The Old and the New, PE,* 7 Jan. 1897 to 30 Dec. 1897.

**Unfinished serialized novel in the *Phrenological Journal*.**

*Why Mar the Image?* Jan.-May, 1877.

# Selected Speeches by Abigail Scott Duniway

Address, San Francisco County Woman Suffrage Association, Dashaway Hall, San Francisco, 4 Jan. 1871. San Francisco *Pioneer,* 5 Jan. 1871.
Address, Twenty-fifth Annual Oregon State Equal Suffrage Association Convention, Portland, 5 Dec. 1896. *Pacific Empire,* 10 Dec. 1896.
Address, U.S. Senate Select Committee on Woman Suffrage, Washington, D. C., 7 March 1884. *New Northwest,* 24 April 1884.
"Ballots and Bullets." National Woman Suffrage Association Convention, Washington, D. C., Feb. 1889. *Path Breaking,* 188-200; *Oregonian,* 9 Sept. 1906.
"Constitutional Liberty and the 'Aristocracy of Sex.'" Illinois State Legislature, Springfield. 19 Jan. 1877. Duniway Papers.
"Eminent Women I Have Met." State Federation of Women's Clubs, Pendleton, OR, 1 June 1900. Pendleton *East Oregonian,* 2 June 1900; Duniway Papers, typescript portions in ASD Scrapbook #2.
"Equal Rights for All." Idaho Constitutional Convention, Boise, 16 July 1889. *Pacific Empire,* 9 June 1898; excerpts in *Path Breaking,* 133-41.
"Home and Mother." Address to Federation of Labor Meeting, Portland, Labor Day, Sept. 1914. Duniway Papers.
"How to Win the Ballot." National American Woman Suffrage Association Convention, Grand Rapids, 2 May 1899. *Path Breaking,* 156-68.

"The Pacific Northwest." World's Congress of Women, Columbian Exposition, Chicago, 1 June
 1893. Duniway Papers, typescript in ASD Scrapbook #2. Published in *The Congress of Women*.
 Ed. Mary Kavanaugh Oldham Eagle. Chicago: International, 1895. 90-96.
"The Powers of Thought." Address to Society of Bible Spiritualists, Portland, 6 Oct. 1907.
 Excerpts in *The Oregonian*, 7 Oct. 1907; Duniway Papers, ASD Scrapbook #1.
Presidential Address, Thirty-Seventh Anniversary of the Oregon State Equal Suffrage Association,
 Portland, Nov. 1908. Duniway Papers, ASD Scrapbook #2.
"Presidents Past and Future." Presidential inaugural address, Portland Women's Club, Portland,
 11 Oct. 1902. Duniway Papers, typescript.
Response and Reading of "Centennial Ode" for Lewis & Clark Exposition, on "Abigail Scott
 Duniway Day," Portland, 6 Oct. 1905. Rpt. *The Woman's Tribune*, 28 Oct. 1905; Duniway
 Papers, ASD Scrapbook #1.
"Success in Sight." National American Woman Suffrage Association Convention, Washington,
 D. C., 14 Feb. 1900. *Path Breaking*, 169-78. Dated as 12 Feb. in Portland *Evening Telegram*, 13
 Feb. 1900; clipping in Duniway Papers.
"Upward Steps in a Third of a Century." Read by Mrs. W. P. Olds at National American Woman
 Suffrage Association Convention, Baltimore, Maryland, Feb. 1906. *Oregonian*, 11 Feb. 1906;
 Duniway Papers, ASD Scrapbooks #1 and #2.
"The Visit of Nicodemus to Jesus by Night." Address to Society of Bible Spiritualists, Salem,
 OR, 24 Feb. 1906. Excerpts in *Salem Journal*, 25 Feb. 1906; Duniway Papers, ASD Scrapbook
 #1.
"The Woman Suffrage Movement and Two Kinds of Prohibition." Liberty Hall, Portland, 5
 Oct. 1914. Duniway Papers, typescript.
"Women in Oregon History." Oregon Legislative Assembly, Salem, in commemoration of the
 fortieth anniversary of Oregon's statehood, 14 Feb. 1899. *Oregonian*, 15 Feb. 1899; *Path
 Breaking*, 144-53.

## Selected Sources on Abigail Scott Duniway

Bandow, Gayle R. "'In Pursuit of a Purpose': Abigail Scott Duniway and the *New Northwest*."
 M. A. thesis, University of Oregon, 1973.
Bennion, Sherilyn Cox. "*The New Northwest* and *Woman's Exponent*: Early Voices for Suffrage."
 *Journalism Quarterly* 54 (Summer 1977): 286-92.
———. "The Suffragists." *Equal to the Occasion: Women Editors of the Nineteenth-Century West*.
 Reno: University of Nevada Press, 1990. 56-71.
Capell, Letitia Lee. "A Biography of Abigail Scott Duniway." M. A. thesis, University of Oregon,
 1934.
Douthit, Mary Osborn. "Abigail Scott Duniway, Mother and Home Builder." *The Souvenir of
 Western Women*. Portland: Anderson & Duniway, 1905. 43.
Duniway, David Cushing. "Abigail Scott Duniway, Path Breaker." *With Her Own Wings:
 Historical Sketches, Reminiscences, and Anecdotes of Pioneer Women*. Ed. Helen Krebs Smith;
 comp. Portland Federation of Women's Organizations. Portland: Beattie, 1948. 202-5.
Holbrook, Stewart H. "No Doll Was Abigail." *Dreamers of the American Dream*. Garden City,
 NY: Doubleday, 1957. 205-12.
Johnson, L. C. "Abigail Jane Scott Duniway." *Notable American Women, 1607-1950*. Vol. I. Ed.
 Edward T. James. Cambridge: Harvard University Press, 1971. 531-33.
Kessler, Lauren. "The Fight for Woman Suffrage and the Oregon Press." *Women in Pacific
 Northwest History: An Anthology*. Ed. Karen J. Blair. Seattle: University of Washington Press,
 1988. 43-58.

———. "The Ideas of Women Suffragists and the Portland *Oregonian*." *Journalism Quarterly* 57 (Winter 1980): 597-605.

———. "A Siege of the Citadels: Access of Woman Suffrage Ideas to the Oregon Press, 1884-1912." Ph.D. diss., University of Washington, 1980.

———. "A Siege of the Citadels: Search for a Public Forum for the Ideas of Oregon Woman Suffrage." *Oregon Historical Quarterly* 84 (Summer 1983): 117-50.

Lake, Randall A. "Abigail Scott Duniway." *Women Public Speakers in the United States, 1800-1925: A Bio-Critical Sourcebook.* Ed. Karlyn Kohrs Campbell. Westport, CT: Greenwood Press, 1993. 393-408.

Larson, T. A. "Dolls, Vassals and Drudges—Pioneer Women in the West." *Western Historical Quarterly* 3 (Jan. 1972): 1-16.

———. "Idaho's Role in America's Woman Suffrage Crusade." *Idaho Yesterdays* 18 (Spring 1974): 2-15.

———. "The Woman's Rights Movement in Idaho." *Idaho Yesterdays* 16 (Spring 1972): 2-15; 18-19.

———. "The Woman Suffrage Movement in Washington." *Pacific Northwest Quarterly* 67 (April 1976): 49-62.

Mansfield, Dorothy M. "Abigail S. Duniway: Suffragette with Not so common Sense." *Western Speech* 35 (Winter 1971): 24-29.

McKern, Roberta O. "The Woman Suffrage Movement in Oregon and the Oregon Press." M. A. thesis, University of Oregon, 1975.

Montague, Martha Frances. "The Woman Suffrage Movement in Oregon." M. A. thesis, University of Oregon, 1930.

Morrison, Dorothy Nafus. *Ladies Were Not Expected: Abigail Scott Duniway and Women's Rights.* NY: Atheneum, 1977. Rpt. Western Imprints, Oregon Historical Society Press, 1985.

Moynihan, Ruth Barnes. "Abigail Scott Duniway: Mother of Woman Suffrage in the Pacific Northwest." *By Grit and Grace: Eleven Women Who Shaped the American West.* Ed. Richard W. Etulain and Glenda Riley. Golden, CO: Fulcrum Press, 1997. 174-97.

———. "Abigail Scott Duniway of Oregon: Woman Suffragist of the American Frontier." 2 vols. Ph.D. diss., Yale University, 1979.

———. "Let Women Vote: Abigail Scott Duniway in Washington Territory." *Washington Comes of Age: The State in the National Experience.* Ed. David H. Stratton. Pullman: Washington State University Press, 1992. 96-112.

———. *Rebel for Rights, Abigail Scott Duniway.* New Haven: Yale University Press, 1983.

———. "Susan B. Anthony, Elizabeth Cady Stanton, and Abigail Scott Duniway: Women's Rights Pioneers." *Heroines: Remarkable and Inspiring Women.* Ed. Sara Hunt. NY: Crescent Books, 1995. 74-79.

———. "Of Women's Rights and Freedom: Abigail Scott Duniway." *Women in Pacific Northwest History: An Anthology.* Ed. Karen J. Blair. Seattle: University of Washington Press, 1988. 9-24.

Nash, Lee. "Abigail versus Harvey: Sibling Rivalry in the Oregon Campaign for Woman Suffrage." *Oregon Historical Quarterly* 98 (Summer 1997): 134-63.

Richey, Elinor. "Abigail Scott Duniway: Up from Hard Scrabble." *Eminent Women of the West.* Berkeley: Howell-North, 1975. 73-96.

———. "The Unsinkable Abigail." *American Heritage* 26 (1975): 72-89.

Roberts, Leslie McKay. "Suffragist of the New West: Abigail Scott Duniway and the Development of the Oregon Woman Suffrage Movement." B. A. thesis, Reed College, 1969.

Shein, Debra. "'No Canada for Fugitive Wives': Five Novels by Abigail Scott Duniway, Voice of Equal Rights (1834-1915)." 2 vols. Ph.D. diss., University of Oregon, 1998.

Smith, Helen Krebs. *Presumptuous Dreamers: A Sociological History of the Life and Times of Abigail Scott Duniway*, Vol. I, 1834-1871. Lake Oswego, OR: Smith Publishing Co., 1974.

Thomas, Mrs. E. H. "The Pacific Northwest." *Phrenological Journal*. Dec. 1877. 436-39.

Ward, Jean M. "The Emergence of a Mentor-Protégé Relationship: The 1871 Pacific Northwest Lecture Tour of Susan B. Anthony and Abigail Scott Duniway." *Proceedings of the 1982 Northwest Women's Heritage Conference Sponsored by the University of Washington and the Ford Foundation*. Seattle: University of Washington, 1984. 120-45.

————. "Women's Responses to Systems of Male Authority: Communication Strategies in the Novels of Abigail Scott Duniway." 2 vols. Ph.D. diss., University of Oregon, 1989.

————, and Elaine A. Maveety, eds. "Abigail Scott Duniway." *Pacific Northwest Women, 1815-1925: Lives, Memories, and Writings*. Corvallis: Oregon State University Press, 1995. 209-19.

## Selected Other Newspapers

*Evening Telegram*, Portland. Ed. Catherine A. Scott Coburn, 1883-88. Oregon Historical Society, Portland. Microfilm.

Oregon City *Argus*, 1855-60. Oregon Historical Society, Portland. Microfilm.

*Oregon Farmer*, Portland, 1859-62. Oregon Historical Society, Portland. Microfilm.

*The Oregonian*, Portland. Oregon Historical Society, Portland. Microfilm.

*The Pioneer*, San Francisco. Originally the *California Weekly Mercury*. Ed. Emily Pitts-Stevens, 1869-73. University of California, Berkeley. Microfilm.

*Statesman*, Salem. Oregon Historical Society, Portland. Microfilm.

*Woman's Exponent*, Salt Lake City, 1872-1914. Ed. Lula Greene Richards, 1872-77; Emmeline B. Wells, 1877-1914. University of Utah. Microfilm.

*The Woman's Pacific Coast Journal/Pacific Journal of Health*, San Francisco, 1870-72. Ed. Carrie Fisher Young. United States National Library of Medicine. Microfilm.

*The Woman's Tribune*, published in Portland, 1905-1909. Ed. Clara Bewick Colby. Oregon Historical Society, Portland. Scattered issues for 1905, 1906, 1908.

## Selected Other Sources

Additon, Lucia H. Faxon. *Twenty Eventful Years of the Oregon Woman's Christian Temperance Union, 1880-1900, Statistical, Historical, and Biographical*. Portland: Gotschall Printing Co., 1904.

*American Newspaper Annual Directory*. Philadelphia: Ayer, 1883, 1885, 1886, 1887.

Anderson, Martha E. *Black Pioneers of the Northwest, 1800-1918*. n. p. [Washington]: Martha E. Anderson, 1980.

Anthony, Susan. *Account of the Proceedings of the Trial of Susan B. Anthony on the Charge of Illegal Voting at the Presidential Election in Nov. 1872*. Rochester, NY: Daily Democrat and Chronicle Book Print, 1874.

Bancroft, Hubert Howe. *History of Oregon, Vol II, 1848-1888*. San Francisco: The History Publishing Co., 1888. [See Frances Fuller Victor]

————. *History of Washington, Idaho, and Montana, 1845-1889*. San Francisco: The History Publishing Co., 1890. [See Frances Fuller Victor]

Beeton, Beverly and G. Thomas Edwards. "Susan B. Anthony's Woman Suffrage Crusade in the American West." *Women in the West*. Ed. Glenda Riley. Manhattan, KA: Sunflower University Press, 1982.

Belknap, George A. *Oregon Imprints, 1845-1870*. Eugene: University of Oregon Books, 1968.

Bennion, Sherilyn Cox. "Enterprising Ladies: Utah's Nineteenth-Century Women Editors." *Utah Historical Quarterly* 49 (Summer 1981): 291-304.

———. *Equal to the Occasion: Women Editors of the Nineteenth-Century West.* Reno: University of Nevada Press, 1990.

———. "*The Pioneer:* The First Voice for Women's Suffrage in the West." *The Pacific Historian* 25 (Winter 1981): 15-21.

———. "Woman Suffrage Papers of the West, 1869-1904." *American Journalism* 3 (1986): 125-41.

———. "The *Woman's Exponent:* Forty-two Years of Speaking for Women." *Utah Historical Quarterly* 44 (Summer 1976): 222-39.

———. "Women Editors of California, 1854-1900." *The Pacific Historian* 28 (Fall 1984): 30-43.

Bergquist, James M. "The Oregon Donation Land Act and the National Land Policy." *Oregon Historical Quarterly* 58 (March 1957): 17-35.

Blair, Harry C., and Rebecca Tarshis. *Colonel Edward D. Baker: Lincoln's Constant Ally.* Portland: Oregon Historical Society, 1960.

Blair, Karen J. *Northwest Women: An Annotated Bibliography of Sources on the History of Oregon and Washington Women, 1787-1970.* Pullman: Washington State University Press, 1997.

———, ed. *Women in Pacific Northwest History: An Anthology.* Seattle: University of Washington Press, 1988.

Blocker, Jack S., Jr. *Give to the Wind Thy Fears: The Women's Temperance Crusade, 1873-74.* Westport, CT: Greenwood Press, 1985.

———. "Separate Paths: Suffragists and the Women's Temperance Crusade." *SIGNS: Journal of Women in Society and Culture* 10 (Spring 1985): 460-76.

Bloomer, Amelia. *Life and Writings of Amelia Bloomer.* Ed. D. C. Bloomer. 1895. Rpt. NY: Schocken Books, 1975.

Bordin, Ruth. *Woman and Temperance: The Quest for Power and Liberty, 1873-1900.* Philadelphia: Temple University Press, 1981.

Braude, Ann. *Radical Spirits: Spiritualism and Women's Rights in Nineteenth-Century America.* Boston: Beacon, 1989.

Buhle, Mari Jo, and Paul Buhle, eds. *The Concise History of Woman Suffrage: Selections from the Classic Work of Stanton, Anthony, Gage, and Harper.* Urbana: University of Illinois Press, 1978.

Bureau of Municipal Research and Service. *Population of Oregon Cities, Counties and Metropolitan Areas 1850 to 1957: A Compilation of Census Counts and Estimates in Oregon.* Information Bulletin No. 106. Eugene: University of Oregon, April, 1958.

Campbell, Karlyn Kohrs, comp. *Man Cannot Speak for Her,* Vol. II. NY: Praeger, 1989.

Clark, Hugh. *Portland's Chinese: The Early Years.* Ethni-City Series. Portland: Center for Urban Education, 1975; rev. 1978.

Clark, Malcolm H., Jr. "The Bigot Disclosed: Ninety Years of Nativism." *Oregon Historical Quarterly* 75 (June 1974): 109-86.

———. "The Lady and the Law: A Portrait of Mary Leonard." *Oregon Historical Quarterly* 64 (June 1955): 126-139. Rpt. in *The War on the Webfoot Saloon & Other Tales of Feminine Adventures.* Portland: Oregon Historical Society, 1969. 25-39.

———. "The War on the Webfoot Saloon." *Oregon Historical Quarterly* 58 (March 1957): 48-62. Rpt. in *The War on the Webfoot Saloon & Other Tales of Feminine Adventures.* Portland: Oregon Historical Society, 1969. 5-24.

Corbett, P. Scott, and Nancy Parker Corbett. "The Chinese in Oregon, c. 1870-1880." *Oregon Historical Quarterly* 78 (March 1977): 73-85.

Corning, Howard McKinley, ed. *Dictionary of Oregon History.* Portland: Binfords & Mort, 1956.

Cross, Mary Bywater. *Treasures in the Trunk: Quilts of the Oregon Trail.* Nashville: Rutledge Hill Press, 1993.

Deady, Matthew P. *Pharisee Among Philistines: The Diary of Judge Matthew P. Deady, 1871-1892.* Ed. Malcolm Clark, Jr. Portland: Oregon Historical Society, 1975.

Decker, Fred W. "Letter to the Editor Discovered: A Photo and More Facts about Mary Leonard, Oregon's First Woman Lawyer." *Oregon Historical Quarterly* 78 (June 1977): 174-77.

Douthit, Mary Osborn, ed. *Souvenir of Western Women.* Portland: Anderson & Duniway, 1905.

Edwards, G. Thomas. "Six Oregon Leaders and the Far-Reaching Impact of America's Civil War." *Oregon Historical Quarterly* 100 (Spring 1999): 4-31.

————. *Sowing Good Seeds: The Northwest Suffrage Campaigns of Susan B. Anthony.* Portland: Oregon Historical Society Press, 1990.

Epstein, Barbara Leslie. *The Politics of Domesticity: Women, Evangelism, and Temperance in Nineteenth-Century America.* Middletown, CT: Wesleyan University Press, 1981.

Evans, Sara. *Born for Liberty: A History of Women in America.* NY: MacMillan, 1989.

Flexner, Eleanor. *Century of Struggle: The Woman's Rights Movement in the United States.* 1974. Rev. ed. Cambridge: Belknap Press of Harvard University Press, 1975.

Foner, Eric, and John A. Garraty, eds. *The Reader's Companion to American History.* Boston: Houghton Mifflin, 1991.

Gaston, Joseph. *The Centennial History of Oregon, 1811-1912.* 4 vols. Chicago: S. J. Clarke, 1912.

————. *Portland: Its History and Builders.* 3 vols. Chicago: The S. J.Clarke Publishing Co., 1911.

Goldsmith, Barbara. *Other Powers: The Age of Suffrage, Spiritualism, and the Scandalous Victoria Woodhull.* NY: Alfred A. Knopf, 1998.

Haarsager, Sandra. *Organized Womanhood: Cultural Politics in the Pacific Northwest, 1840-1920.* Norman: University of Oklahoma Press, 1997.

Harmon, Rick. "Thomas Condon and the 'Natural Selection' of Oregon Pioneers." *Oregon Historical Quarterly* 99 (Winter 1998-99): 436-71.

Harper, Ida Husted. Th*e Life and Work of Susan B. Anthony.* 3 vols. Indianapolis: The Hollenbeck Press, 1898, 1908. Rpt. Salem, New Hampshire: Ayer, 1983.

"Harvey W. Scott Memorial Number." *Oregon Historical Quarterly* 14 (June 1913).

*History of Tazewell County, Illinois.* Chicago: Chapman, 1879.

Hitchman, Robert. *Place Names of Washington.* Tacoma: Washington State Historical Society, 1985.

Holden, Margaret K. "Gender and Protest Ideology: Sue Ross Keenan and the Oregon Anti-Chinese Movement." *Western Legal History* 7 (1994): 223-43.

Horner, John B. *Oregon Literature.* 2nd ed. Portland: Gill, 1902.

James, Edward T., ed. *Notable American Women, 1607-1950: A Biographical Dictionary.* 3 vols. Cambridge: Harvard University Press, 1971.

Johnson, David A. "The Donation Land Act and the Making of Modern-Day Oregon." *Oregon Humanities* (Winter 1995): 8-11.

Josephy, Alvin M., Jr. *The Nez Perce Indians and the Opening of the Northwest.* New Haven: Yale University Press, 1965.

Kirk, Ruth, and Carmela Alexander. *Exploring Washington's Past: A Road Guide to History.* Seattle: University of Washington Press, 1990.

Kraditor, Aileen A. *The Ideas of the Woman Suffrage Movement, 1890-1920.* 1965. Rpt. NY: W. W. Norton, 1981.

Lamar, Howard R., ed. *The New Encyclopedia of the America West.* New Haven: Yale University Press, 1998.

Laurie, Clayton D. "'The Chinese Must Go': The United States Army and the Anti-Chinese Riots in Washington Territory, 1885-1886." *Pacific Northwest Quarterly* 81 (Jan. 1990): 22-29.

Liestman, Daniel. "'The Various Celestials among Our Town': Euro-American Response to Port

Townsend's Chinese Colony." *Pacific Northwest Quarterly* 85 (July 1994): 93-104.

———. "'To Win Redeemed Souls from Heathen Darkness': Protestant Response to the Chinese of the Pacific Northwest in the Late Nineteenth Century." *Western Historical Quarterly* 24 (May 1993): 179-201.

Lockley, Fred. "Documentary: The Case of Robin Holmes vs. Nathaniel Ford." *Oregon Historical Quarterly* 23 (March 1922): 111-37.

———. *The Lockley Files: Conversations with Pioneer Women.* Comp. and ed. Mike Helm. Eugene: Rainy Day Press, 1981.

———. "Some Documentary Records of Slavery in Oregon." *Oregon Historical Quarterly* 17 (June 1916): 107-15.

MacColl, E. Kimbark. *The Shaping of a City: Business and Politics in Portland, Oregon 1885 to 1915.* Portland: Georgian Press, 1976.

———, with Harry H. Stein. *Merchants, Money, and Power: The Portland Establishment 1843-1913.* Portland: Georgian Press, 1988.

McClintock, Thomas C. "Seth Lewelling, William W. U'Ren and the Birth of the Oregon Progressive Movement." *Oregon Historical Quarterly* 68 (Sept. 1967): 197-220.

McLagan, Elizabeth. *A Peculiar Paradise: A History of Blacks in Oregon, 1788-1940.* Portland: The Oregon Black History Project, Georgian Press, 1980.

Merriam, Paul G. "The 'Other Portland': A Statistical Note on Foreign-Born, 1860-1910." *Oregon Historical Quarterly* 80 (Fall 1979): 258-68.

———. "Urban Elite in the Far West: Portland, Oregon, 1870-1890." *Arizona and the West* 18 (1976): 41-52.

Mumford, Esther Hall. *Calabash: A Guide to the History, Culture & Art of African Americans in Seattle and King County, Washington.* Seattle: Ananse Press, 1993.

———, *Seattle's Black Victorians, 1852-1901.* Seattle: Ananse Press, 1980.

Nash, Lee. "Refining a Frontier: The Cultural Interests and Activities of Harvey Scott." Ph.D. diss., University of Oregon, 1961.

———. "Scott of the *Oregonian*: The Editor as Historian." *Oregon Historical Quarterly* 70 (Sept. 1969): 196-232.

———. "Scott of the *Oregonian*: Literary Frontiersman." *Pacific Historical Review* 45 (Aug. 1976): 357-68.

Nelson, Herbert B. *The Literary Impulse in Pioneer Oregon.* Corvallis: Oregon State University Press, 1948.

O'Donnell, Terence, and Thomas Vaughan. *Portland: A Historical Sketch and Guide.* Portland: Oregon Historical Society, 1976.

Papachristou, Judith. *Women Together: A History in Documents of the Women's Movement in the United States.* NY: Alfred A. Knopf, 1976.

Powers, Alfred. *History of Oregon Literature.* Portland: Metropolitan Press, 1935.

Richard, K. Keith. "Unwelcome Settlers: Black and Mulatto Oregon Pioneers, Parts I and II." *Oregon Historical Quarterly* 84 (Spring/Summer 1983): 29-55; 173-205.

Rowell, George P. *American Newspaper Directory.* NY: Rowell, 1873, 1880, 1882, 1884.

Ruby, Robert H., and John A. Brown. *Indians of the Pacific Northwest: A History.* Norman: University of Oklahoma Press, 1981.

Schwartz, E. A. "Sick Hearts: Indian Removal on the Oregon Coast, 1875-1881." *Oregon Historical Quarterly* 92 (Fall 1991): 229-64.

Scott, Harvey Whitefield, ed. *History of the Oregon Country.* 6 vols. Compiled with an appendix by Leslie M. Scott. Cambridge, MA: Riverside Press, 1924.

———. *History of Portland, Oregon.* Syracuse, NY: Mason, 1891.

Sinclair, Andrew. *Era of Excess: A Social History of the Prohibition Movement.* NY: Harper and Row, 1964.

Smith, Helen Krebs, ed. *With Her Own Wings: Historical Sketches, Reminiscences, and Anecdotes of Pioneer Women.* Portland: Beattie and Co., 1948.

Snowden, Clinton A. *History of Washington: The Rise and Progress of an American State.* 4 vols. NY: Century History Co., 1909.

Solomon, Martha M., ed. *A Voice of Their Own: The Woman Suffrage Press, 1840-1910.* Tuscaloosa: University of Alabama Press, 1991.

Spalding, Helen F. "Mrs. Catherine A. Coburn." *Souvenir of Western Women.* Ed. Mary Osborn Douthit. Portland: Anderson & Duniway, 1905. 173.

Stanton, Elizabeth Cady, Susan B. Anthony, Matilda Joslyn Gage, and Ida Husted Harper, eds. *The History of Woman Suffrage.* 6 vols. Vols. I-III, ed. Stanton, Anthony and Gage. Rochester, NY: Mann, 1881, 1882, 1886. Vol. IV, ed. Anthony and Harper. Indianapolis: Hollenbeck, 1902. Vols. V-VI, ed. Harper. NY: Little & Ives, 1922. Rpt. of 6 vols. NY: Arno and The *New York Times,* 1969.

Suttles, Wayne, ed. *Handbook of North American Indians,* Vol. VII. Washington, D. C.: Smithsonian Institution, 1990.

Taylor, Quintard. "The Emergence of Black Communities in the Pacific Northwest, 1864-1910." *Journal of Negro History* 64 (Fall 1974): 342-54.

————. *In Search of the Racial Frontier: African Americans in the American West, 1528-1990.* NY: W. W. Norton & Co., 1998.

Tracy, Charles A., III. "Police Function in Portland, 1851-1874, Parts II and III." *Oregon Historical Quarterly* 80 (Summer & Fall 1979): 134-35; 287-322.

Turnbull, George S. *History of Oregon Newspapers.* Portland: Binfords & Mort, 1939.

United States Bureau of the Census. *Negro Population in the United States, 1790-1915.* Washington, D. C.: Government Printing Office, 1918.

Victor, Frances Auretta Fuller. *All Over Oregon and Washington.* San Francisco: John H. Carmany & Co., 1872.

————. *History of Oregon 1848-1888.* San Francisco: The History Publishing Co., 1888. [See Bancroft]

————. *The Women's War with Whisky; or, Crusading in Portland.* Portland: G. H. Himes, 1874.

Ward, Jean M., and Elaine A. Maveety, eds. *Pacific Northwest Women, 1815-1925: Lives, Memories and Writings.* Corvallis: Oregon State University Press, 1995.

Warren, Sidney. *The Farthest Frontier: The Pacific Northwest.* NY: Macmillan, 1949.

West, Oswald. "Reminiscences and Anecdotes: Political History." *Oregon Historical Quarterly* 50 (Dec. 1949): 243-50.

Wynne, Robert Edward. "Reaction to the Chinese in the Pacific Northwest and British Columbia, 1850 to 1910." Ph.D diss., University of Washington, 1964.

# Acknowledgements

We owe a debt of gratitude to those who assisted in making *"Yours for Liberty"* possible. In particular, we recognize the generosity of the late David C. Duniway, who shared his grandmother's and family papers with us, arranged for us to obtain a full microfilm set of *The New Northwest*, and provided many of the photographs that appear in this volume. Sharon M. Howe, Photographs Cataloger of the Oregon Historical Society, was most helpful in locating additional photographs and securing permissions. Ruth B. Moynihan, biographer of Abigail Scott Duniway, shared our enthusiasm for this collection of Duniway's writings, and we value her friendship and collaborative efforts with us over the years. We also value our continued association with the Oregon State University Press and deeply appreciate the professionalism and good humor of Jo Alexander, Managing Editor. Finally, research grants from Lewis & Clark College were instrumental at various stages in development of this book.

To our husbands, Paul and Pat, loving thanks for sharing our commitment to this project and for your patience when our households were sometimes in chaos. And, to Jean's grandson Benjamin, who was born while this work was underway, thank you for reminding us by your presence in our lives that generations to come can appreciate Abigail Scott Duniway's efforts to make this world a better place for all.

Jean M. Ward and Elaine A. Maveety
Lewis & Clark College

# Photographs

# Index